THE
MANAGEMENT
PROCESS

AN INTEGRATED FUNCTIONAL
APPROACH

THE IRWIN SERIES IN MANAGEMENT

Consulting Editor JOHN F. MEE *Indiana University*

THE MANAGEMENT PROCESS

AN INTEGRATED FUNCTIONAL APPROACH

William McNair Fox, Ph.D.

*Associate Professor of Industrial Relations
and Management,
University of Florida*

1963
RICHARD D. IRWIN, INC.
HOMEWOOD, ILLINOIS

to ELSE

PREFACE

This book presents new and traditional subject matter in a *different context* because it is felt that greater emphasis should be given to the *interaction* of the management functions. All managers plan, organize, and control the work of others, but *not* in a simple, sequential pattern. Managing is a continuous operation or process involving the interaction of these functions. Managers must plan for planning activity, organize for it, and control it. They must plan for organizing activity, organize for it, and control it, and they must perform these same functions for control. It is felt that practicing managers *do*, in effect, think in these terms. Consequently, an analysis of traditional and other materials *in this context* should not only be more *realistic* but also more *meaningful* to the student or practitioner. Reference to the chapter headings in the Table of Contents will illustrate the way in which this *interaction approach* provides a basic framework for the organization of this book.

An attempt has been made to avoid the obvious by presenting only those principles from the management literature which seem to deserve that designation. Also, they have been interpreted in the light of current concepts.[1] In the way of new material, attention is devoted to the role of probability in decision making, the formulation of organic subfunctions of planning, organizing, and controlling, and the new planning and control system known as PERT. A number of behavioral concepts, tersely stated and then discussed, are included so that the reader may more readily draw upon this important area of theory and research. So often, behavioral concepts are presented in such an abstract or generalized form, that the student of management finds it difficult to relate them to actual business situations.

---

[1] A listing of all of the principles used in this book is presented in Appendix I, pp. 415-19.

This is not a book on quantitative techniques in management; however, the *usefulness* and *general character* of such techniques is discussed at length, for the modern manager must hire, evaluate, and collaborate with quantitative experts and draw upon some knowledge of these techniques in planning for the future. The computer is an important tool for quantitative analysis and other uses in business. Consideration is given to the characteristics, present usefulness, organizational impact, and potential capability of this remarkable machine. For example, the rationale of the General Problem Solver Program, which renders a computer capable of creative thinking, is discussed in some detail.

Throughout, stress is placed on the concept that management is an *adaptive* as well as a *creative process* which requires the judicious application of fundamentals to unique situations. The material presented is pertinent to the management of various types of organizations of varying sizes and to the management of various departments or subunits within these organizations. An important goal of this book is to contribute toward the development of the criteria and understanding required for students and practicing managers to analyze and evaluate particular organizations and recognize means for strengthening them.

As a text this book is intended for a first course in management, or a more advanced course, depending upon the characteristics of the curriculum in which it is used. No *specific* course preparation, however, need be regarded as prerequisite to its use.

This book represents a venture down a new path, and I hope that in reading it you will find some measure of the stimulation I have found in undertaking it.

WILLIAM FOX

Gainesville, Florida

ACKNOWLEDGMENTS

I wish to take this opportunity to acknowledge my debt to an outstanding pioneer in the development of management thought, Professor Ralph C. Davis, who, as my teacher, first exposed me to the possibilities of a general theory of management.

I am grateful to the Ford Foundation which has made it possible for me to attend its faculty seminars on New Developments in Business, Simulation and Business Games, and Applications of Mathematics to Business. These have yielded much provocative information and many stimulating contacts with colleagues from other schools of business administration.

The manuscript has profited greatly from the critical comments of Professors John Mee of Indiana University, Cyril Ling of the University of Cincinnati, and Charles Klasson of the University of Texas. I am also indebted to Professors John Bishop of Harvard, Samuel Goldberg of Oberlin, Clare Griffin of Michigan, Wilton Anderson of Oklahoma State, and Lawrence Benninger of Florida for their valuable assistance.

Finally, I wish to thank William Wilmot, Jr., my department head, for facilitating matters through the considerate adjustment of teaching assignments, and Ann Bernos and the typing pool for the many hours devoted to the manuscript.

WILLIAM FOX

CONTENTS

SECTION III. CONTROL OF MANAGING

APPENDIXES

INDEXES

Chapter 1
INTRODUCTION TO THE STUDY OF MANAGEMENT

THE VALUE OF STUDYING MANAGEMENT

School of "Hard Knocks"

There are successful managers in business, government, and else-where who have never attended a college of business administration or, perhaps, even read a book about management. However, much that they have learned about management has been learned the "hard way," that is, they would have learned it more readily from well-organized courses or books about management. In addition, the "school of hard knocks" teaches some things incorrectly and completely fails to teach other things that would help them to do significantly better jobs as managers. This discrepancy between what they have learned and what they could have learned through formal training is growing every day as a result of the rapid advances being made in management theory and practice. The advent of the computer, the formulation of new quantitative techniques, and the refinement of organization theory on the basis of new insights provided by the behavioral sciences are examples of the kinds of advances that are contributing to the *science* of management, that is, the body of accumulated knowledge about management systematized and formulated with reference to general truths.

Managers also must be very much concerned with the *art* of management: *skill in applying* the science and techniques of management. Experience is the best teacher of this, *provided* the learner is equipped with the *right* concepts and techniques to practice. To the extent that they are misinformed about, or unaware of, basic

1

aspects of management, the "untrained" managers referred to above would have gained much more from their experience if it had been *preceded* by more extensive and accurate knowledge about management. Such knowledge is best gained through study that is strongly *interdisciplinary* in character, that is, study of concepts and techniques from such fields as economics, mathematics, psychology, sociology, and cultural anthropology. Such study provides a set of conceptual tools and an approach to problem solving that prepare the student for tackling effectively *all* problems of management, not just familiar ones.

Management by Imitation

Frequently, the "untrained" manager of a company, or the manager of a department or work group within a company, will try to match the success of a competing unit through *imitation*. More often than not this is poor management, for it is unusual for different organizations, or for different units within an organization, to have identical objectives and problems. For example, consider the role of organization structure—the way in which functions, people, and equipment in a company are interrelated for the purpose of achieving its objectives. To imitate the structure of a successful competitor is to miss the point that organization structure, policies, procedures, and duty assignments are all *means to an end*—tools for the achievement of company objectives.

Even two competing firms in the same industry usually will have different objectives. One automobile manufacturer wishes to emphasize economy and durability in his product, so he must build the kind of organization required to create such values. Another, who wishes to produce the highest quality, elegance, and luxury in his car, will have to follow a different approach with different kinds of personnel, policies, controls, and equipment.

Role of Fundamentals

The experienced manager who is well grounded in management fundamentals will be equipped to plan intelligently the future course of his company and to develop the kind of organization that will more effectively follow that course. He will be better able to *anticipate* problems and to *plan* for effective organizational growth. In addition, he will be prepared to plan for the *new* organizational patterns and adjustments required for the efficient utilization of automation, operations research, and decision-by-model techniques.

The "sound barrier" for many organizations is that point in growth beyond which one-man management is unworkable. Crossing it can be most hazardous for managers who do not know how to provide for effective delegation of authority, staff activity, or over-all control. The problem is compounded by the fact that complexities of organization increase at a faster rate than do numerical increases in personnel, and the costliness of management error increases at an even faster rate. Good management does not just happen; it is usually associated with those students of management who have drawn heavily upon the insights and experience of the past. Since so many responsible jobs in our complex society require managerial skill, those who are not preparing consciously for management positions can profit, also, from the study of management fundamentals.

WHAT IS MANAGEMENT?

The Organic Functions

Whenever someone attempts to achieve a goal through the directed efforts of others, he becomes a manager. Let us examine the kind of activities implied by this statement. First, a particular manager must decide on a goal or the means for achieving it, or both (depending on whether or not a specific goal were handed to him from above); he must see to it that the persons and physical factors necessary for the work to be done are present and related to each other as planned; and he must see to it that the goal is actually achieved as planned. In effect, he engages in the functions of *planning, organizing,* and *controlling* the work of others in addition to his own work. These are the three *organic functions of management.*[1] By "organic" we mean that all three are *invariably* basic to, and inherent in, managerial activity, whenever and wherever it is performed.

Planning. Planning has to do with the determination of *what* is to be done, *how, where, when,* and by *whom.* Obviously, it must precede execution if an activity is to proceed in an efficient, coordinated manner. Except by chance, the quality of action cannot exceed the quality of the planning on which it is based. There are

---

[1] They were first identified and published privately as *The Organic Functions of Management* by Ralph C. Davis in 1934. See R. C. Davis, *The Fundamentals of Top Management* (New York: Harper & Bros., 1951), pp. 154, 645.

important concepts and techniques in the area of planning that are well worth the reader's attention. These are discussed in chapter 2. Effective planning for the performance of the organizing and controlling functions is discussed in chapters 2–8.

Organizing. Organization planning "sets the stage" for performance of the organizing function by determining what functions, people, physical factors, and the interrelationships between these will be required to carry out organizational objectives. Organizing is the *actual work* of carrying out these activities as planned. Planning for the effective performance of the organizing function is discussed in chapters 5 and 6.

Controlling. Controlling is concerned with making events conform to plans. This is a most challenging function of management, which draws heavily on the *art* as well as the *science* of management. The art of management is especially involved in the area of personal leadership: the effective understanding and motivation of the individual. For managers must control people as well as things! Planning for control is discussed in chapters 7 and 8.

Differences among Authorities

This classification of the organic functions of management seems plausible to the author and serves as one of the bases for the organization of this book. However, to avoid confusion on the part of the reader when he looks elsewhere, it should be pointed out that there is no real agreement among authorities as to how the organic functions of management should be classified, though there is general agreement as to what these basic functions are. For example, many agree that managers everywhere must *plan, organize, control, staff, direct, command, supervise, motivate, train, coordinate, delegate, evaluate, and correct.* They do not agree, however, as to which of these should be listed as organic functions and which as organic subfunctions.[2] The author believes that there are serious "overlaps" as well as omissions of important subfunctions in the various lists that are found in the management literature. It is believed that the list given above can be logically accommodated by the organic functions of *planning, organizing,* and *controlling* as follows:

---

[2] For the results of a survey of managers in a firm to determine what they perceive as basic management functions see Robert J. House and John M. McIntyre, "Management Theory in Practice," (*Advanced Management,* October, 1961). Vol. 26, No. 10.

Planning	Organizing	Controlling (the work of others)
	staffing	delegating
	training	directing
		motivating
		coordinating
		evaluating
		correlating

Of course, there is definite overlap or duplication in this listing of subfunctions, since the items for it were drawn from various sources. But there are gaps, too. The author has attempted to formulate *complete* lists of organic subfunctions for each of the three organic functions of management. The organic subfunctions of planning are discussed in chapter 2; the organic subfunctions of organizing in chapter 5; and the organic subfunctions of control in chapter 7.

THE MANAGEMENT PROCESS

Designating the *organic functions* of *management* as planning, organizing, and controlling, is, in effect, setting up an arbitrary, three-part classification of all managerial activities. This is done for the purpose of facilitating analysis and conceptualization on the part of the student of management. It should *not* be assumed, however, that unique, completely independent compartments are represented by the organic functions. Actually, a manager must *plan* for the performance of the *organic functions;* he must *organize* for the performance of the *organic functions;* and he must *control* the performance of the *organic functions.* We could just as easily talk about the "management" of planning, the "management" of organizing, and the "management" of controlling! *In reality, managing is a continuous operation or process involving the interaction of the organic functions.*

The chief value of separating the organic functions is one of *emphasis:* to assure that *adequate attention* will be devoted to each important phase of managerial activity and to stress the need for attention to the *sequence* of performance. For example, planning must precede organizing and controlling, but it is certainly influenced by these phases. If a particular event does not conform to plan, this will lead to replanning the event, and often to some organizing activity. Much of the *science* of management is concerned with the development of conceptual tools, techniques, and analytical skills that will improve our performance of the organic functions.

The *art* of management is more concerned with the management process, the interplaying and balancing of the organic functions to assure their proper interaction. Because this continuous interaction of the organic functions—the management process—represents the reality with which managers must cope, it provides the primary basis for the organization of subject matter in this book.

BACKGROUND TO MODERN MANAGEMENT

We tend to take for granted the right to engage in private enterprise, public attitudes about business, and the modern manager's concern with good public relations. Actually, what *is* the basis of the right to engage in private enterprise, anyway? Have public attitudes as to the proper place and role of business in society always been the same? Are modern businessmen concerned with good public relations simply because their predecessors learned many years ago that this is good for business? Do we have the same feelings about the values of unrestrained business activity as did our forefathers, and, if not, why? An understanding of these questions and their answers is closely related to an understanding of the present and future roles of private enterprise in our society.

Business and Society

The right to engage in private business stems from the right of private property, and this right may be modified, extended, or withdrawn as society desires. At times in the past, society has been confused as to the proper role and reward for businessmen. At one time, for example, the charging of interest for the use of funds was regarded as an evil and gave rise to the cry, "Chase the money lenders from the temple!"

Ancient traders were praised for the goods and information they brought from afar and were cursed for the exorbitant profits they realized—profits that often were fair reward for the extreme personal risks they faced and just as often were the result of questionable monopoly rights and highly suspect business practices.

Time and again attempts have been made to displace private enterprise with communal or carefully regulated public enterprise only to find the personal greed and abuses of the private entrepreneur replaced by the political graft and gross inefficiency of the nonprivate manager.

Limitations of Classical Doctrines

Why was it that unrestrained private enterprise capitalism created social ills? If it did, why was it permitted to operate? Actually, the framers of the Constitution knew that unlimited power corrupts businessmen as well as politicians. However, they supported the classical economic doctrines of laissez faire because of the belief that free competition would provide the necessary restraint to assure survival only to those businesses which would *serve* society's needs. Though early American enterprise did reward their expectations with superb dynamic qualities, it produced, also, abuses that could not be tolerated.

In the simple economy of early America it was easy to overlook very real *limitations* to certain basic assumptions, upon which classical economics was founded and upon which it depended for the restraint of abuses and monopolistic practices.

Perfect Mobility of Labor. It was assumed that workers would be financially, emotionally, and technically equipped always to move to optimal employment opportunities for themselves. Most workers were not so equipped, and most had inadequate knowledge of alternative employment opportunities.

Perfect Competition among Employers. It was assumed that healthy competition would be maintained through perfect mobility of labor, adequate consumer knowledge as to competing products, full knowledge on the part of businessmen as to competitor activities, and the possibility of immediate entry by new enterprises into any industry. Obviously, these requirements were realized only partially in practice.

Equality of Bargaining Power. The assumption was made that there was equality of bargaining power between employers and workers *without* the provision of collective bargaining rights and other protections for the worker. The inadequacies of this assumption have been clearly revealed in the history of early American labor relations.

Short-run Application of the Concept of Intelligent Selfishness. There was much merit to the idea that, for the long run, the businessman would maximize his personal gain, and, for that matter, remain in business, only to the extent that he truly served the needs of society. But overlooked were the possible rewards for "unenlightened" selfishness in the short run—the opportunity for the shrewd operator to get in and get out fast and to make his "killing" through the deliberate misrepresentation of his product or service, consumer ignorance, and the time required to expose him. Society has come to realize that it must supplement the pressures of competition with other means to assure that only socially desirable business activity will be engaged in.

The "Economic Man" Concept. Along with the foregoing assumptions went the oversimplified "economic man" concept of human motivation, which carried over into the scientific management movement (which will be discussed) and limited its effectiveness.

Misgivings of Adam Smith

Surprisingly enough, Adam Smith—who presented this early economic theory in his classic *Wealth of Nations*, published in 1776—perceived many of its limitations, limitations that we "moderns," for the most part, have appreciated only in the last fifty years! It is true that he was overly optimistic about the ability of his self-regulating "system" to govern itself and gave relatively little attention to the ways in which supplemental restraints on the system or economy might be devised and applied. Nevertheless, he did recognize the *need* for supplemental restraints, a fact for which he is rarely given credit. It will be worthwhile to review briefly his contribution in this regard.

Remember, now, that Smith taught the doctrine of laissez faire, economic liberalism or freedom from governmental interference. He saw in the drive of self-interest the economic mainspring of men and the basis of a natural order for the attainment of the greatest good available to society. He was one of the first to stress the fundamental role of specialization as a key to greater productivity. However, as was pointed out above, he was aware of the possible ill effects that might result from specialization and did not assume that the built-in checks of the laissez faire approach—competition and self-interest will force optimal service to the community—would prevent them. If anything, he overstated the case in the following excerpts from his book:

> The man whose whole life is spent in performing a few simple operations, of which the effects too are, perhaps, always the same, or very nearly the same, has no occasion to exert his understanding, or to exercise his invention in finding out expedients for removing difficulties which never occur. . . . His dexterity at his own particular trade seems, in this

manner, to be acquired at the expense of his intellectual, social, and martial virtues, but in every improved and civilized society this is the state into which the labouring poor, that is, the great body of the people, must necessarily fall, unless government takes some pains to prevent it.[3]

He provided additional evidence of the need for business ethics, a sound philosophy of management, and protective legislation when he wrote:

To widen the market and to narrow the competition, is always the interest of the dealers. To widen the market may frequently be agreeable enough to the interest of the public; but to narrow the competition must always be against it, and can serve only to enable the dealers, by raising their profits above what they naturally would be, to levy, for their own benefit, an absurd tax upon the rest of their fellow-citizens. The proposal of any new law or regulation of commerce which comes from this order, ought always to be listened to with great precaution, and ought never to be adopted till after having been long and carefully examined, not only with the most scrupulous, but with the most suspicious attention. It comes from an order of men, whose interest is never exactly the same with that of the public, who have generally an interest to deceive and even to oppress the public, and who accordingly have, upon many occasions, both deceived and oppressed it.[4]

Servants, labourers and workmen of different kinds, make up the far greater part of every great political society. But what improves the circumstances of the greater part can never be regarded as an inconveniency to the whole. No society can surely be flourishing and happy, of which the far greater part of the members are poor and miserable. It is but equity, besides, that they who feed, cloath and lodge the whole body of the people, should have such a share of the produce of their own labour as to be themselves tolerably well fed, cloathed and lodged.[5]

What are the common wages of labour, depends every where upon the contract usually made between those two parties, whose interests are by no means the same. The workmen desire to get as much, the masters to give as little as possible. The former are disposed to combine in order to raise, the latter in order to lower the wages of labour.[6]

It is not, however, difficult to foresee which of the two parties must, upon all ordinary occasions, have the advantage in the dispute, and force the other into a compliance with their terms. The masters, being fewer in number, can combine much more easily; and the law, besides, authorises, or at least does not prohibit their combinations, while it prohibits those of the workmen. . . . Many workmen could not subsist a week, few could subsist a month, and scarce any a year without employment.

---

[3] Adam Smith, *The Wealth of Nations* (1776) (New York: Random House ed., 1937), pp. 734, 735.
[4] *Ibid.,* p. 250.
[5] *Ibid.,* pp. 78, 79.
[6] *Ibid.,* p. 66.

In the long-run the workman may be as necessary to his master as his master is to him, but the necessity is not so immediate.[7]

But Adam Smith probably provided the most revealing statement about his basic outlook when he wrote:

> It appears, accordingly, from the experience of all ages and nations, I believe, that the work done by freemen comes cheaper in the end than that performed by slaves. It is found to do so even at Boston, New York, and Philadelphia, where the wages of common labour are very high. . . .[8]

It would be folly to assert, on the basis of these fragments from The Wealth of Nations, that Smith possessed an integrated, coherent philosophy of management, as has been evolved in some quarters today. But it is interesting that this man had such glimpses of an age to come. It is especially significant that these observations were not the protests of a "utopian socialist" but were the insights of an economist looking for ways to increase the wealth of nations.

Reform in America

For many years we were not forced to consider these limitations of the classical doctrine very seriously. For the rate of growth of industry in early America generated sufficient competition for labor among employers that many American workers were spared the hardships they would have encountered in parts of industrial Europe. Also, frontier opportunities provided a workable alternative to many as well as a counterforce to discourage abuse. But the shenanigans of the medicine-show men, the watered-stock promoters, and other get-rich-quick artists were much in evidence and should have convinced some that unrestrained free enterprise has its limitations. Perhaps part of the explanation rests in the fact that, from all evidence, society was much less sensitive to social injustices than it is today. For example, some unions complained bitterly about women and children working twelve hours a day for half the union pay scale, *not* out of compassion for their lot in life but because they felt that this constituted unfair, sweatshop competition for them! And for years our courts refused to curb this kind of exploitation by arguing that they were duty bound to protect the "right" of women and children to enter into such employment as guaranteed them by the Constitution!

However, a growing awareness of the need for supplemental restraints finally led to the passage of the Sherman Antitrust Act of

---

[7] *Ibid.*
[8] *Ibid*, p. 81.

1890, the Pure Food and Drugs Act of 1912, and the regulation of labor relations, security transactions, and other activities in more recent times. The stock market crash of 1929 and the ensuing depression disillusioned many people as to the competence and integrity of many businessmen. And the general failure of business leaders to propose useful solutions to the trying social problems of the depression years did not add to their stature in the eyes of the public. The experimentation of the New Deal years, progressive income taxation, and the current interest in welfare benefits via "non-actuarial" premiums all demonstrate that the public can and will alter the right of private property.

BUSINESS AND THE PUBLIC TODAY

In view of these developments, few business leaders today would be willing to express the sentiment, "the public be damned," which was uttered by an eminent businessman of yesteryear. The increased social awareness of the public, the impressive power of organized labor, and the regulatory activities of the government have made it virtually impossible for businessmen to believe that the conduct of a business is strictly a private affair—that there is some inalienable right by which they may continue to do as they please. Business leaders have come to see more clearly their role in relation to society, the need for a system of business ethics and a sound philosophy to guide them in the practice of management.[9] They know that society is quite sensitive and reactive to those who abuse the *privilege* that it has *conferred* to engage in business. And our better-informed business leaders know from experience and observation, both here and abroad, that the advantages of our free enterprise system are well worth preserving and should not be jeopardized by disservice to the public. They realize that private enterprise, properly restrained within the framework of our constitutionalism, continues to provide the greatest degree of initiative and productive efficiency obtainable and that it also provides one of the best protections against the loss of individual liberty arising from political over-centralism.

THE SCIENTIFIC MANAGEMENT MOVEMENT

We have described some of the developments that have led to the increased social awareness and service orientation of today's business leaders. What about the revolution in managerial concepts

---

[9] Ethical standards are discussed in chap. 7, "Planning for Control." The nature of philosophy and its role in business are discussed in the next chapter.

and techniques that has taken place in the last fifty years? The scientific management movement was undoubtedly the most significant contributor to this revolution. It successfully challenged existing modes of management and laid the groundwork for the development of management as a profession. The "management science" of today has its roots in this movement. Because of the importance of its role in the development of management thought, its origin and character will be discussed in some detail below.

Initial Successes

The full-blown launching of the scientific management movement in the latter part of 1910 produced a public sensation. Harrington Emerson testified in November of that year before the Interstate Commerce Commission that the railroads of the United States might save a million dollars a day by devoting attention to efficiency in their operations.

At the Santa Fe Railroad, the care of shop machinery belting, which was important in those days, was transferred from workmen to specialists, with a resultant saving of 70 per cent in the cost of belt maintenance. In the Santa Fe president's annual report for 1906, data were given indicating a saving of some 1½ million dollars as a result of improved cost accounting practices and the introduction of scientific management.

And there were many other dramatic achievements attributable to the introduction of scientific management. When applied to the simple operation of loading a railway car by hand with pig iron, the performance of the individual worker increased from 12½ to 47 tons per day. When applied to shoveling coal, it doubled or trebled the performance of the shoveler. In machine shop work it developed in certain operations increases in production ranging from 400 to 1,800 per cent. In bricklaying the day's accomplishment rose from 1,000 to 2,700 bricks. And, when applied in the manufacture of machinery, 75 men in the machine shop with 20 in the planning department did two or three times as much work as 105 men in the machine shop had done previously.

Father of the Movement

These results were due largely to the successful separation of *planning* functions from *doing* functions and to the systematic study of business problems by *specialized* personnel. The guiding spirit in this approach was Frederick W. Taylor, who is generally acknowledged throughout the world as the "father" of scientific management. Many investigators before Taylor had given him reason to be impressed by the value of the scientific approach to problems.

Leonardo da Vinci, Copernicus, Kepler, Galileo, Newton, Watt, Fulton, Faraday, and innumerable others had demonstrated what systematic observation, experimentation, and theorizing could accomplish. Their work led to the development of the mechanical deterministic concepts that paid off so handsomely in the achievements of nineteenth-century physics and chemistry. It seems only natural that an attempt would be made by men like Taylor and his pioneering colleagues to apply this same approach in the business world.

The idea of using this method in industry had a tremendous emotional appeal, too. Frederick Taylor was tireless, self-demanding in his work, and of unquestioned integrity, but he was somewhat quick-tempered and diffident in his dealings with others. Like many managers of his day who had had difficulty in coping with large doses of frustration and employee-management conflict, Taylor seemed to long for the security of a "logical" business environment devoid of error, inefficiency, and human conflict. After all, the scientific approach had been so successful in the physical sciences, would it not also rationalize human relationships and somehow dispense with the need for negotiation and compromise in industry? Pursuit of this idea led to increasing distrust on the part of labor and to drastic revision in the logics of the movement later on.

The Systematic Approach

Taylor made it clear that management must first systematically study its work for the purpose of identifying and defining various principles. Then it must develop adequate procedures for applying them. He indicated that to work according to scientific laws, management would have to take over and perform much of the work currently being performed by the men; almost every act of the workman would be preceded by one or more preparatory acts of management that would enable him to do his work better and quicker than he could otherwise have done.

Taylor stated that scientific management comprises a combination of four great underlying principles of management: (1) the development of a true science; (2) the scientific selection of workmen; (3) the scientific education and development of workmen; and (4) intimate friendly cooperation between management and and the men.

He listed various tools to serve these principles, such as time study, functional foremanship, standardization of tools and movements of workmen for each class of work, planning rooms or departments, the "exception principle"[10] in management, slide rules and other time-saving implements, instruction cards for the workmen, the task idea in compensation with bonuses for above-average performance, the mnemonic classification system, routing systems, and cost accounting techniques.

In a specific situation, say a metalworking plant, the introduction of the Taylor system would entail the following steps: (1) the development and introduction of standards throughout the works and office; (2) the scientific study of unit times on several different kinds of work; (3) a complete analysis of the pulling, feeding power, and proper speeding of the various machine tools throughout the place with the view of making a slide rule for properly running each machine; (4) the work of establishing the system of time cards by means of which ultimately all the desired information would be conveyed from the men to the planning room; (5) overhauling the stores issuing and receiving system so as to establish a complete running balance of materials; and (6) ruling and printing the various blanks that would be required for shop returns and reports, time cards, instruction cards, expense sheets, cost sheets, pay sheet, and balance records, and preparing other forms that would be required in the storeroom, for the "tickler" file, and for the maintenance of standards throughout the plant.

Functional Foremanship

Taylor indicated that if the plant were a large one, the man in charge of introducing the system should appoint a special assistant in charge of each of the foregoing functions. He felt that the most important and difficult task of the organizer would be that of selecting and training the various "functional foremen" who would lead and instruct the workmen.

Eight of these "functional foremen" or specialist bosses replaced the single foreman when the Taylor system was installed. Taylor's idea was to introduce the advantages of division of labor and of

---

[10] This is discussed on page 172.

specialized training and experience at the supervisory level. He regarded four of the eight as "executive functional bosses" who handled the active work of the shop: the gang boss, the speed boss, the inspector, and the repair boss. The other four "functional bosses" were located in the planning room. They were: the order of work and route clerk, the instruction card clerk, the time and cost clerk, and the shop disciplinarian.[11]

The least successful of the innovations that Taylor introduced was the use of "functional foremen." Though his work did emphasize the glaring need for more specialized study and skill in industry, he inadvertently selected the least desirable way of introducing it.

"Functional foremen" were skilled specialists, but they were also human. No one of the eight was clearly responsible when production bogged down. Interpersonal friction within the group was virtually assured by the impossibility of accurately defining where one man's jurisdiction ended and another's began. And we can only imagine the bewilderment of the worker confronted with eight bosses.

Other Contributors

Taylor admits that workers frequently commented when they first came under the system, "Why, I am not allowed to think or move without someone interfering or doing it for me!"[12] However, through the "functional foremanship" scheme he *did* dramatize the need for managerial specialization. This was subsequently provided in industry through the widespread utilization of staff specialists in the framework of the "line and staff" form of organization. Harrington Emerson was one of the early leaders in scientific management who recognized and advocated the superiority of the "line and staff" approach.[13]

And, of course, there were many others, both here and abroad, who made significant contributions to the scientific management movement. Among them were such men as Horace Hathaway, Carl Barth, Henry Gantt, and Morris Cooke, who were closely associated with Taylor; Sanford Thompson and Frank Gilbreth, who

---

[11] For a full discussion of his system see Frederick W. Taylor, *Shop Management* (1903) and *The Principles of Scientific Management* (1911). Fortunately, these along with his *Testimony before the Special House Committee* (1912) are printed in one volume: F. W. Taylor, *Scientific Management*, (New York: Harper & Bros., 1947).

[12] *The Principles of Scientific Management*, p. 125.

[13] The "line and staff" form of organization is discussed on p. 94.

did so much to develop the art of time and motion study in the
building trades, and Henri LeChatelier, of France, who introduced
the teachings of Taylor to large areas of Europe.

Intangible Values

Despite the striking successes achieved by it during the early
years, perhaps the most important long-range value of scientific
management to society was not efficiency but the provision of a
basis for the development of professional pride on the part of
business leaders. By supplying them with a growing body of principles and professional techniques, by challenging them to develop
these further and for the right purposes, business leaders were given
a sense of direction, achievement, and worthwhileness in the eyes
of society.

Taylor understood this, for he never stopped pointing out that
the mechanisms of management must not be mistaken for its essence or underlying philosophy. Probably his best expression of
what scientific management meant to him was given in 1912 in
response to hostile criticism from a congressional committee:

> Scientific management is not any efficiency device, . . . nor is it any
> bunch or group of efficiency devices. It is not a new system of figuring
> costs; . . . it is not holding a stop-watch on a man, and writing things
> down about him; it is not time study; it is not motion study . . . ; it is
> not the printing and ruling and unloading of a ton or two of blanks by
> a set of men saying "Here's your system; go to it." It is not divided
> foremanship or functional foremanship; it is not any of the devices which
> the average man calls to mind when scientific management is spoken
> of . . . .
> Now, in its essence, scientific management involves a complete men-
> tal revolution on the part of the working man engaged in any particular
> establishment or industry, . . . And it involves the equally complete
> mental revolution on the part of those on the management's side. . . .
> I have never said that scientific management could be used for bad
> [ends]. It is possible to use the mechanism of scientific management for
> bad [ends], but not scientific management itself. It ceases to be scien-
> tific management the moment it is used for bad [ends].[14]

Limitations

But, generally, Taylor and the other pioneers did not know how
to translate effectively their ideals into practice. Their first error

---

[14] *"Testimony before the Special House Committee,"* pp. 26, 27, 191, in Taylor,
Scientific Management. (This is a reprint of public document, *Hearings before Special Committee of the House of Representatives To Investigate the Taylor and Other
Systems of Shop Management under Authority of H. Res. 90,* Vol. III. pp. 1377–
1508).

was in claiming that theirs was an "exact science." In 1916 Gantt wrote: "The substitution of fact for opinion is the basis of modern industrial progress, and the rate of this progress is controlled by the extent to which the methods of scientific investigation supplant the debating society methods in determining a basis for action."[15]

In his testimony before the congressional committee in 1912 Taylor pointed out that "both sides must recognize as essential the substitution of exact scientific investigation and knowledge for the old individual judgment or opinion, either of the workman or the boss, in all matters relating to the work done in the establishment."[16]

These are typical of the comments made by many of the early leaders. The difficulty is that in industry instances in which fact may be substituted for judgment are far fewer than these men believed. Even if restricted to such specific procedures as time and motion study, methods analysis, and job evaluation, such statements remain misleading, for these activities are far from being based on an "exact science." Collaborative judgment plays an important role in the development and implementation of these procedures for any particular application. Modifying them to meet organizational needs, allowing for the human element in their operation, and preparing the organization for their introduction are hardly matters of exact procedure.

Nevertheless, many of these leaders believed that exactness could be achieved in all areas of activity. They thought, for example, that compromise and negotiation could be entirely discarded in labor management relations. This conviction rested on the assumption that the worker was essentially the emotionless, nonexistent, "economic man" of classical economic theory. If the employer could scientifically determine a fair day's pay, if the employee were told the best way to do his work and were permitted to earn a bonus for above-average performance, and if the employer's intentions were honorable, then "What more could the worker expect or want?"

Frank Gilbreth claims that Taylor told him that the "instruction card can be depended upon to carry the work of the master or the manager without a line of translation in the way of the human element."[17] The logics of this approach suggest that, as long as

---

[15] Henry Gantt, *Industrial Leadership* (New York: Association Press), p. 89.

[16] Testimony before the special House committee (*op. cit.*), p. 31.

[17] Louis D. Brandeis, "Scientific Management and Railroads (Being Part of a Brief Submitted to the Interstate Commerce Commission)," *Engineering Magazine*, 1911, p. 11.

management wishes to be fair, unions are superfluous; that the complexities of the "science" dictate that it be *unilaterally developed* and *administered* by experts; that any grumbling or discontent on the part of workers under well planned scientific management is due solely to a misunderstanding on their part as to the objectives of the movement. Recognition of the human element usually took the form of pointing out the pride and stimulation a worker derives from competing with and outdoing his fellow-workers.

There can be little question as to Taylor's sincerity when he wrote:

> No system of management, however good, should be applied in a wooden way. The proper personal relations should always be maintained between the employers and men. . . . The employer who goes through his works with kid gloves on, and is never known to dirty hands or clothes, and who either talks to his men in a condescending or patronizing way, or else not at all, has no chance whatever of ascertaining their real thoughts or feelings. . . . The opportunity which each man should have of airing his mind freely, and having it out with his employers, is a safety-valve; and if the superintendents are reasonable men, and listen to and treat with respect what their men have to say, there is absolutely no reason for labor unions and strikes.[18]

But, in practice, Taylor did not provide an approach or create an organizational environment designed to exploit these insights. In the scheme of scientific management there was little protection for the employee against unreasonable supervisors and little basis for employee participation in, or identification with, the work of the organization. And the need for participation became more pronounced as the planning room displaced the worker as the custodian of job knowledge—knowledge that was to be "returned" to the worker only piecemeal.

It is easy to see, then, how this movement gave impetus to "paternalism" in industry: the giving of benefits, bonuses, and gifts by employers, with the hope that they would get unquestioning obedience, hard work, and nonunion shops in return. For scientific management left little room for negotiation—we do not negotiate scientific facts—and the unschooled worker could hardly be expected to participate intelligently in scientific planning and analysis. If a worker grumbled openly, he was a "bad egg," to be sternly disciplined or dismissed. After all, the rationality of scientific man-

---

[18] *Shop Management*, p. 184.

agement *assured* the satisfaction and well-being of *normal* employees.

It is easy to see how unscrupulous employers who wished to exploit scientific management by using it to take advantage of their workers encountered little opposition. Organized labor was not strong enough to combat them, and labor legislation at that time gave little protection. And the public of that day embraced the laissez faire philosophy with the notion that if an employee did not like a particular situation, he could move on to another or set up shop for himself.

Organized labor strongly opposed scientific management through fear of the "speed-up" and rate-cutting. Also, workers experienced growing frustration in their inability to have some say-so about things that affected them and in their realization that scientific management did not deal in exact procedures after all. This kind of reaction often has been blamed on those employers who openly "perverted" the basic philosophy and intent of Frederick Taylor, and upon them only. This does not seem accurate. For, just as often, distrust of the movement and perversion of its goals was due to the failure of it sincerest advocates adequately to tackle the human factors involved.[19]

Early Human Relationists

But rejection of the oversimplified notion that economic incentives largely explain employee behavior and acceptance of the idea that there is still much *art* required in management did not have to await the classic Hawthorn experiments started by Elton Mayo in 1927[20] or the development of post-World War II research in group dynamics and human relations.

In 1924 Oliver Sheldon, an Englishman, wrote *The Philosophy of Management,* which was widely adopted as a textbook in both England and the United States. His theme was that, though Taylor-

---

[19] Two of the better works on scientific management are: Horace B. Drury, *Scientific Management: A History and Criticism* (New York: Columbia University Press, 1922), and Robert F. Hoxie, *Scientific Management and Labor* (New York: D. Appleton & Co., 1915). For additional biographical data on the key men who participated in the movement see L. Urwick (ed.), *The Golden Book of Management: A Historical Record of the Life and Work of Seventy Pioneers* (London: Newman Neame Ltd., 1956).

[20] See "The Fruitful Errors of Elton Mayo" in William Fox (ed.), *Readings in Personnel Management from "Fortune"* (New York: Henry Holt & Co., 1947), or *Fortune,* November, 1946.

ism had helped greatly in the development of a science of management, such work had in no way detracted from the predominantly human job of the manager to manage. He felt that, insofar as management deals with things, its methods can be reduced to terms of scientific principle but that there can be no science of cooperation.

Mary Parker Follett, an outstanding business philosopher of the time, agreed with Sheldon as to the need for emphasizing human factors in management. but disagreed by thinking that a science of cooperation could be developed some day.[21] She saw in her "Law of the Situation" a means for bridging the gap between the ideals of scientific management and the unilateral practice of it.

In a paper delivered in 1925 she explained this "law" as a means for depersonalizing order-giving and uniting all concerned in a study of the situation to discover the "Law of the Situation" and obey that. In effect, she proposed the development of objectives, plans, and "facts" through the same kind of collaborative effort between leaders and their subordinates as usually takes place between leaders of the same rank. She went even further to say: "From one point of view, one might call the essence of scientific management the attempt to find the 'Law of the Situation'!"[22]

Starting around 1925, a four-year study of personnel problems in one of the largest mercantile establishments in the United States was undertaken by a group of psychiatrists, psychologists, and psychiatric social workers. They were organized into a well-integrated unit and utilized a broad clinical and social case type of approach to various problems.

In 1926 Sam Lewisohn wrote *New Leadership in Industry,* which provided a new view of the responsibility of personnel specialists for the maintenance of good human relations in an organization. "What does the worker want?" he asked, and answered: "Justice, status, and opportunity." Should a specialist be given the chief role in meeting these needs? Lewisohn wrote: "The management of human relations must finally rest in the hands of line officials."[23]

---

[21] There are many today who think that this will evolve ultimately on the basis of research in the behavioral sciences.

[22] Henry C. Metcalf and L. Urwick (eds.), *Dynamic Administration: The Collected Papers of Mary Parker Follett* (New York: Harper & Bros., 1940), p. 59. The "Law of the Situation" will be considered in greater detail on p. 216.

[23] (New York: E. P. Dutton & Co.). pp. 207, 217, 89.

Scientific Management Today

Today, scientific management has come of age. If anything, the technical phases have been largely displaced from the limelight by the clamor over group dynamics and human relations in industry. However, the advent of automation, operations research, and formalized decision making in industry may soon reverse this emphasis. Management has learned many things since the early days of "Taylorism." Few industrial leaders now question the inadequacy of the "economic man" approach to behavior or the basic need for employee participation at all levels in the organization.

They recognize that participation is necessary to provide the basis for identification with company goals and a feeling of worthwhileness on the part of employees. They realize that workers as well as they themselves will resist and fight changes that they believe threaten their well-being, regardless of how logical the changes may appear to others. Also, management has a greater tendency to regard such resistance today as the result of poor participation and communication practices rather than as a sign of disloyalty on the part of workers.

In addition, the work of men like Einstein, Planck, and Heisenberg has helped to explode the mechanical-deterministic view of the universe that nurtured the dogmatism of many of the pioneers in the scientific management movement. Today, the evolution of a statistical-probability concept has done much to discourage claims for absolutism in any field of study.

Analysis of the defects and oversights in the early pioneering work has permitted management to build on the basically sound foundation laid by Taylor and the other leaders. Today, scientific management, introduced with the spirit of collaborative inquiry and honest negotiation on the part of both labor and management, holds before us the promise of a golden age of progress in the creation of human as well as economic values.

OTHER INTERDISCIPLINARY CONTRIBUTORS

We have presented only a partial "sketch" of the background to modern management. As Haynes and Massie point out, "The 'scientific management' movement in the United States has had an enormous influence, mostly to the good, but is only one strand of ideas important to the managers of the future."[24] They list people from various disciplines who have contributed to present-day management (see Fig. 1-1). Of course, one can debate the relative importance of the names mentioned, but such a chart does drama-

FIG. 1-1
Streams of Thought on Management*

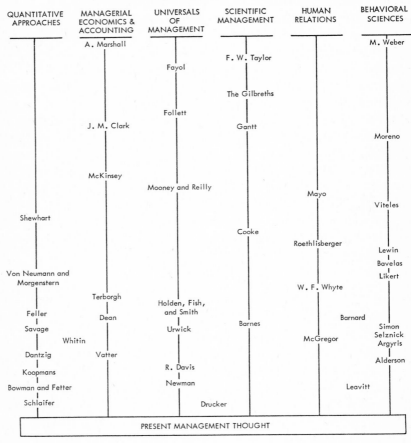

*W. W. Haynes and J. L. Massie, *Management: Analysis, Concepts and Cases* Englewood Cliffs, New Jersey: Prentice-Hall, Inc., 1961, p. 3.

tize the *interdisciplinary* character of the management movement and it suggests many good men with whom the student of management should develop a reading acquaintance!

---
[24] W. W. Haynes and J. L. Massie, *Management: Analysis, Concepts and Cases* (Englewood Cliffs, New Jersey: Prentice-Hall, Inc., 1961), p. 2.

DESIGN OF THIS BOOK

The central purpose of this book is to present modern management concepts, eclectically derived, in a framework that reflects the nature of the *management process:* the continuous *interaction* of the *organic functions of management.* Thus in chapters 2–8, *planning* for the performance of the organic functions will be discussed. This discussion will consider the new tools and techniques of planning that are contributing so much at present and, with continuing development, promise so much more for the future! Also discussed will be those factors which should be considered in organization planning, and planning for the performance of the organizing and controlling functions.

Chapters 9-12 will discuss the important area of *organization* for the performance of the organic functions. The new tools and techniques of planning have created *new* organizational and control problems and requirements. These are confronting managers *today,* and tomorrow they will become overwhelming if not properly handled. Certainly, an important goal of this book is to contribute to the development of the understanding and criteria necessary for students and practicing managers to analyze and evaluate particular organizations and recognize means for *strengthening* them and *adapting* them to changed conditions.

Chapters 13–15 consider important factors bearing on *control* of the organic functions. Again, stress is placed on the *interaction* between control and what is being controlled. There are unique requirements involved when one considers control of planning as contrasted with control of organizing and control of control itself.

Though this is not a book on quantitative techniques in management, one of its purposes is to discuss the *usefulness* and *general character* of these techniques. For modern managers must hire, evaluate, and collaborate with quantitative experts and draw on some knowledge of these techniques in planning for the future. As these techniques become more powerful and pervasive in application—and this is only a question of time—knowledge of them will become essential to the man who aspires to advancement in a company, whether as a specialist or as a general manager.

Some descriptive material is necessary in any fundamentals book. But the overriding objective of this book is to equip the reader with conceptual tools and a broad, realistic frame of reference that will enable him to approach the practice of management, now and in the future, with some analytical skill and enhanced *potential* for superior managerial skill.

QUESTIONS

1. Distinguish between the *art* and the *science* of management. Is it likely that the art of management will be learned most effectively in in the same way as the science of management? Discuss.

2. Is it correct to say that the study of modern management is "interdisciplinary" in character? Explain. Give examples.

3. Why does your author believe that "the 'sound barrier' for many organizations is that point in growth beyond which one-man management is unworkable?" Explain.

4. What are the three *organic function of management?* Explain what each entails. Do all management authorities agree with this listing of three *organic functions?* Why or why not?

5. What is meant by the expression "management process"? Explain.

6. What is the source of the right to engage in private business enterprise in America? Why is it important for managers to identify this source? Discuss.

7. Did unrestrained private enterprise capitalism create social ills? If so, why was it permitted to? Should it be "traded in" for some other basically different system? Why or why not?

8. Discuss the *contributions* and the *limitations* of the scientific management movement. Do you think that we have "come full circle" with the present-day emphasis on "management science"? Discuss.

9. Do you think that the practice of management today is a profession? Why or why not?

Section I

PLANNING
FOR
MANAGING

In chapter 2, planning is more rigorously defined and its organic sub-functions are discussed. Certain new planning techniques and uses of the computer as a tool of these techniques are examined. Chapters 3–8 consider the important areas of organization planning and planning for the performance of the organizing and controlling functions.

Chapter 2

PLANNING FOR PLANNING

NATURE OF PLANNING

Planning involves both *problem solving* (identification of alternatives) and *decision making* (selection from alternatives). *To plan is to search for alternatives, then to select from these alternatives to determine general and specific objectives and the detailed means for achieving them.*

It is difficult to overemphasize the importance of planning to an organization, for planning is necessary before effective organizing and control activity can take place. Since an organization is but a vehicle for carrying out plans, the character of the organization should be *planned* on the basis of previously planned company objectives. Control is concerned with making events conform to plans, and we must have the products of planning in the form of approved policies, procedures, budgets, plans, and programs before control can occur. Also, planning determines the *manner* in which control functions will be performed. Obviously, organizing and controlling activities can be no better than the planning activities that have preceded them.

Important new developments have contributed significantly to the quality and speed of planning. Managers who are capable of using such new planning tools as PERT and other "operations research" techniques will enjoy an increasing competitive advantage over those who do not profit from these developments.

Areas of Planning

Planning not only determines company objectives, organization structure, and the manner in which control will be carried out, as

27

noted above, but also determines policies, procedures, budgets, plans, and programs for various areas of company activity, such as sales, production, finance, personnel, public relations, and so on.

And within these areas of company activity there are further breakdowns. For example, in the sales area we should have clearly defined objectives, policies, procedures, etc., with regard to such subareas as product line, pricing, sales promotion, distribution, and market research. There are production "subareas," such as research and design, procurement, production stability, buy or make, inventory. In the personnel area are such "subareas" as recruitment, selection, training, wage and salary administration, medical services, safety, and labor relations. In the finance area consideration must be given to such "subareas" as costing, capital procurement depreciation, owning versus leasing, the development of cash forecasts and other tools. Also, there must be plans for the *Organic Management Functions* of Planning, Organizing, and Controlling the work of others. It is apparent, then, that good planning should lay the foundation for and permeate all phases of business activity.

Ethics and Planning

The *Generic Planning Premise* states that **planning requires a selection from alternatives for the establishment of goals and the means for achieving them. Since the evaluation of alternative goals presupposes a value system, planning involves ethics.**[1] This is true because the development of a value system requires that judgments be made as to what is desirable and undesirable; it is a philosophical undertaking. And philosophy is that discipline which comprises logic, ethics, aesthetics, metaphysics, and the theory of knowledge. The implication is clear: business planning is a direct reflection of the business philosophy that underlies it, though this may not always be understood by the businessman. Many may reject the idea of a close relationship between ethics and planning, yet demonstrate it in practice.

Business leaders today no longer define "profit" to managers and employees in purely monetary terms. Extensive research and experimentation with new approaches to labor-management relations show that there are other values of greater importance to

---

[1] A provocative discussion of the relation of ethics to planning is provided by Professor C. West Churchman, "How Is Planning Possible?" in J. F. McCloskey and J. M. Coppinger (eds.), *Operations Research for Management*, Vol. II (Baltimore: Johns Hopkins Press, 1956). See also Herbert A. Simon, *Administrative Behavior* (New York: Macmillan Co., 1957), pp. 47-60.

personnel than money—as purchasing power—which the organization should supply.[2] This leads to the need for a distinction between the goals and needs of the firm and the goals and needs of
the firm's personnel, and a determination of the proper "mix" between these goals. Very real ethical judgments are involved.

And business leaders are becoming increasingly aware of the
ethical implications of "unenlightened" selfishness in the short run
when the shrewd operator makes his "killing" at the expense of his
employees and the public. They see that, though businessmen do
not want a "planned economy," they are indirectly "planning" the
economy every day. For society *confers* the right to engage in
business because it expects that this will result in the creation and
distribution of *desired* utilities, and the manner in which it will
shape the economy of tomorrow will be influenced greatly by the
character of over-all business planning today.

Of course, there are no exact standards with which the ethical
factors in planning may be measured. Each age has had its own
convictions as to what is desirable business activity and as to the
proper role and reward for businessmen. We have come a long
way in the development of our understanding of economics since
the time when the charging of interest was regarded as a completely
unjustified and evil activity. Yet it would be folly indeed to assume
that future generations will or should maintain precisely the viewpoint that we have.

This does *not* mean that ethical factors in planning cannot be
measured or that they can be measured *only* in terms of the current
convictions and viewpoints of planners, for there is a long-term
trend in business values and goals that has unfolded and is unfolding as the profession of management develops. Also, the growing interdependence between factors in our economy and the strug-
gle with international communism have forced business leaders to
be even more concerned wtih the long-standing ethical imperatives
of our system of government. The business planner will have his
ethical standards when he has developed a philosophy of manage-

---

[2] For examples of research findings see Dorwin Cartwright and Alvin Zander,
Group Dynamics, and Morris Viteles, *Motivation and Morale in Industry.* For new
approaches to labor-management relations see "Causes of Industrial Peace" (National
Planning Association, Bulletin No. 14); and Frederick G. Lesieur (ed.), *The Scanlon
Plan* (Cambridge: The M.I.T. Press, 1958). Of course, money itself can become a
potent motivator of people who are convinced that they can *buy* satisfactions they
are denied in their daily lives, but little will be gained by the employer who encourages this illusion. And, as will be discussed later, money can be very important when
it serves as a status symbol or is associated with other non-monetary values.

ment based on an extensive study of the history of business and of our form of constitutionalism.[3]

That is not to say, however, that the administrator will or should develop a philosophy of management because society has coerced him into doing it. As was pointed out above, the profit motive is but one—and not necessarily the most important one— of a complex of motives that account for behavior in a business organization. Businessmen are striving toward self-realization and a sense of personal worth as much as the rest of us are; yet, traditionally, they have been expected to explain all their actions in terms of cold, narrow, personal profit making.

James C. Worthy, of Sears, Roebuck and Company, wisely observes: "The harmony between individual and general interests is more profoundly true than classical theory imagined—but in reverse. It is not that individual selfishness makes for general good but that *unselfishness* makes for *personal* good."[4] Certainly, this agrees with our best current psychological theory. Marshall E. Dimock, an experienced administrator also, suggests that consideration of what is in the long-range interests of the firm, or "what is good for the service," is most meaningful for top-level planners. He believes that the most effective administrators throughout history have been men of character and points out that "values, not techniques, were the eventual determiners of action"[5] in all administrative situations that he has reviewed.

Specific Objectives of Planning

Planners must decide: *What* is to be done—general and specific objectives; *how* to achieve these general and specific objectives; when to carry out various activities; where various activities should take place; and *who* should perform the activities.

To determine these things, planners must *search* for available alternatives and then *select* from them. If the average business planner were asked, "Just what do you do when you plan?" the chances are that he would not be very articulate as to *all* the steps— both conscious and unconscious—that he follows. He might say:

---

[3] The matter of ethical standards will be discussed at greater length in chapter 7.

[4] James C. Worthy, *Big Business and Free Men* (New York: Harper & Bros., 1959), p. 30.

[5] Dimock, *A Philosophy of Administration* (New York: Harper & Bros., 1958), p. 56. For a provocative discussion of the ethical responsibilities of management see chap. 6, "To Whom Is Management Accountable," in Ernest Dale, *The Great Organizers* (New York: McGraw-Hill Book Co., 1960).

"Well, first I try to have a clear idea of just what it is I wish to accomplish—as they say, I try to define the problem at hand. Then I try to focus on those key things which must be done or satisfied before I can achieve my objective (I know that I can't possibly consider all variables in the situation, so I concentrate on those which seem to me to be most significant). Then I think of the alternative ways in which these key things can be done; determine which is most practical and desirable and then try it out. You may ask how I determine which way is most desirable. Well, sometimes I can find out by collecting enough factual information and expert opinion as to the different alternatives so that an answer becomes rather obvious—this is especially true for what you might call objective problems, where most of the factors involved are understood and can be measured easily. Other times, when the situation is not so easy to analyze, I suppose I use what you might call intuition—a given approach just feels better, seems to be a better bet."

Organic Subfunctions of Planning

My hypothesis is that *all planning*, whether the informal type described above or the more formal type encountered in "operations research," involves the performance of the same basic or *organic subfunctions of planning*. The only difference—and, granted, it is a considerable one as to degree—between formal and informal planning is that the former signifies more adequate, conscious, and balanced attention to each of the *organic subfunctions*.[6] These *organic planning subfunctions* are:

1. Determination of key environmental factors and the interrelationships among them.

2. Search for and identification of *relevant* alternative objectives and determination of all the *relevant* possible consequences associated with *each* alternative objective.

3. Determination of objectives (the result of subfunctions 1, 2, 5, 6, 7, and 8).

4. Search for and identification of *revelant* alternatives for the achievement of objectives and determination of all the *relevant* possible consequences associated with *each* alternative.

---

[6] I readily concede that except for certain problems being handled today this scheme is closer to being a "normative" model (what ought to be done) than to being a "descriptive" model (what is done). However, this is only with regard to the thoroughness with which each of the organic planning functions listed below is performed. With the further development of computer technology and computer practice, I expect that within a few years this scheme will be far more *descriptive* than *normative* for significantly large areas of business planning.

5. Assignment of numerical value to the consequences of each alternative in terms of their positive or negative contribution.

6. Ordering of those consequences which are *dependent* (and those which they are dependent on) in terms of one or more natural sequences and the assignment of *conditional* probabilities to them. Assignment of probabilities to independent consequences.

7. Determination of the *expected value* for each alternative (this will equal the sum of the expected values for the branches of the dependent consequences "tree" added to the expected values for consequences not in the "tree").

8. Determination of the optimal alternative or set of alternatives from those which have been identified in view of the objectives and the risks involved.[7]

It is thought that even the informal planner mentioned earlier incorporates all these steps in his planning under uncertainty, even though some of them, unquestionably, are included on a *partially satisfied, casual, subconscious* basis, and the informal planner is *highly susceptible* to irrational premises and perceptual distortions and is likely to deal with only a *small portion* of those alternatives and consequences which are relevant to his operations at any given time.

Principle of Limiting Factors. This principle is most useful in planning. It is stated as follows: **In approaching a problem situation with a well-defined goal, it is productive to identify and analyze the sequence of** *limiting factors* **involved. These are factors that if properly satisfied in appropriate order, will permit the accomplishment of the goal.** It will be recalled that our "hypothetical" informal business planner said: "Well, first I try to have a clear idea of just what it is I wish to accomplish. . . . Then I try to focus on those key things which must be done or satisfied before I can achieve my objective. . . . " These "key things" are, in effect, the *limiting factors* that he perceives. They are requirements that must

---

[7] For a discussion of the problems and limitations involved in this approach see chaps. 1–4, 5, 7, 9, 10, 21, 22, 33, and 38 of Robert Schlaifer, *Probability and Statistics for Business Decisions* (New York: McGraw-Hill Book Co., 1959). By "optimal" here is *not* meant maximizing in the sense that all *possible* relevant alternatives were treated to produce the final decision. Of course, the cost of searching for and identifying alternatives or of creating them must be offset against the expected value of finding them. It appears that this type of maximizing is far more prevalent in business decision making than in personal decisions, where there is a strong inducement *not* to search beyond the first alternative that meets, at least in a minimal sense, our various requirements. But even in business there is a strong inducement for managers to seek a *satisfactory* share of the market, a *satisfactory* rate return, and so on. See H. Simon, "Theories of Decision-making in Economics and Behavioral Science," in Fremont Shull, Jr., and A. L. Delbecq (eds.), *Selected Readings in Management* (Homewood, Illinois: Richard D. Irwin, Inc., 1962), pp. 134-145.

be satisfied *before* he can achieve his objective. These limiting factors must be identified before relevant alternatives can be determined. For the purpose of an alternative course of action is to satisfy one or more limiting factors and thereby permit the achievement of a goal. Consequently, the identification of limiting factors is an important *precondition* for the performance of organic planning subfunction 4 (search for an identification of relevant alternatives).

Of course, the *broader* the statement of the initial goal, the greater the likelihood that a *sequence* of limiting factors will have to be satisfied before the goal is achieved. The satisfaction of this sequence of limiting factors presents, in effect, a sequence of subgoals to be achieved. Thus we get a glimpse of the *dynamic process* of planning in the real world. Most of our major goals are not immediately attainable without the achievement of a series of subgoals that relate to the satisfaction of a sequence of limiting factors. And, in the pursuit of this process, it is rare that the end goal remains unchanged. For there are errors of omission as well as commission in the identification of limiting factors, and there are unforeseen consequences that result from the application of selected alternatives, not to mention the obvious fact that other factors, unknown to us or beyond our control, will constantly influence our planning environment with the passage of time. Consequently, each "step" of the way we will be creating—and will have created for us—new conditions, which at best we can only partially anticipate. And each step of the way we will be confronted with the job of redefining major goals and their subgoals in the light of newly identified limiting factors![8]

Use of Subfunctions Illustrated. Examining a simple application of the *organic subfunctions of planning* will help clarify what is meant by the term. Assume that we have established the objective of making a business trip to City X with *minimum expense* in terms of the *key* factors: ticket expense, safety, being on time, and speed advantage (we established this objective either by going through subfunction 3 or by having it *given* to us).

---

[8] For additional discussion of the *Principle of Limiting Factors* see Chester I. Barnard, *The Functions of the Executive* (Cambridge, Mass.: Harvard University Press, 1938), pp. 202-11 and 246-51. Barnard refers to limiting factors also as "strategic factors." For example, on page 203, he points out: "The limiting (strategic) factor is the one whose control, in the right form, at the right place and time, will establish a new system or set of conditions which meets the purpose."

The first part of subfunction 4 requires that we identify all *relevant* alternatives for achieving the objective. As was pointed out in the previous section, we must first identify the *limiting factor* or *factors* in the situation before we can determine which alternatives will be *relevant* (of course this is not the *only* criterion for determining the relevance of an alternative; it must also be *reasonable* in terms of our goal criteria). For our simplified problem we can identify the limiting factor of *physical distance separating us from City X*. Given our location, let us assume that there are only two feasible (relevant) alternatives for successfully dealing with the limiting factor and hence permitting achievement of our goal: (1) going by plane or (2) driving a car. The second part of subfunction 4 requires that we determine all the *relevant* consequences associated with each of these alternatives. We decide that a reasonable approximation to reality will be afforded by the following list of consequences:

With regard to safety in the car or plane: severe accident, moderate accident, and no accident.

With regard to being on time (car or plane): very late, little late, and not late.

Speed advantage of plane depending on degree of lateness.

Ticket expense is fixed for going by plane.

Ticket expense for the car will most likely be 8 or 10 cents per mile.

Subfunction 5 requires that we assign a numerical value to each consequence in terms of its positive or negative contribution to getting to City X with minimum expense. So we will *estimate* the dollar cost we believe should be associated with each consequence and note it as a minus value.[9]

	Alternative 1 (plane)	Alternative 2 (car)
Ticket cost (provided by airline)	−$70	−$80 or −$100
Severe accident	−7000	−5000
Moderate accident	−3000	−2000
No accident	0	0
Very late	−500	−500
Little late	−100	−200
Not late	+300	0

The first part of subfunction 6 requires that we "order" the dependent consequences, and those which they are dependent on, in

---

[9] The one exception in the listing being the +300 dollars for not being late by plane. This and the reduced cost of being a little late by plane (as compared with going by car) reflect the value placed on the speed advantage of the plane.

one or more natural sequences or sets of relationships. In looking over our list of consequences, we see two that do not affect or are not affected by the others: ticket expense for the plane and "ticket" expense (gas, oil, etc.) for the car.[10] What appears to be a logical ordering, for our purposes, of the remaining consequences is presented by the "tree" diagrams in Figures 2-1 and 2-2. We assume that the car and the plane leave for City X on time.[11]

Three consequences can occur in going by plane or by car—severe accident, moderate accident, and no accident—which in turn *affect* the likelihood or *probability* of occurrence of three arrival consequences—very late, little late, and not late. These are the *conditional probabilities* referred to in subfunction 6. As can be seen in Figure 2-1, if the plane has a severe accident it seems reasonable to assume that the passengers will be very late in arriving at City X, and the probability that they will be a little late (given the severe accident) is so small that it should be ignored. Consequently, the probability of being very late, given a severe accident, is 1 (or 100 per cent) and the probabilities of being a little late and not late are "zero." However, if there is no accident, the probability of being very late is estimated to be .30 (or 30 per cent); for being a little late, .20; and for not being late, .50. As can be seen, there are only three possible consequences in the "tree" after plane—severe accident, moderate accident, and no accident—and the probabilities for these (which are non-conditional in the diagram presented) *must* add up to 1, or 100 per cent. The same is true for each set of possible consequences, *given* one of the three just mentioned. For example, the conditional probabilities for the three states of lateness, given a moderate accident, add up to 1, or 100 per cent (.90 + .08 + .02).

There is no need to assign probabilities to various possible costs associated with the independent consequence of plane-ticket cost. This is assumed to be $70 *certain* and, after we have added up the expected values for the branches of the plane alternative "tree," we will merely add this —$70 to that minus total to get the total expected cost of the plane alternative. However, for the car alterna-

---

[10] We are making the simplifying assumption of a new, tuned-up car which has no likelihood of mechanical failure.

[11] Of course, the assumption that you may not leave on time is perfectly plausible and another "tree" diagram could be constructed for this (with states of lateness being listed right after plane or car and then the other dependent consequences). This is why subfunction 6 prescribes "one or more" natural sequences. The evaluation of several sequences or "trees" for each alternative might well enter into the evaluation of alternatives. Obviously, the cost of any refinement in procedure must be weighed against the contribution of that refinement.

tive there are two possible costs and their estimated probabilities of occurrence listed for the independent consequence of car-"ticket" cost. The expected value or cost for this consequence is $90 (.50 times $80 + .50 times $100) .

We are now ready to satisfy subfunction 7 by determining the expected value (or expected cost in this case) of the two alternatives: going by plane or going by car. To get the expected cost for a given "branch" of the "tree," we multiply the first probability of that branch times the second probability of that branch times the third

FIG. 2-1

Consequences Tree for Alternative 1 (Going by Plane)

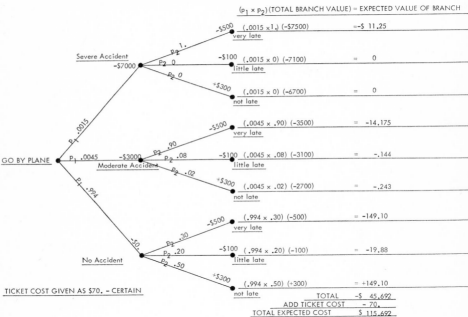

probability of that branch and so on (in our example, we have only two probabilities for each branch). We then take the result of this multiplication and multiply it by the algebraic sum of the values (or costs) of the given branch. This procedure is illustrated to the right of the tree diagrams in Figures 2-1 and 2-2. For example, to compute the expected cost of the branch "severe accident—very late" in Figure 2-1, we multiply the estimated probability of a severe accident (.0015) times the estimated probability of being very late, given a severe accident (1). Then we multiply this product (.0015 times 1 = .0015) by the algebraic sum of the costs of the branch

($-\$7,000$ plus $-\$500 = -\$7,500$), and we get $-\$11.25$ as the *expected cost* of this branch.[12] The expected cost for each alternative is found by adding the ticket cost to the total of the expected branch costs. In this example, with the objectives we have established and the estimated values and probabilities we have assigned, the plane looks like the better alternative (expected cost of $\$115.692$ for the plane vs. $\$633.25$ for the car).

FIG. 2-2
Consequences Tree for Alternative 2 (Going by Car)

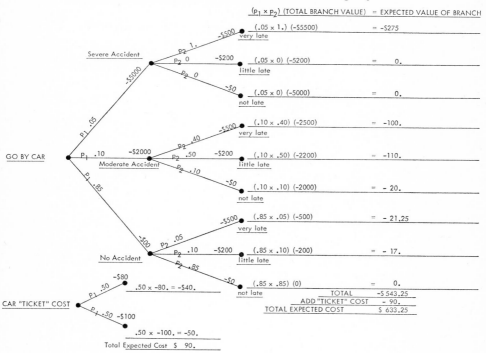

Formalization in Practice. Though greater formality in planning promises much for the future, we should not make the mistake of assuming that informal judgment or intuition in planning have become, or will become, unimportant. For example, performance of subfunction 4 (search for an identification of relevant alternatives and relevant consequences) requires the exercise of considerable

[12] Another way to think of this is as follows: Assume that there is only one other branch in the tree (probability .9985) and its occurrence costs "zero". Then, 15 times in 10,000 we will have to pay 15 times $\$7,500$ or $\$112,500$. However, the other 9,985 times in 10,000 we pay nothing. Consequently, the *average* cost is $\$112,500$ divided by 10,000, or $\$11.25$.

judgment in identifying limiting factors and determining which alternatives—and consequences—are relevant to them. And informal judgment or intuition provides the *only* basis for performing subfunctions 5 and 6 with regard to the *majority* of consequences: estimating their values, ordering them, and estimating their probabilities. In addition, no one should become a slave to algebraic summations of expected values. Most of us will be willing to *use* the expected value approach for only a certain *range* of consequence values. That is, we will think in terms of the greatest possible loss and the greatest possible profit we are willing to sustain before we will *abandon* the use of expected value as the primary basis for our decision.

For example, if you offer me the opportunity to spin a wheel one time only with a 10 per cent chance of losing $500 and a 90 per cent chance of winning $1,000, the expected value of this for me would be +$850 (.10 times −$500 plus .90 times +$1,000). However, I may well decline to play simply because I cannot afford to lose $500! Or suppose that you offer me $1,000,000 certain as opposed to an 80 per cent chance to get $2,000,000 and a 20 per cent chance to get nothing. I personally will take the $1,000,000, though the expected value of the second option is higher by $600,000 (.80 times $2,000,000 plus .20 times $0). Going to the other extreme, I will be happy to use the expected value approach and flip you for a cup of coffee! Somewhere in between these two positions I have abandoned expected value as the primary basis for my decision. If there is some consequence that I as the planner cannot afford to accept, whatever its probability of occurrence, then an *absolute* rather than a relative restriction is imposed on the solution or choice of alternatives.

It is my hypothesis that the trend toward greater formalization of planning activity does not represent a change in the organic character of planning. Rather, it is the result of developments that have made much greater thoroughness and accuracy in planning feasible for the first time. The advent of electronic computers, refinements in model building and simulation, and the development of other operations research techniques have all contributed significantly to this trend toward formalization. It will be worthwhile to discuss the nature of these new planning tools and techniques and the way in which their use permits us to perform the organic subfunctions of planning with greater speed and effectiveness than was ever before possible. An attempt will be made to define "operations research," followed by a discussion of computers, model building, and other tools and techniques.

NEW PLANNING TOOLS AND TECHNIQUES

Operations Research Defined

There is no single definition of "operations research" that enjoys widespread acceptance, but following are several definitions from authoritative sources:

"Operational research" (as I understand it) is concerned with optimizing the performance of a system regarded as given for the purposes of the problem.

Historically, the first such problem to receive the name was concerned with how to set the time fuse of a bomb to be dropped from an aircraft onto a submarine.[13]

Operations are considered as an entity. The subject matter studied is not the equipment used, nor the morale of the participants, nor the physical properties of the output; it is the combination of these in total, as an economic process. And operations so conceived are subject to analysis by the mental processes and the methodologies which we have come to associate with the research work of the physicist, the chemist, and the biologist—what has come to be called "the scientific method."[14]

As I see it, operations research is a point of view or method of approach to the study of the operation or functioning of a complex organization, including both men and machines. The essential feature of it is that it always studies the organization in operation . . . the operations researcher always looks at whatever element he is considering as a whole and he not only studies the whole of it, but also tries to understand at least a little of how it fits into its larger background.[15]

As a rule, the "team" approach is used so that a problem may be attacked with expertise in each of the disciplines that are relevant to its solution.

Generally, operations researchers first determine the purpose of a given system or organization. Then they attempt to devise some means for measuring the effectiveness of the system and its components to discover likely places for improvement. Or, if accurate measurement is not feasible, an experimental approach may be used by which factors are varied in an attempt to find a more productive combination. As we shall see, one form of simulation for this is

---

[13] The Earl of Halsbury, "From Plato to the Linear Program," *Journal of the Operations Research Society of America,* Vol. III, No. 3 (August, 1955), p. 239.

[14] Leroy A. Brothers, "Operations Analysis in the United States Air Force," *Journal of the Operations Research Society of America,* Vol. II, No. 1 (February, 1954), p. 1.

[15] Omond Solandt, "Observation, Experiment, and Measurement in Operations Research," *Journal of the Operations Research Society of America,* Vol. III, No. 1 (February, 1955), p. 4.

called *the Monte Carlo method.* An important tool for implementing it and other Operations Research activities is the computer.

Computers

A modern electronic computer *is* a "glorified computational machine." But it is also much more—it has a *memory.* For this reason it is often called a "mechanical brain," for much that we label "intelligence" involves nothing more than pulling appropriate material from our memories for a particular application.

We see this in the case of a doctor who must diagnose a disease. Basically, he looks for a familiar pattern of symptoms. The computer, when properly programmed, can do this too. In fact, the computer can remember much more than the doctor and can do so with complete accuracy of retention for an indefinite period of time! Of course, the computer will be no more accurate than the data with which it is programmed, but the programming can be done by a group of leading specialists, and this contribution need never be lost.

Because of its memory capacity and high rate of computation, the computer can do many things that were not practical before. In the General Electric Company it was found that certain calculations relating to the design of efficient steam turbines could be performed by a computer in an hour or less. If conventional methods of calculation had been used, from *one to three years* of error-free work would have been required.[16]

There are two basic types of computers:

The Analog Computer. This computer is based on *simulation* and therefore is *non-numerical* and does not employ a *memory.*[17] A slide rule on which distances simulate the logarithms of numbers is one; so are the Link Trainer for flyers and the common thermostat for controlling house temperature.

The Digital Computer. This is a computational machine that uses *numbers* and has a *memory.* It can be a general purpose machine, large or medium sized, or a special-purpose machine, for example, a machine designed especially for an insurance company to make complex actuarial computations for each policy. A general-purpose machine could do this, but a special-purpose machine is

---

[16] This example is taken from R. K. Gaumnitz and O. H. Brownlee, "Mathematics for Decision Makers," *Harvard Business Review,* Vol. XXXIV, No. 3 (May–June, 1956).

[17] Though some analog computers are equipped with "holding devices" that perform limited memory functions.

cheaper and faster. Of course, an *analog system* may incorporate a digital computer.

Because of its computational speed and flexibility, the digital computer can be of great value in the mathematical work associated with organic planning functions 3–5, especially if the planner must deal with a large number of alternatives and consequences. A thorough analysis of many problems would produce such a complex of factors that solution would be impossible or impractical without the computational assistance of the computer. One of the greatest contributions of the computer, however, has been in connection with organic planning function 1 (determination of environmental factors and the relationships between these factors). Only to the extent that we can forecast the environmental "givens" with which we will have to contend, and the way in which these given factors interact, will we be able to identify and quantify relevant alternatives and their consequences. Often such understanding can come only through the simulation, experimentation, and model building made possible by the use of computers.

Model Building [18]

A model, through necessity, is a *simplified* representation of reality. The model builder must limit himself to the number of factors and the level of complexity with which he can work effectively. He achieves simplification by building into the model only those factors which he thinks are most essential. As the model is refined and improved, additional factors may be incorporated up to a point of manageable complexity or to a point at which increases in accuracy are not worth the cost of obtaining them. The basic steps in model building are:

1. Determination of the relevant factors in the problem.
2. Numerical measurement of the factors.
3. Formal, mathematical expression of relationships between factors.
4. Validation of the model.
5. Refinement of the model.

Through analysis of the problem or system, an attempt is made to identify the most essential factors or variables involved. Then these factors are measured, not only individually but as they relate to one another. Rough formulations are made as to how these factors affect

---

[18] Much of this material is taken from George Kozmetsky and Paul Kircher, *Electronic Computers and Management Control* (New York: McGraw-Hill Book Co., 1956), chap. 6.

one another, and these are "tested" conceptually or logically. Next, the expression of these relationships is formalized by statement in mathematical terms and validation of the model is undertaken. Appropriate historical data may be fed into the model to see whether the model will produce results that agree with actual historical outcomes. Last—and this indicates the "circular" character of model building—continuing efforts are made to improve on the validity of the model. This may be done through the measurement and inclusion of new factors and the more accurate restatement of old factors in the model.

These are the steps for developing a "descriptive" model—a model that describes mathematically the relationships that seem to exist in a situation. Probably the best example of a "descriptive" model in business is the accounting system, which is a symbolic representation or model of what is happening. Basically, systems of production control, inventory control, and time study are "descriptive" models.

A "descriptive" model becomes a "predictive" model when *forecast* data are used for one or more of the factors; to the extent that the model is accurate, the other factor or factors can be predicted. The most common example of a "predictive" model in business is the budget. "In mathematical terminology, budgets are built up from the 'independent variables' in the situation. The other factors are 'dependent variables.' The former are the basic estimating factors, the forecasts of the strategic elements in the business situation. The latter are expected to follow if the forecast is correct."[19]

When several "predictive" models are *grouped* with some criteria for selecting from among them the one that best fulfills the objectives at hand, a "decision" model is created. "Decision" models "have been used to tell the businessman where to ship; what, where, and how to produce; and where to sell. These models often use the new technique known as 'linear programming.'"[20]

Simulation

"Descriptive" and "predictive" models can be used productively to simulate or imitate the realistic functioning of a system. This is especially helpful when the expense and time required for actual tests are prohibitive. Take the design for a new jet airliner, for ex-

---

[19] Kozmetsky and Kircher, *op. cit.*, p. 134. For a different classification of models see Edward H. Bowman and Robert B. Fetter, *Analysis for Production Management* (Homewood, Illinois: Richard D. Irwin, Inc., 1957), pp. 20–30.
[20] *Ibid.*

ample. Physical models can be flown in the wind tunnel, and mathematical or analog models can be "flown" on a computer to yield much valuable data about flight characteristics and operating and maintenance requirements. In other cases, problems may be so complex that the mathematical model required cannot be developed fully. For this situation, a physical or analog model of the *mathematical model* can be constructed and studied to analyze the behavior of the mathematical model. On the basis of the findings obtained, the mathematical model can be enlarged and refined and then used to study the original problem. The Monte Carlo method permits this kind of system simulation when problems are too complex to analyze and program from an over-all viewpoint or when the use of another method is too costly. As we shall see, the method is based on repetition and probabilities.

In one sense, non-physical model simulation is not new. Whenever management planners have put before their colleagues alternative investment or product plans along with their expected costs and returns, they have, in effect, simulated the alternatives. However, the introduction of new mathematical concepts and high-speed computers has significantly increased the potential of the simulation approach.

The Monte Carlo Method. If a problem is too complex to admit of formal analysis and mathematical expression, an approach based on simulated experience—*the Monte Carlo method*—may be used. It is a form of simulation providing *experimental* rather than *theoretical* answers to problems that involve the complex interaction of numerous random factors. It is a process whereby some form of random number generation is used to produce sequences of numbers having the same statistical characteristics as data drawn from actual experience. "In this way an inexhaustible fund of simulated experience is available which can usually be secured at much lower cost than further actual experience. So long as the statistical model continues to represent the facts of the situation, the simulated experience is safely usable for a wide variety of purposes."[21]

The army has used the Monte Carlo method to simulate battles between opposing forces of tanks and infantrymen. It would be impossible to program a computer for the large number of combinations that would characterize the over-all battle. But the computer can be programmed on the basis of authoritative military opinion in

---

[21] Bowman and Fetter, *op cit.*, p. 298.

terms of specific probabilities associated with specific events. For example, if a tank should meet an infantryman in an open field with no place for the infantryman to conceal himself, chances are that he would be shot by the tank. If two tanks meet, the nature of the terrain will determine the likelihood of whether or not the lighter weight but greater speed of one will be an asset or a liability. The computer program can then be sequential: if Red Force loses its tanks, it will do such and such; but, if the tanks get through, it will do such and such. Since the outcome of the battle is based on probabilities, one victory is not very meaningful. But the advantage of the Monte Carlo method is that the same battle can be fought 1,000 times in a relatively short period of time. All other things being equal, if a change in tank design for one force produces 800 out of 1,000 victories, then there is valid statistical reason for regarding this as a superior design feature.[22]

Given realistic assumptions as to how some phase or phases of an actual enterprise operate under day-in and day-out competition and the use of a computer, top business planners could use this method to simulate "battle" with their competitors. Such interaction would be too complex to formulate mathematically, but they could use the step-by-step Monte Carlo calculations to play out action and re-action with their "enemies." As Lindsay points out, the Monte Carlo method can be applied to many kinds of problems:

> Complicated queuing or waiting-line problems often can be solved more easily by this means than by mathematical means. Transportation, production, inventory, and distribution problems usually have random factors that are too complicated for formal mathematical treatment, even when the individual probabilities can be represented by standard probability equations.[23]

The Business Game. One of the most interesting forms of simulation for the business student and one holding out much promise for the future is *decision simulation* in the form of the business game. At present it is used primarily as a training tool. A "descriptive" model of a fictitious firm is constructed. Management "teams" compete with each other by feeding decision inputs into the model and then making new decisions on the basis of the outcomes fed

---

[22] Richard E. Zimmerman, "A Monte Carlo Model for Military Analysis" in McCloskey and Coppinger (eds.), *op. cit.*, p. 376. Other good operations research examples are given also.

[23] Franklin A. Lindsay, *New Techniques for Management Decision Making* (New York: McGraw-Hill Book Co., 1958), p. 100.

back to them by the model. Usually, the model is programmed in a computer to facilitate the necessary computations. The models currently in use are *highly simplified* representations of reality and are not intended to simulate *actual* firms, though they provide a high degree of training realism. The day may not be too far off when models for a specific firm may be developed, validated, and used for testing various management strategies prior to execution, leading to the ultimate development of an over-all "decision" model for the firm. But this is a long, long way off. New mathematical short cuts and new ways for combining factors based on greater knowledge of the firm will have to materialize before the over-all model will be approachable. But on a more limited basis the use of model building and simulation has produced impressive results and has been especially helpful with regard to *organic planning subfunction 1:* Determination of environmental factors and the interrelationships between these factors.

The Logic Theorist. Three men—A. Newell, J. C. Shaw, and H. A. Simon—have developed and refined a computer program to simulate substantially human problem-solving behavior.[24] Their first program, *the Logic Theorist,* was designed to discover proofs for theorems in basic symbolic logic through the use of techniques similar to those used by humans. They describe a most impressive achievement of the program:[25]

Now no one would deny that Whitehead and Russell were creative when they wrote *Principia Mathematica.* Their book is one of the most significant intellectual products of the twentieth century. If it was creative for Whitehead and Russell to write these volumes, it is possibily creative for the Logic Theorist to reinvent large portions of Chapter 2—rediscovering in many cases the very same proofs that Whitehead and Russell discovered originally. Of course the Logic Theorist will not receive much acclaim for its discoveries, since these have been anticipated, but subjectively although not culturally, its product is novel and original. In at least one case, moreover, the Logic Theorist has discovered a proof for a theorem in Chapter 2 that is far shorter and more elegant than the one published by Whitehead and Russell.

---

[24] For more detailed discussion of this work see the following papers authored by these men and published by the Rand Corporation of Santa Monica, California: *The Processes of Creative Thinking* (January, 1959); *Report on a General Problem-solving Program* (February, 1959); and *A Variety of Intelligent Learning in a General Problem Solver* (July, 1959).

[25] *The Processes of Creative Thinking,* p. 9. See also "Elements of a Theory of Human Problem Solving," *Psychological Review,* Vol. 65, (1958), pp. 151-66, for additional discussion of the Logic Theorist by these three men.

The General Problem Solver. The General Problem Solver program represents further development and refinement of the Logic Theorist. Newell and Simon point out that it

. . . was devised to simulate the behavior of some specific human subjects solving problems in symbolic logic in a task situation devised by O. K. Moore and Scarvia Anderson. . . . GPS . . . is called "general" because it is not limited to the task for which it was originally devised. Hand simulation indicates it can also solve the Whitehead and Russell logic problems, do trigonometric identities, perform formal integration and differentiation, and with a small extension to the program, solve algebraic equations . . . in its present form it constitutes an unequivocal demonstration that a mechanism can solve problems by functional reasoning.[26]

Since the GPS is designed to simulate human problem-solving behavior, it is patterned after a descriptive model of such behavior. In building such a model, Newell, Shaw, and Simon employed certain specialized terms:

Heuristic: any principle or procedure which may aid in problem solving but which offers no guarantee of a solution. As contrasted with the term
Algorithm: any principle or procedure which if followed properly in problem solving will assure a solution.
Difference: The contrast between a starting state and the desired solution or "ending state."
Operator: an algorithm or heuristic which is appropriate to the reduction of a particular difference (problem) with which we are dealing.

Also, they made certain basic assumptions:

The theory of problem solving is concerned with discovering and understanding systems of heuristics.
No clear distinction between learning and problem solving appears . . . learning is change in the repertoire of heuristics itself.
Dramatically viewed, problem solving is the battle of selection techniques against a space of possibilities that keeps expanding exponentially.
There are three things which a human (or machine) must know or discover to solve problems: what are possible differences, what are permissible operators, and which operators are relevant to which differences.[27]
Humans will "satisfice"; i.e., they will search until they find a solution which meets all of their requirements—which satisfies them—and

---

[26] *The Simulation of Human Thought* (Rand Corporation, June, 1959), pp. 20, 21.
[27] These definitions and assumptions were taken from the previously cited works by Newell, Shaw, and Simon.

not necessarily until they find the best attainable or optimal solution within the conditions given.[28]

The functional scheme of the descriptive model of human problem solving (which provides the basic rationale of the GPS) is as follows:

Evaluate the problem to determine the *difference* between (a) state description of one or more starting points (where we are) and (z) a state description of one or more solutions (where we wish to be).

Determine the list of allowable processes or *operators* which may be applied to reduce the difference between where we *are* and where we wish to be (there are different kinds of operators for different kinds of differences). Progress toward a solution will be indicated by net[29] difference reduction. Continue "loop" as long as it continues to produce some net progress.

Eliminate the difference between (a) and (z) via a one-step transformation of (a) into (z) by the application of an appropriate operator, or:

Reduce the difference between (a) and (z) by the establishment and reduction of easier sub-goal states along the way (i.e., transform (a) into (b); (b) into (c) and so on until (z) is reached), or if this does not work:

Abstract the state description of (a) and the state description of (z) and the operators which are associated with them by omitting certain details and getting down to basics. If one-step transformation won't work, set up easier abstracted sub-goal states. When a sequential application of operators produces the abstracted (z) then apply the same plan or sequence to non-abstracted (a) using non-abstracted operators.

As can be seen, when necessary, a principle of sub-goal reduction is followed: "Make progress by substituting for the achievement of a goal the achievement of a set of easier goals."[30] (Actually, this and the use of abstraction are both excellent heuristics.) Also, there may be operators which are applied to several states as inputs, producing one or more states as output (e.g., joining four beams to produce a frame.)[31]

It will be recalled from the discussion of the *organic sub-functions of planning*, that *sub-function 4* has to do with "search for and identification of *relevant* alternatives for the achievement of objectives . . .," which is the *problem-solving* phase of planning (the other phase is *decision making*: selection from alternatives). Before we

---

[28] Though this assumption is implicit in the work cited above, it is explicitly given in James March and H. A. Simon, *Organizations* (New York: John Wiley & Sons, 1958), p. 140.

[29] "Net" because sometimes we must take two steps backward to make one forward. (This, incidentally, is a good *heuristic!*)

[30] Newell, Shaw, and Simon, *Report on a General Problem-solving Problem*, p. 8.

[31] Newell and Simon, *The Simulation of Human Thought*, p. 22.

can determine which alternatives are *relevant* to the achievement of a goal, we must have a goal and identity the *limiting factor* or *factors* that must be satisfied to achieve the goal. Then we can determine which alternatives are relevant to the satisfaction of the limiting factor (or factors), select and apply the most appropriate one, and achieve our goal.

To the extent that the General Problem Solver program can be supplied with an increasing store or "memory" of possible alternatives (heuristics and algorithms), it will provide an important tool for the performance of *organic planning subfunction 4:* "search for and identification of *relevant* alternatives for the achievement of objectives." For in the GPS program our *goal* is represented by the "ending state" desired. Our *limiting factor* is represented by the "difference" between the beginning state (where we are) and the ending state (where we wish to be). And the *relevance* of an alternative (heuristic or algorithm) to the limiting factor (difference) is evidenced by its ability to "reduce the difference" (satisfy the limiting factor). Thus, we may see the day when a GPS-like program will be able to print a list of relevant alternatives for us for any set of limiting factors. Or perhaps this will merely serve as input for another computer program that will perform the other *organic subfunctions of planning* to make the *selection* from alternatives for us also—and we can go fishing!

Advantages of Simulation. Some of the major advantages of simulation given by Franklin A. Lindsay are:

1. The ability to handle very complex problems and to find either the precisely or the approximately best answers.

2. The ability to analyze—at least to some extent—the implications of competitive situations and the relative merits of alternative strategies.

3. The ability, through computers, to try out literally hundreds of alternative assumptions, strategies, and decision rules.

4. The ability to analyze dynamic situations in which each decision sets the conditions under which the following decisions must be made.

5. The ability to make "sensitivity analyses" by means of which one can determine whether a small change in a single factor will result in a major or a minor change in the outcome. If the former, the simulation model will show the degree to which the critical factor must be controlled to avoid violent fluctuations.

6. The ability to analyze quickly new and unexpected situations so that decisions to take advantage of opportunities can be made promptly.

7. Finally, the great advantage of simulation is that it is not restricted by the requirement that the model be solvable mathematically. It is this requirement that today places the ceiling on the usefulness of many of

the strictly mathematical solutions to management problems—by forcing the analyst to depart from a realistic and accurate model in order to make a mathematical solution possible.[32]

Other Operations Research Techniques

Linear Programming. Some problems are so complex that a direct enumeration of all solution possibilities is out of the question. Calculus cannot always be used to handle questions involving maximization or minimization applied to the scheduling of activities and the allocation of resources. *Linear programming* is a planning technique that permits some objective function to be minimized or maximized within the framework of given situational restrictions. Bowman and Fetter list some of the problems that can be solved with its application:

A product or good is composed of several ingredients yielding the desired characteristics of the product and with varying cost. The least costly mix of ingredients which meets the characteristic requirements of the product is obtained.

A number of jobs or products must be handled by various men and/or machines. The least costly assignment is made. The army has used linear programming to assign men to jobs, while industry has used it to assign orders to machines.

Limited capacity is allocated to products in order to yield maximum profits.

An uneven sales demand is met by a production schedule over a period of time with given penalties for storage and overtime, or "undertime," production.

The simplex method may be used to select a least costly shipment schedule from various plants with given capacities and costs to various distribution centers with given demands and given costs of transportation.

Where a number of jobs must be done and it is possible to buy or sub-contract some of the parts or jobs, linear programming can help choose between the firm's own departments and outside suppliers in order to accomplish the whole job at minimum cost, or minimum time if this is the important variable.

The simplex method automatically assigns values to unused slack variables (capacity completely used, or restriction exactly satisfied). It, therefore, indicates the value to the firm of increasing by a unit each limiting capacity. This might be useful in investment decisions. It would also indicate the least cost per unit of additional weight placed in a package.

It is also possible to determine the difference in costs or profits between the "best" solution and some other solution. . . .[33]

[32] Lindsay, *op. cit.*, p. 94.
[33] Bowman and Fetter, *op. cit.*, p. 99.

However, linear programming cannot always be used. As its name implies, it requires the assumption that all the relationships with which it deals are linear, or are nearly so for the range required so as not to introduce excessive error into the solution. As with model building, in dealing with a highly complex problem, care must be taken in simplifying the problem for mathematical expression so that some of its *essential* characteristics are not destroyed.

Dynamic Programming. This is a technique applicable to the solution of multistage programming problems where the decisions at one stage supply the conditions that govern succeeding stages in stepwise fashion; an optimum solution is carried forward each time rather than all of the previous stages. Bellman summarizes the concept in one of our basic planning principles, the *Principle of Optimality:* **An optimal policy has the property that whatever the initial state and initial decision are, the remaining decisions must constitute an optimal policy with regard to the state resulting from the first decision.**[34] Lindsay lists the types of multistage problems that may be suitable for dynamic programming:[35]

1. Long-range capital budgeting.
2. Timing of equipment replacement.
3. Machine loading in job shops.
4. Transportation scheduling to meet shifting demands.
5. Smoothing of production levels to meet variable demands.
6. Allocation of limited resources between current consumption and reinvestment to increase future output.

PERT. PERT (Program Evaluation and Review Technique)[36] is a form of dynamic programming that provides important aid for the planning and control of projects. The planning aspects will be discussed here and the control aspects in chapter 7. PERT helps in planning for the allocation of resources—equipment, space, materials, man-hours, superior leadership, etc.—*given* a series of interrelated objectives (a project), *given* the functions to be performed to achieve them, and *given* three time estimates (optimistic, most likely, and pessimistic) for the completion of *each* objective (or subproject). These objectives in proper sequence and the three estimated time requirements for their completion are shown in a network as depicted in Figure 2-3. The three estimated time requirements—optimistic, most likely, and pessimistic—are shown on top

---

[34] Richard Bellman, "Some Applications of the Theory of Dynamic Programming—A Review," *Journal of the Operations Research Society of America*, August, 1954, p. 285.

[35] Lindsay, *op. cit.*, p. 78.

[36] Also known as CPM (critical path method) time-network analysis.

of the arrow shafts. The "expected time" requirement for the achievement of each objective (which is obtained through statistical treatment of the three time estimates) is shown below the arrow shaft.[37]

Usually, the event (or objective) descriptions shown in the circles are replaced with numbers for easier reference, and the *cumulative* total of expected times between the start of the network through

FIG. 2-3

Completed PERT Network*

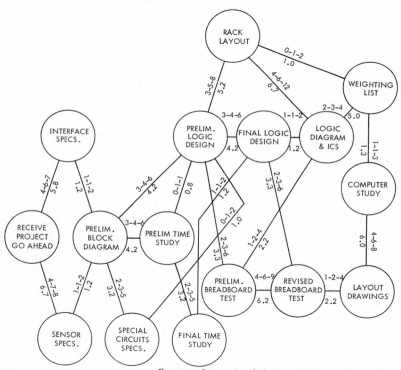

Courtesy: International Business Machines Corporation

* Taken from *General Information Manual PERT*, Data Processing Division IBM, 112 East Post Road, White Plains, New York.

completion of any given event or circle is written under the circle. For example, the event labeled "Receive Project Go Ahead" might be numbered event 21; the event labeled "Sensor Specifications," 20;

---

[37] For discussion of the assumptions and statistical procedures involved, as well as a more detailed examination of the entire procedure, see *General Information Manual PERT* (Data Processing Division IBM, 112 East Post Road, White Plains, New York) and Robert Miller, "How To Plan and Control with PERT," *Harvard Business Review*, March-April, 1962, pp. 93-104. A trade-off relationship between time and cost is discussed in the DOD-NASA guide, *Pert Cost* (U.S. Printing Office, June, 1962), 75 cents.

and the event labeled "Preliminary Block Diagram," 18. The cumulative total expected time under event 20 would be 6.7 weeks (the expected time to go from "Receive Project Go Ahead" to completion of "Sensor Specifications"). The cumulative total under event 18 would be 7.9 weeks (6.7 weeks to go from 21 through 20 plus 1.2 weeks to go from 20 through 18).

The "critical" path through the network is the one from start to finish that requires the *greatest* cumulative expected time. In Figure

FIG. 2-4
PERT Network Showing "Slack"*

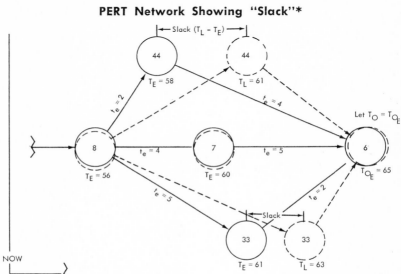

Courtesy: International Business Machines Corporation

* *General Information Manual PERT,* Data Processing Division IBM, 112 East Post Road, White Plains, New York.

2-4 the critical path from event 8 to 6 would be 8—7—6. The letters *TOE* under event 6 signify total expected time from beginning to completion of the final objective (in this instance, event 6). The small *te* above each arrow shaft in Figure 2-4 represents the expected time required to go from completion of one event to completion of the next event. And the large TE under each circle represents the cumulative total of expected times up through completion of that event. If we go from 8 to 6 via 44, we find that the expected time required is 62 weeks, less than the 65 required for going from 8 to 6 via 7. Also, we see that the expected time for going from 8 to 6 via 33 is less; so the 8—7—6 path *is* the longest or *critical* one.[38] It is expected that 6 weeks will be required to get from 8 to 6 via 44 and 9 weeks will be required to get from 8 to 6 via 7. Now there is *no* choice of paths (all events must be completed to finish the project), but the *difference* of 3 weeks for 8–44–6 as compared with the critical path is called "slack" for event 44. That is, the latest allowable time (TL) for completion of event 44 can be 61 weeks without delaying the completion of the whole project. Or, looking at it another way, we can miss our expected time of 58 weeks for completing event 44 by "overshooting" 3 weeks and still not miss the finish date for the entire project.

From a planning standpoint, what are the reasons for doing all of this? Well, to begin with, the formulation of the network itself forces a type of analysis that might otherwise be neglected. As Miller points out:

. . . the kind of planning required to create a valid network represents a major contribution to the definition and ultimate successful control of a complex program. It may surprise some that network development and critical path analysis do, in fact, reveal interdependencies and problem areas which are either not obvious or not well defined by conventional planning methods. The creation of the network is a fairly demanding task, and is a surefire indicator of an organization's ability to visualize the number, kind, and sequence of activities needed to execute a complex program.[39]

In addition, once we know the critical path (or paths) and the amount of "slack" associated with each event, we are in an excellent position to allocate our resources effectively and to plan for economical control.

With regard to resource allocation PERT facilitates the use of the *Principle of Limiting Factors* and thus the identification of *revelant* alternatives; for the critical path identifies the *limiting factors* or the most likely places for potential "bottlenecks" or delays that may prevent project completion on time.[40] To provide greater assurance for meeting our schedule, we may well decide to assign more of

---

[38] It is perfectly possible to have more than one critical path in a network.

[39] Robert Miller, *op. cit.*, p. 96.

[40] The *Principle of Limiting Factors*, it will be recalled, is stated as follows: "In approaching a problem situation with a well-defined goal, it is productive to identify and analyze the sequence of *limiting factors* involved. These are factors that, if properly satisfied in appropriate order, will permit the accomplishment of the goal." Actually, PERT facilitates the visualization of the sequence of limiting factors involved in a project and consequently facilitates the visualization of the subgoals and their interrelationships that are involved.

our resources, or at least our better resources, to these places (diverting them from events with slack, which can take more time to compensate for the loss of resources). On the other hand, we know that if the critical path is *shortened* by a certain amount of time, we can finish the total project sooner by that same amount. Some time reduction might be possible through diversion of resources from slack events. However, we do not wish to squeeze all the slack out of the system, for all our time requirements are based on estimates and we need margin for error. But we could muster additional resources to the extent that the value of total project time reduction would defray the cost of additional resources. PERT dramatizes what we must do to accomplish a project on time or to reduce the total time and makes it possible for us to allocate resources and plan our schedules accordingly. Actually, it provides for the "graphic simulation" of courses of action!

All expected times for the completion of events are computed through statistical treatment of the three time estimates given in the original planning of each event. The data from these estimates also permit computation of the risk (probability) involved in on-schedule completion of an event, a project segment of several events, or the entire project. The advantage of this is that it permits the *adjustment of risk,* through schedule modification, to a level that is acceptable to the planner.

Miller reports:

> The PERT approach is usefully introduced in such diverse situations as planning the economy of an under developed nation or establishing the sequence and timing of actions to effect a complex merger. . . . A very considerable amount of research now is taking place on the "extensions" of PERT . . . into the areas of manpower, cost, and capital requirements. As an ultimate objective, "trade-off" relationships between time, cost, and product or equipment performance objectives are being sought.[41]

As these developments are realized, there is little question that PERT will become an increasingly important tool of planning and control.

Critique of Various Techniques. Lindsay provides a good critique as to the current relative value of some of the other tools and and techniques of operations research:

> Some analytical tools are of proven value, others are of considerable potential value, while still others will have little practical application unless and until the theoretical work is pushed considerably beyond

---

[41] Robert Miller, *op. cit.,* pp. 94, 95. See p. 51, footnote, for time-cost reference.

its present point. Linear programming, queuing theory, probability theory, Monte Carlo methods, and simulation techniques are of proven value. Dynamic programming, quadratic programming, and operational gaming (e.g., the business game) have been used successfully in a few cases to solve practical problems and appear to have considerably greater potential application. Symbolic or mathematical logic, input-output analysis, and search theory have today limited application to special problems. Formal game theory appears to have little or no practical application in its present state of development.

It is my own belief that probability theory, simulation, and operational gaming (e.g., the business game) will have a major impact on management over the next few years.[42]

It is beyond the scope of this book to attempt a more thoroughgoing treatment in the area of operations research. Some discussion of tools and techniques that show promise has been provided to whet the reader's appetite. It is hoped that he will be stimulated to explore further.[43]

Mathematical Background Required

Can managers who do not have extensive training in mathematics and statistics effectively utilize these techniques through collaboration with operations research specialists? The answer is "yes." However, a conceptual understanding of techniques and the mathematical approach to business problem solving will obviously facilitate matters. In the attempt to identify variables, assign weights and probability estimates, and speculate as to relationships between factors, managers will draw upon their extensive experience and knowledge of the business—not mathematics. However, a conceptual understanding of the role of the mathematician-statistician on their part will provide for more fruitful collaboration and will give them a better basis for *appraising the effectiveness* of such specialized staff personnel.

Limitations to the Formalization of Planning

We have seen how the development of new mathematical techniques and the advent of the computer have changed the depth and scope of planning activity. These new planning procedures have so much potential that it seems only a matter of time before the majority of managers—at least those of large scale operations—will be forced to formalize their planning activities as a matter of competitive necessity.

---

[42] Lindsay, *op. cit.*, p. 168.

[43] For example, read David Miller and Martin Starr, *Executive Decisions and Operations Research* (Englewood Cliffs, New Jersey: Prentice-Hall, Inc., 1960).

However, *complete* formalization of planning, as was suggested earlier, is not likely to occur in the foreseeable future. In the area of personal relationships, the need for judgment, a sense of timing, and intuition is apparent. *Complete* knowledge of the present and the future remains unattainable, so the need for adjustments and emergency decision making will continue. And prospects for the development of an over-all model of the firm are still remote. Also, as a generalization, plans and solutions should have what is called "face validity," i.e., should appear reasonable for the purposes to which they will be put; and this "face validity" should yield only to the strongest type of properly developed statistical validity. In all decision making, adequate consideration must be given to the extent and implications of probable error in outcomes.

Engineering, despite its relative freedom from the human element, remains predominantly an art rather than a precise application of immutable laws. And there are few scientists, indeed, who claim infallibility for their disciplines. In business, individual differences as to "expected values" of ethical and social issues, along with other human factors, will make heavy demands on the *art* of management for many years to come.

PLANNING PREMISES

Planning premises are assumptions about environmental factors and policies that will prevail in the future and set the boundaries within which planning must take place.[44] How many people will there be? What types of markets? What kind of political and regulatory climate? What kind of labor relations and what level of wages? What kind of consumer preferences, taxes, and technological innovations? What kind of basic values and philosophy will the public and our particular organization regard as essential to adhere to?[45] These and many other factors that will "set the stage" for intelligent planning will have to be dealt with. The determination of planning premises for the firm is, in effect, the performance of *Organic Planning subfunction* 1 (determination of environmental factors and the interrelationships among these factors) for the over-all situation.

---

[44] Much of this presentation is based on the sound analysis of planning premises and forecasting appearing in Koontz and O'Donnel, *Principles of Management* (New York: McGraw-Hill Book Co., 1959), pp. 477–513.

[45] This is the point at which planning is most influenced by "subjective" factors— i.e., the role expectations of organizational members, their personal values or philosophies, and other social influences will help to shape the framework of planning premises and, thereby, planning.

The rationale for the very existence of a business organization is the carrying-out of the organization's objectives. All planning— other than to define these objectives in the first place—is designed for the purpose of determining the tools (e.g., the functions, types of trained people, physical facilities, procedures, policies, rules, and organization structure) necessary for achieving the objectives. Planning premises not only influence planning for the implementation of organizational objectives but also influence the determination of the objectives themselves. The determination of planning premises is the result of *forecasting*. Forecasting is a form of planning, so planning premises, themselves, are the product of planning.

Classification of Planning Premises

Koontz and O'Donnell provide an excellent classification and analysis of planning premises; the following classification system and comments are taken from their work:

Premises External to the Firm: The General Business Environment

Political Stability: The questions of war, cold war, armed truce, or peace are usually uppermost in a planner's mind because of their permeating effect upon other factors of the business environment.

Government Controls and Enterprise Freedom: The difficulty arises for the manager, not only in the premising of the immediate future of such controls, but in the forecasting of their probable character and effect for a longer term. Naturally, this difficulty is the greater, the more a business is subject to controls and the less stable the controls.

Government Fiscal Policy: When the Federal government spent less than 5 percent of the national income, as it did three decades ago, the effect of government fiscal policy on business was considerably less than it has been in the past decade, when the expenditures ran to approximately 20 percent. When the government becomes a major factor in income distribution, taxation, and investment, practically every business manager in the nation must premise government fiscal policy in developing his plans.

Population Trends: Among the best indicators of future markets for most businesses are population estimates, whether in terms of totals, composition, or location.

Employment, Productivity, and National Income: Given a certain population growth and some knowledge as to the age and sex composition of the population, and assuming that public policy will not permit more than a given level of unemployment, the total number of persons employed in all undertakings, both government and private, can be forecast. From employment data and estimates of annual increases in output per man-hour and of changes in the work week, one can calculate a gross national product for the future at present levels of prices.

Price Levels: . . . in the short term—approximately one or two years —through calculating the impact of deficit financing and the utilization of credit institutions, both government and private, the probable trend of prices is subject to a reasonably accurate estimate. But the fact remains that accurate price-level forecasting is largely a matter of prophesying government policy.

Premises External to the Firm: The Product Market

Industry Demand: For most industries, there are a number of statistical series available through government sources, trade associations, or special economic studies showing product output, prices, employment, and, occasionally, costs. While these are usually of a historical nature, they often furnish a basis for forecasting industry demand, especially if factors such as new processes and techniques, shifts in customer tastes, national economic welfare, population changes, and similar items are considered. Moreover, for certain industries, comprehensive forecasts of demand have been worked out for the future.[46]

Individual Firm Demand: Every firm needs to know who its potential customers are, where they are, and what are the most effective means of selling them. Few enterprises are so small that they cannot take advantage of existing data, whether this be from government sources, from publications available in libraries, or from material collected by business associations.

Premises External to the Firm: The Factor Market

Business Location: It is preferable from the standpoint of business management . . . to refer to the factor market as applying to business location, the labor market, the sources of materials and parts, and the availability of capital . . . location may be dictated by a balance between the costs of transporting raw materials and the cost of shipping finished goods to the market. A second force strongly influencing location is the existence of complementary industry.

The Labor Market: In addition to the importance of availability of skills in an area, a prominent consideration in planning is the nature of the labor market in terms of the quality, stability, and adequacy of the labor supply.

Sources of Materials and Parts: Sources become of major importance when transportation costs are controlling factors in the economics of the firm. Despite transportation efficiency, cost differentials do exist. Furthermore, the nearness of a source of supply makes it possible to better control design, quality and delivery.

Capital Availability: Capital availability is often the controlling external premise of planning. Particularly with small and medium-sized businesses, the limits to availability of capital are reached at a relatively

---

[46] For research findings as to the impact of industry demand on individual company growth and the importance of "corporate environmental surveillance" see Robert B. Young, "Keys to Corporate Growth," *Harvard Business Review,* November–December, 1961.

low level, and often far sooner than the enthusiasm of their expansion-minded owners will admit.

Premises Internal to the Firm

The Sales Forecast: To a very real extent, the sales forecast is the basic planning document of the typical firm. It is, in a sense, both a plan and a planning premise. Business expenses, capital outlays, and policies of all kinds are made for the purpose ordinarily of maximizing profits obtainable from expected sales. Whether this forecast is for a period of months or for a period of years, it is the key to future business plans.

Capital Investments . . . in developing plans for the future, a business enterprise must weigh carefully the commitments that have already been made in capital equipment and modify these plans to make the best possible use of this equipment.

Basic Policies: Plans for the future are also subject to conditions that arise as the result of basic policies. Product policies, distribution policies, and many others are often fixed, in the sense that they cannot be readily changed.

Supply Factors: One of the more significant areas of premises external to the enterprise are those that have to do with sources of materials and parts. To some extent, however, these sources may be within the control of the firm and hence may be premises internal to the firm . . . whether the sources of supply are obtained through integration or through conscious development, they furnish a significant area of planning policy that may be internal to the firm as well as external in nature.[47]

Of course, there are other important factors to consider. Have the significant strengths and weaknesses of the firm and its competitors been evaluated realistically? Have plans been made for future reverses? Has an adequate appraisal been made of the capacity of each part of the firm to support its phase of the program in the future? This last question gets into the area of organization planning which is the subject of the next chapter.

FORECASTING

Forecasting is a form of planning in that it requires an identification of probable future alternative conditions and a selection from among these alternatives. The determination of planning premises is the result of forecasting. The *sales forecast* is the firm's basic planning document. This is true because the sales forecast sets the stage for all other types of internal planning. The following discussion of forecasting will be about sales forecasting, since it is so essential and the steps involved are basically the same as for other types of forecasting.

---

[47] Koontz and O'Donnell, *op. cit.*

Five Basic Approaches

Looking back, we can discern five basic approaches (or a combination thereof) with which sales forecasts have been developed:
1. Intuitive judgment or guessing.
2. Opinion sampling or polling of executives, sales personnel, and consumers.
3. Time-series or trend analysis to provide projections of historical data.
4. Correlation of sales with other variables or national indexes.
5. Model building.

Approaches 1 and 2 may represent an extreme form of subjective, biased planning or a productive form of informal planning, depending upon the extent to which data obtained are based on "ulterior" motives rather than on careful consideration of relevant factors. Consumers, for example, to satisfy the "logical requirements" of an interview or questionnaire and their own status needs, often profess intentions that are not confirmed later by their buying behavior. Salesmen and sales executives may have various reasons for submitting "padded" or "diminished" estimates.

Trend Analysis. Trend projections are based on the assumption that past rates of change will continue into the future; they supply correct estimates a surprisingly large part of the time. This occurs because prior conditions do tend to persist *except* at turning points and major shifts in growth rates. But that is the rub, for these turning points and major shifts provide the biggest opportunities for success or failure to the firm. Consequently, the ability to predict these turning points and shifts accurately is the characteristic that distinguishes a sophisticated from a naïve method of forecasting. Sophistication will be achieved only when all the factors significantly relevant to future sales and their interrelationships are properly considered.[48]

However, the use of "pressure indexes" does provide one refinement to the trend projection method. These are ratio and difference measures that can indicate pending change and its direction, though they are not very good for indicating the magnitude of such change. The ratio of raw materials inventory to new orders for finished goods, for example, is a "pressure index" that might be used in predicting shifts in raw materials prices. Shifts in the long-term demand for new housing may be anticipated with the help of an-

---

[48] Here we have another illustration of the *process* of planning. We forecast to produce planning premises relevant to future sales, then we forecast future sales in part on the basis of these premises.

other "pressure index": the difference between the rate of family formation and the rate of increase in housing inventory.[49]

Correlation Analysis. Correlation analysis is a widely used approach in forecasting. The basic objective of the firm's forecasters is to find some national or industry index or series that varies with—correlates with—their sales. *Ideally,* they would like to find one that "leads" or "lags" their sales figures by a constant period of time. The value of a predictor that would indicate, let us say, the level of company sales six months hence (within narrow margins for error) would be obvious. Even if the correlation is not high, such a predictor—like a "pressure index"—may be used to warn of shifts and turns (though it may not accurately indicate the magnitude of change). Gross national product, national income, and consumer's disposable income are three indexes that have been used. G. H. Moore found the following eleven series to have lead characteristics, where the figures in parentheses represent the average lead in months at business cycle peaks and troughs, respectively:[50]

Business failures—liabilities (10.5) (7.5)
New orders for industrial durables (6.9) (4.7)
Residential building contracts (6.2) (4.5)
Common stock prices (6) (7.2)
Commercial and industrial building contracts (5.2) (1.7)
Average hours worked per week (3.8) (2.6)
Passenger automobile production (3) (4)
Wholesale prices, BLS index (2.6) (3.2)
New incorporations (2.5) (3.5)
Pig iron production (2) (3)
Steel ingot production (1) (4)

Though a given firm may find good correlation between one of these series and its sales, none of these, used singly or in conjunction with others, can be counted on for consistent general economic forecasting; lead times are not consistent enough with the passage of time and changing economic conditions.

The Forecast Model

When trend and correlation analyses bear fruit, then it is time to give consideration to a further refinement in forecasting methodology: model building. As was pointed out earlier in this chapter,

---

[49] For an excellent discussion of this and other aspects of forecasting see chaps. 2 and 5 of M. H. Spencer and L. S. Siegelman, *Managerial Economics* (Homewood, Illinois: Richard D. Irwin, Inc., 1959).

[50] *Ibid.,* pp. 33 and 34.

models are very useful planning tools. A model is a simplified representation of reality; it attempts to describe mathematically how the
various factors in a system interrelate with each other. After such a
"descriptive" model has been validated, forecast data may be fed
into it to make it a "predictive" model. Spencer and Siegelman describe a number of interesting models for predicting demand. Part

FIG. 2-5

**Actual and Calculated Motor Fuel Consumption
(In Millions of Barrels)**

Source: Econometric Institute, Inc.

of their report of a study concerned with the demand for gasoline
follows:

What are the controlling forces affecting the demand for gasoline:
Total sales of gasoline can be expressed as a function of three classes of
factors: (1) the number of gasoline consuming units in use, which includes passenger cars, trucks, airplanes, buses, tractors, and other miscellaneous sources; (2) the average number of miles per unit, which in turn
depends upon the composition of motor vehicles in use, changes in super-
numerary income (i.e., disposable income less living costs), and gasoline
prices; and (3) the average number of miles per gallon. A fourth vari-

able, such as a time trend, is also needed as a measure of the influence of other factors not included in the above three. This embraces the average of all other miscellaneous influences that affect average mileage. The forecast equation is then given by the formula:

$$G = \left\{ 1.66T + [C + 5.5B] \, [.458 \, (3.15I) \, ^{.165}] \, 4.74P{-}^{.52} \right\} 17TT$$

where G = gasoline consumption in millions of barrels per calendar year

     T = trucks in use July 1

     C = cars in use July 1

     B = buses in use July 1

     I = supernumerary income

     P = price of gasoline in cents per gallon (average per calendar year)

    TT = time trend, which is a measure of those factors not otherwise included in the formula.[51]

The report goes on to discuss the significance of each of the variables as demand-controlling factors.[52] Figure 2-5 provides striking proof of the validity of this model.[53]

A Multi-Method Approach Needed

Until the necessary insights and data for model building are developed, the forecaster will do well to use a combination of the other four approaches that have been discussed. Even after a valid, refined model has been created, these other approaches should not be abandoned, for no model is infallible, and none to date have been all-inclusive. Constant checks must be made to test for continuing validity, and a model must be used with the same judgment and care as any of the other planning tools that have been discussed. Important developments are taking place in the field of planning, and it is hoped that this introductory material will encourage further exploration on the part of the reader.

QUESTIONS

1. What is "problem solving"? What is "decision making"? How are the two related to define "planning"?

2. In your own words state the *Generic Planning Premise.*

3. From the standpoint of benefit to society, what is the difference between action based on short-term and long-term selfishness on the part of the businessman. Explain.

---

[51] Spencer and Siegelman, *op. cit.*, chap. 5.

[52] *Ibid.*, p. 163.

[53] For additional material see Milton Spencer and Theodore Mattheiss, "Forecasting Sales of Consumer's Durable Goods," *California Management Review*, (Spring, 1962), Vol. IV, No. 3, pp. 75–101.

4. What is the difference between "formal planning" and "informal planning" as to the functions involved? As to the way in which these functions are performed? Discuss.

5. Explain the *Principle of Limiting Factors*.

6. "The rational manager will now base all his business decisions on a comparison of the expected values of the alternatives involved." What is your reaction to this statement? Why?

7. Try to define "operations research." Compare your definition with those presented on page 39.

8. What distinguishes a modern digital computer from a "glorified computation machine"? Explain.

9. What is the distinction between a "descriptive" model and a "predictive" model? What is a "decision" model?

10. If a new tank design were being tested via the Monte Carlo method of simulation, what would one battle victory signify? What kind of proof would you want before you would be willing to assume that the new design is really significant?

11. Can computers be made to think? Discuss.

12. In what way could the General Problem Solver program assist a business planner in his problem solving? Explain.

13. What is PERT? In what ways does it facilitate planning? What is the significance of the "critical path"?

14. Will all successful managers of the future, by necessity, have to be competent mathematicians? Discuss.

15. What are "planning premises"? What role do they play in business planning?

16. What are the five basic approaches to sales forecasting? Which approach is best? Why?

17. What is a "pressure index"?

18. Outline the steps you would follow to construct a "forecast model."

Chapter 3

ORGANIZATION PLANNING: PART I

The general character of management has been examined, and the organic management function of planning has been discussed at some length. This chapter and the next will consider a type of planning—organization planning—that is vital for the proper performance of managerial activity and the effective functioning of an enterprise as a whole.

Once a firm's objectives are determined, the need for organization planning comes to the fore. What functions will have to be performed? When, by whom, where, and how? What equipment and facilities will be required and by whom shall they be utilized? What kinds of relationships should be encouraged among organizational personnel and what provisions in the way of policies, procedures, communication systems, and so on will be needed to facilitate the effective coordination of effort? What kinds of informal group and individual values will contribute to the achievement of company objectives, and how can their development be encouraged? What informal group and individual values will *detract* from this effort, and how can their development be discouraged?

Organization planning is concerned with all these questions and many more. It is concerned with the specification of desired authority, responsibility and communicative relationships among functions, physical factors, and personnel for the purpose of achieving company goals.

In chapter 1, it was pointed out that there are very few owner-managers who can successfuly "grow all the way" with an expanding firm. Often this is due to personal problems that make it difficult

for them to relinquish or delegate authority. But, even if they are
capable of delegation, they run into major difficulties as the firm
increases in size, if they do not have a basic understanding of how
an organization should grow and adapt to changes in personnel,
physical factors, and the general business environment. Unfortunately, organizations do not grow in desirable patterns by chance,
and attempts to imitate the pattern of another company—even in
the same industry with "similar" goals—are usually fruitless.

Organization planning, based on sound concepts, must be made
an important and continuing activity of the enterprise if it is to
avoid the heavy costs of letting "nature take its course." For, when
the inadequacies of a given situation—which was not anticipated by
and provided for by adequate organization planning—finally "force"
a change, it is usually after a long period of inefficiency and de-
moralization, possibly involving losses of key personnel in addition
to a serious wasting of resources.

There are many disagreements and misconceptions as to how an
enterprise should be organized. Some people are quite confused
as to a *workable* and *useful* distinction between "line" and "staff"
positions. Some claim that there are basically only two types of
organization: the "functionalized" organization and the "divisionalized" organization. Others argue that, once an organization structure that is a "winning combination" for a company has been found,
the basic design of the structure should never, under any circumstances, be tampered with. Is there really a basic theory that will
place these questions in some sort of perspective? Can we make
any useful generalizations about organizations at various stages of
growth? The following discussion will attempt to develop a set of
concepts and a frame of reference that, it is hoped, will assist an
organization planner in dealing productively with these and many
other organizational matters.

FORMAL VS. INFORMAL ORGANIZATION

*The "formal" organization structure of a company comprises the
authority, responsibility, and communicative relationships among
functions, physical factors, and personnel that are prescribed by
owners or their delegates for the achievement of organizational
objectives.*

*"Informal" organization structure comprises the authority, respon-
sibility, communicative, and associative relationships among functions, physical factors, and personnel that are supplemental to the*

"formal" organization structure and may be "for," "against," or "neutral" with regard to the achievement of organizational objectives. These informal relationships are influenced by the social values, attitudes and customs of organizational members and groups and, in turn, influence behavior as they become codified in the form of informal organizational cultures and subcultures. "Informal organization," then, is a term used to indicate interpersonal and other kinds of relationships that exist in an organization and are essential to its functioning but are not spelled out in formal organization charts or are necessarily consistent with the formally planned scheme.

There has been a tendency on the part of some students of human relations and group dynamics to "debunk" the study of traditional, formal organization theory on the grounds that reality is described by informal not formal organizational concepts. On the other hand, many formal theorists claim that the study of informal without formal concepts would be analogous to the study of an animal with its skeleton removed. The most productive approach in the opinion of your author is the one that attempts to synthesize the best concepts from both formal and informal theory, for it is believed that this is the one most likely to approximate reality.

In an actual firm we can observe constant interaction between the formal and the informal organizations. Obviously, formal assignments of authority and responsibility have a profound impact on individual status and influence as well as on organizational efficiency and sources of power in the company. But such assignments are immediately and persistently modified by the "informal" expectations and values of employees. As we shall see, formal authority is *not* synonymous with *effective* authority; formal communication is not the only form of communication; and the traditional "economic man" concept of motivation is rather naïve.

Due attention to individual and group needs must be given to assure productive placement and teamwork in an organization. However, the business firm and all the activity it encompasses are but *means* to the end of achieving organizational goals that are predominantly *formal goals.* Good placement, counseling, and human relations practices are provided, *not* as ends in themselves, but as *means* for facilitating the achievement of primary company objectives. In our discussions we will consider both formal and informal organizations in this context; as *means* to the end of achieving company goals. Good formal structure encourages a high level of motivation and task orientated coordination on the part of all personnel.

It must be made an effective complement to desirable informal structure and vice versa. In this regard, good formal structure and leadership will encourage the development of informal organization along constructive lines.

Simon provides a useful statement as to the values of *formal* structure and *informal* structure in facilitating the achievement of organizational objectives:

1. Organizations and institutions permit stable expectations to be formed by each member of the group as to the behavior of the other members under specified conditions. Such stable expectations are an essential precondition to a rational conideration of the consequences of action in a social group.
2. Organizations and institutions provide the general stimuli and attention-directors that channelize the behaviors of the members of the group, and that provide those members with the intermediate objectives that stimulate action.[1]

Another reason for stressing the importance of formal goals (and therefore the importance of formal organization) was suggested in chapter 1. The right to engage in private business stems from the right of private property, and this right may be modified, extended, or withdrawn as society desires. A firm must be concerned with formal goals—service to society—if it wishes to survive and prosper.

ROLE OF OBJECTIVES

Is the concluding sentence above, "a firm must be concerned with formal goals—service to society—if it wishes to survive and prosper," really true? Can we equate formal goals with service to society? Undoubtedly, we can think of some instance in which a businessman or promoter has taken advantage of the public and this relation did not hold. But for the business that must operate over a period of time against active competition, the statement provides a valid and useful generalization. For the success and sustained existence of such a firm in our society depend on its ability, relative to the ability of other producers, to meet the needs of customers efficiently.

One of the chief contributions of the entrepreneur or legitimate promoter results from his ability to perceive *new* or *more effective ways* for meeting the needs of consumers. The successful establish-

---

[1] Herbert A. Simon, *Administrative Behavior* (New York: Macmillan Co., 1957), pp. 100–101.

ment of any business requires money, physical equipment, and some knowledge of business administration. But, more than anything else, it requires the satisfactory answer to one of two questions: What *salable* values can be provided that are not currently available? How can currently available values be supplied more effectively than they are now being supplied? The salable values that a business plans to create and distribute are defined by its *primary service objectives.*

Not only is the clear definition of sound objectives vital to the very existence of a business, it is an absolute prerequisite to effective organization planning. For organization planning is concerned with the specification of desired authority, responsibility, and communicative relationships among functions, physical factors, and personnel *for the purpose of achieving company objectives.* There is no such thing as organization structure that is good or ideal in and of itself! The value of any structure must be measured in terms of its contribution to, or detraction from, the effective achievement of company goals. These observations are plausible, and it would seem that they would be obvious to the average businessman. Yet it is surprising how few of them in practice clearly define their objectives at the outset, consciously design their organizations in view of these objectives, and periodically review the need for modification of structure in the light of carefully considered changes in objectives!

Primary Service Objectives

The *salable* values that a business plans to create and distribute are defined by its *primary service objectives.*[2] An automobile company, for example, converts raw materials into finished cars and then distributes them to customers. Specifically, what kind of car or cars does the company plan to make? The finest quality regardless of price? Or the most durable and economical to own and operate? Or, of course, some combination of features that comprises a compromise? Carefully formulated *primary service objectives* present a detailed enumeration of the salable values that a firm plans to create and distribute. They provide a frame of reference within

---

[2] For the classification of objectives used and many other concepts of organization the author has borrowed freely from the classic work of Ralph C. Davis, The *Fundamentals of Top Management* (New York: Harper & Bros., 1951), and his *Industrial Organization and Management* (3d ed.; New York: Harper & Bros., 1957).

which *collateral* and *secondary objectives* must be developed and
within which organization structure should be designed.

Collateral Objectives

Primary service objectives are objectives of the *organization; collateral objectives* are those of the *people* associated with the firm,
without whom *primary objectives* could never be attained. As
Davis puts it: "Collateral personal objectives are just what the term
suggests—values that individuals and groups within the organization, or associated directly with it, seek to acquire for and distribute
among themselves."[3] Who are these people? They are owners or
stockholders, board members, managers, members of the community
in which the firm operates, customers, and employees.

An immediate reaction may be that *collateral objectives* must
have to do with money, for isn't this why people work for or associate themselves with a business organization? There is little
question that money *is* important! However, it is perhaps most important, at least in our society, in ways that have not been sufficiently recognized in the past. And even when these non-traditional
roles of money are properly considered, it soon becomes apparent
that money is "the tail and not the dog." Traditionally, money has
been thought of primarily in terms of its purchasing power, its
ability to buy off-the-job satisfactions and necessities. In fact, one
of the off-the-job satisfactions that has been given considerable
weight in the past has been retirement—accumulation of enough
money to permit abandoning the job altogether!

Today, on the basis of research findings and more acute observation, we realize that on-the-job satisfactions are extremely important
for the well-being as well as effective contribution of all the firm's
employees. As we will discuss at greater length later (especially in
chap. 8), these on-the-job satisfactions are created largely through
the fulfillment of individual and group *needs,* which in our society
are predominantly non-monetary in character. True, money in its
"other" role cannot be divorced from these needs, for pay is a status
symbol—a way of keeping "score" as to relative performance—and a
source of pride and self-respect, as well as a measure of the fairness
of an employer or boss. But the non-monetary means for meeting
on-the-job satisfactions are undoubtedly more important than the

---

[3] Davis, *The Fundamentals of Top Management,* p. 103.

monetary means, given a reasonably "in line" rate structure to begin with.

One of the great truths we are beginning to grasp in industry, is that these on-the-job needs are beyond the conscious control of employees. That is, even if they honestly *wish* to accept higher pay in lieu of non-monetary sources of satisfaction and sign agreements to this effect, the effort is usually futile except for the briefest of periods. For, with the extended passage of time, deterioration of morale and performance is inevitable despite the sincerest of resolutions! People are attracted to that work environment which holds out the best promise of meeting their non-monetary needs: status, rewarding social intercourse with others, feelings of worthwhileness and achievement in what they are doing, and protection from ridicule, unfair treatment, and undue insecurity.

Absentee stockholders may be primarily interested in dividend policy and earnings, but other personnel associated with the firm think of "wages" in a much broader context, in terms of psychic as well as monetary income. These values that the organization must create to induce the proper implementation of *primary service objectives* are defined by the *collateral objectives* of the business. They include community, political, and public relations values in addition to the personal values listed above.

Secondary Objectives

Last, there are *secondary objectives*. These have to do with the implementation of *primary* and *collateral objectives* with maximum economy and effectiveness. As we shall see, *line* agencies are chiefly concerned with *primary objectives,* whereas *staff* agencies are primarily concerned with *collateral* and *secondary objectives*. *Staff* agencies exist for the primary purpose of assisting line agencies in their "line" work of creating and distributing salable values or utilities.

At times a staff agency may have to operate at less than optimal efficiency (for example, be overstaffed) in order to assure that the line agencies it serves can operate at optimal efficiency. This situation is described by the *Limitation of Staff Economy Principle*. It **is usually necessary that staff functions be performed with less than maximum economy in order that the line functions which they serve may be performed with maximum economy and effectiveness.** An example of this principle in operation would be provided by a maintenance or trouble-shooting crew that is deliberately "over-staffed" relative to its normal work load in order to provide prompt and effective service in the event of a major breakdown.

The Objectives Pyramid

In the same way that staff efficiency often must be subordinated to line efficiency, *collateral* and *secondary objectives* must be developed in *support of* and within the framework defined by *primary service objectives.* In turn, all divisional, departmental, group, and individual work objectives should be developed in support of and within the framework defined by the *primary objectives* of the next higher organizational level within the same chain of command. In

FIG. 3-1

The Objectives Pyramid

this fashion an "objectives pyramid" may be visualized as depicted in Figure 3-1.

To lay the groundwork for adequate implementation, objectives must be stated in terms of *degree* as well as *kind;* for example, to say that our objective will be to emphasize quality in a particular undertaking is not enough, the extent to which this is to be done—quality specifications—must also be given.

Harmonizing Organization and Personal Goals

The distinction made between goals of the firm *(primary service objectives)* and the personal goals of those associated with the firm *(collateral objectives)* is a very useful and realistic one. With the passage of time the firm develops a certain character or corporate image; employees as well as the public begin to associate certain values and methods of doing business with particular organizations. Obviously, the firm's *primary service objectives* are fashioned by people, but the pressures of competition, the power of the public to control the sanction to engage in business, and the desire for continuity within the framework of precedent encourage the formulation of *primary objectives* that are *not* merely an extension of the personal goals of the planners. There is little question, however, that there is *interaction* between personal goals and *primary* goals; *primary objectives* are influenced by the personal needs and values of the planners, *but within a very definite framework of restrictions dictated by the past and present.*

At times, some employees can find significant personal satisfaction in identifying with and achieving company goals. There is evidence that this was the case at the Ford Motor Company during its early years. Henry Ford would proclaim with all sincerity his belief that a cheap, durable car, within the reach of every family, would revolutionize American society, that it would bridge the gap between the farmer and the city dweller and encourage better unity of purpose and understanding throughout the nation. To show that he "meant business" Ford reduced the price of his touring car from $950 in October, 1909, to $600 in October, 1912, and to $360 in August, 1916, while, at the same time, making significant improvements in its quality! We are told that this sense of mission was infectious and that many of his men caught it and shared his enthusiasm and zeal.[4] Men in military service during wartime and scientists today engaged in the "race to space" often derive considerable personal satisfaction from close identification with the formal goals of their organizations.

But, realistically, even with good selection procedures that minimize the chance of conflict between organizational goals and personal goals, we usually find it difficult to generate much spontaneous enthusiasm on the part of employees and others for the *primary service objectives* of their firm. Absentee stockholders are probably the only profit seekers in the narrow, traditional sense. Many of them have no idea of the problems or even the products of "their" firms and couldn't care less as long as their stock investment properly appreciates in value. But it is unlikely that the average board of directors member is so oriented. And, when we consider top

---

[4] See Allan Nevins, *Ford, the Times, the Man, the Company* (New York: Charles Scribners' Sons, 1954). (The automobile prices are presented in the appendixes.)

managers, middle managers, foremen, and others associated with an enterprise, we realize that their *personal* goals not only differ, in all likelihood, from the goals of the enterprise, but differ, also, from group to group and individual to individual!

If this is true, how can we ever hope to harmonize organization goals *(primary service objectives)* with these diverse group and personal goals? The answer provides one of the greatest challenges to the modern manager. He must first be able to *perceive* the character of individual and group needs and then so manipulate various factors under his control—job assignments, praise, censure, titles, pay, working relationships, promotions, and so on—that these needs are met, and some constrained, *in the process* of carrying out the work of the firm. If an employee cannot derive personal benefit, in other than purely monetary terms, from his work environment, then management has failed either to formulate sound *primary* and *collateral objectives* or to associate the worker with appropriate organizational activity. This means, of course, that management must devote considerable skill and attention to initial personnel selection and the continuing determination of individual and group needs so that the formulation of company objectives and the plans for their implementation can be realistic and productive.

The basic rationale of our discussion is summarized in the statement of the *Principle of Harmony of Objectives:* **Though the personal goals of the people associated with an organization frequently are not the same as primary organization goals, organization goals often can be conceived and implemented in such a way as to satisfy these personal goals within the framework of necessary organizational constraints.** Chapter 5 and 8 are particularly concerned with concepts and techniques that lend support and meaning to this statement.

TOOLS OF IMPLEMENTATION

The point has been made that all business activities (functions) are merely means to the end of attaining *primary, collateral,* and *secondary objectives* (ultimately, *primary service objectives*). Thus, functions are determined by the character of these objectives and, as we have pointed out, in turn influence the character of *formal* organization structure (the authority, responsibility, and communicative relationships among functions, physical factors, and personnel for the achievement of organization objectives) and *in-*

formal structure (the authority, responsibility, communicative, and associative relationships among functions, physical factors, and personnel that are supplemental to formal structure and may be "for," "against," or "neutral" with regard to the achievement of primary objectives). There are other important "tools" for implementing objectives that deserve mention at this point.

Procedures

A *procedure* prescribes the complementary and sequential relationships between functions, physical factors, and personnel for the accomplishment of specific subgoals within the framework of *formal* structure. For example, most companies have procedures for processing in-coming orders, handling requests for vacations or leaves of absence, for ordering supplies, for requisitioning personnel, for obtaining pay increases for subordinates, and so on. Perhaps you have encountered the expression, "Oh, that's SOP," by someone in service or someone who has been in service. It stands for "Standard Operating Procedure." Yes, the armed forces, along with all other types of organizations, find the formulation of procedures to be of value.

Procedures, along with *rules* and *policies* permit the routinization of certain organizational work and provide some assurance of uniformity of performance throughout the organization as well as through time. This permits organizational resources (especially experienced executive talent) and time to be conserved. Many activities can be initiated and performed by less skilled employees without recourse to higher-level order giving and supervision when provision is made for soundly conceived procedures, rules, and policies.

Rules and Policies

Rules are specific prescriptions for action, which leave no room for interpretation or discretion in application. "Do not walk on the grass" or "No smoking in this room" are examples of rules. Often the inclusion of an explanation for a rule renders it more palatable and meaningful. "No smoking—high explosives" is likely to be more effective than simply "No smoking"!

Policies are guides to action that require interpretation and discretion in application. For example, a company may have the following policy: "Decentralized divisions are expected to buy supplies

from other company divisions *unless* they can obtain superior quality for the same price or the same quality for a lower price outside
the company." At first glance, this may appear to be like a rule, but
when we consider the problems of applying it we can see that
judgment is involved. Determination of the quality of a product,
especially if there is an element of style present, can require considerable interpretation and judgment. It is useful if statements of
policy also include an explanation of the underlying reason or
rationale for their existence. In the example given above it would
be useful if the policy statement had been preceded by the phrase:
"In order to encourage the sale of our products, yet *not* make our
decentralized divisions less flexible and competitive. . . ."

Unity of Objectives

In addition to organization structure, rules, policies, and procedures, there are other "tools" for implementing objectives, such as
plans, reports, techniques of organizing, communication and control,
and various principles and concepts, which will be discussed
throughout the remaining chapters of this book. The *essential* point
we wish to make here is that *none of these is an end in itself; all
must operate in concert for the achievement of organization objectives.*

This desirable relationship between tools for implementation and
company objectives is expressed in the *Principle of Unity of Objectives:* **The organization as a whole as well as each of its parts
provides merely a tool for the achievement of organizational objectives; therefore, *all* organization activity should contribute to
the attainment of these objectives.** This concept is presented
graphically in Figure 3-2.

There is a strong temptation on the part of many managers to
take the policies, rules, procedures, and other tools of successful
firms and "transplant" them intact to their own organizations. We
have already mentioned the fallacy of this "management by imitation" with regard to copying organization structure. Since all these
"tools" are employed solely for the purpose of fulfilling objectives
that are *unique* to a particular firm, it follows that they should be
developed and *refined* by personnel of that firm with this in mind.
Of course, they can benefit greatly from the experience and theorizing of others, but they must judiciously *tailor* borrowed techniques
and ideas to the special requirements of their own company.

THE ORGANIC BUSINESS FUNCTIONS

Identification

One of the most important prerequisites to effective organization planning for any enterprise is accurate identification of its *organic business functions. These are the major functions that define how a firm creates and distributes salable utilities; they are the sources of all line organization.* Once *primary service objectives* are determined, the stage is set for the identification of *organic business functions.*

FIG. 3-2

"Ends" and "Means"

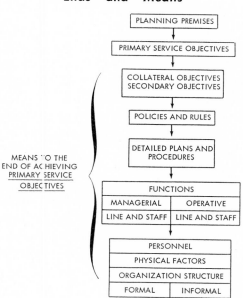

Assume, for example, that our *primary service objectives* have to do with the manufacture and sale of various types of automobiles; our *organic business functions* or major functions for achieving these objectives will be *production* and *sales* (see Fig. 3-4). Suppose that our *primary service objectives* have to do with the operation of a retail hardware store, then our *organic business functions* are *buying* and *selling.* An integrated oil company, for example, might have the *organic business functions* of *production, refining, transportation,* and *marketing.* More research is needed to determine what the *or-*

ganic business functions are, or should be, for various types of business concerns. Figure 3–3 lists those we have mentioned along with other possibilities.

Of course, some companies, such as General Motors, are really a "federation" of separate businesses. In addition to manufacturing automobiles, GM top management oversees the General Motors Acceptance Corporation (financing) and GM Overseas (in part an export corporation). In such cases, each "separate" business in the company will have its own *organic business functions*.[5] Also, as can be seen by reference to Figure 3-3, a firm may have more than two *organic business functions* for the creation and distribution of

FIG. 3-3
Types of Concerns and Their Organic Business Functions

TYPE OF CONCERN	ORGANIC BUSINESS FUNCTIONS (MAJOR FUNCTIONS FOR CREATING AND DISTRIBUTING SALABLE VALUES)
MANUFACTURING	PRODUCTION, SALES
SMALL RETAIL STORE	BUYING, SELLING
LARGE DEPARTMENT STORE	OPERATIONS AND MERCHANDISING
TELEPHONE	PLANT, OFFICE, AND COMMERCIAL
INTEGRATED OIL CO.	PRODUCTION, TRANSPORTATION, REFINING, MARKETING
CONSULTING	PROJECT OR ENGAGEMENT ACTIVITY

its salable utilities, as is the case for the telephone company, which has three *organic business functions: plant, traffic,* and *commercial.* Of course, a number of line "subchief executives" will be created when the firm employs a *product* or *service, customer,* or *regional* basis for departmentation in addition to the universal *functional* basis that we have been discussing. See Figure 3-5 for an example of the *regional* basis.

Line-Staff Distinction

We have indicated that the *organic business functions* are the *sources of all line organization. Line positions* in an organization are those concerned *directly* with the creation and distribution of

---

[5] See chap. 12 for discussion of the General Motors Corporation.

salable utilities or with the management of such activity. In addition, *line positions* are concerned with *staff* activities (which comprise all non-line activities that must be performed and which contribute *indirectly* to the creation and distribution of salable utilities). It is important to remember that this is a *dynamic classification;* a *line position* in one type of concern may be a *staff position* in another. And a position in a given firm may *change* from line to staff or vice versa with a change in the firm's *primary service objectives!*

FIG. 3-4

A Manufacturing Concern

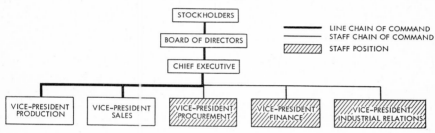

FIG. 3-5

Regional Departmentation of a Manufacturing Concern

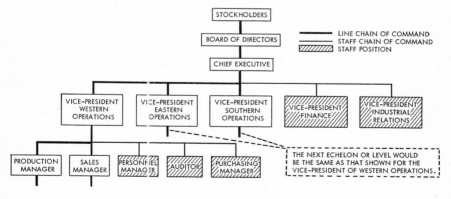

When an organization is small, there may not be enough work or need for specialization to warrant differentiating staff functions from a line position and placing them in a separate *staff position* under the supervision of a line manager. But as the organization grows in size and complexity, this need does arise. Figure 3-5, for example, shows that the staff positions of personnel manager, auditor, and purchasing manager have *evolved* from the line organization under the supervision of the regional line vice-presidents. All staff personnel report either to a line manager or to a higher staff chief who in turn reports to a line manager. Staff personnel are concerned predominantly with the performance or supervision of those functions which *indirectly* contribute to the creation and distribution of salable utilities, *except* when they exercise functional authority.[6] The nature and use of functional authority are discussed later in this chapter.

We see, then, that line personnel may perform both line and staff functions and that they have line bosses. Staff personnel perform primarily staff functions, except when exercising functional authority, and report directly to line bosses or to staff superiors who report to line bosses. All this may be quite clear, but two important questions arise: Do the formal authority relationships between a vice-president, his subordinates, and the chief executive *change* as a result of labeling his position line or staff? If not, why is the determination of *organic business functions* and the consequent distinction between line and staff activities and positions of value, anyway? Certainly, no two questions are more important to the student of organization planning!

It is true, that formal authority relationships among a vice-president, his subordinates, and the chief executive do *not* change as a result of the line or staff "label." In Figure 3-5 the vice-president of industrial relations (whose position we have labeled "staff") has the *same* formal authority relationships with his subordinates and the chief executive as the vice-president of western operations (whose position we have labeled "line"). The value of the line-staff distinction, however, stems from *purpose* and *philosophy of performance*.

First, a sense of direction and proper emphasis is given to planners when those functions *which justify the existence of the business* are clearly designated and assigned priority. Second, this sets the stage for answering the key question, *"Who serves and supports whom in the organization?"* It is not the primary responsibility of a line vice-president to gain the confidence of his fellow vice-presidents

---

[6] Actually, a few specific staff functions assigned to staff personnel may *directly* create salable utilities. For example, the staff purchasing agent in an automobile plant may buy the finished tool kits that are placed in finished cars. However, it is unlikely that the majority of his purchases are of this type—direct creation of utility—and his role in the organization is clearly that of a staff person. Of course, if an automobile company both manufactured and imported cars, it would be plausible to regard those who purchase raw materials, etc., for manufacturing and other divisions as *staff* buyers and those who buy cars for resale as *line* buyers. In this instance, there would exist two distinct means by which the firm creates salable utilities.

and other managers so that he may study their problems and be permitted to serve them effectively. But this is the primary job of a staff vice-president or any staff officer. For staff agencies and staff functions exist for the chief purpose of assisting line personnel in the work of creating and distributing *salable* goods or services.

Customers will not "buy" a good training program or accounting system. They will buy, however, the improved product values that are made possible by these products of soundly conceived staff activity. Line functions are the "pay-off" functions that create and distribute those salable values which account for sales and revenue. Staff positions "earn their way" only so long as they contribute more to line operations than the cost of maintaining them. In this regard, all staff activity is just as essential as line activity. No staff activity should be pursued as an end in itself. The ultimate test of its value is its contribution to the achievement of *primary service objectives*.

This emphasis is crucial to the incumbent of a staff position, for it indicates the "role" that he is expected to assume. It is predominantly *his* job to gain acceptance, for himself and his ideas, from those in the organization he is supposed to serve—to persuade, not impose. His role in the organization is analogous to that of a medical specialist with his patient. The patient seeks the specialist out and pays for his expert skills and advice for the purpose of being helped. Normally, the patient is the final judge as to whether or not his advice will be acted upon and whether or not he has, in fact, been "helped." Certainly in an impasse, after due appeals to higher line authority have been made (if the urgency of the matter seems to warrant it), staff personnel should defer to the ultimate authority of the line. If a staff specialist finds himself constantly at odds with higher line management or organizational objectives, probably he should seek employment elsewhere.

FUNCTIONALIZATION AND DEPARTMENTATION

When a man starts a hot-dog stand by himself, he cannot afford the advantages of specialization and personal assistance. He alone must perform all the activities, line and staff, that are required for the successful conduct of his business. With success and growth, however, it will not be long before he will be physically unable properly to perform all functions; he will have to seek help. At this point he must become concerned with *functionalization* (the grouping of functions for job assignment purposes) and, later on, with *departmentation* (the grouping of jobs into departments or other organizational units and the development of chains of command).

Guides for Functionalization

There are certain guides for the proper grouping of functions. As R. C. Davis points out:

The similar or complementary characteristics of functions are the basic considerations that determine what functions will be grouped together in what relationships, depending on the requirements of the particular functional problem. . . . Similar functions may be defined as those that have like objectives and work characteristics; that in consequence give rise to similar problems involving similar factors, forces and effects; that require similar background, training experience, intelligence, and personality in the personnel assigned for their performance.[7]

We all have different aptitudes (basic inborn abilities) and interests. These help to determine the kind of formal training and practice we pursue and, in turn, the type of work at which we are most adept. In this broader framework we all specialize.

The values of specialization have not been discovered just recently. From the beginning of time, among the most primitive of tribes, certain forms of specialization have been practiced. The outstanding pottery maker, hunter, or arrow maker was often relieved of other duties so that he could concentrate his efforts in his area of skill to the benefit of all. The advent of the industrial revolution paved the way for the widespread introduction of specialization in the factory. In fact, machine and mass production techniques have made possible the development of specialized job assignments to an *extreme,* where the benefits of increased production resulting from specialization per se are forfeited as a result of the psychological impact of such job assignments on workers.

The skilled surgeon does not have this problem, even though he is a specialist, because there is sufficient variety and challenge in his work to sustain his interest. The average worker may not need as *much* variety as the surgeon does—owing to differences in basic ability and intelligence—but there is growing evidence that he needs more than he is often given in industrial job assignments if he is to produce at his optimal level. This observation, of course, does not invalidate the concept of specialization; it merely points up the need to use functionalization in setting up jobs with discretion.

In this regard, it is useful if certain jobs can be "enlarged" so that a worker can carry out a *meaningful* set of operations from

---

[7]Davis, *The Fundamentals of Top Management, op. cit.,* pp. 220, 223.

beginning to end. Just as the surgeon completes an operation from start to finish, it is useful for a clerk to do *all* the work required to process an order or arrange a ticket reservation. In other words, when possible, let the arrow maker fashion the whole arrow rather than just sand the shaft or glue on the feathers! Along this same line, for more complex undertakings, specialists may find greater meaningfulness in their work if they are assigned to project or task teams and work on a particular undertaking from beginning to end. Or, when individual work assignments by necessity—say, on certain production assembly lines—are too simple, provisions for job rotation and socialization on the job can help to alleviate stultifying effects.

Guides for functionalization are found in the *Principle of Functional Emergence:* **The tendency of a given function toward differentiation and independent grouping tends to vary directly with (1) the degree of dissimilarity between the particular function and the functions with which it is grouped, (2) the degree of correlation between its growth and development and the growth of the organization as a whole, and (3) the tendency of the function to become increasingly complex and technical with growth.**[8]

Obviously, the first criterion given in this principle is based on the rationale we have just discussed: making provision for specialization through the grouping of similar functions. The second criterion relates to the dilemma of our individual hot-dog-stand proprietor faced with the growth of his business. As the *burden* of activity becomes too great for him with increased sales, he must seek help. Those functions which are affected the most by the increase in sales and have the greatest growth potential for the future, other things being equal, are logical ones for him to differentiate and incorporate into new positions.

Last, the third criterion deals with the tendency of a function to become complex and technical with the growth of the firm. Consider personnel functions, for example. When our hot-dog-stand proprietor personally manages his business with the help of several operative employees, the costs of poor selection and training practices on his part will be less severe, proportionately, than were he applying those same practices to the selection and training of *numerous* employees—both operative and managerial—who would not be under his personal surveillance and supervision. Also, growth of an

---

[8] *Ibid.,* p. 375.

organization *creates* problems of control, communications, collective bargaining, motivation, wage and salary administration, and so on, which require the services of specially trained personnel for proper handling.

We have discussed above one limitation to the concept of grouping similar functions; if possible, we do not wish to push specialization to such an extreme that a job holds little interest for *any* worker. Another limitation is presented by the frequent need to separate functions, which might otherwise be grouped in the same work assignment, to discourage dishonesty—for example, separation of the functions of handling cash from those of recording the transactions involved. In most organizations of any size, bookkeepers and accountants are not also given the duties of receiving and disbursing cash.

On the other hand, sometimes it is very difficult to affix responsibility unless *dissimilar* functions, which otherwise might be separated, are grouped together in the same position! In some retail stores, for example, one man is responsible for *both* buying and selling merchandise. This is done to avoid divided control of sales and inability to hold anyone accountable for poor performance. The level of sales attained will be significantly affected by both the caliber of buying activity and the quality of sales effort. Without this arrangement, we can easily visualize the buyer and the person responsible for sales blaming each other for reduced volume and the owner not knowing what to do, short of firing them both!

As is true about organization planning in general, when we approach the work of functionalization, we draw predominantly on the art rather than the science of management. A thoroughgoing analysis *for* every job in an organization should be made initially, and subsequently a periodic analysis *of* every job should be made. As we have seen, there are a number of "ifs," "ands," and "buts" involved, and discretion must be used in applying these various guides.

Perhaps one other observation deserves mention before we move on to departmentation: other things being equal, functions may be assigned to individuals who have shown the greatest interest in them or the best capacity for implementing them, without bias, in the manner originally intended. Of course, "other things" rarely are equal and such concessions to personal attributes must not be pushed to a point at which the basic rationale of organization structure becomes confused.

Guides for Departmentation

How shall jobs be grouped into departments or other organizational units for the development of chains of command? There are several bases and guides that will be considered. Not surprisingly, because of the advantages of specialized effort, the *functional* basis for departmentation is *universal;* it is used somewhere at or near the top and the bottom of every organization! *Product or service, customer,* and *regional* bases for departmentation may be, and usually are, used in *combination* with the universal *functional* basis. They may be used for upper, middle, or lower levels of departmentation in the organization, depending on the unique demands of each area and level of operations. In addition to these bases, *process or equipment* may be used as a basis for the departmentation of lower-level operations. It may be useful to examine examples for each of these bases for departmentation:

Functional: In terms of functions to be performed (production, sales, procurement, finance, personnel management) or their subfunctions (recruitment, selection, training, etc., in the case of personnel management).

Product or service: The Cadillac, Pontiac, Oldsmobile, Buick, and Chevrolet divisions of General Motors represent product departmentation; the home-furnishings, hardware, and candy departments of a department store represent product departmentation. The washing and greasing "departments" of a filling station and the brake relining and engine tune-up departments of a garage represent service departmentation (as well as functional departmentation, it may be argued).

Customer: An advertising agency that establishes a different "department" or account executive for each client or class of customers; the department store that sells men's, women's and children's shoes.

Regional: English operations, German operations, and French operations; southern operations, western operations, and eastern operations.

Process or equipment: The processes in a chemical manufacturing plant. Departmentation on the basis of machine functions rather than product in a "job-order" shop.

In view of the fact that most businesses utilize *several* of these bases for departmentation in combination, we must be careful about using any one as a "label" for an organization. In Figure 3–4 we see a *functional* basis immediately under the chief executive, but it is very possible that a *product* basis could exist under the vice-president of production and that a *regional* or *customer* basis might be desirable under the vice-president of sales. In Figure 3–5, we see *both regional* and *functional bases* used at the level under the chief executive! And a functional basis prevails immediately under the regional vice-presidents. Some might characterize the company depicted in Figure 3–4 as being "functionalized" and the one in Figure 3–5 as being "divisionalized." Actually, as was pointed out above, it is quite likely that *both* firms are "divisionalized" *and* "functionalized" as well as being a number of other things to boot!

A common problem of departmentation has to do with the placement of a staff position or agency that is supposed to serve all areas of the business, for example, the position of personnel manager in a manufacturing concern. A logical place for the *initial* placement of this position is under the production head, for this will be the point of *most use* as the organization grows in size (normally, in a manufacturing concern the production organization grows at a faster pace than the sales division or other organization units.) But, as the company grows larger and there is greater need for impartial service to all divisions, this arrangement becomes increasingly inadequate, as will be seen in the discussion of staff organization in the next chapter.

Personal vs. Organizational Demands

Some business leaders go so far as to avoid *planned* functionalization and delegations of authority and responsibility. They say that, realistically, we must deal with individuals and their capacities; let each man define his areas of responsibility and authority through his own efforts. What you put on paper will never agree with the actual "informal" situation anyway.

It is very true that a compromise must be struck between the quality of personnel and equipment at hand at any particular time and the functions to be performed and the way in which they are to be performed. However, in the long run personal inadequacies and tenure must yield to the performance demands placed on the company by its objectives and competitive pressures. Improved selection, development, and motivation of personnel can go a long way toward closing the gap between formal performance demands and actual results.

It is hard to see how the organization that encourages each man to "stake out his claim" can avoid the inefficiencies and conflicts that inevitably result when personal goals are permitted to displace or take precedence over business objectives. It is essential that all activity in the firm be directed toward the achievement of company objectives, that personal goals be satisfied via collateral objectives that operate within the objectives pyramid or framework defined by *primary service objectives.*

In practice, of course, functionalization and departmentation cannot take place without the development of "gaps" and "overlaps" in responsibility and function. When those occur, we must look to informal organizational values—individual initiative, a sense of teamwork, and self-coordination—to sustain performance. If every man in an organization were to meet only the minimum requirements of his job assignment and do only what he is ordered to do, the failure of the enterprise would be assured!

Because of limitations in the qualifications of personnel and our inability to predict all developments, ideal plans for functionalization and departmentation are rarely attained. At any given time, concessions will have to be made to the personal attributes of employees and to physical resource limitations. But the "trick" is to keep these concessions as just that: *concessions* to well-conceived, ideal plans, which do not grow to the point that they become the "tail that wags the dog."

In developing these ideal plans for functionalization and departmentation, organization planners should not try to solve their problems merely by copying the patterns of successful firms in their industry. The work of others can provide good "leads" and ideas, but until these are adapted to meet the unique requirements of a specific organization they should not be used.[9] We must be concerned not only with the uniqueness of the organization as a whole but with the uniqueness of each part at each level. The various guides for functionalization and the bases for departmentation must be used in combination and on the basis of knowledge gained from detailed analysis of the enterprise being developed and the physical factors and personnel that will be available to it. Unfortunately, there are no precise rules or formulas for this important work.

AUTHORITY AND RESPONSIBILITY

When functions are grouped to form jobs, and the physical factors to be associated with them are determined, a basic framework is established within which *authority* and *responsibility* may operate. Authority and responsibility are vital to the sustained successful operation of any organization. They provide part of the "glue" holding any organization together in concerted action, and they spark effort and provide a basis for effective planning and control.

---

[9] Good survey data as to those practices which companies actually have followed may be obtained from two books: Ernest Dale, *Planning and Developing the Company Organization Structure*, Research Report No. 20 (New York: American Management Association, 1959), and Paul Holden, L. S. Fish, and H. L. Smith, *Top Management Organization and Control* (New York: McGraw-Hill Book Co., 1951).

This section will consider the various dimensions of authority and responsibility and the proper relationships that should exist between them.

Formal Authority

"Formal authority" may be defined as the right, derived from a "legitimate" source and exercised within the framework of prescribed organizational constraints, that is delegated to an individual to plan and execute certain activities utilizing physical resources of the organization, and employ certain organizational penalties and rewards (both tangible and implied) to induce compliance on the part of subordinate personnel with his directives and those of the organization.

The word "legitimate" is presented in quotation marks because in different societies it means different things. In our society, we usually associate the word with "that which is lawful." Formal authority in private American business flows from the right of private property, conferred by our society, through owners and their delegates. In addition, it is based upon a legally enforceable contract for the personal services of the subordinate, and this right to contract is a property right also subject to revision by our society. Last, but certainly not least, the presence and effective usage of formal authority in our business organizations is supported by long-standing custom and certain basic values in our society.

Formal authority derived by this process provides the "backbone" of formal organization, the unbroken "chain of command" that has always been associated with organized human economic activity. This "chain of command" may be visualized as follows:

Organized Society
↓
Right of Private Property
↓
Stockholders
↓
Board of Directors
↓
Administrative Management
↓
Divisional or Departmental Management
↓
Operative Management
↓
Operative Performance

Reference is made to it by *The Scalar Principle:* **An unbroken chain of direct authority relationships from superior to subordinate must be developed from the top to the bottom of the organization.** This principle is simple but important. It provides that every employee of an organization is subject to the formal authority—sometimes called "line" authority—of a superior (or group, in the case of a president reporting to board members or board members reporting to stockholders). If an individual is not subject to such formal or "line" authority, he is not an employee of the organization. It is based on the realization that organized human economic activity cannot be carried on through time *without* the arrangement of an organization's personnel into an unbroken hierarchy based on graduated allocations of formal authority. Purely voluntary association is not adequate to the task!

Nor is this a unique requirement of business activity. Hundreds of societies, both primitive and advanced, have been studied and *none* to date has been found that does not utilize *government* based on *The Scalar Principle.* Philosophical anarchists and communists who talk about government withering away notwithstanding, government is a *universal* requirement of all societies. This is an important point, for we should never regard the *existence* of formal authority in industry as "antidemocratic," nor should we equate the introduction of more democracy in industry with the *elimination* of this authority.

By giving managers the right to employ certain organizational penalties and rewards (both tangible and implied) to induce compliance with directives on the part of subordinates, formal authority provides an important source of *power.* We can say that we possess *power* over someone to the extent that we can grant rewards or impose penalties that are *meaningful* to him. In our definition of formal authority, the phrase "induce compliance," rather than "assure compliance," is used intentionally. Formal authority does not give a superior the right to *make* someone do something in any absolute sense, but it does provide important penalties and rewards in the form of promotions, job assignments, disciplinary action, status symbols, recognition, pay increases, and so on, which give him a very real measure of *power* over his subordinates.

Of course, the potency of this power in a purely negative sense depends on general economic conditions and the ease with which subordinates feel that they might obtain comparable or better employment elsewhere. And it may be counteracted to some degree by those who wield power from other sources: the union leader who can pull employees off the job, the customer who buys 20 per cent of our output, or the employee who has skills, knowledge, or contacts that would be difficult if not impossible to replace.

Authority through Acceptance

There is little question that an organization would fall "flat on its face" if everyone did only what he was ordered to do! This is illustrated by a rather unusual "strike" of postal employees that took place in England a few years ago. The employees did not leave their jobs or stop working; they simply did what they were told to do and *scrupulously* observed all the regulations that applied to their work! Hopeless backlogs of mail sacks backed up all along the line, and there was nothing but utter chaos. Packages that were not properly tied were returned to their senders "through channels" and postal truck drivers who normally had double-parked to expedite deliveries would circle a block for hours, if necessary, waiting for a parking place.

Admittedly, most competitive business enterprises would not have as much unworkable "red tape" for their employees to contend with, but, if their employees were in this same frame of mind, they would find it difficult to keep things going effectively and to compete with firms not so afflicted. It has been said many times, but it is worth repeating: You can buy a man's physical presence and minimum compliance with orders, but you *cannot* buy his loyalty, enthusiasm, and initiative—those must be earned!

Though the power derived from formal authority is a force to be reckoned with, its use will never tap—certainly not in the long run—the real potential of most subordinates. Experienced leaders agree that the superior who must rely solely on his formal authority in his dealings with subordinates is in a barren and unenviable position indeed. A leader cannot hope for a high degree of long-range success without the *acceptance* and *respect* of his subordinates. For inducing *effective* compliance with directives as well as the kind of cooperative effort and initiative that cannot be commanded, the leader needs the *influence* that comes from acceptance in addition to the *power* derived from his formal authority.

What is influence? As used here, the term means the favorable or "objective" impact that the suggestions and reactions of one person have on the behavior of another person or group owing to *voluntary* acceptance on the part of the recipient rather than orientation to penalties and rewards. All of us are influenced, favorably or unfavorably, in our daily contacts with people, often unconsciously. We may readily accept the influence of those whom we admire and respect by acting on their advice or emulating them, with the feeling that such identification will enhance our self-respect and sense of worthwhileness. Or, other things being equal, we may give preference to the requests and needs of people who are influential with us, simply because we like them. And we will tend to give their requests and communications the "benefit of the doubt" in instances when we might otherwise interpret them unfavorably or in the "wrong way." Though extremely important to all managers, the use of influence is, or should be, the *primary* basis of operations for the staff person in his dealings with other members of the organization.

Actually, at times it is difficult to try to determine where *power* stops and *influence* begins, though we know that both are present. Take the boss who feels that a subordinate has a problem and "invites" him to step into his office. It may very well be that the subordinate feels that his boss is a warm, helpful person and will admit afterward that the interview was beneficial. But would he have stepped into any warm, helpful person's office at that moment? Or did he regard the boss's "invitation" as more than just an invitation? Undoubtedly, he did! And this is all right, as long as the boss is *perceptive* of the difference and uses the negative power of his formal authority as a last resort and not as a "way of life." Chapter 8 will consider means by which a supervisor may hope to strengthen his influence with his subordinates.

Parity with Responsibility

What is *responsibility?* R. C. Davis provides the following definition: "Functions are derivatives of objectives. Business responsibilities are primarily derivatives of business functions. They are the obligation of the individual to perform properly the functions and duties that have been assigned to him, to the best of his ability and in accordance with the directions of the executive to whom he is accountable."[10] Obviously, good practice and equity require that a man not be made responsible for more than he can reasonably be expected to control, that he not be given more formal authority than is necessary for meeting his responsibilities. This concept is expressed in the *Principle of Parity of Authority and Responsibility:*

---

[10] Davis, *The Fundamentals of Top Management, op. cit.,* p. 243.

The responsibility of any manager or employee should correspond with his authority.

This principle is not meant to imply that a *literal* equality between formal authority and responsibility can *consciously* be provided by management. In an organization of competent leaders no manager will be able fully to meet his responsibilities *solely* through the exercise of formal authority; he will need, also, the influence provided by the acceptance and respect of his men. Yet formal authority is all that we can delegate to him; we cannot *give outright* any amount of influence through acceptance. We can only establish conditions for him that will be *conducive* to the gaining of adequate influence by giving him formal authority, an appropriate title, adequate support, pay, privileges, and information tailored to his needs. After setting the stage in this manner, it is up to him to gain, through effective personal behavior, the acceptance and respect he will need to be a successful leader and to meet fully his managerial responsibilities.

Of course, the *new* manager will often assume his duties with formal authority and the kind of "stage setting" assistance just discussed as the only tools for meeting his responsibilities. A perceptive superior will make adjustments in his performance expectations, knowing that it takes time for anyone to establish himself with a new group and gain its acceptance. However, sooner or later, depending on the circumstances at hand, this period of "grace" will have to end, and the only way in which the new manager will be able to meet the *increased* responsibilities confronting him will be through the exercise of influence that he has largely *earned*.

Functional Authority

Functional authority has the same force as formal or "line" authority; in fact, it is a "slice" of such authority. It may be given to anyone in an organization, whether or not he is in the same chain of command as the subordinates who will be subject to it, and the primary purpose for its use is to bring specialized skills, experience, and controls to bear upon certain activities.

For the most part, Frederick W. Taylor was responsible for the introduction of functional authority into industry as part of the system of scientific management discussed in chapter 1. He replaced the single foreman of a machine shop with eight "functional foremen" or specialist bosses. His idea was to introduce the advantages of division of labor and of specialized training and experience at the supervisory level. Four of the eight foremen were "executive functional bosses" who handled the active work of the shop: the gang boss, the speed boss, the inspector, and the repair boss. The other four "functional bosses" were located in the planning room. They were: the order of work and route clerk, the instruction card clerk, the time and cost clerk, the the shop disciplinarian (see Fig. 3–6).

"Functional foremen" were skilled specialists, but they were also human. No one of the eight was clearly responsible when production bogged down; accountability—the ability clearly to affix responsibility—could not be established. Interpersonal friction within the group was virtually assured by the impossibility of accurately defining where one foreman's authority ended and another's began. And we can only imagine the bewilderment of the worker con-

FIG. 3-6
Taylor's Functional Foremanship

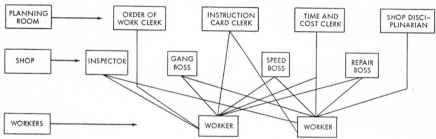

fronted with eight bosses! This approach clearly violated the common-sense notion that each employee should have only *one* boss, which for years has been stated as the "principle of unity of command." It is hard enough for an employee to try to *please* one individual, let alone be subjected to the conflicting orders and demands of several bosses.

Functional foremanship in practice also violated the *Principle of Parity of Authority and Responsibility,* which was discussed just prior to this section. All the functional foremen enjoyed delegations of formal authority, but *none* in reality could be held responsible for the performance of the shop; accountability could not be established.

The dramatic failure of Taylor's functional foremanship caused widespread apprehension as to the usefulness of functional authority and led some to proclaim that its use *under any conditions* would be a violation of good management practice. Actually, Taylor made a real contribution by pointing up the *need* for specialization in managerial activity; the separation of *planning* from *doing*, as he put it. His mistake lay in the *excessive* or *injudicious* use of functional authority, certainly not in his recognition of its value as a means for introducing specialized skills.[11] Harrington Emerson, another scientific management pioneer, recognized Taylor's mistake and encouraged the introduction of specialization into the traditional "line" type of organization via the use of staff personnel. This was a sound move, for many of the functions that Taylor assigned to functional foremen can be performed by staff specialists just as well and without the chaos he created by throwing responsibility out of the window and creating an incubus of conflicting orders.

However, the *need* for functional authority is not entirely removed by the use of the "line and staff" form of organization. There are certain situations for which its use is more appropriate than any other arrangement. For example, a "staff" chemist from a research department may be given functional authority to supervise men of a "line" foreman *only* with regard to the loading of certain chemicals into dye vats for testing purposes, when the amounts to be introduced are dependent on the highly developed technical judgment of the chemist (see Fig. 3–7). The "line" foreman concerned understands the need for this arrangement. Time is of the essence in such an operation, and, if the chemist was required to relay his instructions *through* the foreman, it could result in unduly slow corrective action as well as non-productive use of the foreman's time. In view of this, the foreman is unlikely to give conflicting orders to the loaders during the loading period unless an emergency arises, and then it is understood by the chemist that supervision of the men will revert to the foreman. Men so supervised are not likely to regard the chemist as their boss, for he will have nothing or little to do with counseling them or with making pay or promotional recommendations for them.[12]

---

[11] Taylor's idea about separating planning from execution is still quite valid. In fact, many current articles can be found about management's basic job of planning and control. However, there is real value in the refinement of splitting Taylor's "execution" into organizing and control. Thus we have the organic functions of management—planning, organizing, and controlling (the work of others)—which are presented in this book.

[12] Another illustration of the use of functional authority is given on page 295 in the discussion of decentralized staff activity.

When used judiciously, as outlined in the illustration above, functional authority provides for the application of specialized skills in situations for which the use of staff advice is inappropriate, *without* the disadvantages that come from an *indiscriminate* violation of the unity of command concept. When it is applied *only* to those activities for which some other arrangement is inadequate, its scope is carefully specified, and a successful understanding of the nature and purpose of its use is reached by those concerned, "We can have our cake and eat it too!" That is, we can most effectively utilize our specialists in *all* situations without creating the very real problems that result from a *meaningful* violation of the sound concept of unity of command. With these qualifications in mind, the *Principle*

FIG. 3-7
The Use of Functional Authority

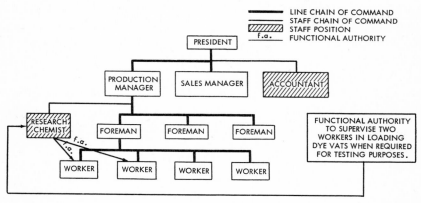

of Unity of Command is stated in this book as follows: **An employee should receive orders from one "regular" superior only, unless they result from specific functional authority delegations which are clearly understood by the "regular" superior, the employee, and the functional superior.**

So, in a sense, we have come "full circle" back to Taylor's use of functional authority, but in a way that avoids the very serious problems created by his functional foremanship approach. We recognize, as he did not, that the use of such authority must be limited to specific applications that are justified on the basis of careful and continuing study. We realize that we can and should meet *most* of the organization's needs for specialized skills through the proper utilization of line and staff positions and personnel. For this will permit maintenance of the "integrity" of the line organization, provision of adequate means for ascertaining accountability, and improved morale for all concerned.

In this regard, staff personnel will only begin to make their optimal contribution, as was suggested earlier, when they see their basic mission as one of serving the needs of the line organization. This is not likely to occur without careful observance of the *Principle of Staff Authority:* **A staff executive should *not* have authority to supervise line personnel (only his own personnel) or issue orders to the line unless he is authorized to do so by a specific allocation of functional authority.**

And it might be added that delegation of functional authority to staff personnel should be based on a determination of need made by persons other than those affected! For the mission of a staff person is at times a frustrating one indeed, and it is easy to see how he may succumb to the notion that a little more formal authority in his hands will ease the way. It is easy for him to lose sight of our sound proposition that all staff agencies and personnel exist for the primary purpose of assisting—not dictating to—line agencies in their work of creating and distributing salable utilities.

In modern industry this use of the "line and staff" form of organization incorporating *limited* delegations of functional authority has provided the best vehicle yet devised for the conduct of complex business activity.

SPAN OF CONTROL

In the 1920's and 1930's attempts were made to define the optimal number of subordinates or "span of control" that managers at "high" and "low" levels in an organization should have. In more recent times, this work and the findings derived from it have been subject to serious attack. The nature of this work will be briefly reviewed and then some of the bases for current dissatisfaction with it will be examined. Then an attempt will be made to draw some conclusions that are applicable to current practice.

Graicunas

In 1933 V. A. Graicunas, in an article in the *Bulletin of the International Management Institute,* described three kinds of subordinate-superior relationships with which a superior must contend: (1) direct single relationships between the superior and each of his immediate subordinates individually; (2) direct group relationships, relationships between the superior and each possible combination of his immediate subordinates; and (3) cross-relationships developed by subordinates consulting with one another. He developed a mathematical formula showing how the number of relationships increases in a geometric manner as the number of subordinates increases arithmetically; for example, with two subordinates Graicunas computed 6 relationships; for four subordinates 44; for six, 222; for eight, 1,080; and so on. Actually, he omitted some possible relationships and included others that at times would not be of concern to the superior, but these data dramatize the kinds of limits that exist for effective span of control on the part of supervisors.

Set Ranges and Actual Experience

On the basis of this work and the opinions of certain military leaders, a number of management authorities concluded that from three to six subordinates was the maximum range for higher-level managers and from six to twelve was the maximum desirable range for lower-level managers. Two later developments, however, cast serious doubt upon these standards. In 1952 Ernest Dale reported the findings of the American Management Association's survey of span of control in industry. One of the tables is reproduced in Figure 3–8.[13]

Dale points out:

The companies selected were all known to have good organizational practices. The median number of subordinates supervised by the president is between eight and nine. To this responsibility should be added the president's contacts with the Board of Directors, a more or less large number of company committees, important customers, suppliers, financial interests, government, local community, etc. The number of executives reporting to the president is clearly larger than the number advocated by several writers on the subject.[14]

The other development that has challenged the validity of the earlier standards for span of control has been the very successful experimentation on the part of many leading firms with decentralization, in part achieved by *broadened* spans of control. It has been found that decentralized operations provide for greater organiza-

---

[13] Dale, *op. cit.*, p. 77. For the results of another survey of practice, see Doris Entwisle and John Walton, "Observations on the Span of Control," *Administration Science Quarterly*, Vol. 5, No. 4 (March, 1961), pp. 522–33.

[14] Dale, *op. cit.*, p. 76.

tional flexibility with which to meet changing conditions, superior recognition and development of new leaders, and improved employee morale.[15]

Of course, there would be very little progress if ideal practice were always defined by whatever is conventional practice at any given time; the mere fact that a number of leading firms do and

FIG. 3-8

Number of Executives Reporting to President in 100 Large Companies (Over 5,000 Employees)

No. of Executives Reporting to President	No. of Companies	
1	6	
2	—	
3	1	
4	3	
5	7	
6	9	
7	11	
8	8	
		Median
9	8	
10	6	
11	7	
12	10	
13	8	
14	4	
15	1	
16	5	
17	—	
18	1	
19	—	
20	1	
21	1	
22	—	
23	2	
24	1	
Total	100	

like something does not make it right. However, re-examination of earlier work that was prompted by such experience has revealed some important deficiencies.

The basic problem confronting the supervisor has to do with the *frequency* and *severity* of contacts with subordinates more than with the absolute number. Also, it is most important to distinguish

---

[15] For a report on the now famous Sears, Roebuck and Company studies see J. C. Worthy, "Organization Structure and Employee Morale," *American Sociological Review,* Vol. 15 (April, 1950), and his *Big Business and Free Men* (New York: Harper & Bros., 1959), pp. 102–18. The subject of decentralization will be taken up in chap. 11, "Organization for Control."

between subordinates who have *access* to the superior (but normally work with his assistant or his staff personnel) and those who *report to* the superior. And it may be that a "tighter" span of control *is* necessary for a military organization—for it must deal with that continuing series of emergencies known as war—but that such centralization is neither necessary nor appropriate for peacetime business activity.

Factors Affecting Span of Control

To an excessive degree the mathematical analysis by Graicunas *oversimplified* the problem. What is the proper span of control for each situation is to a great extent dependent on *many unique factors* in that situation. Some of these factors are:

1. *Superior's capacity for supervision:* His emotional capacity to delegate, his ability to counsel and develop his subordinates, his endurance.

2. *Capacity of subordinates:* Level of competence, knowledge of relevant objectives, policies, and practices.

3. *Nature of work supervised:* Is the work varied and complex as a result of continuing organizational growth or technological innovation, or is the work relatively simple, homogeneous, and stable in character. Graicunas did recognize this as a qualification to his formulation. He realized that if the work was such as to require little teamwork or few working contacts between subordinates, the number of cross-relationships with which the superior would have to contend would be proportionately smaller. This is undoubtedly one reason why he and others at the time prescribed more subordinates for foremen than for higher-level managers. The nature of work at the foreman level usually requires fewer cross-relationships.

4. *Capacity of line or staff assistants of superior:* Their competence; their knowledge of relevant objectives, policies, and practices; their ability to work with others.

5. *Development of control through well-defined standards of performance:* For further discussion of this factor see that part of chapter 11, "Organization for Control," that deals with criteria for effective decentralization.

The Optimal Span

Excessively "narrow" spans of control can lead to excessive overhead for supervisory salaries relative to the size of the work force, undue rigidity in action at lower levels, status and communication problems resulting from the undue number of echelons or levels that must be created to meet the requirements of the narrow span, and frustration for less dependent subordinates who want more opportunity for experimentation and growth in their jobs. On the other hand, an excessively "broad" span of control can preclude the development of any *real* relationship between superior and subordinate and can force the superior to operate continuously at the very peak of his physical and mental capacities with little or no margin for reflection, long-range planning, and unexpected developments.

Determination of the optimal span of control for any given supervisor should be made on the basis of a careful analysis of the given situation in terms of the kinds of factors we have discussed. There are no hard and fast rules. Though Graicunas' mathematical formulation suffers from certain deficiencies and is of little help in organization planning, his essentially valid *Theorem* is of interest and should be presented. It states: "The complexities of managing tend to increase in geometric progression as the number of subordinates increases in arithmetic progression."

QUESTIONS

1. What is organization planning? Should it be engaged in *before* or *after* the definition of a firm's objectives? Explain.
2. Why not just wait until organizational problems appear and then solve them quickly and efficiently? Wouldn't this save a lot of the unnecessary effort and expense that are required to try to anticipate them? Explain your thinking.
3. What is meant by *formal* organization structure? *Informal* organization structure? Discuss the differences between the two. Do you think that we need *both* in an organization? Why or why not.
4. Discuss the role of objectives in a business undertaking?
5. Distinguish between *primary service objectives, collateral objectives,* and *secondary objectives.* Are any of these subordinate to another? Why or why not?
6. Discuss the role of money in motivating good work in an organization.
7. What is the purpose of the objectives pyramid?
8. Generally, would you say that the goals of a firm are the same as the goals of the people who are associated with the firm? If this is not true, why do people work at attaining the goals of the firm—solely in response to fear of losing their jobs and other penalties? Explain.
9. What is a procedure? How would you distinguish your definition of it from your definition of formal organization structure?

10. Distinguish between a *rule* and a *policy*. How would you describe what is a good rule or policy for *any* company?

11. What are *organic business functions?* Why is it important to identify them?

12. Distinguish between *line* and *staff* positions. Is there any significant difference as to *mission* between line and staff personnel; or would it be correct to say simply that both are striving to achieve successfully the objectives of the firm? Explain.

13. Can a line position in one firm legitimately be a staff position in another firm? Explain. Can a position in the same firm legitimately change from line to staff or vice versa? Explain.

14. What is meant by the terms "functionalization" and "departmentation?"

15. Give the essence of the three essential parts of the *Principle of Functional Emergence.*

16. Discuss exceptions or qualifications that we should keep before us in utilizing the concept of grouping similar functions together for job assignments.

17. What are the bases for departmentation given in the text? Give examples of each.

18. How far should we go, in your opinion, in modifying ideal organization structure to accommodate the personal characteristics of organizational personnel? Explain the reasons for your position.

19. Define formal authority. What are its sources in our society? Can its character be altered by our society? If you say yes, explain how and give examples.

20. Distinguish between *power* and *influence*. Discuss the *sources* of each in an organization.

21. State the *Principle of Parity of Authority and Responsibility*. Can we apply it *literally?* Why or why not?

22. Define *functional authority*. Where should it be used? Does its use violate the *Principle of Unity of Command?* Explain.

23. What is the *Principle of Staff Authority?* In what way should we be cautious in applying it?

24. What is "span of control"? Discuss the factors that affect span of control. How would you go about determining the *optimal* span for any given supervisor? Explain.

25. State *Graicunas' Theorem.*

Chapter 4

ORGANIZATION PLANNING: PART II

In the preceding chapter distinction was made between line and staff positions. In this chapter further elaboration on the distinction will be made, the nature and development of staff organization will be discussed, the stages of over-all organizational growth will be traced, and the attributes of the three levels of top management will be considered.

STAFF ORGANIZATION

With company growth, staff functions are differentiated from line functions and then grouped to form staff positions, which "sprout" from the line organization as branches from a tree. Staff organization *evolves* from the line organization as a result of the line manager's need for help in handling his growing burden of work and the need to bring specialized skills to bear upon the solution of more complex or economically significant problems. The line chains of command are lengthened by the process of *devolution*—downward growth. After a staff position has *evolved* from a line primary chain of command, with further organizational growth a secondary chain of command may develop from it through the process of *secondary devolution*. These processes are illustrated in Figure 4-1.

As was pointed out in chapter 3, staff personnel are chiefly concerned with *collateral* and *secondary objectives;* they justify their existence primarily through the assistance they provide the line organization in its crucial job of creating and distributing salable utilities.

Collateral objectives have to do with the values that the organization must create to meet the personal needs of its personnel in order to induce them to do the work required to attain the firm's *primary service objectives.* It is quite a job, even with the help of staff specialists, to understand these personal needs and to devise ways for meeting them that *at the same time,* will contribute to the attainment of primary objectives. As an organization grows, this problem becomes more complex, because of increased "social distance" and physical distance between workers and over-all planners and greater difficulty in maintaining effective communications and coordination of effort. And when employees fail to identify with primary service objectives as a basis for meeting their personal needs and feel that they can better satisfy their needs *outside* the

FIG. 4-1
Evolution of Staff Organization

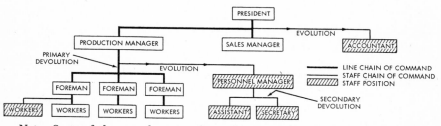

Note: Some of these workers may be performing staff operative functions rather than line operative functions, e.g., the worker who primarily cleans spray gun nozzles is a staff operative, the worker who sprays paint on the product is a line operative who is directly creating salable values.

framework defined by these objectives, strong forces, destructive to the company, are set into motion. As a company grows and these problems become more pronounced, the need for staff organizations to cope with them becomes apparent.

Secondary objectives are the province of staff personnel, too, for they are concerned with the attainment of primary and collateral objectives with a maximum of economy and effectiveness. Efficiency engineers, production scheduling departments, safety committees, and many other individuals and agencies in a firm are concerned with finding ways to achieve more and better-quality output, and improved distribution of that output, at reduced costs. The opportunities for making such improvements increase significantly as a firm grows larger, for, with such growth, waste and inefficiency can increase at an alarming rate if not properly controlled. The need for staff personnel to deal with secondary objectives becomes pressing, indeed, as organizations grow in size.

Baker-Davis Study

Professor R. C. Davis formally expresses this concept of increasing organizational complexity with company growth in the *Law of Functional Growth:* **The complexity of functional relationships tends to increase in geometric progression as the volume of work that the organization must handle increases in arithmetic progression.**[1] He hypothesizes that this increasing complexity with company growth is handled by staff organizations growing faster than line organizations, since organizational growth has practically no effect on the percentage requirements for line executives.[2]

A questionnaire survey of 211 Ohio firms was made by Baker and Davis to test three hypotheses: [3]

1. As the total number of direct workers (line) in a manufacturing company increases arithmetically, the total number of indirect (staff) workers tends to increase geometrically.

2. As the total number of direct workers in a manufacturing company increases arithmetically, the number of indirect workers in *each function tends* to increase geometrically.

3. As the total number of direct workers in a manufacturing company increases arithmetically, each indirect function becomes increasingly differentiated.

Hypothesis 1 is not supported by the empirical data obtained. It was found that the total number of staff workers for the 211 firms tends to increase *arithmetically* as the total number of line workers increases arithmetically. Hypothesis 2 is supported only in part by the survey data; a number of relationships were found. As the total number of line workers increases arithmetically, it was found that the number of staff workers in each of the following areas increases arithmetically too: purchasing, tool handling, personnel, accounting, time and motion study, and production control func-

---

[1] R. C. Davis, *The Fundamentals of Top Management* (New York: Harper & Bros., 1951), p. 232.

[2] *Ibid.,* p. 355.

[3] A. W. Baker and Ralph C. Davis, *Ratios of Staff to Line Employees and Stages of Differentiation of Staff Functions: A Study of Ohio Manufacturing Companies* (Bureau of Business Research, Ohio State University, Research Monograph No. 72, 1954). A similar but more recent survey of some 155 companies has been made. See Bruce E. DeSpelder, *Ratios of Staff to Line Personnel: A Study of Small and Medium Size Manufacturers of Metallic Automotive Parts* (Bureau of Business Research, Ohio State University, Research Monograph No. 106, 1962).

tions. There is also a linear relationship between growth in the number of supervisors and executives of line workers and growth in the number of staff workers. The number of top management executives and staff personnel engaged in plant protection and shipping and receiving increases at a *decreasing* rate with increases in the total number of line workers.[4]

However, in each of the following areas the number of staff workers *increases* at an increasing rate with increases in the total number of line workers: inspection, cafeteria, maintenance, engineering, tool and patterns manufacturing, and tool design. Findings with regard to hypothesis 3 are of interest:

Insofar as the third aspect of the study is concerned the results are a little more positive. Almost every industrial function utilized in this survey tends to go through successive stages of development and differentiation as the size of the company increases. It is evident in the data that functional differentiation proceeds at varying rates as far as various functions are concerned. The following functions are generally completely differentiated by the time the size of the company reaches 75 to 99 direct workers: maintenance, purchasing, shipping and receiving, accounting, and engineering. The indirect functions of production control, time and motion study (industrial engineering), inspection, and personnel, do not reach this stage until a company employs 100 to 499 direct workers. Finally, there is a tendency for some functions to become completely differentiated only in relatively large companies or those employing 500 or even 1,000 direct employees. These include tool design, cafeteria, tool and patterns manufacturing, tool handling, and plant protection.[5]

These patterns as to points at which functional differentiation takes place in practice are of interest but certainly do not constitute standards for practice. Such functions should be separated *before* absolute necessity forces differentiation; however, this cannot happen unless top management engages in organization planning and acts upon its findings. The findings of this study are far from conclusive because of the presence of several serious limitations in its conduct. As Baker and Davis point out, *they were unable to study the growth characteristics of particular firms throughout a period of time;* they had to use data obtained at one point in time from firms of varying size representing different industries and types of production. This is a serious defect, for, among other factors, it seems reasonable to assume that the age, size, and type of

---

[4] See the Baker and Davis study for charts and specific data.
[5] Baker and Davis, *op. cit.*, pp. 58–59.

the firm are factors that will influence its internal growth rates. Finally, the use of questionnaires as the sole basis for obtaining data introduces the likelihood of error resulting from misinterpretation of terms, etc.

Haire Study

A most provocative and useful study throwing further light on this matter of growth patterns is one reported by Mason Haire.[6] At first, Professor Haire gives a biological analogy by pointing out that

. . . in the organism, the proportion of skeleton needed to support the mass grows faster than the mass itself and puts a limit on size as a function of the environmental forces playing on it. Similarily, it is suggested that, as the size of a firm increases, the skeletal structure (needed to support it against the forces tending to destroy it) grows faster than the size itself, and hence comes to consume a disproportionate amount of the productive capacity of the organization. . . . It seems reasonable to argue that the relative growth of staff to line provides a parallel to the shelf bracket or the bridge arch—the organization grows fastest where the force tending to destroy it is strongest; the shape of the support is a diagram of the forces acting against the structure.

On the basis of a detailed study of the growth histories of four firms, Haire obtained qualified support for the first Baker-Davis hypothesis: "As the total number of line workers in a manufacturing company increases arithmetically, the total number of staff workers tends to increase geometrically." His findings are:

In the early years while the line grows linearly, the staff grows by some exponential function (though no single one seems to describe the curve well). Later, in another period of growth, they grow at quite similar rates. In terms of rough averages, during the period when the line first doubled, the staff grew about six times as large. When the line next doubled, the staff grew about five times; the next doubling of the line was accompanied by a tripling of the staff, and from then on they (approximately) each doubled. Early, the staff grows geometrically as the line grows linearly, but this relation tapers off to parallel growth.[7]

As Haire points out, these are only the first results—based on the study of just four firms—of a research project designed to study organizational growth. Perhaps, as a tentative statement, we can say that in response to the *Law of Functional Growth,* the total

[6] "Biological Models and Empirical Histories of the Growth of Organizations," in Mason Haire (ed.), *Modern Organization Theory* (New York: John Wiley & Sons, 1959), pp. 272–305.

[7] *Ibid.,* p. 292.

number of staff workers tends to increase geometrically as the total number of line workers increases arithmetically *during a certain initial period of organizational growth.*[8] Professor Haire suggests that a logistic equation, often applied to population growth, may eventually be used (when certain modifiers can be determined) to predict organizational growth for ten to thirty years on the basis of known growth for two or three years.[9] We can look forward to additional research findings in this area with genuine anticipation.

Active vs. Passive Staff

"Active" staff organizations develop to provide assistance to managers, both line and staff, in the performance of the organic functions of management: *planning, organizing and controlling.* A staff position or organization serving a line manager is known as *primary* staff, whereas a staff position or organization serving a staff manager is known as *secondary* staff. For example, a blueprint department that serves a staff product planning department would be *secondary* staff. A discussion of the organization structures for "active" staff organizations will be found in the chapters on organization for planning, organization for organizing, and organization for control. These are referred to as "active" staff organizations, for they must take the initiative in planning, organizing for, and carrying out their programs of assistance to others.

In addition to the three "active" types of staff activity there is a fourth "passive" type. It is concerned not with the initiation and conduct of programs of assistance but only with the provision of expert skills or advice. A group of employee counselors who are sought out by troubled employees who want someone to talk with and know that their conversations will be held in confidence provides "passive" staff assistance. The same would be true of a lawyer who is retained merely to advise management and employees about legal rights and procedures when his opinion is sought. Whereas there are different organizational forms for the "active" types, there is no unique organization form for the "passive" type. However, there is such a significant difference in the role or mission of "passive" staff personnel as contrasted with "active" staff personnel, that it seems worthwhile to establish this fourth category of staff activity.

---

[8] It is interesting to speculate as to what the effects of increased reliance on automation, mechanization, and operations research techniques will have on this relationship.

[9] *Ibid.,* pp. 277–87.

Stages in the Development of Staff Organizations

The growth of staff organization may be traced through several distinct stages.[10]

1. *Integration with line*—all staff functions assigned to line positions.

2. *Differentiation*—certain staff functions are separated to form a staff position which is attached to the organization as in (a) or (b):

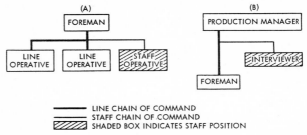

3. *Secondary devolution*—a secondary chain of command devolves from the evolved staff position.

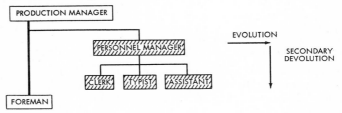

4. *Duplication*—the same staff functions—for example, the personnel functions of selection and training—are differentiated and developed for more than one chain of command.

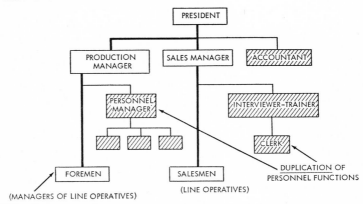

---

[10] See Davis, *op. cit.*, pp. 376-84. For a good discussion (with charts) of the detailed functionalization and departmentation that occur with the growth of a manufacturing concern see his other book: *Industrial Organization and Management* (3rd ed.; New York: Harper & Bros., 1957).

5. *Integration*—consolidation of the duplicated functions into one agency. In the case of consolidated personnel functions the manager will probably report to the head of production because this is the point of "most use" where, in all likelihood, the first personnel position was established.

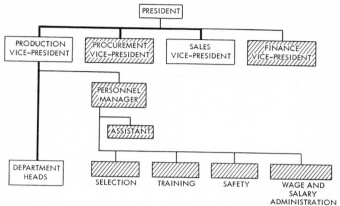

6. *Elevation*—when some or all of the functions of a staff organization are separated from it and reattached to the line at a higher level. A personnel manager, for example, and his department would be separated from a subordinate position under the vice-president of production and set up to operate with the personnel manager as a vice-president of industrial relations reporting to the president. Often this step is taken because the personnel manager argues effectively that the head of a company-wide personnel program should be permitted to participate in top-level decision making. Also, it is apparent that as long as he *reports* to one of the vice-presidents, he cannot serve all of them equally without fear or favor.[11]

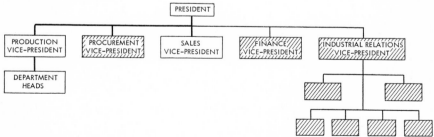

---

[11] The point should be made, however, that not all staff agencies must go through the stages of development outlined here to reach the top divisional level of the organization. The relative *importance* of the staff activity to the over-all well-being of the company *at the outset* has an important bearing upon its initial placement. For example, a staff financial position may well initially evolve at, and remain at, the top level of an organization. In the textile industry the purchase of wool is highly speculative and demanding; competence in it often spells the difference between profit and loss for a company. It is not surprising that the staff position of the chief wool buyer frequently is found immediately under the president.

Criteria for Distinguishing Staff from Line Positions

On the basis of our discussion of line and staff organization we can now summarize certain standards or criteria for *distinguishing staff from line positions.* It is important to make this distinction to facilitate unity of command, preserve the integrity of the line chains of command, and to indicate to personnel *who should serve whom.*

1. Line organization stems from the owners to the chief executive and through the Organic Business Functions of *creation* of salable values and *distribution* of salable values.

2. Line operative functions *directly* create salable values for the firm, whereas staff operative functions, for the most part, do not directly create salable values.

3. Line managers manage the work of line and staff managers and operatives; staff managers do not manage line managers or line operatives except as provided for by specific delegations of functional authority. Of course, staff managers have "line" or formal authority over subordinates in their staff departments.

4. If a line manager is removed from the organization, the number of echelons or levels in a *line* chain of command is reduced by one, or a "gap" in the chain of command is created. No reduction in the number of levels or "gap" occurs in a *line* chain of command if a staff manaager is removed (though a "gap" will be created in a staff chain of command if one had devolved beneath him), because his position is *appended to* the line as a branch to a tree.

5. Though staff managers often advise line managers, line managers have, or should have, the final say-so on organization objectives and the policies, procedures, and rules developed to facilitate their attainment.

6. Line managers are *directly* concerned with primary service objectives (in addition to collateral and secondary objectives in the absence of staff personnel); staff managers are *directly* concerned, primarily, with collateral and secondary objectives.

THE STAGES OF ORGANIZATION GROWTH

We have seen how, with company growth, the development of organization structure is necessary to provide for division of labor and effective coordination. We have observed that various parts of the structure do not necessarily grow at the same rate. Also, we have discussed functionalization and departmentation—how line organization devolves and staff organization evolves—and we have examined various principles of organization that are closely related to these processes. It should prove helpful now to trace the step-by-step growth of a manufacturing company—Mr. Smith's E-Z Shine

Automobile Wax Company—from sole proprietorship to a level at which several staff positions have evolved. In the following diagrams a *line* authority relationship will be shown by a solid line, a *functional authority* relationship by a solid line with "f.a." written on it, and an *advisory* relationship by a broken line.

An organization may be viewed as a group of interacting people engaged in coordinated activity under leadership for the achievement of certain objectives. When Mr. Smith first starts his business, he has no organization and must perform all line and staff functions himself. He has no *managerial* function, for management involves planning, organizing, and controlling *the work of others* in addition to one's own work (which all employees must do to some extent).

> MR. SMITH'S
> SOLE PROPRIETORSHIP

Normally, more effort is required to produce a product than to sell it. Chances are that the first functionalization—differentiation and grouping of functions—will apply to certain production functions. Smith will now assume the managerial duties of planning, organizing, and controlling the work of his first subordinate, though the major part of his time will still be devoted to non-managerial activity.

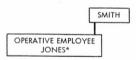

With continued growth, Smith will probably increase his production personnel, hire a salesman, obtain the services of a local accountant (on a fee basis) to help him set up his accounting and records systems, and hire a secretary-bookkeeper (the first differentiation and grouping of staff functions to establish a full-time staff position).

Smith may still call on certain customers. He has permitted his first employee to assume managerial functions on a limited basis as a working "straw boss" in his absence. Not all men have the

---

*Though Jones is in a line position, he may, like Smith, perform staff functions in addition to his line work of creating a salable value (product). Non-managerial (operative) staff personnel do *not* perform line functions in addition to their staff functions. Staff managers do *not* manage line employees except with specific functional authority to do so.

ability to handle the increasing responsibilities of the devolving "pyramid" under them as a company grows. But if a man can grow with the job, he has an unparalleled opportunity to enjoy rapid promotions with a new, developing organization by "just staying in one position."

As the business continues to grow, Smith will wish to devote more time to *administrative* as opposed to *operative* management. That is, he will be concerned with planning for the future, the procurement of capital, and the welding of his production manager, sales manager, and accountant into an effective team for the accomplishment of company goals. He will become less concerned with the day-to-day work of meeting production schedules, etc. Then, as a means for facilitating the procurement of capital, limiting his personal risks with regard to the business, drawing upon the

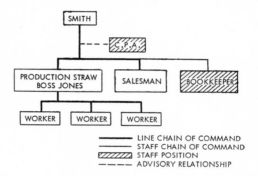

LINE CHAIN OF COMMAND
STAFF CHAIN OF COMMAND
STAFF POSITION
ADVISORY RELATIONSHIP

seasoned experience of others, and providing for the indefinite continuity of the company, he decides to incorporate.

With further growth of the company, there may be established a *controller's position* to handle the accounting, auditing, budget control, and financial analysis functions and a *treasurer's position* to handle the receipt, custody, and disbursement of funds. Later, these two positions may be coordinated under a vice-president of finance.

As a company grows, there is functional *differentiation*. When it is faced with permanent or long-term contraction of operations there should be functional *integration* in the *reverse order* with which functionalization took place with growth. This is easier said than done; for much resistance will be given by those who are threatened with layoff and demotion. However, only to the extent that the company can effectively contract will it remain competitive.

In the way of a brief summary, the stages in the growth of the E-Z Shine Company can be traced as follows:

1. One-man business—no organizational problems because there was no organization! All functions, both line and staff, were performed by one man: the owner.

2. Owner hired a man to help out—first appearance of *managerial* as opposed to *operative* activity (though the owner still did much operative work, too).

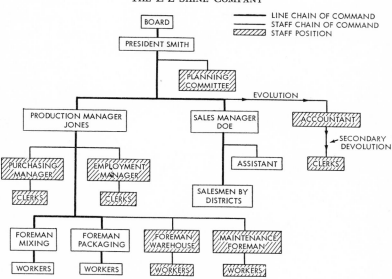

THE E-Z SHINE COMPANY

Note: In organization planning it is important to separate the designation of positions from the designation of personnel to fill them. One man may fill two positions, and it is important that he know and attempt to meet the requirements of each. When the production manager, sales manager, and accountant serve on the planning committee, they act in a dual capacity as staff advisers to the president. The objectives of the two positions are quite different. Jones, for example, as the line production manager, should be primarily concerned with the work of his division. But as a member of the planning committee, he should be primarily concerned with developing a balanced view of the over-all needs and problems of the company. Normally, anyone who fills a line managerial position regardless of his staff activities is referred to as a line executive.

3. Further growth led to division of labor at the managerial level on a *functional basis* (the organic business functions for the company appear as *production* and *sales;* these would serve as the wellsprings of all line organization). The staff position of bookkeeper *evolved* from the line, and provision was made for more specialization, if it were desired, at the operative level. That is, one man could specialize in mixing the wax, another in packing it, and so on, if this seemed desirable.

4. Additional growth led to further *evolution* of staff positions from the *devolving* line chains of command and then to *secondary devolution,* which formed staff organizations.

5. Distinction grew between levels of management—both line and staff—such as *administrative management* and *operative management.*

6. Continued growth leads to additional stages in the development of staff organization and further differentiation of top management functions, as will be discussed in the following pages.

These stages of growth are depicted in Figure 4-2.

FIG. 4-2

Stages of Organizational Growth

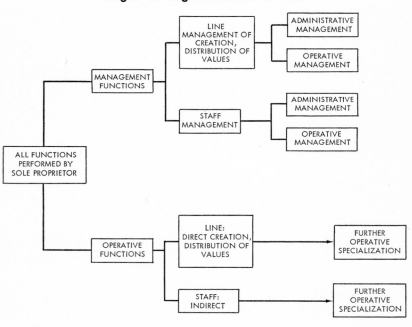

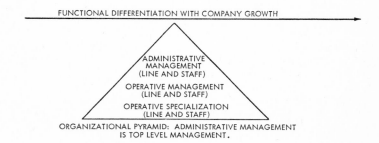

THE THREE BASIC LEVELS OF TOP MANAGEMENT

As a company grows larger and is incorporated, the need for three distinct strata of top management activity becomes clearer:

Level I. For trustee functions (usually performed by the board of directors).

Level II. For general management functions (several solutions for performance).

Level III. For major division or department management (performed by division or department heads).[12]

As Holden, Fish, and Smith point out:

In many companies these three fundamental and separable levels of top management appear to be indistinct and confused. In some instances two or even three of these fields are administered by the same identical group of executives, as in the case of some managing boards. . . . It is believed that a clear conception of the proper functions, responsibilities, and relationships of these three levels of management affords an effective basis (a) for testing the adequacy of any company's plan of top organization, (b) for making sure that each field is entrusted to a "team" whose composition and qualifications are best adapted to do that particular job, and (c) for passing the burden of management detail down to those in the best position to assume it.

Trustee Level

Trustee functions are *judicial* in character and *intermittent* in performance; they have to do with *appraisal* and *approval*. Owners of the business (stockholders) look to the board of directors to safeguard their interests. In addition, the board should:

1. Appraise over-all results and approve major plans.
2. Control major organizational matters with regard to plant and equipment, large financial outlays, the selection of the chief executive and approval of key personnel appointments.
3. Decide dividend policy.
4. Coach and advise management.

Many companies fail to recruit the right kind of board personnel to begin with, or fail fully to utilize a competent board. It is difficult for a small company to find a more desirable source of expert

---

[12] This classification of top management levels and functions is based on an analysis of the practices of 31 companies given on pp. 15–29 of Paul Holden, L. S. Fish, and H. L. Smith, *Top Management Organization and Control* (New York: McGraw-Hill Book Co., Inc., 1951).

consultation than will be provided by a well-selected board. However, it is most important to define clearly the role of any board so that there will not be undue encroachment upon, or conflict with, the general management area.

General Management Level

General management functions are *executive* in character and *continuous* in performance; they have to do with the *over-all* management of the company. They include the *initiation* and *formulation* of changes in objectives, over-all operating policies, and plans; and:

1. The maintenance and development of sound organization and other tools for the implementation of plans.
2. Coordination and appraisal of divisional or departmental work.
3. Counseling of division or department managers.

In a very small business, general management functions, along with many other functions, must be performed by the owner-manager. But as soon as the organization develops to the point at which competent managers head up major line and staff departments, it is most desirable that the chief executive form these department heads into a staff council or executive committee to advise him with regard to general management functions. This can do much to produce better decisions based on a more balanced consideration of the major line and staff functions of the business. Also, it can do much to develop departmental executives and to give them a greater sense of participation and worthwhileness.

However, it is difficult for departmental or divisional managers to "wear two hats"—to switch from the parochial view that they must have as departmental managers to the over-all view that they should display as committee members. And as the organization grows bigger and "both jobs" become more complex, the use of the executive committee to assist with the performance of general management functions becomes inadequate. At this stage, if circumstances are favorable, serious thought should be given to the idea of general management via a council of *general executives;* men who devote all their time to the performance of general management functions.

Not only will these men find it easier to identify psychologically with the over-all needs and objectives of the organization; they will be *rewarded* rather than *penalized* for doing so—for example, a divisional executive goes to bat for the over-all needs of the company and is criticized by his own personnel for not protecting their interests sufficiently in executive committee deliberations.[13] The use of general executives has obvious advantages if the organization is big enough to carry the overhead involved.[14]

This kind of analysis of top managerial activity is perhaps more important today than ever before. In chapter 2, reasons why were suggested. Many of the tools of operations research are still in their infancy, and many, undoubtedly, are merely awaiting birth. The top management group that organizes itself *effectively* for performance of the activities outlined in this section will be in an advantageous position to exploit the *new* tools and techniques as they develop as well as to get the most "mileage" out of existing tools and techniques. Organization for the key planning activities of the general management level will be considered in some detail in chapter 9, "Organization for Planning."

SOME CONCLUDING OBSERVATIONS

Desirable organizational growth occurs only as the result of careful organization planning and implementation. As we have seen, organization structure, along with related policies, rules, procedures, and systems of communication and control,[15] are but "means" for attaining company objectives, and they must be specifically tailored to meet the requirements of those objectives. Good initial organization will assure greater opportunity for the firm's success and growth; knowledge of how the organization is *likely* to grow and how it *should* grow can do much to facilitate effective *anticipation* and solution of problems that otherwise might constitute impassable barriers to further growth with efficiency.

We need very much the further development and refinement of dynamic organization theory. Fortunately, a good start has been made in this direction, and there is growing interest and research activity. As Professor Haire has pointed out: "It would be delight-

---

[13] See page 222 for the results of an experimental study relating to this.

[14] The Du Pont Company goes even further; it has made a "plural executive" of the executive committee and has general managers reporting to the committee. This can be done because Du Pont's general managers function as presidents of "independent businesses" rather than as divisional managers. See W. H. Mylander, "Management by Executive Committee," *Harvard Business Review*, Vol. 33, No. 3 (May, 1955), for a full discussion of the Du Pont approach.

[15] Systems for communication and control are discussed in the chapters on organization for planning, organization for control, and elsewhere.

ful if it were possible to observe two years of growth (of a firm) and predict the next fifteen." [16] Yes, it would be delightful! And who knows, it may not be long before we will be able to use formulas, derived from the kind of research Haire has done, to project "target organizations" for the future and predict, with surprising accuracy, the capital, personnel, and physical requirements needed for their effective implementation.

Such formulas will be most helpful, too, for "flexible budgeting." Sales forecasts are subject to error. Because of this, we use *flexible budgets* which are based on analyses of costs as a function of volume—to project requirements with varying volumes of sales. Obviously, such budgeting will be greatly facilitated by improved knowledge as to how each line and staff organization in the firm grows and contracts. As we have seen, with good practice they grow and contract at *different* as well as *changing* rates with over-all company growth. It will be a real achievement when we can determine with some precision the actual rates involved for a given firm.

Organization planning is a never-ending process. Existing structure and other "tools" for the implementation of company objectives must be constantly analyzed and appraised in the light of *current* definition of these objectives. An ideal organization should be fashioned with the understanding that it will provide direction but will never be fulfilled. Goals change and concessions must be made to the capacities and needs of the company's personnel. Also, concessions must be made to informal organizational values and the need for "practical" operational flexibility.

For example, "cross-contacts" between subordinates in different chains of command are desirable and necessary for the carrying-out of organizational projects. As long as subordinates keep their respective superiors informed as to what of consequence takes place, the "integrity" of each chain of command will be preserved. Jasinski illustrates the need for "cross-contacts" with his description of the problems facing an assembly-line foreman in an automobile factory:

Theoretically, the foreman can report any deficiency in service from supporting groups to his general foreman. This procedure is formally and clearly defined. Time on the assembly line, however, is crucial; cars pass a given work station at the rate of one every 1.5 minutes. Unless an

---

[16] Haire, *op. cit.*, p. 281.

error is corrected immediately, the consequences can be far-reaching. The foreman cannot afford to spend time hunting down the general foreman; he has to attend to the matter immediately and directly. To do so he has to deal with other foremen (on the horizontal plane) and also with materials handlers, maintenance men, inspectors, and other foremen's workers (on the diagonal plane).[17]

There are several ways to facilitate "cross-contacts" and effective coordination. A "product" rather than "process" basis for departmentation may be used. Other ways are provided by the use of:

1. Project management.
2. Expediters.
3. Functional authority.
4. Over-all or project incentive plans.
5. Special communications equipment, such as intercoms, discussion-group phone hookups, and in-plant television.
6. Standard operating procedures.[18]

Determination of the most appropriate approach will, of course, depend on the particular circumstances. The most important requirement, however, will remain the presence of good informal relationships between interdependent personnel.

There is little question that informal organization serves to strengthen as well as to subvert formal organization. If formal leadership is weak, informal leaders will often emerge to fill the breach; if formal communication of intentions is inadequate, the "grapevine" will "smoke" with rumors; if employees feel that the company is exploiting them, they will take measures to defend themselves and strike back. As a broad generalization, it seems accurate to say that unionism thrives on mismanagement. Fuller discussion of these topics is provided in other parts of this book.

Considerable care must be given to the ways in which change is introduced. If changes are perceived by employees as *inconveniences* or, more importantly, as threats to their *status* or *security* rather than as means to a better realization of their needs, they will openly or covertly resist them. Of course, some people may have to be removed or dealt with firmly, but this does not require the creation of a general atmosphere of uncertainty and fear. As is discussed in chapter 8, on supervision, there is ample evidence today

---

[17] Frank Jasinski, "Adapting Organization to New Technology," *Harvard Business Review*, Vol. 37, No. 1 (January-February, 1959).

[18] Some of these "means" will be discussed in the chapters on control.

to support the idea that the way with which change is introduced is just as important, if not more important, than the nature of the change.

Finally, a few comments about committees. We have made a number of references to the important role of committees in our discussion of organization planning, yet the committee is a frequently maligned organizational tool in the management literature. Many people take a dim view as to the value of a committee for *any* decision making that must cope with time limits. Long lists of advantages and disadvantages associated with the use of committees can be found in many books. But such analyses seem to assume that all committees are essentially *alike*.

Actually, it is the *caliber* of the committee that is really the decisive factor. Most of us, unfortunately, have been associated with *mediocre* committees, which either lack decisive purpose or are sabotaged by unprepared members who use committee time for the pursuit of purely personal goals. Contrast this with the functioning of a *permanent* committee of *seasoned* executives—each drawn from a major activity area of the business and each selected on the basis of his *emotional maturity* and *human relations skills* as well as his *knowledge* and *experience*. Assume that each member has been supplied with all available data relating to the coming agenda by a competent staff, which has presented the data in the most appropriate form well in advance of the meeting. Assume that each member has the *time, motivation,* and *ability* to study thoroughly and speculate about such data before each meeting. Such a committee does not "just happen," it is the result of careful planning. Do such committees exist? Yes, at Du Pont and a number of other firms! In chapter 12 the role of committees at General Motors will be discussed.

QUESTIONS

1. What is meant by "secondary devolution?"
2. Give an example of a staff operative function and an example of a line operative function. What must you do first? Explain why.
3. What is the chief limitation to the value of the Baker-Davis study? Did Haire overcome this? How?
4. Explain Haire's "biological analogy."
5. What is a *secondary* staff position? Give an example.
6. What distinction is made in the text between "active" and "passive" staffs? Explain.

7. List and explain each of the stages in the development of staff organization. Must every staff position go through these stages to reach eventual placement at the top of an organization? Why or why not?

8. List four of the six criteria for distinguishing staff from line positions.

9. Trace the probable stages in the growth of a hardware store from the sole proprietor, one-man state through incorporation. Explain the nature and purpose of each stage that you give.

10. In organization planning, is it useful to separate the designation of positions from the designation of personnel to fill them? Why or why not?

11. What are the three basic levels of top management? Describe the functions that are associated with each level. What organizational provision should be made at each level for the performance of these functions? Discuss.

12. As a special assignment, write a report on one of the topics discussed in the "Concluding Observations" section of this chapter.

Chapter 5

PLANNING FOR ORGANIZING

Part I: Procurement of Factors

The function of *organizing* is one of the three organic management functions of *planning, organizing,* and *controlling.* As was pointed out in chapter 3, organization planning "sets the stage" for *organizing* by determining what personnel, physical factors, and functions—and the interrelationships between them—will be required to carry out company objectives. *Organizing* is the actual work of carrying out such plans: the actual procurement of physical factors as planned, the procurement and training of personnel, the delegation of authority as planned, and so on.[1] *Controlling* is that management activity concerned with seeing that events conform to plans. *Organizing* activity must be controlled as well as *planning* and *controlling* activity.

The *organic subfunctions* of *organizing* have to do with the procurement of factors, the establishment of interrelationships among factors, and the development of factors, as follows:

Procurement of Factors (as Planned)

Procurement and maintenance of required capital.

Procurement and maintenance of required plant, equipment, and materiel.

Procurement and maintenance of required personnel.

---

[1] R. C. Davis defines *organizing* as "an advance provisioning and proportioning of basic factors and potential forces as specified by the plan." *The Fundamentals of Top Management* (New York: Harper & Bros., 1951), p. 23.

Establishment of Interrelationships among Factors (as Planned)

Assignment of duties.

Arrangement of machine and/or equipment layout.

Delegation of authority and responsibility.

Activation of a communications system, procedures, rules, policies, and others bases for accountability and control.

Development of Factors (as Planned)

Development of sources of capital.

Development of plant, equipment, and sources of materiel.

Development of personnel.

The first organic subfunction of organizing, the procurement of factors, will be discussed in this chapter, and the last two, the establishment of interrelationships among factors and the development of factors, in the next chapter. Let us now consider the *procurement of factors*.

PROCUREMENT OF REQUIRED CAPITAL

Planning Capital Requirements

The first step in planning for the procurement of capital is concerned with an accurate forecast of capital needs. This, in turn, will flow from a determination of the primary service objectives of our company: what salable utilities we plan to create and distribute; whether we plan to "make or buy"—lease or own; an accurate prediction of sales-price mix and anticipated revenue; and due consideration to various tax aspects and the "costs" associated with each source of funds. Money will be required for "permanent" investment in plant and equipment. Working capital—the excess of current assets over current liabilities—will be required for financing inventories, accounts receivable, and various day-to-day cash needs.

Also, provision must be made for the initial organizing period, when many expenses will be incurred but little if any revenue will be realized by the still "non-productive" enterprise. In addition, promotional expenses and the prospect of losses should be anticipated for the company's early period of operation. Actually, all expected expenditures and revenue should be projected well into the future in the form of an expense and revenue forecast. In this, all *accrued* as well as current transactions are considered. From the expense and revenue forecast and an analysis of those few expenditures and disbursements that do not appear in it—for example, repayment of loans, cash from sale of assets, etc.—we may determine not only how much money will be needed but also, and this is of equal importance, *when* it will be needed. The latter need is shown by the development of a cash forecast that is formulated after the expense and revenue forecast has been well developed.[2] The cash forecast records the anticipated month-to-month, week-to-week, or even day-to-day "out-of-pocket" and "in-pocket" cash flow to indicate net cash position at any given time.

Figure 5-1 presents a simplified expense and revenue forecast. It is simplified in that it omits many operating and non-operating items that must be considered in a real business. By being concerned with the first year's operations of a firm "starting from scratch," it avoids the matter of inventory carry-over and the computation of cost of goods sold. However, in conjunction with Figure 5-2 it will serve the purpose of dramatizing part of the planning process that competent managers must constantly engage in. The expense and revenue forecast and the cash forecast are not *independent* projects to be tackled, completed, and then set aside. They are tools of planning and should be used interdependently. To illustrate this point, Figures 5-1 and 5-2 have been left incomplete. The cash forecast shows that the company will face a cash deficit of $330 in August if anticipated expenses cannot be pared, anticipated revenue raised, or an adequate loan arranged. Any one of these "solutions" will affect the final make-up of Figure 5-1. For example, if a loan is decided upon, the interest charges associated with it will affect the computation of net income before income tax, estimated income tax, and net income in Figure 5-1. The amount of the loan, the timing of its receipt, and the interest payment schedule, obviously, will affect a number of items at the bottom of Figure 5-2. One forecast without the other would prove most inadequate. They complement each other very well. The cash forecast points up various problems and constraints with which the expense and revenue forecast must cope. On the other hand, the expense and revenue forecast provides a means for helping to gauge the relative profitability of various courses of action.

Of course, the data for the forecasts are based on estimates and are subject to error. They should be adjusted *regularly* on the basis

---

[2] If we add forecast balance sheets to these forecasts, we have the essential tools for over-all financial planning. For financial planning is largely the business of deciding how to raise needed funds or to productively utilize excess funds that are estimated for any given period by these forecasts.

FIG. 5-1

Ajax Manufacturing Company Expense and Revenue Forecast—First Year (Simplified)

	May	June	July	Aug.	Sept.	Oct.	Nov.	Dec.	Jan.	Feb.	March	April	Total
Estimated sales in units	500	1,000	1,500	2,000	3,500	5,500	6,000	4,000	2,500	2,000	2,700	3,000	34,200
Gross operating revenue at $10/unit	$5,000	$10,000	$15,000	$20,000	$35,000	$55,000	$60,000	$40,000	$25,000	$20,000	$27,000	$30,000	$342,000
Estimated operating expenses:													
Direct labor*	$2,000	$4,000	$6,000	$8,000	$14,000	$22,000	$24,000	$16,000	$10,000	$8,000	$10,800	$12,000	$136,800
Materials†	1,000	2,000	2,250	3,000	3,500	4,125	4,500	4,000	2,500	3,000	2,700	3,000	35,575
Indirect labor	1,700	1,700	2,050	2,050	2,050	2,450	2,450	2,050	2,050	2,050	2,050	2,050	24,700
Sales commission (20%)	1,000	2,000	3,000	4,000	7,000	11,000	12,000	8,000	5,000	4,000	5,400	6,000	68,400
Depreciation	400	400	400	400	400	400	400	400	400	400	400	400	4,800
Insurance and taxes	50	50	50	50	50	50	50	50	50	50	50	50	600
Heat, light, water	30	30	30	30	30	40	50	60	60	60	50	40	510
Advertising	2,000	1,000	1,000	3,000	4,500	4,500	3,000	1,000	1,000	1,500	1,500	1,000	25,000
Rent	600	600	600	600	600	600	600	600	600	600	600	600	7,200
Total	$8,780	$11,780	$15,380	$21,130	$32,130	$45,165	$47,050	$32,160	$21,660	$19,660	$23,550	$25,140	$303,585
Net income from operations	-$3,780	-$1,780	$ 380	-$1,130	$ 2,870	$ 9,835	$12,950	$ 7,840	$ 3,340	$ 340	$ 3,450	$ 4,860	$ 38,415
Add other income	--	--	--	--	--	--	--	--	--	--	--	--	--
Deduct other expenses:													
Interest expense	--	--	--	--	--	--	--	--	--	--	--	--	--
Net income before income tax‡	- 3,780	- 1,780	380										
Estimated income tax‡	--	--	380										
Net income													

*Direct labor computed at $4 per unit.

†Estimated cost of materials on the basis of the following schedule:

Quantity in Units	Price per Unit
0–1,000	$2.00
1,001–2,000	1.50
2,001–4,000	1.00
4,001 and over	0.75

‡Technically, this should be computed on a month-by-month basis, but for the planning purposes of the forecast it is not worth the effort (especially if months with losses are involved). A practical solution is to assign 1/12 of the estimated annual tax to each month.

FIG. 5-2

Ajax Manufacturing Company Cash Forecast—First Year (Simplified)

	May	June	July	Aug.	Sept.	Oct.	Nov.	Dec.	Jan.	Feb.	March	April	Total
Cash receipts from sales*	--	$ 5,000	$10,000	$15,000	$20,000	$35,000	$55,000	$60,000	$40,000	$25,000	$20,000	$27,000	$312,000
Cash disbursements:													
Direct labor	$2,000	$ 4,000	$ 6,000	$ 8,000	$14,000	$22,000	$24,000	$16,000	$10,000	$ 8,000	$10,800	$12,000	$136,800
Materials	1,000	2,000	2,250	3,000	3,500	4,125	4,500	4,000	2,500	3,000	2,700	3,000	35,575
Indirect labor	1,700	1,700	2,050	2,050	2,050	2,450	2,450	2,050	2,050	2,050	2,050	2,050	24,700
Sales commissions	1,000	2,000	3,000	4,000	7,000	11,000	12,000	8,000	5,000	4,000	5,400	6,000	68,400
Depreciation†	--	--	--	--	--	--	--	--	--	--	--	--	---
Insurance and taxes	--	60	--	--	--	--	--	60	--	--	--	480	600
Heat, light, water	30	30	30	30	30	40	50	60	60	60	50	40	510
Advertising	2,000	1,000	1,000	3,000	4,500	4,500	3,000	1,000	1,000	1,500	1,500	1,000	25,000
Rent	600	600	600	600	600	600	600	600	600	600	600	600	7,200
Income tax	--	--	--	--	--	--	--	--	--	--	--	--	
Total	8,330	11,390	14,930	20,680	31,680	44,715	46,600	31,770	21,210	19,210	23,100	25,170	298,785
Cash gain or loss (−) from operations	-$8,330	-$ 6,390	-$ 4,930	-$ 5,680	-$11,680	-$ 9,715	$ 8,400	$28,230	$18,790	$ 5,790	-$ 3,100	$ 1,830	$ 13,215
Loans received (+) or paid (−)	--	--	--	--	--	--	--	--	--	--	--	--	
Other cash receipts	25,000 (cash from owner)												
Other disbursements:													
Interest expense‡	--	--	--										
Cumulative cash balance	16,670	10,280	5,350										

*We have made the simplified assumption that customers will pay cash for their purchases 30 days after they are made.

†Depreciation is a "non-cash" expense and therefore is not reported in the cash forecast.

‡Unless the owner is willing to supply more cash, it is apparent that he will have to borrow to cover the expected $330 deficit facing him in August. In real life he might have to arrange the loan a month or two in advance and pay a fee for each month to reserve it. Here, we have made the simplified assumption that there will be no loan or interest charges for the months of May, June, and July.

of actual experience and, as each month passes, an additional month's projection into the future should be made so that the projection in time of the forecasts will remain constant. Allowance should be made in interpreting all forecasts for the amount of estimating error that past experience and judgment deem wise. Any action that will improve the accuracy of forecasting, and thus reduce the amount of estimating error, will contribute to more efficient operation if the expense required is not excessive. In chapter 2 techniques for improved forecasting were discussed. A simple but very effective tool is the use of "post mortem" sessions to analyze thoroughly why deviations from the forecast occurred. These problems of control will be discussed at greater length in later chapters specifically dealing with control.

Failure adequately to plan capital requirements at the outset can be deadly, even for a business that has the potential for being highly successful. The kind of close race with disaster than can be run is well illustrated by the experience of the infant Ford Motor Company trying to produce its first car in 1903:

> But for a few weeks at the start the company ran a neck-and-neck race with bankruptcy. On June 26, with a bank balance of $14,500, it had to disburse $10,000 to Malcomson to cover payments made by him to the Dodge Brothers; $5,000 to the Dodge Brothers for engines; $640 to the Hartford Rubber Works for sixty-four tires; and some smaller sums. This would have left the company account overdrawn but for the fact that on the same day J. W. Anderson paid in his $5,000. Five days later payments for salaries and services had to be made to Ford, Couzens, Wills, Gould, Wandersee, and others; and between July 7 and July 11, a payment of $5,000 to Dodge Brothers and checks for rent and other expenses brought the balance down to $223.65. The company was skirting the edge of ruin! As yet not a car had been sold; unpaid bills were mounting; the suppliers of parts were growing clamorous. Happily, Malcomson and Ford were able to bring pressure to bear on Albert Strelow, whose stock subscription was not yet covered. On the 11th his check for $5,000 arrived—and loud must have been the sighs of relief. Then, in the nick of time, came the first orders.[3]

Of course, if people had *known for certain* about the tremendous success his cars were to enjoy, there would have been little financial difficulty for the new firm. On the contrary, investors would have flocked to his door from miles around, cash in hand, with the hope

---

[3] Allan Nevins, *Ford: the Times, the Man, the Company* (New York: Charles Scribner's Sons, 1954), p. 240.

that they could get in on such a good thing. But in life it rarely happens that way. The new firm, struggling to "get off the ground," often is seriously limited as to sources it may tap for funds. As the owner-managers demonstrate their staying power and competence along with reasonable expectations for future profits, previously unavailable sources wil become available to them. This should be kept in mind when viewing the list of sources below. Determination of which of these will be available to a particular firm at any given time and the proper combination and timing of their use by the firm will depend on the unique characteristics of the company and its industry coupled with current conditions inside aud outside the firm. When we realize that these sources can be used in various combinations, we can see that the range of choice is wide indeed! A thorough analysis of the bases for making such choices intelligently is beyond the scope of this book; it is the provocative subject matter of corporation finance.

Sources of Capital

The following list is not meant to be exhaustive, but it does include the more common sources of capital:

Sources of Intermediate and Long-Term Capital (for periods of more than one year)
    Owners
        Contribution of cash or other assets (includes cash from sale of
            stock)
        Retained earnings
    Long-term indebtedness
        Bonds and other credit instruments
        Term loans
        Leases

Sources of Short-term Capital (for periods of one year or less)
    Owners
        Cash loans
    Creditors
        Banks
        Customers
        Suppliers
        Relatives and friends
        Lessors
    Other
        Cash balances
        Working capital turnover
        Turnover of fixed assets

The *capitalization* of a corporation represents the total of stocks, bonds, and long-term notes outstanding; *capital structure* refers to the relative proportion of these factors comprising the company's capitalization, including retained earnings. As we suggested above, one of the most important and challenging areas of financial planning has to do with the determination of capital structure. Careful analysis at the outset can save money and provide management with greater freedom of action in the future.

Some students of management have pointed out that an important source of working capital is the depreciation reserve. This is often misunderstood. First, of course, to have such a reserve you must have sufficient revenue from operations to cover all expenses including depreciation. Second, the depreciation reserve accrual does not necessarily imply the holding of cash—unless the depreciation expense has been *funded,* and this introduces undesirable rigidity in the area of financial planning. The sum in a depreciation reserve, however, does stand for the *preservation* of assets or the *reduction of debt;* for that part of revenue which is allocated to depreciation charges is represented on the balance sheet by an off-setting increase in other assets or a reduction in debt.

A good question, then, is: Where will the money come from to replace a particular piece of equipment if no sinking fund is set aside for this specific purpose? One possibility would be to take that portion of assets which represents the accumulated depreciation for a piece of equipment and convert it to cash, "borrow back" and add to this the amount of depreciation charges used to reduce debt, and use this sum to replace the depreciated item. In actual practice management rarely does this. Company needs and opportunities change. Presumably, depreciation accounting has helped to maintain the financial strength and credit position of the company. A new equipment acquisition would be financed on the basis of this strength and on the basis of *current* depreciation charges for other pieces of equipment that are not to be replaced immediately.

If depreciation expenses are not taken into account, management will *overstate* profits by the amount of depreciation that should have been taken. In effect, without recognition of depreciation expenses, management will tend to weaken the company through depletion of its assets. This will result from the payment of higher taxes than would otherwise be required and the temptation to *disburse* funds derived from operations that should be used to help preserve the assets and, consequently, the strength of the firm.

Trading on the Equity

When a company's income is secure enough and stable enough, it can enjoy the benefits from a high proportion of debt to equity (ownership) financing; it can "trade on the equity." This means that it can take advantage of the fact that it pays a *fixed* charge (interest) for funds obtained through indebtedness. Stockholders (owners) do not have to share with the lenders the earnings (in excess of the interest charge) generated by the borrowed capital. Consequently, as long as the company can earn more through the use of borrowed funds than it must pay for the funds, stockholders stand to gain more than if the funds had been obtained through the sale of additional stock. Of course, this advantage to the stockholders turns into a disadvantage if *less* is earned through the use of the borrowed funds than the interest paid for them. Then, the stockholders must bear a loss, for the lenders are not fellow-owners who will share equally in whatever is in the pot—gain or loss. Figure 5-3 illustrated the advantage and the disadvantage of trading on the equity. We can see that, in a good year, the stockholders of the Marge N. Al Corporation would enjoy a 6 per cent return on their investment of $30,000 without trading on the equity. If, however, half of the capitalization were supplied by the holders of 4 per cent bonds and the stockholders supplied the other half ($15,000), the stockholders would enjoy a 10 per cent return on *their* investment after paying the 4 per cent interest charge to the bondholders for the use of their money. This would be trading on the equity at its best! On the other hand, if the company experienced a loss, it is clear that the stockholders would have been better off without trading on the equity; they would have lost $600 rather than $1,200.

Impact of Taxes

Today, taxes play an important part in the determination of desirable capital structure. If the firm's income tax can be reduced by a dollar, *all* this saving goes to the owners; but if the firm's expenses are reduced by a dollar, only a portion of this, after taxes, will go to the owners. If a building is owned, *part* of the costs of maintaining it may be deductible as a business expense; if the building is leased, all the rental constitutes a deductible expense. As Durand points out, taxes have affected the cost of equity financing:

In choosing a method for raising capital, costs are only one consideration; others include fairness to all parties, company income situation, risk to the firm, and limitations of the money market. Cost of capital should be figured from the point of view of the old common stockholder; any considerations not included in that view may be added separately.[4]

A dollar of earnings available for new stockholders is a dollar less available for old common stockholders, but a dollar of interest paid to bondholders "costs" the old stockholders about 50 cents. This is why corporate income taxes have raised the cost of equity financing. We may

FIG. 5-3

Marge N. Al Service Corporation*

(Dollar data in thousands of dollars)

	Good Years	Normal Years	Poor Years	Worst Years
Investment and total assets	$30,000	$30,000	$30,000	$30,000
Earnings before interest and income taxes:				
A. Amount	$ 3,600	$ 2,700	$ 1,050	$ −600
B. Percentage on investment	12.0	9.0	3.5	− 2.0
Without Trading on the Equity				
Capitalization: Common Stock	$30,000	$30,000	$30,000	$30,000
Income taxes†	$ 1,800	$ 1,350	$ 525	$ 0
Net profit	$ 1,800	$ 1,350	$ 525	$ −600
Rate of earnings on book value				
common stock, per cent	6.0	4.5	1.75	− 2.0
With Trading on the equity				
Capitalization:				
Common stock	$15,000	$15,000	$15,000	$15,000
4 per cent bonds	$15,000	$15,000	$15,000	$15,000
Bond interest	$ 600	$ 600	$ 600	$ 600
Earnings before income taxes	$ 3,000	$ 2,100	$ 450	$−1,200
Income taxes†	$ 1,500	$ 1,050	$ 225	$ 0
Net profit	$ 1,500	$ 1,050	$ 225	$−1,200
Rate of earnings on book value				
common stock, per cent	10.0	7.0	1.5	− 8.0
Common stockholder gain from trading on				
on the equity, per cent	67	56	−14	−300

*Taken from Robert Durand, *Business: Its Organization, Management and Responsibilities* Englewood Cliffs, New Jersey: Prentice-Hall, Inc., 1958, p. 480.
†Income tax assumed at 50 per cent.

make interest and dividend costs comparable by adjusting all to pre-tax equivalents. For example, $50,000 of bond interest or any other expense is $50,000 pre-tax cost, but earnings of $50,000 to be paid to new shareholders requires about $100,000 pre-tax.

---

[4] As Durand indicates elsewhere (p. 473) it has been estimated that underwriting and selling costs for "usual" issues of an established business range from about 3 to 10 per cent of retail price. To this must be added fees for professional services and advice, preparation and printing of the prospectus, and costs of registration with the SEC. The prospectus and forms alone may easily run to $15,000 or $20,000. For new-venture capital, costs are much higher, running up to one-third of net proceeds.

Flotation cost depends on difficulties in selling, risks of underwriting, and the services rendered. Restricted services are much less expensive. Investment bankers acting as intermediaries in private placements of bonds have charged from 0.2 to 1.7 per cent of proceeds.

FIG. 5-4

Comparison of Costs of Financing
Yukon and 40 Mile River Improvement Corporation

(Dollar totals)*

	If the new investment earns		
	15%	25%	40%
Estimated annual earnings before interest and income taxes:			
Old investment of $3,200,000	$ 800,000	$ 800,000	$ 800,000
New investment of $1,000,000	150,000	250,000	400,000
Total	950,000	1,050,000	1,200,000
Bond financing:			
Interest on $1,031,000 issue of new 4% bonds (netting $1,000,000) (cost of capital)	41,240	41,240	41,240
Pre-tax earnings available for common stock	908,760	1,008,760	1,158,760
Pre-tax earnings per share of common stock:			
After expansion	90.88	100.88	115.88
Without expansion	80.00	80.00	80.00
Gain per share for common stock	10.88	20.88	35.88
New investment earnings less finance cost	108,760	208,760	358,760
Preferred stock financing:			
Dividends on $1,136,000 issue of 6% preferred (netting $1,000,000)	68,160	68,160	68,160
Pre-tax dividends (cost of capital)	136,320	136,320	136,320
Pre-tax earnings available for common stock	813,680	913,680	1,063,680
Pre-tax earnings per share of common stock:			
After expansion	81.37	91.37	106.37
Without expansion	80.00	80.00	80.00
Gain per share for common stock	1.37	11.37	26.37
New investment earnings less finance cost	13,680	113,680	263,680
Common stock financing:			
Number of shares of new issue needed to net $1,000,000 *†	(4,230)	(3,680)	(3,080)
Total shares after expansion	(14,230)	(13,680)	(13,080)
Pre-tax earnings available for the new common stock (cost of capital)‡	282,400	282,500	282,600
Pre-tax earnings per share of common stock:			
After expansion	66.76	76.75	91.74
Without expansion	80.00	80.00	80.00
Gain (loss) per share	(−)13.24	(−)3.25	(+)11.74
New investment earnings less finance cost	(−)132,400	(−)32,500	(+)117,400

*Durand, *op. cit.,* p. 487.

†Number of shares needed depends on market price, which, in turn, depends on earnings. Thus price is different for each of the three assumed earnings estimates.

‡Small differences are from rounding share numbers.

FIG. 5-5

Comparison of Costs of Financing
Yukon and 40 Mile River Improvement Corporation

(Percentages)*

	If the new investment earns		
	15%	25%	40%
Estimated annual earnings before interest and income taxes:			
Old investment of $3,200,000	25	25	25
New investment of $1,000,000	15	25	40
Total investment of $4,200,000	22.6	25.0	28.6
Bond financing:			
Capital cost (interest as a percentage) of new capital raised)	4.1	4.1	4.1
New investment earnings less finance cost	10.9	20.9	35.9
Pre-tax earnings for common stock (on its $3,200,000 book value):			
After expansion	28.4	31.5	36.2
Without expansion	25.0	25.0	25.0
Gain to common stock	3.4	6.5	11.2
Preferred stock financing:			
Capital cost (pre-tax preferred dividends as a percentage of new capital raised)	13.6	13.6	13.6
New investment earnings less finance cost	1.4	11.4	26.4
Pre-tax earnings for common stock (on its $3,200,000 book value):			
After expansion	25.4	28.5	33.2
Without expansion	25.0	25.0	25.0
Gain to common stock	0.4	3.5	8.2
Common stock financing:			
Capital cost (pre-tax earnings for new common stock as a percentage of new capital raised)	28.2	28.2	28.2
New investment earnings less finance cost	(−)13.2	(−) 3.2	(+)11.8
Pre-tax earnings for old common stock (on its $3,200,000 old book value)			
After expansion	20.9	24.0	28.7
Without expansion	25.0	25.0	25.0
Gain (loss) to old common stock	(−) 4.1	(−) 1.0	(+) 3.7

*Durand, *op. cit.*, p. 488.

The net capital raised, after deduction of the one-time costs, is the base for computing percentage costs to the old stockholders. Costs of financing by different methods may thus be compared to each other and to the expected rate of return on the new investment.

Because of marketing and preparation costs and administrative expenses, the pre-tax cost to the old common stockholder is somewhat greater than the pre-tax yield to the investor—for all types of new security issues. The investor figures his yield on the selling price of the security; cost is figured on net proceeds.[5]

---

[5] Robert Durand, *Business: Its Organization, Management and Responsibilities* (Englewood Cliffs, New Jersey: Prentice-Hall, Inc., 1958), pp. 484–86.

PROCUREMENT OF REQUIRED PLANT, EQUIPMENT AND MATERIEL

Relation to Organic Business Functions

The organic functions of business are the *creation* and *distribution* of salable utilities. Before we can intelligently plan for the procurement of plant, equipment, and materiel, we must clearly define our primary service objectives: specifically *what* we plan to create and *how* we plan to distribute it. This is not easy, for such planning must go well beyond generalities. For example, if we wish to manufacture automobiles, it is not enough to say that our primary service objectives are to make and distribute cars. What kind of car do we have in mind; for what kind of market? Shall we attempt to make the finest car in the world, irrespective of price? Or shall we try to give the customer the best possible buy in inexpensive, durable transportation? Or are we looking for something in between, a blending of these two extremes? Specific answers to such questions will determine not only the kind of plant, equipment, and materiel needed but also the character of all other organizational factors. For it should be remembered that all functions, policies, rules, procedures, and other organizational factors are but means or tools for carrying out the firm's primary service objectives!

Make or Buy

Assume that we plan to manufacture an automobile. The most desirable approach will be first to design the product, then the processes by which it is to be made, and then to plan for the procurement, layout, and maintenance of required plant, equipment, and materiel. At about this point the decision must be made as to whether we plan to "make or buy." Some of the factors to be considered are:

When To Make
1. When the process or product contains a secret element that the company desires to retain for itself.
2. When a high degree of quality needs to be maintained.
3. When the product, part of service can be produced in the plant at lower cost.
4. When sources of supply are uncertain in terms of delivery, thus raising a question as to whether or not the production schedules can be maintained.

When To Buy
1. When, because of specialization, outsiders can do a better job and at a lower cost.

2. When time is an important factor and the outside specialist is already set up for production of the part.
3. When the demand for the part or service is temporary.
4. When funds for capital expenditures are limited.
5. During periods of high or intense competition. In such circumstances a buyer can often take advantage of a seller's predicament and make a satisfactory purchase. One should not depend on these instances for a supply of parts.[6]

To this list, of course, should be added the important consideration of the impact of the decision on labor-management relations.

Location

Attention must be given to the matter of location, for this will significantly affect the cost of establishing and maintaining our plant as well as our general efficiency of operation. Some of the factors bearing on the location decision are:

1. Accessibility of markets and availability of financing.
2. Availability of suitable labor, raw materials, water, waste disposal facilities, transportation, related service industries, and power or fuel.
3. Construction or lease costs, room for expansion, and national defense.
4. Political "climate": taxes, regulation, and economic outlook of area.
5. Labor-management relations: state or local labor laws and character of local union movement.
6. General living conditions as to climate, recreational and educational facilities, and availability of housing.

Process Planning: Machine Selection Example

Product design is concerned with the specific characteristics and specifications of the products to be produced, whereas process design is concerned specifically with how they are to be produced. According to Davis, the prinicpal phases of process planning are operation layout, machine selection, routing, tool design, plant layout, and materials handling.[7]

Whether we are dealing with a new or an established installation, the matter of machine selection can be a very involved one. As with the investigation of any proposed investment in plant or equipment, there are three major areas of inquiry: the economic attractiveness of the alternative or proposal, the means for financing it, and due consideration to various "intangible" factors, such as impact on labor-management relations, etc. Assuming that our primary service

---

[6] Lyman Keith and Carlo Gubellini, *Business Management* (New York: McGraw-Hill Book Co., 1958), pp. 87, 88.

[7] R. C. Davis, *Industrial Organization and Management* (3d ed.; New York: Harper & Bros., 1956), p. 282.

objectives have been defined, the next step in planning for machine selection would entail a search for alternatives.

Typical of possible alternatives that might exist in the replacement analysis of, say, an ordinary engine lathe, are:

1. The various brands of new engine lathes on the market capable of doing the same job and no more;
2. The various types and brand of new lathes having superior operational characteristics, such as turret lathes or automatic lathes;
3. The acquisition of a used lathe completely adequate and sufficiently reliable to do the job, either from the open market or from intra-company transfer;
4. Complete overhaul of existing lathe;
5. Rebalance machining operations among other existing equipment to eliminate the need for the lathe under study;
6. Eliminate the need for the lathe's function by changing production methods (such as using die castings instead of sand castings to reduce required machining);
7. Estimate the need for the lathe's function by redesign of the product.[8]

Other alternative possibilities could be developed, of course, and a number could be eliminated by cursory inspection. The remaining alternatives could then be subjected to the following kind of analysis (assume two alternatives: machine A and machine B).

		Machine A	Machine B
	Life expectancy	2 years	3 years
	Cost of machine	$2,000	$3,000
(E.R.)	Expected return in excess of variable costs:		
1	First year	1,200	1,500
(E.R.) 2	Second year	800	1,210
(E.R.) 3	Third year	—	700
(S.)	Salvage value at end of second year	237	—
(S.)	Salvage value at end of third year	—	350
(i)	Interest rate	8%	10%

$$\text{Present value} = \frac{(E.R.)1}{(1+i)} + \frac{(E.R.)2}{(1+i)2} + \frac{(E.R.)3}{(1+i)3} + \frac{(E.R.)n+S}{(1+i)\ n}.$$

$$\text{Present value of machine A} = \frac{1200}{1.08} + \frac{800+237}{(1.08)2} = 2000.17.$$

$$\text{Present value of machine B} = \frac{1500}{1.10} + \frac{1000}{(1.10)2} + \frac{700+350}{(1.10)3} = 3152.52.$$

The cost of the machine is the price we have to pay for it. Expected return in excess of variable costs for each year that we anticipate using the machine is based on our estimate of value

---

[8] David A. Thompson, "Machinery Replacement Economy (unpublished Master's thesis, University of Florida, April, 1956), pp. 27, 28.

added by the machine's operation less our estimate of such variable costs as direct labor, power consumption, and maintenance. Depreciation is *not included* because it is already taken into account by the computation of present value.[9] The salvage value is the amount that we realistically expect we can get for the machine at the end of the third year. The interest rate assigned should equal the rate that we know we can realize from alternative investments with the same degree of risk. If we feel that the risk of the machine investment is higher, we should assign a higher rate of interest accordingly! In any event, the interest rate assigned should be as high as the cost of capital to us.

We can see from our computations that machine B is the better investment choice, for its present value is higher than its initial cost. The present value of machine A is just equal to its initial cost. This conclusion, of course, is based on the assumption that the higher interest rate assigned to machine B adequately compensates for the higher risk that may be associated with a longer time span of use or a less flexible piece of equipment.

The present value approach for evaluating investment alternatives is more realistic than the "pay-back" approach or other approaches that do not look far enough into the predictable future. After all, the value of any asset is dependent on the *amount* of its anticipated usefulness and the *period of time* during which it will be useful. Despite the inevitable estimating errors that will be involved, the present value analysis accounts for these future values better than do other approaches. Assume, for example, that we had used the "pay-back" approach with the criterion that an investment must pay for itself within 2 years. With this standard, machine A would be selected in preference to machine B. For machine A will pay for itself in 2 years, while it will take machine B approximately 2½ years.

Often a more convenient approach for comparing investment alternatives is to solve for that rate of return for each which will discount its future returns to the value of the investment (in our example above, the cost of the machine). This will permit a comparison of investment alternatives in terms of differing rates of return. The formula is the same except that we solve for that (i) which will give a present value equal to the amount of the investment. We would have:

---

[9] The present value of some future sum (in our case, expected net return for different years) is that amount which if compounded at the interest rate we have selected will equal the future sum in the prescribed number of years.

$$\text{Cost of machine} = \frac{(E.R.)1}{1+i} + \frac{(E.R.)2}{(1+i)2} + \frac{(E.R.)3}{(1+i)3} + \frac{(E.R.)n+S}{(1+i)n}$$

and solve for i.

With many years of machine usage to compute for, the mathematics can get sticky unless one has access to a computer.[10]

It is not within the scope of this book to go into a more detailed discussion of the kinds of quantitative analyses that can be made with regard to the procurement, layout, and maintenance of required plant, equipment, and materiel. The example given above provides an illustration of the type of approach that as far as the business environment goes, originated in these planning areas. As was pointed out in chapter 2, "Planning for Planning," computers may now be programmed to perform very complex forms of quantitative analysis that were not feasible previously. And now, the quantitative approach has "spilled over" into, and is being elaborated for, *all* areas of planning in the company.

PROCUREMENT AND MAINTENANCE OF DESIRED PERSONNEL

A recent advertising blurb sent to personnel directors and managers in general extols the virtues of a "system" that "guarantees" to tell you how to judge people by their physical characteristics. It points out that such factors as facial features, body build, taste in women, and the shape of a man's hands can tell you all that you need to know to hire the right sort of man for a particular position. Understandably, this appeals to many of us, for we pride ourselves on our "ability to size up people." But, unfortunately, there is no reference to definite and revealing statistical evidence of *validity* for such an approach, and this, too, is understandable; for rarely do such factors *prove* useful in selection.

Validation

Nature and Value of Validation. The combined physiognomical, phrenological, and astrological chart used for personnel placement during the late twenties (shown in Figure 5-6)—and perhaps by some even today—would be amusing were it not indicative of an *approach* that is still all too prevalent: the use of *non-validated* se-

---

[10] For a fuller discussion of the present value approach in comparison with others see W. Haynes and Joseph Massie, *Management: Analysis, Concepts, and Cases* (Englewood Cliffs, New Jersey: Prentice-Hall, Inc., 1961), pp. 300–309. See also Joel Dean, "*Measuring the Productivity of Capital,*" *Harvard Business Review*, Vol. XXXII, No. 1 (January, 1954), pp. 120–30.

lection instruments. Every year hundreds of graduating university seniors are interviewed by company representatives who are making evaluations that are no better than "chance" predictions of success or failure on the job, that is, for the purpose of selection alone—not the

FIG. 5-6
Combination Physiognomical, Phrenological, and Astrological Chart Designed for Personnel Placement Uses

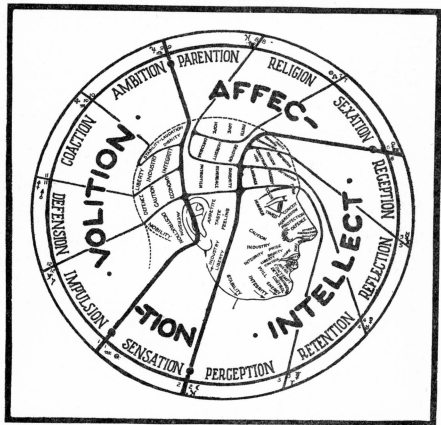

advertising or public relations part of the interviewer's job—the company could save a lot of money by flipping a coin or using some other means of random selection to determine which applicants should be hired![11]

---

[11] Among more than 100 companies interviewed by *Fortune,* only one noted any difference in ability between graduates hired over the counter and recruits painstakingly selected as the "cream of the crop," i.e., men who supposedly combine special and general abilities. Herrymon Maurer, "The Worst Shortage in Business," *Fortune,* April, 1956, or W. M. Fox (ed.), *Readings in Personnel Management from "Fortune"* (New York: Henry Holt & Co., 1957), p. 26.

The results of an experiment in which six district sales managers of the same company interviewed the same thirty-six applicants and ranked them as to their promise for sales work are pre-

FIG. 5-7

**Combined Report of 6 District Managers
As to Ability of 36 Applicants
for Sales Positions***

Applicants			Managers			
	A	B	C	D	E	F
I	5.0†	11.0	2.0	1.5	3.0	2.0
II	8.5	11.0	12.0	3.0	7.5	5.5
III	6.5	18.5	25.0	21.0	15.0	22.0
IV	2.0	2.0	1.0	1.5	1.0	5.5
V	15.0	3.0	4.0	28.0	3.0	14.5
VI	1.0	11.0	5.0	9.0	15.0	3.0
VII	17.5	18.5	19.0	12.0	23.0	26.0
VIII	14.0	18.5	27.0	6.0	15.0	23.0
IX	28.0	11.0	22.0	11.0	3.0	9.0
X	19.0	11.0	16.0	18.0	15.0	10.5
XI	10.5	23.0	18.0	17.0	30.0	4.0
XII	12.0	30.0	22.0	35.0	30.0	14.5
XIII	3.0	23.0	12.0	5.0	15.0	19.0
XIV	4.0	11.0	6.0	24.0	23.0	18.0
XV	31.0	5.0	8.0	4.0	7.5	25.0
XVI	6.5	1.0	7.0	7.0	7.5	7.0
XVII	28.0	30.0	3.0	29.0	23.0	8.0
XVIII	23.5	4.0	9.5	32.5	23.0	1.0
XIX	16.0	6.0	20.0	26.5	34.5	10.5
XX	8.5	11.0	15.0	14.5	30.0	21.0
XXI	21.5	11.0	17.0	8.0	23.0	17.0
XXII	13.0	30.0	30.0	30.0	30.0	24.0
XXIII	35.0	11.0	14.0	25.0	15.0	16.0
XXIV	26.5	16.0	9.5	23.0	23.0	27.0
XXV	34.0	23.0	26.0	14.5	7.5	13.0
XXVI	30.0	23.0	11.0	10.0	15.0	12.0
XXVII	21.5	34.0	34.0	16.0	30.0	32.0
XXVIII	10.5	30.0	23.0	19.0	7.5	28.5
XXIX	25.0	18.5	21.0	20.0	15.0	20.0
XXX	28.0	23.0	29.0	34.0	7.5	28.5
XXXI	23.5	30.0	33.0	13.0	30.0	30.0
XXXII	17.5	30.0	31.0	22.0	23.0	31.0
XXXIII	33.0	34.5	36.0	32.5	15.0	33.0
XXXIV	32.0	26.0	28.0	26.5	34.5	36.0
XXXV	26.5	30.0	24.0	31.0	36.0	34.0
XXXVI	36.0	36.0	35.0	36.0	30.0	35.0

† Rank assigned.

* Scott, Clothier, Mathewson, and Spriegel, *Personnel Management* (New York: McGraw-Hill Book Co., 1941), p. 148.

sented in Figure 5-7. As can be seen, with but few exceptions these seasoned, successful managers were unable to agree as to the relative desirability of the applicants; the important point is that this is *typical, not atypical,* of the situations in which non-validated interviews or other selection instruments are used!

The concept of validation is extremely important for managers and their personnel staff specialists. With regard to selection, for example, it permits us to know "where we've been, where we are, and where we hope to go." To attempt to build a successful personnel procurement program without it would be analogous to trying to learn to shoot well without ever being permitted to see the target! A selection test or interview is valid to the extent that it can predict success or failure on the job. The extent of validity is normally shown by a correlation coefficient. Figure 5-8 illustrates the value of knowing the validity of a test. Assume that a selection test or procedure has "0" validity—a very commonplace occurrence when no attempts at validation have been made—and that 50 per cent or half the people hired turn out to be satisfactory; as can be seen from the top horizontal line in the table, it makes no difference, except in terms of expense to the company, whether we take only the "best" five in a hundred we screen or ninety-five in a hundred—still 50 per cent will be satisfactory. We would do just as well using a random basis for selection: say, taking every even-numbered person who could meet our specific minimum requirements.

However, assume a test with the modest validity of .50 (by squaring it we find that we have only explained 25 per cent of the variance; a correlation of .80 would account for 64 per cent of the variance). Now if we take the best five in a hundred, 88 per cent will turn out to be satisfactory! [12] Some estimates are that the cheapest processing cost for any new employee is around $600. The savings made possible for reduced processing costs alone would more than offset the expense of the validation study. And it is difficult to place a value on the other important savings that result from reduced turnover: better morale and higher productivity in stable work groups, less demand on supervisory time for instructional purposes, less time devoted to grievances, disciplinary action, counseling, transfers, and so on.

---

[12] The decision as to which selection ratio is appropriate will depend upon the supply of applicants relative to the needed number of hirees, and the added cost of screening more to get a few versus the savings that will result from reduced turnover owing to a more discriminating selection ratio. There are other Taylor-Russell Tables for other percentages of randomly selected employees who are satisfactory. Of course, these tables are based on certain assumptions that must be satisfied if they are to be used properly. See M. Smith, "Cautions concerning the Use of the Taylor-Russell Tables in Employee Selection," *Journal of Applied Psychology,* Vol. 32 (1948), pp. 595–600.

Validation Procedure. The surprising thing is that, given an adequate sample to work with, the basic work of validation is neither especially difficult nor expensive. Take, for example, a selection interview that you have used for a period of time but

FIG. 5-8

Taylor-Russell Tables*

Tables of the Proportion Who Will Be Satisfactory among Those Selected, for Given values of the Proportion of Present Employees Considered Satisfactory, the Selection Ratio, and r

Proportion of Employees Considered Satisfactory $= .50$

Selection Ratio †

r‡	.05	.10	.20	.30	.40	.50	.60	.70	.80	.90	.95
.00	.50	.50	.50	.50	.50	.50	.50	.50	.50	.50	.50
.05	.54	.54	.53	.52	.52	.52	.51	.51	.51	.50	.50
.10	.58	.57	.56	.55	.54	.53	.53	.52	.51	.51	.50
.15	.63	.61	.58	.57	.56	.55	.54	.53	.52	.51	.51
.20	.67	.64	.61	.59	.58	.56	.55	.54	.53	.52	.51
.25	.70	.67	.64	.62	.60	.58	.56	.55	.54	.52	.51
.30	.74	.71	.67	.64	.62	.60	.58	.56	.54	.52	.51
.35	.78	.74	.70	.66	.64	.61	.59	.57	.55	.53	.51
.40	.82	.78	.73	.69	.66	.63	.61	.58	.56	.53	.52
.45	.85	.81	.75	.71	.68	.65	.62	.59	.56	.53	.52
.50	.88	.84	.78	.74	.70	.67	.63	.60	.57	.54	.52
.55	.91	.87	.81	.76	.72	.69	.65	.61	.58	.54	.52
.60	.94	.90	.84	.79	.75	.70	.66	.62	.59	.54	.52
.65	.96	.92	.87	.82	.77	.73	.68	.64	.59	.55	.52
.70	.98	.95	.90	.85	.80	.75	.70	.65	.60	.55	.53
.75	.99	.97	.92	.87	.82	.77	.72	.66	.61	.55	.53
.80	1.00	.99	.95	.90	.85	.80	.73	.67	.61	.55	.53
.85	1.00	.99	.97	.94	.88	.82	.76	.69	.62	.55	.53
.90	1.00	1.00	.99	.97	.92	.86	.78	.70	.62	.56	.53
.95	1.00	1.00	1.00	.99	.96	.90	.81	.71	.63	.56	.53
1.00	1.00	1.00	1.00	1.00	1.00	1.00	.83	.71	.63	.56	.53

*From H. C. Taylor and J. T. Russell, "The Relationship of Validity Coefficients to the Practical Effectiveness of Tests in Selection: Discussion and Tables," *Journal of Applied Psychology,* Vol. XXIII, No. 5 (1939), p. 573–78.

†The selection ratio is the proportion hired of those screened

$$\text{S.R.} = \frac{\text{No. of hirees}}{\text{No. screened}}$$

‡r represents the validity coefficient of the selection instrument, e.g., the correlation between test scores and performance scores (our validating criteria).

have never validated. Starting from scratch, here are the basic steps in the validation procedure:

1. Think of the factors that you evaluate the applicant on; such things, perhaps, as appearance, personality, stability, experience, initiative, and so on. How many different degrees or rating levels do you perceive for

each factor? Make up an evaluation sheet that presents all factors and an appropriate rating scale for each.

2. Each time that you interview an applicant, fill in one of these evaluation sheets for him.

3. When you have collected thirty or more of these sheets for people whom you can obtain adequate performance scores for, correlate the interview scores for each factor separately with the performance scores.

4. Discard those factors with no correlation or validity and use multiple correlation analysis to determine the optimal weights to apply to the valid factor scores (this permits the addition of such factor scores into *one* total interview score that will correlate higher with performance scores than any of the factor scores contributing to it).

5. Establish fiducial limits at at least the 5 per cent level of confidence and use the lower limit as the current validity of the selection battery. Recompute as the sample grows larger so that you can "improve" the useful validity by "pulling in" the lower fiducial limit.[13]

6. Convert factor raw scores in the future to standard scores before weighting unless all factor rating distributions have the same variability.[14]

7. Constantly try to improve the validity of the interview by refining existing factors, by searching the literature for promising factors that others have validated for similar purposes, and by just making up likely looking factors to try out. Repeat the "validation cycle" with these new experimental items.[15]

Step 4 in the validation procedure is especially important, and unfortunately it is often overlooked even by those who accept the basic necessity of validation for their selection instruments. There is a fallacy of "safety in numbers" even though some of the numbers (selection factors or instruments) have "0" or unproved validity. To illustrate this, let us assume that selection decisions are made on the basis of the following "battery" of selection instruments:

Instrument	Weight
A. aptitude test	20%
B. personality test	30
C. selection interview	50

---

[13] See the discussion on pp. 369–72 for an explanation of the need for this procedure.

[14] That is, if the weights derived from multiple correlation analysis are "beta" weights. If "B" scores or weights are computed, these may be applied directly to raw scores, for they are adjusted for differences in variability in factor rating distributions.

[15] Review of back issues of such publications as the *Journal of Applied Psychology* and *Personnel Psychology* (the validity exchange feature) will suggest some very worthwhile factors or approaches to try. For a specific example of personal data validation see Howard C. Lockwood and Stuart O. Parsons, "Relationship of Personal History Information to the Performance of Production Supervisors," *Engineering and Industrial Psychology*, Vol. II, No. 1 (Spring, 1960), pp. 20–26.

Unfortunately, in the majority of organizations today such a battery would be used day in and day out with no attempt to validate its parts! But let us assume that research shows us that scores on instrument A correlate .40 with performance or "success" scores so that A has a validity of .40; B has a correlation of "0" or no validity; and C a validity of .20. With this situation the company would have been much better off had it used A (the aptitude test) as the *sole* predictive instrument for selection. By combining the scores for A, B, and C, the validity of A is *diluted* below the .40 level and the weighting system used (which has no relation to the relative predictive worth of the three instruments) exaggerates this dilution even further! Though many managers would immediately protest that using A alone would "obviously" not be as sound as using it *with* B and C—"We don't want to go overboard about this testing business"—this is simply not true, *unless* B and C are valid and are weighted as outlined in step 4.

In this particular case, if B which had "0" validity were dropped, and A weighted more than C (based on the results of multiple correlation analysis), then the validity of the total of the *properly combined* scores would be higher than the .40.[16] Of course, a detailed analysis, factor by factor, of instrument C, the interview, would indicate proper "weeding-out" and weighting so that the total score for the interview would have a higher validity than the obtained .20.

It is difficult to overstate the importance of validation in the development of a sound program of personnel procurement. Without validity coefficients, it is impossible to know where we started, where we are, and how and by what route we may expect to improve. *Any* improvement in the validity of a selection procedure generally is a contribution, for the cost of validation is usually a small portion of the savings made possible. The performance scores or "validation criteria" required must be developed anyway if the organization hopes to promote and reward employees on the basis of their individual contributions.[17] And, since evaluations are being

---

[16] How much higher would depend on the amount of intercorrelation between the two rating factors.

[17] It should not be assumed, however, that the development of adequate performance scores or "validation criteria" is generally a simple matter. See Edwin Ghiselli and Mason Haire, "The Validation of Selection Tests in the Light of the Dynamic Character of Criteria," *Personnel Psychology,* Vol. 13, No. 3 (Autumn, 1960); Stanley Seashore, Bernard Indik, and Basil Georgopoulos, "Relationship among Criteria of Job Performance" (publication of the Institute for Social Research, University of Michigan, August, 1959); and Robert Thorndike, *Personnel Selection* (New York: John Wiley & Co., 1949).

made, the additional step of recording them is not very demanding. Now, with "canned" statistical programs for the computer, the most demanding routines (e.g., multiple correlation with numerous factors) have become quite manageable.

The procedure for validating a selection test would be very similar to that outlined above for a selection interview. In place of the first step, however, we would substitute a search of the literature and our own "creative resources" to provide test items or situations to validate. And we could "short cut" steps 2 and 3 to obtain "preliminary findings" right away by administering the test to those present employees for whom we have performance scores. This is a *preliminary* test of validity, however, for what applies to experienced employees may not apply to applicants. It is still desirable to run the more time-consuming but more accurate procedure of correlating applicant test scores with later acquired performance scores.

Sample Size. We have been discussing situations for which validation is feasible, wherein at least thirty or more employees will be involved in a reasonable period of time.[18] When only a few employees are hired at rather prolonged intervals, probably the best basis for predicting success or failure with your firm will be provided by projecting into the future, the behavior of an applicant for the past five years or so and by looking for people who share the values of the organization and look as if they will be personally compatible with those with whom they will work (a good indication of this latter factor may be obtained by exposing the applicant to the various persons concerned). Though individual behavior is subject to change, it is rare that it changes suddenly or drastically. Generally, for predictive purposes, our past behavioral histories speak much louder than our most sincere resolutions! The real tragedy is that managers have not developed sufficiently high "standards of expectation" with regard to their personnel men, nor are they sufficiently aware of promising areas for useful personnel research in the area of personnel procurement. A few of these will be discussed below.

Some New Approaches to Selection

Situational Tests. From a personnel standpoint, one of the most interesting developments to come out of World War II was the

---

[18] Actually, this small a number is quite marginal, for sampling error increases as sample size decreases. A sample of 100 would be much better. But, at least, good initial indications can be obtained from a sample of thirty, and this sample will be expanded as more employees are included.

procedure evolved by the Office of Strategic Services for the selection of intelligence agents, a procedure that included a series of *situational tests* to assist the assessment staff in making its appraisal of the total man.[19] In addition to probing the candidate's personality, the assessment staff observed his behavior in a number of stress situations. The staff drew upon a most important realization, which has frequently been overlooked by those who place great reliance on personality factors alone: the possession of a neurosis can be *either* an asset or a liability; it can either provide added "steam" or "drive" for achievement or be seriously disabling! As is pointed out by the editors of *Fortune:*

The clinical interview, at which the components of the personality were unearthed, was considered so valuable that some psychiatrists on the staff suggested dropping all other tests. Experience, however, showed that of two men with virtually the same basic personality components, one could be hopelessly inadequate in most life situations, whereas the other, having transformed his neurotic drives so that they led to accomplishment, could be very successful. That was the main reason why the situation tests were so vital to the whole assessment program: they showed how effectively the student had learned to handle his own unconscious patterns. Staff psychiatrists, whose previous experience had been mostly with the mentally sick, were amazed to find that the same unhappy experiences they thought had made their former patients ill showed up in the life histories of healthy, generally successful persons assessed by S. As MacKinnon put it: "The fire that melts the butter hardens the egg." [20]

The situational test idea has not been fully exploited by industry, but it has been used. Informally, it is not uncommon for some firms to "look over" junior executive applicants at a "casual" weekend house party; if the activities are well planned and the observers are perceptive, it is surprising how many behavioral situations may be investigated at such an affair! Dale reports that du Pont has long used a form of situational testing for executive selection:

A program of cross-fertilization, or directed movement of family and nonfamily personnel, among different functions and product departments tested potential leadership; also, candidates were often given varied assignments in manufacturing sales, and research or served as

---

[19] See "A Good Man Is Hard To Find," in *Fortune,* March, 1946, or Fox, *op. cit.,* p. 33. Also read *Assessment of Men* (New York: Rinehart & Co., 1948); William J. Morgan, *The O.S.S. and I* (New York: W. W. Norton & Co., Inc., 1957); and Bernard M. Bass, "The Leaderless Group Discussion as a Leadership Evaluation Instrument," *Personnel Psychology,* Winter, 1954, pp. 470–77.

[20] Fox, *op. cit.,* p. 37.

line and staff officers, as "assistants to" and "assistant managers." They tried out, and benefited from, the counsel of older men with differing ideas regarding different types of management. It was originally Barksdale's idea that the worth of a manager could be established only by trying him out in different groups and not permitting him to take his staff with him.[21]

The situational approach has been used for a number of years in the form of the group oral interview in selecting persons for various civil service positions. Usually, the applicants are given some problem or topic to discuss and then asked to seat themselves about a table for their discussion as raters observe from an unobtrusive corner table. As there is normally no discussion leader appointed or other structuring of the discussion, much can be learned about the interpersonal behavior of the various participants.[22]

Perhaps one of the most fruitful opportunities for situational testing in business will be afforded by the further development of the complex business game.[23] The organizational, motivational, and technical realities of an actual business situation may be sufficiently simulated and compressed in time so that a most revealing and highly valid "work sample" test may be provided. Applicants serving as company team members, competing with other teams under pressure and making decisions over a period of several days (which would represent several years of operations), would reveal much about themselves to the selection observers. In addition, as will be discussed later in this chapter, such a "game" will perform the dual function of providing an excellent training device.

The Non-directive Interview. More attention has been directed in recent years to the potentialities of the *non-directive* interview for selection purposes. The rationale of the traditional *directive* interview is that if one wants objectively to know something about the

---

[21] Ernest Dale, *The Great Organizers* (New York: McGraw-Hill Book Co., 1960), p. 66.

[22] British experience with situational testing has been reported on in several issues of the British Journal *Occupational Psychology*, as follows: A. G. Arbous and S. Marcee, "The Contribution of Two Group Discussion Techniques to a Validated Test Battery for the Selection of Administrative Personnel," Vol. XXV, No. 2 (1951); T. M. Higham, "Some Recent Work with Group Selection Procedures," Vol. XXVI, No. 3 (1952); J. D. Handyside and D. C. Duncan, "Four Years Later: A Follow-up of an Experiment in Selecting Supervisors," Vol. XXVIII, No. 1 (1954); B. S. Morris, "Officer Selection in the British Army," Vol. XXIII, No. 4 (1949).

[23] For an excellent discussion of the background to and potentialities of the complex business game and the dynamic business case see Kalman Cohen and Eric Rhenman, "The Role of Management Games in Education and Research," *Management Science*, Vol. 7, No. 2 (January, 1961).

interviewee, ask him and he will objectively supply the information. Unfortunately, in practice this rarely happens. The interviewee, in his zeal to make a favorable impression and get the job, usually is willing to play a game: "Tell me what you want me to be and I will rummage through my experience and find something that will convince you that I am it!" Or, as a result of his *unawareness* of many subconscious values and needs, the interviewee is truly unable to answer objectively. The non-directive approach is more "foolproof" and is more likely to evoke revealing information. It involves using broad questions designed to get the interviewee talking without providing clues as to just what the interviewer is looking for. For example, if we were looking for initiative in an

FIG. 5-9

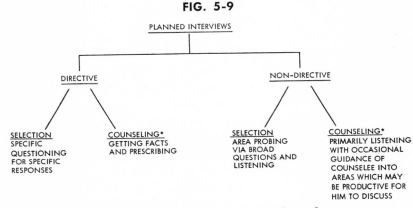

*Directive and non-directive counseling are discussed in chapter 8.

applicant, rather than asking directively, "Do you like a job that requires initiative?" We would ask, "Whom have you enjoyed working under the most? Why?" Through such questions, we would hope to find out whether the applicant *really* prefers a superior-subordinate situation that encourages and requires initiative on the part of the subordinate.[24] Of course, these new procedures, as with the old ones, will be just as useful for selection purposes as they are valid; the same validation procedure must be applied to them as to traditional selection instruments.

Statistical Background Required. Does this mean that personnel directors, as well as managers in general, must be statisticians? No, not really. But it does mean that personnel men should know

---

[24] For a good illustration of this approach in action see Arnold S. Judson, "New Approach to Executive Selection," *Harvard Business Review*, Vol. 32, No. 2 (March–April, 1954). See also the discussion of non-directive theory in Chapter 8, p. 213.

when and how to use such other statistical tools and concepts as the following:

The t-test for tests of significance at various levels of confidence.

Various types of correlation analysis (the meaning of correlation co-efficients and the use of the "z" transformation in establishing fiducial or confidence limits for them).

The use of standard deviation or normalized standard deviation scores in combating unintentional weighting of factors or selection instruments in a battery.

The use of multiple correlation to obtain weights that will optimize the correlation between selection instruments in battery form and performance criteria.

Knowledge of these tools along with understanding of such basic concepts as normal distribution, sampling error, standard error, and reliability should prove adequate for the typical personnel situation. For the higher executive it is important that he realize that these tools exist and that they *must* be intelligently used if any planned progress is to be made in the development of a procurement program. Undoubtedly, one of the chief reasons why so many personnel men do not understand and use these essential tools is that no one has ever demanded it of them!

What Are We Looking for When Selecting Managers?

In the preceding discussion it was pointed out that we would search the literature, the experience of others, and utilize our own creative resources to produce test items, interview factors, or situations to validate. Are there any generalizations that we can make as to what we are looking for that will guide us in our search for valid instruments for the selection of managerial personnel? Yes, research findings suggest some that should prove quite useful.

The Three-Skill Approach. With regard to the possibilities of situational testing via the complex business game or the dynamic business case, the "three-skill approach" for the selection of administrators suggested by Katz may prove most useful. As he points out:

This approach is based not on what good executives *are* (their innate traits and characteristics), but rather on what they *do* (the kinds of skills which they exhibit in carrying out their jobs effectively) . . . a skill implies an ability which can be developed, not necessarily inborn, and which is manifested in performance, not merely in potential. So the principal criterion of skillfulness must be effective action under varying conditions.[25]

---

[25] Robert Katz, "Skills of an Effective Administrator," *Harvard Business Review,* Vol. 33, No. 1 (January–February, 1955).

The three basic developable skills that he suggests are:

Technical Skill—involves specialized knowledge, analytical ability within that speciality, and facility in the use of the tools and techniques of the specific discipline.

Human Skill—ability to work effectively as a group member and to build cooperative effort within the team he leads.

Conceptual Skill—the ability to see the enterprise as a whole; it includes recognizing how the various functions of the organization depend on one another, and how changes in any part effect all the others; and it extends to visualizing the relationship of the individual business to the industry, the community, and the political, social, and economic forces of the nation as a whole.

Presumably, at the foreman level the technical and human skills are most important; at the top administrative level conceptual skill takes top priority. The complex game environment should afford an excellent "testing ground" for sampling these skills. We may find that rather than looking for or attempting to develop these three skills properly proportioned in one individual, it will be more feasible to select and develop a *management team*. Katz comments on this:

This three-skill concept suggests immediate possibilities for the creating of management teams of individuals with complementary skills. For example, one medium-size midwestern distributing organization has as president a man of unusual conceptual ability but extremely limited human skill. However, he has two vice presidents with exceptional human skill. These three men make up an executive committee which has been outstandingly successful, the skills of each member making up for deficiencies of the others. Perhaps the plan of two-man complementary conference leadership proposed by Robert F. Bales, in which the one leader maintains "task leadership" while the other provides "social leadership," might also be an example in point.

The Michigan Bell Study. Alvin Zander and Jay Jackson found that the following characteristics have some validity in predicting the success or failure of service representatives:

It was found that a significantly higher proportion of those with low self-esteem (self-confidence or the value a person places on himself) had departed than of those with high self-esteem. . . .
Ego strength is defined as the ability of a person to control emotional tension and to direct his energy into appropriate channels of action. . . . The higher the ego strength among these participants, the more they produced. . . . It was found that the nature of a person's ego-strength had more effect upon his behavior in groups where persons worked individually than in those in which they were closely interdependent. . . .

When an over-all index of performance is computed for Service Representatives in the Business Office, using all the various criteria upon which SR's contacts are evaluated by management, we find a powerful relationship between over-all performance and an SR's social worth in the Business Office.[26]

General Attributes of Good Supervisors. Generally, from a functional viewpoint, here are some of the things that successful supervisors do but that unsuccessful supervisors do not do, or at least do not do so well. Good supervisors:

1. *Are perceptive to the needs of individuals and are capable of helping them meet their needs.* In addition to being sensitive to human needs, good supervisors are *flexible.* For example, a new, insecure worker may want and need constant and close supervision, whereas the more confident and experienced worker usually welcomes more autonomy and freedom of action in carrying out instructions. In some situations, autocratic leadership intelligently applied is superior to "democratic" leadership. (For further discussion of these points see chapter 8 on supervision.)

2. *Are perceptive of the group as a group and its needs and rationale.* Good supervisors will act in the best interest of the group even if this conflicts with the best interest of an individual in the group.

3. *Gain the confidence of their men.* Good supervisors must be impartial and have personal integrity and the ability to communicate effectively with their men; they must have the ability to gain the confidence of *their* superiors or their attempts to help subordinates with need fulfillment will backfire, that is, it is worse to make recommendations that are consistently ignored than to make none at all![27]

4. *Are "cause oriented" rather than punitive with regard to errors and disciplinary action.* Good supervisors are sufficiently mature and confident to remain objective and avoid personal involvement.

5. *Set high standards of performance in collaboration with their men.* They enforce these impartially for their men and meticulously for themselves.

---

[26] *Summary of Personnel Research at Michigan Bell* (Research Center for Group Dynamics, Institute for Social Research, University of Michigan, January, 1958), pp. 20, 21, 38. Service representatives handle customer complaints and requests for installation of phone equipment.

[27] For further discussion of this point see p. 223.

6. *Have the technical and conceptual ability necessary to plan and organize effectively the work of others in addition to their own work.* They spend most of their time not on "doing" but on "initiation" and "consideration" activities.

7. *Encourage their subordinates to participate.* They encourage their subordinates to participate in decision making and self-development to a degree consistent with subordinate expectations and needs and the situation at hand (e.g., is the group a transient or a stable one?)

8. *Draw upon an identifiable set of human values.* They acknowledge the cooperative spirit, dignity, and importance of the "normal" individual, yet are aware of the influence that negative environmental forces can have upon him and of the hostility and disruptive tendencies of the maladjusted or mentally ill. They see dignity and purpose in their supervisory roles, and they abhor manipulation of others for self-aggrandizement.

It is important to remember, however, that supervision does not take place in limbo. As Zander and Jackson put it:

> In attempting to understand a person's feelings or behavior, it is misleading to ask which is responsible, the person's persistent characteristics, his "personality," or the nature of the situation. Both are always responsible, simply because a person always has certain relatively stable traits which are descriptive of him in any situation, and because a person never behaves in a vacuum: there is always a situation.[28]

We can see, then, that there is no simple answer to the question, "What Are We Looking for?" Best results or higher validities are likely to be achieved if we attempt to assess the candidate in interaction with the environment in which he will work rather than to predict his future chances of success solely on the basis of his past performance or the qualities that he brings to the placement office. Some have suggested that we should select "teams" rather than individuals.[29] Vroom writes: "Relationships can be explained better in terms of the effects of subordinates' attitudes on their perception of their supervisor rather than the effects of supervisors' behavior on the attitudes of their subordinates."[30] In view of these interacting

---

[28] *Op. cit.*, p. 5.

[29] See the reference on page 150 to the idea of creating management teams of individuals with complementary skills. See also Robert Chapman and John Kennedy, "The Background and Implications of the Systems Research Laboratory Studies" (Rand Paper P–740, September 21, 1955).

[30] Victor H. Vroom, "Employee Attitudes," in R. Gray (ed.), *The Expanding Frontiers of Industrial Relations* (Pasadena: California Institute of Technology, 1960).

factors, as was suggested earlier, perhaps one of the most promising avenues for validation for selection purposes in the future will be afforded by the complex business game and the dynamic business case situation.

QUESTIONS

1. What are the organic subfunctions of organizing? Do *you* feel that these really are *organic*, i.e., that *all* of them must be performed whenever we organize for any type of enterprise? Give examples to support your position.

2. What is working capital? What is an expense and revenue forecast? What is it used for? What are the objectives of financial planning?

3. Why did the Ford Motor Company almost close its doors shortly after it was started? What steps might have avoided this difficulty?

4. Do you feel that all the sources of capital listed on page 128 are equally available to a given business? Why or why not?

5. It is often said that an important source of working capital is the depreciation reserve. Is that statement correct or incorrect? Explain.

6. What does the expression "trading on the equity" mean? Would it be wise for all companies to trade on the equity up to the limit of their ability to borrow? Why or why not?

7. Is leasing less expensive than owning? Explain.

8. What relationship is there between the procurement of factors and primary service objectives.

9. What do we mean by "present value"? Is its use preferable to the "pay-back" approach for the purpose of making a choice between two machines? Why or why not?

10. How can we tell whether or not a sales manager is good at "sizing up" applicants for sales positions?

11. What is the selection ratio? How can it be used to assist those responsible for the procurement of personnel?

12. Outline in detail the procedure you would follow to validate a selection interview.

13. How can scores from selection instruments of varying validities be combined so that the validity of the total score will be higher than the validity of any single score contributing to it?

14. Can you think of certain situations that might be developed into useful "situation tests" in industry? Describe them.

15. What advantages may non-directive interviewing have over directive interviewing in selection? Explain why.

16. Review the general attributes of good supervisors starting with page 151. On the basis of *your* experience (working or as a member of various kinds of groups), what do you think of these as to their accuracy and usefulness?

Chapter 6

PLANNING FOR ORGANIZING

Part II: Establishment of Interrelationships among Factors and Development of Factors

The *organic subfunctions of organizing* are: (1) *procurement of factors* (as planned), which was discussed in chapter 5; (2) *establishment of interrelationships among factors* (as planned); and (3) *development of factors* (as planned), which will be discussed in this chapter. First, the *establishment of interrelationships among factors* will be considered.

ASSIGNMENT OF DUTIES

All functions performed in an organization have but one purpose: the implementation of organizational objectives. *Therefore, functions are derivatives of objectives.* Since no one person can perform all the required functions effectively, it is necessary to divide the work into groups of functions or job assignments. In doing this, it is logical to group the functions that draw on similar skills and a relatively uniform level of competence (i.e., it is inefficient and demoralizing to have a highly skilled worker perform an excessive number of unskilled tasks or to perform skilled tasks that do not utilize his special abilities). Actual assignment of duties is greatly facilitated by the use of well-developed *job descriptions* that provide detailed accounting of all the duties of the job. As we go from lower- to higher-level jobs, it is necessary to shift the content of job descriptions from enumeration of detailed specifics to a "functional approach." Figure 6–1 presents a functional job description for a district sales manager.

FIG. 6-1

Sales Department   Job Specification No._____

District Sales Manager*
(Western District)

Basic Function
   Responsible to the general sales manager for distributing and marketing all company products in the Western District (California, Oregon, Washington, Idaho, Nevada, and Arizona).

Scope (figures indicate approximate magnitude)
Business

Potential business	$10,000,000/yr.	Potential accounts	12,500
Business enjoyed	3,000,000/yr.	Accounts served	3,600

Operating Expenditures: $560,000/yr.
Organization: Total personnel, 150

District sales manager	1
Key assistants	2
Branch managers	15
Salesmen	77
Warehousemen	30
Clerks	25

Facilities:

District office	1
Branch offices	15
Branch warehouses	15
Motor vehicles	126

General Objectives and Responsibilities	*Control through*
1. To sell the largest possible volume which can be profitably marketed at the prices prescribed by the home office. Quotas, based on analysis of available business and accounts, to be developed and agreed upon with the general sales manager and incorporated in the annual budget.	Comparison of sales performance against budget.
2. To maintain a high standard of service, with the customers thoroughly satisfied, the company well and favorably known, and no complaints.	Analysis of sales performance and complaints.
3. To maintain all costs and manpower at a minimum as represented by standard costs and reflected in the annual budget.	Comparison of actual against standard costs and budget.
4. To develop and maintain a fully effective organization with fully qualified personnel, thoroughly trained in the requirements of their respective jobs (as specified in the organization manual), and enthusiastically co-operating in their fulfillment.	Analysis of sales performance, rating results, number and caliber of men developed for promotion, turnover, morale, and organization practice.
5. To be active in the promotion of improvements in products, methods and facilities—abreast of the best-known practice.	Number and caliber of improvements suggested or developed.

*Holden, Fish, and Smith, *Top-Management Organizations and Control* (New York: McGraw-Hill Book Co., 1951), pp. 96–97.

FIG. 6-1—*Continued*

Relationships with Other Units of Organization

1. Directly responsible to general sales manager for performance of the above.
2. As member of general sales manager's council, responsible for participation in the discussion, co-ordination, and solution of problems common to all districts.
3. Functionally responsible to sales comptroller for supervision of local clerical activities and for conformance with prescribed accounting practices.
4. Functionally responsible to sales organization and cost-control manager for co-operating in the clarification and co-ordination of organization plans, and for the development and compliance with suitable manpower and cost standards.
5. Functionally responsible to sales personnel manager for co-operating in the general personnel development program.
6. Functionally responsible to general credit manager for conformance with established credit and collection policies.
7. Functionally responsible to sales operating manager for sale and efficient operation and upkeep of warehouses, motor vehicles, and other facilities.

Limits of Authority

1. On expenditures

   All expenditures to be covered by annual or supplementary budget allowances approved by general management. Within this general authorization, further restrictions are imposed as follows:

   New facilities: May approve up to $25; above this, submit to general sales manager (Attn. sales operating manager).

   Maintenance: May approve up to $100; above this, submit to general sales manager (Attn. sales operating manager).

   General sales expense: Limited only by approved budget, except specific items as follows:

   Policy adjustments (returns and allowances): May approve items up to $100; above this limit, submit to general sales manager.

   Disposition of obsolete and excess stock: May approve disposition entailing losses up to $100 per lot; above this limit submit to general sales manager.

   Donations and subscriptions: May approve up to $10; above this submit to general sales manager.

   Purchase contracts, leases, etc.: No authority.

2. On Personnel

   Additions to force: To be anticipated in and limited by budget. Before hiring, clearance to be obtained through sales personnel manager (a) that there are no suitable surplus personnel available in the company, (b) that there are no suitable employees elsewhere who should be considered for promotion to this job, and (c) that prospects for Class F jobs (salesmen, etc.) or higher are properly qualified.

   Promotions and appointments: Full authority to fill jobs below Class F. Class E and F appointments must be approved by the sales personnel committee which will satisfy itself as to the adequacy of the nominee's qualifications and give proper consideration to any markedly better-qualified candidates from elsewhere in the department. Appointments above Class E must be submitted through the general sales manager for approval.

   Dismissals for cause: No limitations.

   Layoff and demotion on account of lack of work: Full authority to lay off personnel below Class F, with under 10 years' service and merit rating below "average." Above this limit, clearance must be obtained from the sales personnel committee to the end that the least-deserving employees in the organization may be released.

3. On compensation

   Wages: Full authority to apply established daily or hourly wage rates for prescribed work. All changes in wage scales must be submitted through general sales manager for approval.

FIG. 6-1—*Continued*

Salaries: Full authority to change salaries for positions below Class F within prescribed policies and bracket limits. All salary changes affecting positions in Class F or higher, and all changes in job classification to be submitted through the general sales manager for approval.

4. On sales prices and contracts
   No authority to determine prices—responsible for maintaining prices established by home office. Has full authority to execute sales contracts in accordance with approved form, terms, and prices.
5. On operating methods and policies
   All changes in branch or district boundaries, plan of organization, or general channels and methods of distribution must be submitted to the general sales manager.
   The district manager is expected, however, to initiate recommendations looking to change of plans or policies wherever, in his considered opinion, this would be to the company's interest.

Note: Classes D, E, F, etc., refer to particular brackets of the company's salary scale. Class D, for example, includes positions with salary evaluation between $250 and $300 per month; Class F, $200 to $225 per month.

Approved (*date*)
    General Sales Manager
    Director of Organization

However adequate the development of job descriptions and the assignment of duties, *continuing review and modification are essential.* An organization is dynamic; it is constantly changing. New jobs are created; old ones are dropped. The process of organizational growth accelerates change through the creation of specialized staff positions and other new jobs. Personnel turnover has an effect, for personalities influence relative emphasis given to duties as well as job content.

DELEGATION OF AUTHORITY AND RESPONSIBILITY

As functions are derivatives of objectives, *responsibilities are primarily derivatives of functions.* Authority is a tool for facilitating the performance of functions, and responsibility is the obligation that should be delegated concomitantly for the proper performance of functions. Actually, as will be discussed further in the next chapter, responsibility exists as a delegated reality only to the extent that *accountability*—the extent to which an individual has discharged his responsibilities—can be ascertained. The primary means for delegating authority and responsibility are appropriately authorized: job descriptions, organizational manuals, organization charts, standard operating procedures or technical orders, and standing orders—and of course, day-by-day oral or written orders and directives.

As Davis points out, important releases of authority and responsibility "should be made or confirmed in writing. Any release should have the approval of the line superior of the individual to whom it is made. Otherwise, there is a violation of the *Principle of Unity of Command.*"[1] It will be recalled that this principle provides that: **An employee should receive orders from one "regular" superior only, unless they result from specific functional authority delegations which are clearly understood by the "regular" superior, the employee, and the functional superior.**

Some have claimed that only authority can be delegated, *not* responsibility. Yet they adhere to the *Principle of Parity of Authority and Responsibility:* **The responsibility of any manager or employee should correspond with his authority.** If responsibility is regarded as an obligation to discharge an accepted assignment of work, then it will vary directly with the amount of authority delegated; thus, *it derives from delegation.* This should be clearly recognized, for there are many instances of individuals enjoying authority without being made accountable for commensurate responsibility; this must be specifically delegated. The opposite is not likely to happen. It is obviously irrational to hold a person responsible for events over which he could not be expected to have any possible control.

Along this same line, the idea that delegation does not relieve the delegator of *any* of *his* authority and responsibility may be misleading. If a bus driver suddenly dropped dead during a run and this caused serious loss of life and property, it is inconceivable that the driver's superior would *fairly* be held responsible if this accident in no way resulted from his imprudence or lack of judgment and foresight. He would be completely exonerated to the extent that it could be shown that he had fully satisfied the organization's physical examination and other requirements and had no reasonable basis for questioning the driver's fitness. In practice, a superior is responsible for subordinate behavior only to the extent that behavior is traceable to his negligence. In this context, there is value in the *Principle of Fixation of Responsibility and Authority:* **The process of delegation relieves the responsible executive of none of his responsibility, authority, or accountability.**

---

[1] R. C. Davis, *The Fundamentals of Top Management* (New York: Harper & Bros., 1951), p. 298.

Activation of a formal communications system, procedures, rules, policies, and other bases for accountability and control is accomplished also through the use of appropriately authorized organization manuals, charts, standard operating procedures, standing orders, day-by-day oral or written orders or directives, and, in addition, policy manuals.

Now let us consider the *development of factors.*

DEVELOPMENT OF SOURCES OF CAPITAL

The development of sources of capital has to do, largely, with gaining the confidence of representatives of sources and supplying them with the information and investment opportunities that meet their particular needs. Confidence is established to a large extent through a record of demonstrated competence, but this is not the whole story. Personal integrity, managerial skill, and a sense of responsibility have induced more than one investor to bet on new enterprises or untried ventures. The ability of a manager to plan well and to present his plans effectively in a "prospectus" for prospective investors or lenders can do much to attract capital.[2] It is equally important to understand the needs of various investor groups and to solicit these groups *selectively* in terms of the kind of opportunity being presented. Often, by trying to match its requirements with a particular type of investor desire, a company can reduce the cost of its capital. One of the most common devices, for example, used by corporations to tap the small investor group is the stock split. By reducing the price per share, the company will often attract many new investors to the market for its stock.

DEVELOPMENT OF PLANT, EQUIPMENT, AND SOURCES OF MATERIEL

Development of Plant and Equipment

As much as we attempt to anticipate the future needs of a company in our original planning of plant and equipment needs, we always seem to leave ample room for the further development of these factors! This is not surprising when we consider the never-ending procession of new problems, new opportunities, and new techniques created by our dynamic economy. More attention is

---

[2] A good prospectus presents the fruits of sound profit and loss, cash, and balance sheet forecasting. It presents a conservative picture of anticipated revenues, expenses, and profits and an explanation of the key assumptions upon which these expectations are based.

being given today to the concept of flexibility in plant design so that the facility may more readily be developed for, or adapted to, changing conditions. Formerly, changes in work processes provided the biggest demand for modifications in plant layout. Now, we have a new area of need: data processing. Advances in computer and business machine technology have made it profitable for many firms to reorganize data flows and clerical processes for the entire organization, not just for the machine room. If anything, the future seems to promise an even faster rate of development in this area! It does not seem too "farfetched" to speculate that the day is coming when plants will be designed with the flexibility of a set of building blocks, and plant development will demand the attention of full-time staff specialists.

The development of equipment and the development of plant are often interdependent, especially with regard to automated production layouts. As for computer and business machine technology, the future seems to promise an even faster rate of development for automation technology. More and more specialized equipment needs are evolving each day and many of these needs are sufficiently unique to a given firm that it cannot reasonably look to others to meet them. Also, we have greater awareness today of the values of "human engineering": the better adaptation of equipment to the physical and psychological needs of humans, both generally and individually. The most publicized work in this area has been done by the designers of specialized maintenance and control equipment for our astronauts. But, behind the headlines, many firms have learned the value of developing their equipment for greater flexibility and compatability with human needs.[3]

Development of Sources of Materiel

The values that we seek and wish to develop most in our suppliers are those of consistent quality in production, dependability of supply, advantageous prices, honesty, and a spirit of accommodation with regard to our needs and any differences that may arise. The likelihood that we will receive preferential treatment from a supplier varies directly with the size and frequency of our orders, no doubt! But it also varies directly with the effort we make to consider and accommodate *his* needs and to keep in mind his "stake"

---

[3] For a good discussion of "human engineering" see Ernest J. McCormick, *Human Engineering* (New York: McGraw-Hill Book Co., 1957). See also Edward Bennett, James Degan, and Joseph Spiegel (eds.), *Human Factors in Technology* (New York: McGraw-Hill Book Co., 1962).

in the relationship. If another supplier offers legitimate advantages that we cannot afford to overlook, we will probably find it worth the effort in the long run to advise our present supplier of the development and give him a reasonable opportunity to match the offer. Many firms have found it productive to provide technical as well as financial assistance to deserving suppliers and to stand by them during periods of stress. Obviously, this is not an argument for blind allegiance to incompetence or obsolescence. Judgment must be exercised. But good human relations *are* important in the company-supplier relationship.[4]

DEVELOPMENT OF PERSONNEL

Our primary problem with rank and file employee training is to determine specific training needs and then to devise effective programs for meeting them. We must determine specific executive training needs, too, but the degree of specificity attainable is usually less. Training is *not,* however, something that management may elect to do or not do. Personnel of any organization must be trained to do what is expected of them. The only choice that management has is to leave training largely to chance and the initiative of the trainee or to make it the product of a carefully planned, effectively organized, formal program. There is little doubt as to which will be the more efficient approach. The informal, *unplanned* program is likely to be much more expensive than the well-planned, formal one, in terms of results obtained!

"Knowledge about" vs. *"Experience with"*

It is useful to identify two primary targets of training activity: (1) Giving trainees "knowledge about" things. (2) Giving trainees "experience with" things. This dichotomy of *theory* and *practice* has utility, for it suggests that what may be good training methodology for imparting "knowledge about" is not necessarily good for developing "experience with." We cannot say, for example, that the *case method* is inherently "better" than the *lecture method.* Both approaches are necessary for an adequate training job to be done.

The successful doctor has been exposed extensively to both "knowledge about" and "experience with" training; he has a firm grasp of both the science and the art of medicine. Through well-

---

[4] See Dean S. Ammer, *Materials Management* (Homewood, Illinois: Richard D. Irwin, Inc., 1962), esp. chaps. 12, 13, and 14.

planned lectures, demonstrations, and text materials, he learned certain terminology and basic concepts. He got the "feel of the scalpel" and the "feel for diagnosis" through *doing*, by being effectively "coached" through numerous case analyses. So it must be with the successful, modern manager! Unfortunately, there is still widespread belief that the three types of management skill—technical, human relations, and conceptual—can be taught exclusively via the text-lecture-demonstration-discussion approach. Though this approach is excellent for imparting the *knowledge* required for developing these skills, it can never substitute for the *experiential* portion of a training program, upon which the actual development of the skills is based.

Job Instruction Training

This basic rationale was incorporated in the now famous Job Instruction Training Program of the Training within Industry Program of World War II. It was simple but quite effective in assuring that the trainee would get both "knowledge about" and "experience with." The foreman was told that he should follow the basic steps below in training his men: [5]

a. Step 1. . . Prepare the worker.
   Put him at ease. ("relax and let me worry about your *learning*. That's *my* responsibility.")
   State the job. (I'm going to teach you how to . . . .")
   Find out what he already knows about the job. (Insist on an answer. If he knows, try him out, make sure. "We do it somewhat differently here. Let me teach you our way.")
   Get him interested in learning job. (Show relation of this job to the whole, the *importance* of it.)
   Place in correct position. (Not so that he will see it backward as in a mirror.)
b. Step 2. . . Present the operation.
   Tell, show, illustrate and question carefully and patiently.
   Stress key points.* (Both positively and negatively.)

* A key point is defined as anything in a step that might . . .
. . . make or break the job.
. . . injure the worker.
. . . make the work easier to do—(including "knacks," "tricks," special timing, bit of special information.)[6]

---

[5] Taken from Ignatius Barnard, "Re-Birth of Job Instruction," *Supervision* magazine, February, March, and April, 1954. See also "Training Manpower," *Fortune*, April, 1951.
[6] The non-profit Training Within Industry Foundation (382 Springfield Avenue, Summit, New Jersey) has continued and further developed the work of the wartime TWI program.

Instruct clearly and completely . . . taking up one point at a time, but no more than he can master. (Repeat information as often as necessary. Say: "Shall I do it again" until he is satisfied.)

c. Step 3. . . Try out performance.

Test him by having him perform job. (Tell him not to bother explaining the key points yet. Correct errors instantly; compliment him on correct part of performance.)

After he is able to perform the operation correctly, have him tell and show you; have him explain key points. (Positively and negatively as you did; correct errors or omissions instantly.)

Ask questions and correct errors.

Continue until you know HE knows.

d. Step 4. . . Follow up.

Put him on his own. Check frequently. (Urge him to work for quality before speed. Above all return *soon*.)

Designate to whom he goes for help. (*You* if at all possible.)

Encourage questions.

Get him to look for key points as he progresses.

Taper off extra coaching and close follow-up.

Human Relations Training

In human relations training we are primarily concerned with *altering* behavior. We do not want human relations trainees merely to be aware of basic concepts or simply to talk about them; we want to make these concepts part of them, tools that they will actually use in coping with day-to-day situations. This is no easy task, for fortunately, human behavior is not so susceptible to influence that it may be remolded at will by either the benevolent or the capricious efforts of others. If this were not true, it would be impossible for each of us to maintain an essentially stable identity through time; we would be schizophrenic indeed! At best, we can only try to create the type of climate that will induce the trainee to re-examine his behavior and then encourage him to explore and experiment with alternative modes that will be more productive for him. And we can structure the "compulsions" of his work environment to reinforce and sustain him in his new behavior.

Irrational Behavior. This approach to human relations training is most frustrating and challenging for the trainer; it is easy to understand why many of us yield to the "easy out" and the "illusion of progress" we obtain with the lecture method. We even have a good rationale to go with this retreat! It goes something like this: "The reason that people do not behave the way they should is simply that they do not know the right way. Tell them what is right and the problem is solved." How wonderful, if this were true! But, unfortunately, we are not this *rational* in our conduct. Much that we do is influenced by needs, prejudices, values, and role expectations of which we are often only dimly aware. As one cynic has put it: the purpose of an education is to obtain better reasons for doing what we were going to do anyway! If we simply tell a group of supervisors *how* good supervisors behave and coach them until they can repeat this information on a test, this provides no assurance that they will *behave differently* back on the job. This would be like saying that a poor student will become a scholar when he can describe how a scholar behaves. As was pointed out above, the best bet is to find a way to induce the trainee to re-examine his own behavior and to gain insight into it, at the same time structuring the compulsions of his work environment to encourage the type of behavior desired. What are the most effective training techniques for doing this, for giving trainees "experience with" good human relations practices? We will now consider a number of the more productive and promising possibilities.

The Case Method.   The case method has been used in legal and medical education for many years; its serious use for business education was pioneered by the Harvard Graduate School of Business Administration in the early 1920's.[7] It is most effective when used with a non-directive approach, that it, the trainer draws heavily upon the ideas of the trainees and tends to guide them through provocative questioning rather than by simply prescribing solutions. Whenever possible, the trainer uses case material that is closely related to the problems and environment that the trainees will work in. This can be done by obtaining the actual case material from the trainees themselves. When appropriate, in the discussion of a particular case, *role playing* may be used to "test" a proposed course of action or to define the problem better—for example: How would a person react in this situation? [8]

Case Method with "Feedback."   The *dynamic business case* and the *complex business game* offer the advantages of the case method coupled with the important value of "feedback." Trainees can find out "what happened," that is, how well their proposals worked. In effect, trainees deal with a "series" of cases. Last month's decisions and their outcomes provide the current case for this month's deci-

---

[7] See Kenneth R. Andrews (ed.), *The Case Method of Teaching Human Relations and Administration* (Cambridge, Massachusetts: Harvard University Press, 1953).

[8] For an excellent "role-playing dynamic case study" see J. M. Jackson, G. E. Jensen, and F. C. Mann, "Building a Hospital Organization for Training Administrators," *Hospital Management*, September, 1956.

sions, and so it goes through simulation of many *years* of monthly (or quarterly) analysis. At Carnegie Tech, students play a complex game that does much to simulate the problem of managing a manufacturing company in the detergent industry. They may have to justify their decisions periodically to a faculty board of directors or defend their financial statements before an inquiring CPA. If team members need a loan, they may be required to prepare a prospectus and present it in person to an experienced banker, or they may have to negotiate wages with a veteran union negotiator! [9]

"On the Job" Supervisory Training

Role of Delegation. But what about the day-in and day-out development of the supervisor or executive? Can we do more of value than merely expose him to the work environment? There is much evidence that we can and that the effort is most worthwhile! Ernest Weir, founder of the National Steel Corporation, thought little of formal training or appraisal activity, but he was "sold" on the value of *real* delegation of authority and responsibility coupled with rigorous accountability as a means of developing executive talent. As Ernest Dale points out:

... He introduced some ideas that organization planners in other companies began to approach cautiously only in very recent times; for example, he delegated both responsibility and authority as far down the line as possible, with control exercised through profit and loss statements rather than through rules regarding set ways of doing things. ...

The "middle manager," who was managing a unit just about large enough for one man to comprehend all the details, was charged with the basic decision making and stood or fell on results.

Weir went much further in this than do many companies that believe they have "decentralized decision making" today. A superintendent of a nearby company once commented:

"I have never been able to understand why we do not have financial authority commensurate with responsibility. I have friends at a competitive company (Weirton) and I know that when they write a good order, they get what they need. ... A general superintendent (in our company) can make a mistake that will cost the company half a million dollars, yet he cannot authorize the purchase of a $5,000 tractor." [10]

---

[9] See Kalman Cohen and Eric Rhenman, "The Role of Management Games in Education and Research," *Management Science,* Vol. 7, No. 2 (January, 1961). Another interesting example of "situational training" is provided by the "in-basket exercise." See Lewis B. Ward, "The Use of Simulation on Business Problems," *Management Record,* June, 1960.

[10] Ernest Dale, *The Great Organizers* (New York: McGraw-Hill Book Co., 1960), p. 133.

The values of extensive delegation for developing executive talent have been dramatized by the findings of the now famous Sears, Roebuck and Company studies.[11] The Sears "flat" stores (broader span of control with fewer levels of management) developed leaders significantly better than the "pyramidal" stores (tighter span of control with more levels of management) for the same size of organization. The use of delegation as a training device can be enhanced further when combined with a carefully planned and controlled understudy program. Cooperation with the understudy idea on the part of line managers can be encouraged by joint planning as well as the understanding that a man will not be eligible for promotion until he has developed some replacement talent.

The Understudy. John Pfiffner points out four significant ways in which the superior may develop his understudy after establishing a good personal relationship with him:

In the first the principal asks the understudy's opinion on particular matters. The hazard attached to this approach consists in not accepting his suggestions. If there is consistent rejection of his ideas, he may feel frustrated, and the training value of asking for them will be minimized. The purpose is to build his confidence and teach him how to think and analyze. Thus, rejection of his ideas should be accomplished obliquely, with explanations and counter proposals rather than through head-on rejection.[12]

The second method gives him a chance to lead people. The principal should instruct him in how to handle relationships with others. The manner in which he handles these relationships should be observed and followed by discussions in which his strength and weaknesses are brought out.

The third approach to the development of understudies consists of impressing upon them the importance of fact-finding. The understudy can become a sort of staff assistant to the principal. When problems come up, he should be expected to gather all of the available data pertaining thereto and then come up with an interpretation. In this way he will be impressed with the importance of facts in arriving at decisions. This is a good training approach because it throws one right into the heart of the materials of which decisions are made without risking the hazards of immaturity. The understudy jumps right into the problems of management without immediately taking the responsibility for decision.

---

[11] For discussion of the findings see J. C. Worthy, "Organizational Structure and Employee Morale," *American Sociological Review,* Vol. 15 (April, 1950).

[12] An interesting and successful training experience that encourages problem solving as well as effective interaction with others is provided by the use of "multiple management," whereby "trainee boards of directors" are formed. For a complete description see Charles P. McCormick, *The Power of People* (New York: Harper & Bros., 1949).

The fourth recommended method gives the understudy the opportunity for contact with those above him in the hierarchy. This not only gives him experience in meeting and dealing with high status people, but also serves as a tool for evaluation. Those whom he meets on higher echelons will inevitably report back any deficiencies in his conduct and demeanor. The device of "sending him upstairs" serves to build confidence and helps him to acquire poise and assurance.[13]

The "Assistant to." Use of the "assistant to" position can greatly facilitate use of all but the second method for developing understudies. In addition to its training value, the "assistant to" position provides for effective "situational testing" on the job and more effective placement of executive personnel. As Ernest Dale points out:

... The "assistant to" has no power to act on his own. Instead he furnishes his chief with information and recommendations which the latter is free to use as he pleases.

The position of the "assistant to" may have the advantage of introducing a new function "under the wing" of the boss. Thus the incumbent of the new function is given a chance to show what he can do. If put on his own, he might fail because of opposition from those in the established functions, particularly if the other top management men felt the new function legitimately belonged to them. . . . Furthermore an "assistant to" the president can learn a great deal more about the company, and more quickly, than if he were on his own. Once in possession of company know-how and accepted as a personality, he can be invested with personal responsibility.[14]

The Trainee Committee. Stanley Seashore, of the Michigan Institute for Social Research, reports that the International Harvester Company

... has had considerable success with a series of committees, composed of candidates for training, that were created to help in defining objectives and needs. These committees have been constituted in various ways to represent different levels of the organization, and different fields of specialization within the company. Useful and ingenious ideas have come from the committees. Furthermore, this procedure has made many people aware of the complexity of training problems.

---

[13] John Pfiffner, *The Supervision of Personnel* (2d ed.; Englewood Cliffs, New Jersey: Prentice-Hall, Inc., 1958), pp. 433, 434.

[14] Ernest Dale, *Planning and Developing the Company Organization Structure,* American Management Association Research Report No. 20, New York, 1959, p. 83. For an excellent discussion of the pros and cons of the "assistant to" position see pp. 83 ff. See also Thomas L. Whisler, "The Assistant-to: The Man in Motley," *Journal of Business* (University of Chicago), Vol. XXIX, No. 4 (October, 1956), pp. 274–79, and Whisler, "The 'Assistant-to' in Four Administrative Settings," *Administrative Quarterly,* Vol. V, No. 2 (September, 1960), pp. 181–216.

The training methods of the company reflect a growing conviction, derived from experience, that one of the principal beneficiaries of a human relations training activity is the trainer himself. Formerly the company relied to a large extent on outsiders to provide training in human relations; they now mainly depend on people from within the organization, and purposely plan to make many different line and staff people engage in some training activity. The idea that an executive should be taken from his regular work for special service in developing and conducting training for others is consistent with research findings and with the company's appraisal of training needs.[15]

Organizational Climate. The general organizational climate must be right; the trainee must receive the kind of behavior from his boss that he is expected to practice with his subordinates. Good human relations must start at the top of an organization and permeate downward, *not* at the foreman level and permeate upward! In fact, with the wrong climate it is quite possible for the supervisor to be less effective *after* human relations training than before it; the training merely confirms his misgivings about the inadequacies of his boss's approach and undermines his confidence in company management. At best, any positive effect that the training may have on his behavior will tend to "wear off" with the passage of time if it is not supported and encouraged by his work environment.[16] Not only does the behavior of an individual supervisor tend to mirror that of his boss, but all supervisors in an organization are significantly influenced by the distinctive "climate" or pattern of leadership that is unique to the organization. In view of this, it may be much better to attempt to train groups of supervisors as organizational units rather than as individuals when basic changes in leadership climate are sought.

The kind of behavior that we wish to train our supervisors for was suggested in the preceding chapter. It will be discussed further in chapter 8, "Planning for Control: Supervision." Here we are primarily concerned with effective training methodology.

---

[15] "The Training of Leaders for Effective Human Relations," *Some Applications of Behavioral Research* (UNESCO 19 Ave. Kleber, Paris 16e, 1957), pp. 11, 12, 16. Somewhat allied to this type of participation is the approach to merit rating that requires the subordinate to develop his *own* program. See chap. 8, p. 205.

[16] For research findings that support these observations and stress the importance of conceptual as well as human relations training for supervisors see Edwin A. Fleishman, Edwin F. Harris, and Harold E. Burtt, *Leadership and Supervision in Industry* (Monograph No. 33, Bureau of Educational Research, Ohio State University) (Columbus, 1955).

Evaluation of Training Activity

The *evaluation* of training permits us to know "where we've been, where we are, and where we hope to go." A training program is successful when it achieves what it is supposed to achieve. If it is the purpose of a particular program to impart certain knowledge or to alter behavior so that the trainee will be more effective on the job, it is essential that we obtain adequate post-training statistical evidence to show the *extent* and *persistence* of change that may be attributed to the training. This is a fundamental requirement for the effective planning and control of training activities. Research has uncovered several cases wherein foremen have been *less* successful after training than they were before, and in comparison with their colleagues who did not receive the training![17] In chapter 14 the problem of controlling the development of personnel will be discussed, and some specific means for evaluating training activity will be examined.

QUESTIONS

1. What are the three *organic subfunctions of organizing?* Does your definition include planning for the performance of these? Should it? Explain.

2. The statement "Functions are derivatives of objectives" is made at the beginning of this chapter. Is this true? Explain. What is your reaction to the statement "Responsibilities are primarily derivatives of functions"?

3. At least six media for delegating authority and responsibility were discussed. List and explain four of these.

4. Distinguish between the *Principle of Unity of Command* and the *Principle of Parity of Authority and Responsibility.*

5. The *Principle of Fixation of Responsibility and Authority* provides that "The process of delegation relieves the responsible executive of none of his responsibility, authority, or accountability." Does this mean that a superior is responsible for *everything* that happens "under his command" *regardless* of the circumstances involved? Discuss.

6. What is the basic rationale or approach for developing sources of capital? Explain.

7. What is meant by the term "human engineering"? Can you think of any examples in everyday life that reflect its application?

---

[17] Harold E. Burtt, "Why Most Supervisor Training," *Management Methods,* January, 1958, p. 28.

8. Is it easier to determine the training needs of rank and file employees than of executives? Why? What is meant by the statement that "training is *not* something that management may elect to do or not do?" Explain. Is formal training usually more or less expensive than informal training? Why?

9. Does learning to drive a car require "knowledge about" as well as "experience with"? Explain. Are both these incorporated in job instruction training? Explain how.

10. "The chief reason that some foremen are not good leaders is that they do not know how good leaders should behave." What is your opinion as to the accuracy of this statement?

11. What is a "dynamic business case" as compared with a "regular" business case? Explain.

12. Discuss the advantages and disadvantages of each of the four methods for developing understudies presented on pages 166–67. Are any of these methods applicable to the training of an "assistant to"? Explain.

Chapter 7

PLANNING FOR CONTROL

Control has to do with making events conform to plans. It is the *organic management function* of coordinating the action of others according to plans so that *primary, collateral,* and *secondary objectives* will be achieved. This and the following chapter will discuss some of the developments that have influenced current thinking about and practice of control, will examine the *organic sub-functions of control,* and will discuss standards, without which control is impossible.

ORIGIN OF THE MODERN CONTROL CONCEPT

Frederick Taylor was concerned at the turn of the century by the widespread failure of managers to separate, at least conceptually, the *organic management function* of planning from that of control, or "planning" from "doing," as he put it. Since his time, we have introduced the further refinement of dividing the "doing" function into the two separate *organic management functions* of *organizing* and *controlling.*[1] It will be recalled from chapter 5 that organizing is that part of the "doing" which is concerned with "getting ready" to create and distribute the organization's salable utilities (paving the way for the performance of the organization's *organic business functions*). Organizing has to do with the actual procurement of planned capital, personnel, and physical factor requirements and with the maintenance and development of these factors.

---

[1] For an interesting discussion of the *evolution* of scientific management see John F. Mee, "Management Thought: Its Genesis and Historical Development," in Fremont A. Shull, Jr., and André L. Delbecq (eds.), *Selected Readings in Management* (Homewood, Illinois: Richard D. Irwin, Inc., 1962), pp. 29–37.

Taylor and his colleagues recognized the need for experimentation and study so that they could better define standards of performance and develop more effective means for controlling performance. To facilitate the work of defining work standards, they gave attention to the standardization of tools and movements of workers for each class of work. They set the stage for more effective control through the development of the task idea in compensation with bonuses for above-average performance, standard instruction cards, routing and scheduling procedures, cost accounting techniques, and various types of periodic reports. Also, they recognized the value of the *Exception Principle* in control. It has been rephrased for this book as follows: **To conserve the time and ability of executives, each decision should be made by the lowest manager in the organization who has the necessary competence, authority, and prestige. Also, only significant deviations of actual from planned performance should be brought to the attention of the responsible executive.**

Of course, this principle applies to the control of planning activity as well as to control of performance. It is based on the sound premise that control cannot be feasible and economical unless it is *selective*. For example, we are not only interested in limiting our attention to *significant* deviations; these should be obtained *only* for *key* factors and operations. *Key* factors and operations are those which are especially relevant to the attainment of objectives, *those which, if properly controlled, are likely to assure adequate control of many related subsidiary factors and operations.* In chapter 11, "Organization for Control," some of the actual key factors around which control systems may be developed will be discussed. Another important aspect having to do with the economics of control is the problem of "overcontrol." This will be discussed in chapter 15, "Control of Control."

Actually, Taylor and other pioneers perceived the basic character and many of the demands of control, but they did not have the "tools" and, consequently, the incentive to push the analysis and refinement of control activity beyond a certain point. In their day the *time*, alone, required to process data presented a very real limitation. In addition, a compromise had to be struck between the *cost* of processing data and the value of supplying data to various data customers in the organization in a form most suitable to their needs. Of course, it is true that data users did not push too hard for such accommodation, since they realized that the time requirements of data processing would *prevent* the delivery of reports in time to significantly affect *current* planning and control. As a result, traditional modes of processing data that effectively served the needs of only a minority of managers became entrenched, and other data users in the organization were expected to adjust to the "standard" reports as best they could.

But now a significant revolution in data processing methods and concepts has been brought about by the advent of the computer! Time and cost limitations have been whittled down to size, and the ideal of adapting the mode of data processing to the unique planning and control needs of data users is truly feasible for the first time. In chapter 9 the concept and implementation of "integrated data processing" will be discussed, and new data processing functions that accounting departments should undertake will be examined. There is a definite need for accounting personnel to "break with the past" so that they may more readily recognize and serve the diverse needs of various data customers in the organization.

We now have a better grasp than the pioneers had of the *organic subfunctions* involved in control. The nature of these will be discussed in this and the next chapter and appropriate organization for their performance will be considered in chapter 11. Finally, new techniques such as PERT have made an important contribution to modern control practice. The nature of PERT and its contribution to planning were discussed in chapter 2. Later in this chapter important ways in which it facilitates the performance of certain of the *organic subfunctions of control* will be considered.

As more sophisticated computer programs are developed and the sensing capacity of computers is broadened (so that they may react to a larger range of stimuli), we can expect to see a greater application of the "servomechanism" or "automatic feedback system" approach to control in business.[2] In simple form, such a system provides for the measurement of deviation from planned performance and the initiation of corrective action to eliminate the deviation. An everyday example of this is provided by the household

---

[2] "Feedback" in electronics refers to the process of feeding back part of the output to the input at the proper time to alter future output. For our purposes, "feedback" has to do with the process of eliminating future deviation from planned action on the basis of knowledge of current deviation. "Feedback information" permits us to compare where we are with where we wish to be and thus be prepared to take corrective action to get back on course or engage in new planning.

thermostat-furnace system. The thermostat detects deviations (cooling of the house) and initiates corrective action (turns on the furnace) to eliminate the deviation (warm the house back to the desired temperature level). Of course, for many undertakings, when certain deviations occur, it is impossible to get back on course or to "get back" without a change in plans, and corrective action may entail the replanning of objectives and/or the means for achieving them. In the areas of automated production and missile guidance, the "automatic feedback system" approach to control has *already* been refined to the point that certain *replanning activities* in addition to amazingly accurate and fast *deviation correction activities* are being handily performed by computers. We may not have to wait very many years before we shall be able to assign additional control functions to non-human control systems that will be applicable to a much broader range of activities!

THE ORGANIC SUBFUNCTIONS OF CONTROL [3]

There are six *organic subfunctions* of *control*. These are programming, scheduling, dispatching, supervision, comparison, and corrective action. It is assumed that *all* these subfunctions must be performed wherever a manager engages in the *organic management function* of *controlling* (the work of others), whatever the setting or type of organization. Each of the *organic subfunctions* will be discussed in turn below, with the exception of supervision, which will be considered at length in the next chapter.

Programming

Programming is concerned with the *routine* collection, sorting, and assignment of data: the plans data, organization data, and control data that are required for the controlled execution of plans. It is a preparatory function. In involves the collection of information—often from various sources in the organization—that the user (executor of the plan) will require, and the recasting of the information (on a pre-planned basis) into the form most useful for the user. Programming should not be confused with the *organic management function* of *planning* (the work of others). As used here, the term "programming" does not imply the *creative effort* that is associated

---

[3] The author has drawn heavily upon the work of R. C. Davis in developing these *organic subfunctions of control*. See his *Fundamentals of Top Management* (New York: Harper & Bros., 1951).

with planning. Planning involves problem solving and decision making. Problem solving has to do with the search for relevant alternatives and decision making with selection from alternatives. Programming is concerned with the *routine* collection, sorting, and assignment of data *as planned*. It may involve decision making (on a preplanned basis), but it does not involve problem solving.

Scheduling

Scheduling has to do with the specification of *dates* and times based on planned requirements for the performance of functions and the implementation of plans. *Planned time requirements and completion dates are translated into actual calendar times and dates.* This is a simple but essential control function that provides specific calendar time targets for the completion of plans and their subplans.

Dispatching

Dispatching is concerned with the *release of authority:* authority regarding *how* to act as well as *when* to act. The mechanics of delegating authority are supplied by the dispatching function. The release of approved technical orders, standard operating procedures, policies, standard practice directives, specifications, and other such instruments indicates to organization members *how* they are authorized to act when the time comes for them to act. Authority as to *when* to act is released via the dispatching function in the form of written or verbal operating orders and standing orders. A schedule, for example, has the force of an operating order when it is approved by proper line authority.

Comparison

Comparison is the *organic subfunction of control,* which has to do with evaluation of completed action to see how well it has conformed to plans or other standards. When an inspector measures a manufactured part to see whether it conforms to specification, he performs the comparison function; when a supervisor checks the actual output of his department against the production schedule or compares the actual development of a trainee with his planned development, he performs the comparison function. As discussed earlier in the chapter, faster feedback of performance data is made possible by the computer. This greatly facilitates control by reducing the time span between actual performance and comparison for many phases of operations. When comparison reveals a discrepancy between actual and planned performance, the stage is set for activation of the last *organic subfunction of control:* corrective action.

Corrective Action

Corrective action is concerned with getting things back on course or, if that is not feasible, changing the course or schedule through new planning. Often it leads to new planning, also, for the purpose of making organizational changes to assure that the same deviation from plans will not recur in the future. Not only must we have *standards,* and *comparison* of performance against them to assure effective corrective action, but also we must have an adequate means for establishing accountability (for *affixing responsibility* for action). Objectives, along with legitimate operating and technical orders, approved plans, policies, procedures, rules, and technical specifications, are all examples of *standards.* A standard is a criterion with which an object or activity may be evaluated. Corrective action is brought into play when we have *deviations* from planned performance or conditions. Obviously, deviation can occur only when we can compare actual performance or conditions with some criterion or standard of desired performance or condition. If we cannot establish *accountability*—the extent to which people have discharged their responsibilities—we will be greatly hampered in our ability to take effective corrective action. For corrective action often will require a modification of behavior, and clearly we must know *on the part of whom.*

Corrective action often involves routine decision making (selection from well-defined alternatives on a preplanned basis). For example, a foreman is faced with a common type of machine breakdown. He is well acquainted with the several relevant alternatives available to him and with their "costs." He also is equipped with a set of criteria for deciding which alternative is most appropriate, given the circumstances of that moment. Of course, there are times when human or machine problems arise for which there are no well-defined solution procedures. When this occurs, then corrective action entails new planning: creative problem solving and decision-making. Or in other instances, corrective action may involve merely the routine adjustment of a cutting blade or the replacement of a fuse!

Chapter 11, "Organization for Control," will discuss the organizational setting in which the six *organic subfunctions of control—*

programming, scheduling, dispatching, supervision, comparison, and corrective action—should be performed.

STANDARDS

As was pointed out earlier, standards are the criteria with which we evaluate past or present performance and condition. Objectives and the policies, plans, procedures, etc, for carrying them out are all standards. Obviously, a business cannot function without them, and quality of results will be influenced significantly by the *thoroughness* and *manner* with which they are formulated. Careful analysis of operating conditions, in the areas to which the standards will apply, will help make them more realistic. Opportunity for those affected to participate in the *formulation* of standards will do much to gain their acceptance and to encourage compliance with them. Some standards deserve additional discussion or explanation.

Ethical Standards

In the past there has been a tendency to regard business ethical conduct as a personal, individual matter involving the corporation only to the extent that, in particular instances, the firm reflected the personal code of a strong leader. Appeals for better ethics in business were directed at individual businessmen rather than at the "impersonal" corporation. The public tended to expect—and to settle for—behavior "within the law" from the corporation as an entity.

Today, the large corporation has become so interwoven in the fabric of our society, with so much influence for good or bad, that a more perceptive public has begun to think in terms of the *social responsibilities of the corporation as well as of the primary individuals managing it*. A factor contributing to this trend is the increasing difficulty of associating the large, widely held corporation with any owner or group of owners. In certain respects, we have come to look upon the modern corporation as a quasi-public institution and have become increasingly concerned with the ethical integrity of the organization itself. It is more important than ever before that managers distinguish *organizational ethics* from *individual ethics* in the same way that organizational goals should be distinguished from the personal goals of those associated with the organization. Eells and Walton observe that:

As government and unions circumscribe its vast entrepreneurial activities by making demands on its wealth and setting limits to the powers of that wealth, the management of an economic organization must move out of the ethical vacuum of pure economic theory and into the main stream of human existence. For the rise of large business organizations, and the need for men to manage them, has inevitably led to a demand that the holders of economic power employ it for other than exclusively economic ends.[4]

Corporate management's failure to give adequate attention to the growing demand for corporate ethical standards was dramatized by the "scandals" of 1961. There was the electrical equipment price-fixing conspiracy involving such respected companies as Westinghouse and General Electric. A major conflict-of-interest exposé embarrassed the Chrysler Corporation, and evidence turned up by congressional investigation of the pharmaceutical industry's pricing practices did not tend to reassure the public. Testimony from the electrical equipment price-fixing hearings is quite revealing.

Time reported that some of the witnesses believed that they had to go along with clandestine price fixing if they wanted to get ahead in their company. Others thought that this was necessary, despite proclaimed company policy against such a practice, just to hold their jobs. A former departmental sales manager who went over the head of his immediate superior to complain was informed that it was necessary to talk prices with competition. He did; a fellow executive who did not was transferred to a lesser job.

A departmental manager of another company stated at the hearings that he was aware of the price-fixing activities of his immediate superior and subordinate. He said that he knew these actions were illegal but did nothing because he felt caught in the middle. A fellow executive of the same company testified that part of his new job as department sales manager was to get acquainted with executives from other companies at price-setting sessions in hotels.[5]

Obviously, businessmen have the obligation to exercise privileges of private property in such a way as to serve society. Otherwise, these privileges will be seriously curtailed or withdrawn altogether. The awareness of this obligation on the part of many business lead-

---

[4] Richard Eells and Clarence Walton, *Conceptual Foundations of Business* (Homewood, Illinois: Richard D. Irwin, Inc., 1961), p. 429. Note: There are a number of provocative sections in this book that deal with the ethical and social responsibilities of business.

[5] *Time,* April 28, 1961, p. 92. See Richard Smith's two part article, "The Incredible Electrical Conspiracy," *Fortune,* April, May, 1961.

ers is one of the significant reasons for their growing interest in the development and enforcement of business ethics in America today. Henry Ford II, chairman of the board of Ford Motor Company, is one business leader who is well aware of these implications. In a talk before a Junior Chamber of Commerce, he said:

There is really only one thing for top executives to do at such a time as this. That is to forget the alibis and the explanations and have the fortitude—the plain guts—to stand up and say: "This is our failure. We are chagrined and sorry. It will not happen again." . . . Too fast and too close together for comfort we have had a series of falls from grace involving some of our oldest and most respected business firms. . . . I think that what has happened has very grave implications for all of us in business.[6]

Ford pointed out that if companies themselves fail to keep their own houses in order,

. . . the house-cleaning job certainly will be put in less friendly hands. . . . I suggest we look not only at the obvious areas of danger, where we may run afoul of the law, but also at those borderline areas of corporate action which might have unfortunate social consequences for our fellow man.[7]

He went on to point out that companies and industries must establish formal standards of ethical practice in addition to effective means for self-policing. But he added: "I recognize that no amount of law, no amount of written codes of ethics or pious promises will take the place of a rigorous and unshakeable integrity in the total conduct and in the ideals of industrial management." [8]

It seems appropriate to repeat here several observations that were made in chapter 2. There are no exact permanent standards with which the ethical factors in planning may be measured. Each age has its own convictions as to what is desirable business activity and what are the proper role and reward for businessmen. We have come a long way in the development of our understanding of economics since the time when the charging of interest was regarded as a completely unjustified and evil activity. Yet it would be folly, indeed, to assume that future generations will or should maintain precisely the viewpoint that we have. However, this is *not* to imply that reasonable ethical standards for an organization are unattainable. For there is a long-term trend in business values and goals that has unfolded and is unfolding as the profession of management

---

[6] *Time*, April 28, 1961, pp. 90, 91.

[7] *Ibid.*, p. 90.

[8] Reported in *Gainesville* (Florida) *Daily Sun*, June 25, 1961, p. 32.

develops. Also, there are certain long-standing ethical imperatives associated with our economic system and our system of government. The business planner will be able to fashion ethical standards for his organization when he has developed a philosophy of management based on an extensive study of the history of business, our economic system, and our form of constitutionalism!

It is interesting that Secretary of Commerce Hodges established the Business Ethics Advisory Council in 1961, to recommend a code of principles to serve as a guide to ethical business conduct. The council presented its first report to President Kennedy during a White House meeting on January 16, 1962. The following excerpts are taken from this report, which is entitled: "A Statement on Business Ethics and a Call for Action." [9]

The ethical standards of American businessmen, like those of the American people, are founded upon our religious heritage and our traditions of social, political, and economic freedom....Immutable, well-understood guides to performance generally are effective, but new ethical problems are created constantly by the ever-increasing complexity of society. In business, as in every other activity, therefore, men must continually seek to identify new and appropriate standards.

... Business enterprises, large and small, have relationships in many directions—with stockholders and other owners, employees, customers, suppliers, government, and the public in general. The traditional emphasis on freedom, competition, and progress in our economic system often brings the varying interests of these groups into conflict, so that many difficult and complex ethical problems can arise in any enterprise. While all relationships of an enterprise to these groups are regulated in some degree by law, compliance with law can only provide a minimum standard of conduct. Beyond legal obligations, the policies and actions of businessmen must be based upon a regard for the proper claims of all affected groups.

Moreover, in many business situations the decision that must be made is not the simple choice between absolute right and absolute wrong. The decisions of business frequently must be made in highly complex and ever-changing circumstances, and at times involve either adhering to earlier standards or developing new ones. Such decisions affect profoundly not only the business enterprise, but our society as a whole. Indeed, the responsible position of American business—both large and small—obligates each participant to lead rather than follow.

... In the final analysis, however, the primary moral duty to establish high ethical standards and adequate procedures for their enforcement in each enterprise must rest with its policymaking body—its board of directors and its top management.

---

[9] Booklet published by the U.S. Department of Commerce, Washington 25, D.C.

... We urge all enterprises, business groups, and associations to accept responsibility—each for itself and in its own most appropriate way—to develop methods and programs for encouraging and sustaining these efforts on a continuous basis.

To assist each organization in developing and applying to its activities a meaningful set of ethical standards, the council formulated "Some Questions for Businessmen" (these are presented in Appendix II on page 420). The Council regards the publication of its report as only a starting point; it plans to undertake a long-range program of encouragement and assistance to help business improve ethical performance. As the Council indicated to the President:

This program will involve working with key businessmen and association leaders in industry to encourage adoption, updating, and activation of company and industry codes. Schools of business administration and the major religious groups will be asked to increase awareness and study of problems of business ethics by businessmen, students, and the public at large. In addition, foundations and universities will be asked to sponsor studies in depth of various ethical problems of business. The aid of government agencies will also be sought in some of these efforts.[10]

Standard Costs

Standard costs are *normative* for a given firm: costs that *should* have been incurred in the performance of any functions or phase of operations. A standard cost represents the attainable ideal for a given set of circumstances, it does not represent the ultimate in efficiency that could be achieved, given the most modern plant and equipment, etc. Because of this, standard costs are subject to modification whenever basic changes are made in the organizational environment. For any given period of operations, there may be a *variance* between the actual cost incurred and the standard cost that should have been incurred. The maintenance of variance accounts in the accounting system greatly facilitates the performance of the comparison function. As Anthony points out, "The variance accounts may or may not be closed at the end of the accounting period. Companies that leave variance accounts open from one period to another do so with the expectation that over a period of time unfavorable variances will be offset by favorable variances, and the balance in the account will therefore become zero." [11]

---

[10] *Ibid.,* p. iv.

[11] Robert Anthony, *Management Accounting* (Homewood, Illinois: Richard D. Irwin, Inc., 1956), p. 180.

Analysis for standard costs helps dramatize the excessive cost of short runs and frequent changes in production, the cost of failure to cut back on clerical and other indirect help with declining production, and the cost of failure fully to utilize facilities and manpower. For standards on items of indirect labor, etc., are based on *minimum* requirements for different levels of production. Participation in the development of standards costs helps sensitize foremen and other managers to the *dynamics* of their organizations in operation. Variance account balances provide them with feedback information as to the direction and degree of deviation from "ideal" performance.

Financial Ratios

Ratios, such as the *current ratio* (current assets to current liabilities), the *quick ratio* or *acid test* (cash, accounts receivable, and marketable securities to current liabilities), *receivables* turnover (annual credit sales to average accounts receivable), *inventory turnover* (cost of goods sold to average inventory), *total debt to net worth, times-interest-earned* (after-tax, before-interest earnings to interest charges), and others, provide standards of operation—when based on historical firm data and industry data—which are of interest to those within the firm as well as those outside the firm, for example, prospective suppliers of funds to the firm. As long as the *purposes* of ratio analysis are kept in mind and one does not forget the ease with which ratios may be manipulated to "look good," such analysis provides a useful tool for evaluating performance.[12]

Procedures, Rules, and Policies

A *procedure* is a set of complementary and sequential relationships among functions, physical factors, and personnel for the accomplishment of specific subgoals within the framework of formal organiaztion structure. As with a *rule,* a *procedure* is a specific prescription for action and is most useful for assuring uniform compliance with good practices throughout the organization. Also, it conserves managerial time in that subordinates are provided with guidance they would otherwise have to seek from their superior. Often, approved procedures are codified in manual form and called

---

[12] For an illustrative analysis see Robert Johnson, *Financial Management* (Boston: Allyn and Bacon, 1959), pp. 60–75.

standard practices, technical orders, or standard operating procedure.

Policies are guides to action that require interpretation and discretion in application. It is highly desirable that the underlying reasons or rationale for *rules* and *policies* be stated with them, to facilitate acceptance and intelligent implementation. Policy manuals published in loose-leaf form provide a convenient means for disseminating policy, with minimum effort and expense to accomodate changes. Since *procedures, rules* and *policies* are developed for the purpose of implementing objectives that are unique to a particular firm, it follows that they should be developed and refined by personnel associated with each particular firm. In the formulation of standards, one can benefit greatly from the experience and theorizing of others, but he must judiciously tailor transplanted ideas to the unique requirements of his primary, collateral, and secondary objectives.

Budgets

A budget—for example, the cash budget or forecast—is a tool of planning, and, when it becomes an approved plan, it is also a standard for control. Initially, budgets may be formulated in nonmonetary as well as monetary terms. It is often more convenient to start with budgets in terms of man-hours of work, pounds or tons of raw material, physical sales volume, and so on, though eventually these will be translated into monetary terms for financial planning and control. Budgets provide useful media for quantifying departmental and divisional objectives and for synthesizing all these into over-all, company-wide, quantified objectives.

If developed properly, with adequate participation by those concerned, budgetmaking encourages more thoroughgoing planning and the raising of one's sights to higher attainment. One problem with the budgetary approach is that all budgets ultimately are based on the sales forecast or anticipated level of sales activity for the coming period. When actual experience does not jibe with the sales forecast, it is often quite laborious to recalculate budgets on the basis of revised expectations. A good solution to this problem is provided by the use of *flexible budgets:* a series of budgets for the same department or activity, each for a *different* level of sales. Though better forecasting techniques will provide for significant improvements in accuracy in the future (see chapter 2) and the *hedging function* of flexible budgeting may decrease in importance, flexible budgeting will still have a very real value; as with analysis for standard costs, it will help to sensitize managers to the dynamics of their organizations in operation. The important matter of organization for effective budgetmaking is discussed in chapter 11, "Organization for Control."

Policies, budgets, and other standards discussed above provide guides to action that help managers at every level to utilize the *Exception Principle*. In addition to providing for economy through selective control, as was discussed earlier, application of the *Exception Principle* also provides for better utilization of seasoned talent and better executive motivation and development.

Standards of Performance for Staff Agencies

Though it is difficult to establish quantitative performance standards for those phases of staff activity which deal with the creation of *intangible values* for the organization, much can be done with those areas of staff activity which do admit of quantitative formulation. There are definite quantitative standards that may be applied to the performance of financial staff functions. In the area of personnel work, adequate data relating to validation, reliability, turnover, measured effectiveness of training, and other factors, supply the basis for establishing realistic standards for performance and improvement. There are similar opportunities associated with all staff work, and it is the responsibility of management to explore these with staff personnel concerned and, through collaboration, to fashion meaningful standards.

It is true that Operations Research staff groups and other research-oriented groups pose a more challenging problem. For their objectives often have more to do with *function* than with specific, well-defined targets. Even so, adequate control of such activity requires that management place as much emphasis on the collaborative development of *functional goals* with these groups as it places on the development of quantitative goals for other agencies in the organization. For example, an adequate written record of the instructions given to such a group—as to either a specific research undertaking or a general, agreed-upon mission of exploration—will do much to affix responsibility and avoid subsequent misunderstanding. This record could take the form of an *instruction manual,* with copies prepared for the group leader and other relevant personnel. In addition, weekly or monthly progress reports should be required and prior agreement in writing should be made as to *stop* or *completion points* so that a balanced allocation of research resources may be made. These standards—when supplemented by adequately formulated policies, rules, procedures, and budgets—will do much to encourage organizationally productive effort on the part of such staff agencies.

Standards for Individual Performance

It is useful to have subordinates, in collaboration with their superiors, formulate their *own* criteria for *present performance* and *growth*. To assure some degree of continuity and company-wide uniformity in such a program, some staff agency—probably the personnel department—should be supplied with copies of all individual performance programs so that it may *advise* managers of deviations from company-wide standards. For example, an individual subordinate's program might be overly demanding or overly vague relative to the majority of other individual programs. The staff agency should arrange periodic conferences with managers to discuss the setting of general standards. These can be clarified through discussion of sample individual programs.[13] For additional control there should be adherence to the *Principle of Personnel Coordination:* **Promotions, wage changes, and disciplinary action should always be approved by the executive immediately superior to the one directly responsible.**

Standards for Over-all Performance

There is a widespread belief that the primary objective of business is to "maximize profits." Not only is this a harmful generalization—often voiced by businessmen who do not follow it in practice—it is an erroneous one. In our society today more than ever before, a business not only must be competitive but must constitute a satisfactory *social entity* for the people associated with it as well as for society. It is realistic and useful to distinguish between the goals of the firm—its primary service objectives—and the goals of the various people who are associated with the firm. The firm's primary service objectives *are* fashioned by people, but the pressures of competition, the power of the public to control the sanction to engage in business, and the desire for continuity within the framework of precedent encourage the formulation of primary objectives that are *not* merely an extension of the personal goals of

---

[13] See p. 381 for further discussion.

the planners. There is little question, however, that there is inter-action between personal goals and primary goals: primary objectives are influenced by the personal needs and values of the planners, but within a very definite framework of restrictions dictated by the past and present.

It is true that public ignorance, lack of competition, and inade-quate federal or state control can produce get-rich-quick enter-prises that are primarily oriented to profits. Usually, the promoters associated with these ventures are primarily oriented to profits also in a personal sense. But these firms represent a minority of busi-nesses and usually are short-term operations. Even for these, it seems incorrect to say that *profit maximization* is the profit goal. It would seem more realistic to say that profit "satisficing" or profit "adequacy" is the goal! [14] There are certain seemingly profit-oriented firms, such as real estate syndicates, speculator groups, and stock underwriters, which, to the extent that they perform the legitimate functions of creating and stabilizing organized markets, really are creating and distributing salable utilities that are socially desirable; they do not properly belong in the former category.

In most cases, in the long run, the efficiency with which a firm creates and distributes socially legitimate salable utilities is indi-cated, to a large extent, by its return on total investment (total in-vestment being the total assets at its disposal made possible by equity or debt capital).[15] The following breakdown of return on total investment is often useful and revealing:

(For a manufacturing concern)
Return on investment = Capital turnover × Earning rate

$$\text{Capital turnover} = \frac{\text{Sales}}{\text{Total investment}}$$

$$\text{Earning rate} = \frac{\text{Earnings}}{\text{Sales}}$$

Note: In practice, there is little agreement as to what should constitute total investment for return computations, i.e., some managements exclude idle cash or idle facilities, etc., to make a better showing on paper.

---

[14] On this question of maximizing see the discussion of the *organic subfunctions of planning* in chap. 2, p. 31. For additional discussion of this, as well as the value of distinguishing organizational goals from personal goals, see Robert Anthony "The Trouble with Profit Maximization," *Harvard Business Review*, November, 1960.

[15] For managerial analysis it may be desirable also to compute return against the *replacement value* of the assets. This rationale is applied to elements of the organiza-tion in the form of "Profit Center Control," which is discussed in chap. 11, "Organi-zation for Control."

But even for the long run this is not the sole criterion, for industries are not static, society is not static, and there are many long-term factors, external to the firm, with which it cannot cope or can only partially cope. Some of the other criteria that should be used in evaluating the long-term over-all performance of a firm are:

Philosophy and quality of management.
Market position.
Reputation and status.
Organization viability: quality and adaptability of personnel, plant, and equipment.
Organization unity and morale coupled with high standards of individual performance.

In the short run, there are important criteria of over-all performance that have a significant impact on long-term success or failure:

Profits and conservation of assets.
Quality of planning.
Personnel training and development.
Customer and public relations.
Efficiency of plant and personnel.
System of rewards and penalties: Does it encourage productive leadership and individual growth?
Innovation and research.
Labor relations.
Social legitimacy of primary objectives.

All the foregoing criteria are related to the firm's capacity for, and success with, the creation of salable utilities that are socially legitimate. No one knows the *relative importance* of these criteria in ascertaining a firm's capacity for achieving, or success in achieving, its primary service objectives. Though, for comparative purposes, the best single criterion of over-all performance is, undoubtedly, return on total investment.[16]

In ending this discussion of standards, the point should be made that the most effective standards of all are those that are self-imposed through an understanding of goals and a firm identification with them. Understanding can come about only through an effective communications effort; organized group activity is impossible without it (think of the plight an orchestra would be in were it deprived of an effective system of communication)! Firm identifica-

---

[16] A good discussion of the dangers of using too few criteria for evaluative purposes is provided by two selections in Shull and Delbecq (eds.), *op. cit.*: Frank Jasinsky, "Use and Misuse of Efficiency Controls," and V. F. Ridgway, "Dysfunctional Consequences of Performance Measurements,"

tion with goals is most likely to result from the kind of managerial leadership that perceives individual needs and manipulates organizational factors so that those needs will be satified *when* and *as* the individual performs his organizational mission.

PERT[17] AND CONTROL

Chapter 2 discussed how PERT, through the plotting of expected times in an activity network, permits the identification of *critical paths* and the *amount of slack* associated with various network events. This activity aids planning by forcing a type of analysis that might otherwise be neglected and by providing a sound basis for the allocation of resources. How PERT facilitates planning for more effective control of operations and contributes to the actual implementation of more effective control will be discussed here.

To begin with, control (making events conform to plans) is greatly facilitated by realistic schedules based on sound time requirements. PERT requires a kind of analysis that is likely to produce better time estimates and, consequently, more realistic schedules than would otherwise be obtainable. This is especially true for "one shot" programs, such as those in defense work, for which well-defined time and resource *standards* are not readily available. In addition, as was discussed earlier in this chapter, control must be *selective* if it is to be both feasible and economical; it should deal with deviations from planned performance or condition with regard to *key* factors and operations (those which, if properly controlled, are likely to assure adequate control of many related subsidiary factors and operations). It is often difficult in recurring projects, and especially so for one-of-a-kind projects to *identify* key factors and operations. PERT provides for this readily through the identification of critical paths and events that are associated with significant amounts of slack. These *are* the *key* factors and operations that should be watched with special care and from which more frequent and concise feedback information should be obtained.

The reason that a critical path is a *key factor* for control is that its total time requirement is the same as the total project's time requirement. Any extension or reduction in critical path expected time means an equivalent extension or reduction in total project time. Therefore, control of critical paths will do much to assure successful

---

[17] If necessary, review the general discussion of PERT (Program Evaluation and Review Technique), which is presented in chap. 2 (pp. 50–54).

completion of the total project on time. *Key operations* are represented by events that are associated with slack, for a large part of corrective action required to control critical paths will involve these operations in the following ways: (1) diversion of resources from events with slack to critical path events that are offschedule and (2) the making of tradeoffs (e.g., of management personnel) between events with slack and off-schedule critical path events. Of course, effective corrective action for controlling critical paths will also entail special investigation and trouble-shooting of *key* organizational units (those associated with critical path events or events with slack) and the allocation of new resources (such as additional equipment, manpower, or extra "overtime") to *key* organizational units as needed.

The periodic determination of the current amount and location of slack in the network greatly facilitates the performance of the comparison function for complex project control, by letting us know whether the total program and each of its parts is on, ahead of, or behind schedule. Through the use of periodically adjusted expected times for the completion of future events in the project, we can determine, also, the probability at any given time that an "ahead of" or "behind" schedule condition will persist.

PERT facilitates the application of the *Exception Principle* to control. Since it provides for the identification of critical paths, subproject heads within the same organization, as well as subcontractors outside the organization who are all working on the same project, may selectively control their parts of the total project on a decentralized and intelligent basis. That is, they can handle corrective action for off-schedule events without recourse to the over-all project director as long as they do not affect critical path schedules. Without PERT it would be difficult, if not impossible, to identify these project-wide critical paths. There is little question that, as PERT is developed further along the lines discussed in chapter 2, it will make important additional contributions to project control!

QUESTIONS

1. What contribution did Frederick W. Taylor and his colleagues in the scientific management movement make to modern control theory and practice? Discuss.

2. The statement is made that "control cannot be feasible and economical unless it is selective." Do you believe that this is true? Explain.

3. What impact has the computer had on control? Discuss.

4. What is "feedback"? What is "feedback information"? In what form should feedback information be presented?

5. What are the *six organic subfunctions of control?* Define the five that are presented in this chapter. Do you think that all six are truly *organic* to control, that is, that the organic management function of control cannot be performed unless *all* six of these organic subfunctions are performed? Give examples to support your view.

6. What is a standard? Is it correct to say that control cannot occur without standards? Why or why not? Explain.

7. Do you believe that business ethical conduct, generally, is better or worse than it was fifty years ago? Discuss.

8. Is it correct to say that *standard costs* define the lowest achievable costs of performing certain operations under the best known conditions existing anywhere? Why or why not?

9. What is a rule? What is a policy? Effectively distinguish one from the other.

10. Do you believe that the primary objective of business is to maximize profits? Explain.

11. Turn to the standards for over-all performance on page 187. Discuss the relevance of each of these to over-all performance. Do you think that some are relatively more important than others? Why? Would this evaluation hold for any type of business? Why or why not?

12. In your opinion, what is the major contribution of PERT to project control? Explain.

Chapter 8

PLANNING FOR CONTROL: SUPERVISION

Up to this point, the nature of control and the six *organic sub-functions of control* have been discussed, with the exception of one: supervision. It has been separated from the others for discussion because it has to do with the effective motivation of men—the face-to-face direction of individuals and groups—and this is undoubtedly one of the most demanding and challenging functions for the modern manager. To supervise successfully, a manager must have a large measure of self-knowledge, an understanding of individual and group behavior, and the character, courage, and skill to profit therefrom. This sounds like a "big order," and it is!

This chapter will discuss the hypotheses about individual and group behavior that seem especially relevant to supervision and certain supervisory concepts and practices that appear to be supported by these hypotheses. We will call them *generic* hypotheses to denote that they are presumed to be *universal* in their applicability and not limited to particular groups. We call them hypotheses, for they are explanations about behavior that either are purely speculative or are not, as yet, fully proved (or disproved).[1] For the most

---

[1] On the basis of these criteria the term "generic hypothesis" could just as well be applied to many of the more traditional "principles" presented elsewhere in this book. But the statements of the generic hypotheses in this chapter are new to the management literature, and there is some value in distinguishing them.

part, the hypotheses we will discuss *are* supported by evidence, though it is by no means conclusive. In many respects, we can only scratch the surface of a broad and still largely unexplored area. But significant research efforts are being mounted by behavioral scientists, and their findings will confirm and extend our knowledge about behavior at an increasing pace in the years ahead. The reader can profit greatly by keeping abreast of these developments as they are reported.

GENERIC HYPOTHESIS I (UNIVERSAL NEEDS)

Though employees act in terms of their *belief systems* (and effective leadership must operate through these systems), they have the *same basic needs* (ends are more universal than the means for achieving them, for means are largely determined by local culture). These universal need characteristics support a *pattern* of leadership that can be applied successfully in a wide range of activity.

This hypothesis lays the groundwork for a "functional" approach to supervision that is useful because it is dynamic, that is, it is adaptive to a wide range of group situations and to change through time. It is significantly superior to the "traitist" or "descriptive" approach to the study of leadership that is *static,* that is, attempts to identify specific leader traits or descriptive attributes with leadership success. After much exhaustive work the traitist researchers have failed to produce useful lists of specifics. What success they have had has been in the direction of identifying certain effective *functions* that are performed by leaders who represent a diversity of personal traits.

Common and Unique Characteristics

When we say that people have the *same basic needs,* we do not mean to imply that they are alike as to the strength of each need or that they lack *other unique characteristics.* One who has been deprived of love and acceptance throughout his childhood will have a greater need for acceptance than one who has not been so deprived. In addition, we have important individual differences as to physical strength, visual and hearing acuity, coordination, intelligence, finger dexterity, and other aptitudes. Also, the way in which each individual attempts to meet his needs is influenced by the interplay of the values of his culture with his own role expectations, skills, beliefs, environmental conditioning, and past satisfaction of needs. But it is true that the uniform pattern of basic needs, coupled with the standardizing pressure of cultural values, provides a framework within which a *universal functional mode of leadership can fruitfully operate.*[2]

Individual Needs and Organizational Goals

One of the primary challenges to the modern manager is to develop the capacity for perceiving the individual and group needs of his subordinates and to plan for the implementation of organization goals so that these individual and group needs are satisfied in the process. The *Principle of Harmony of Objective* states: **Though the personal goals of the people associated with an organization frequently are not the same as primary organization goals, organization goals often can be conceived and implemented in such a way as to satisfy these personal goals within the framework of necessary organizational constraints.** The manager has a variety of "tools" at his disposal for doing this. In the first place, he can contribute to the formulation of *primary, collateral,* and *secondary* goals for the organization that are legitimate and defensible. He can attempt to select people whose values are consistent with these goals or, at least, are not in opposition to them. Then he can use work assignments, penalties, interpersonal relations, training, praise, promotions, titles, and other forms of recognition in a way that meets individual subordinate needs and at the same time achieves organizational goals.[3]

We do not expect the goals of those associated with the organization to be the same as organization goals. Certainly, absentee owners have different expectations—largely monetary—from their association with the enterprise than non-owner directors, profes-

---

[2] For an interesting discussion of basic worker needs see Whiting Williams, *The Mainsprings of Men* (New York: Charles Scribner's Sons, 1925). The author collected his data while working as a laborer.

[3] In discussing this, Summer and Newman point out that "we can design many jobs so that they provide a man who fills them with direct personal satisfactions. Job enlargement, for example, increases opportunity for self-assertion and a sense of achievement. 'Task-teams' provide sociability while allowing considerable self-regulation. Committee assignments open the way for give-and-take communication and often add prestige to individual members. Decentralization, too, creates major opportunities for self-expression and personal growth. Such direct satisfactions tend to increase a man's willingness to cooperate with his boss." William Newman and Charles Summer, Jr., *The Process of Management* (Englewood Cliffs, New Jersey: Prentice-Hall, Inc., 1961), p. 499.

sional managers, foremen, or employes.[4] On the other hand, customers and the public have another set of expectations based on the enterprise's ability to produce and distribute, competitively, salable utilities. The solution is not to make these diverse expectations uniform—an impossibility—but to satisfy all of them within the framework prescribed by the *primary service objectives* of the organization.

A good analogy, perhaps, is afforded by the Marine Corps. What are its primary objectives? Presumably, to fashion one of the finest fighting forces in the world, an organization prepared to tackle military assignments that impose personal hardships and risks greater than those which an average military organization could or would impose on its members. Is it likely that the typical marine is looking for an improved opportunity to have his head blown off? It seems much more plausible to argue that the corps functions in such a way as to satisfy important personal needs of its members—for feelings of acceptance, worthwhileness, etc.—in the process of preparing to carry out, and in carrying out, its hazardous assignments. The "price of admission" for marines to stay in the Corps—and to continue to enjoy the satisfaction of needs that they believe only the Corps can satisfy so well—is to do the work of the Corps, to identify with its objectives, in a manner consistent with its high standards of excellence.

Of course, in a young organization that is growing rapidly and "shooting for the moon" there may be *transient* identification with company goals on the part of personnel and willingness on their part to *tolerate* each other as well as autocratic leadership due to the impact of dramatic company successes. But this is a phase of

---

[4] Chester I. Barnard, a man of extensive experience in top management positions, writes: ". . . my observation in several well-managed businesses convinces me that business decisions are constantly being made that are not based on economic motives. This is something that businessmen seldom admit, and of which they are frequently unaware. Prestige, competitive reputation, social philosophy, social standing, philanthropic interests, combativeness, love of intrigue, dislike of friction, technical interest, napoleonic dreams, love of accomplishing useful things, desire for regard of employees, love of publicity, fear of publicity—a long catalogue of non-economic motives actually condition the management of business, and nothing but the balance sheet keeps these non-economic motives from running wild. Yet without all these incentives I think most business would be a lifeless failure. There is not enough vitality in dollars to keep business running on any such scale as we experience it, nor are the things which can be directly purchased with money an adequate incentive." *Organization and Management* (Cambridge, Massachusetts: Harvard University Press, 1948), pp. 14–15. Support for this view is provided by the results of a *Fortune* survey of some 221 management men. See William H. Whyte, Jr., "How Hard Do Executives Work?" William M. Fox (ed.), *Readings in Personnel Management from "Fortune"* (New York: Henry Holt & Co., 1957), or *Fortune,* January, 1954.

growth which cannot be sustained indefinitely. Sooner or later the organization's approach to human relations will have to be placed on a sounder foundation and the longer this is delayed the more difficult a task it will become.

Basic Needs and Behavior

But before managers can meet the needs of their subordinates, they must be able to *perceive* them. As Generic Hypothesis I implies, we can *generalize* about human needs and then *adapt* these generalizations to the *individual*. It seems reasonable to assume that all people share the following basic needs: [5]

The Need for Security: protection from threat, some degree of mastery over one's environment.

The Need for Acceptance: love, a sense of belonging.

The Need for Self-Expression: an outlet for one's natural impulses, tensions, and creative urges. [6]

The Need to Understand: to satisfy curiosity, to acquire knowledge.

The Need for New Experience: for the stimulation of variation in routine, for new problems and challenges.

The Need for Feelings of Worthwhileness: status, prestige and self-esteem.

The satisfaction of these needs leads to individual self-realization: the feeling that an individual has become what he is capable of becoming. It permits him to be socially productive by channeling his energy into learning, coping (problem solving), and acceptable, expressive behavior. Frustration of these basic needs will divert the individual's energy and his tension-created energy into defensive behavior—to protect him from further need deprivation—and more stereotyped, non-need-fulfilling, coping behavior. In extreme cases, frustration of needs may lead to mental illness, for example, the psychopathic personality, which becomes *indifferent* to the need for acceptance.

Maslow does not regard these basic needs as instincts but rather as "instinctoid impulses." That is, they are weaker than animal instincts; they may be more readily negated or perverted by extreme

---

[5] The author has drawn heavily upon the important theorizing of A. H. Maslow for this discussion of basic needs. See Maslow, *Motivation and Personality* (New York: Harper & Bros., 1954).

[6] Gordon Allport suggests: "When the ego is not effectively engaged the individual becomes reactive. He lives a life of ugly protest, finding outlets in complaints, strikes, above all in scapegoating; in this condition he is ripe prey for a demagogue whose whole purpose is to focus and exploit the aggressive outbursts of non-participating egos." "The Psychology of Participation," *Psychology Review*, Vol. LIII, No. 3, pp. 119–27.

or prolonged *threatening* deprivation (deprivation per se is not bad unless it is *perceived* as deprivation by the individual. The healthy person who has enjoyed basic need gratification during his early years achieves a degree of independence from his environment; he can better live with need deprivation—and, paradoxically, better savor need fulfillment—than can the individual who was ungratified in his youth). In the healthy person, *rationality* and *impulse* are *synergic* rather than antithetic, that is, they cooperate with and complement each other rather than oppose each other. In the unhealthy individual this is not true, and, as we shall see, that mode of supervision which is appropriate for the healthy individual is inappropriate, quite often, for the unhealthy individual!

Maslow points out that an individual has *multiple* not *single* drives or needs at any given time; that a particular desire may be a channel through which several other desires express themselves. Conflict or frustration with regard to non-basic needs does not lead to mental illness. A scheme of the factors contributing to behavior and the kinds of behavior that may be evoked could be sketched as follows:

Character Structure
(shaped by needs, frustrations, emotional and intellectual attitudes)

Role Expectations
(behavior associated with various roles in our society)

Cultural Pressures
(ways in our society by which self-esteem and other needs may be legitimately achieved and expressed)

Immediate Situation or Field as Perceived
(a speeding car, collapsing bridge, or glandular disorder. Rewards or penalties. . . . You say "dog," I think of a dog)

Learning Residuals
(conditioned reflexes, associations, problem solving, irrational responses, etc.)

Biological Heritage
(the basic physical characteristics and aptitudes with which a person is born)

Learning Behavior

Coping (need-oriented) *Behavior**

Expressive Behavior

Associative Behavior

Conditioned Reflex

Protective or Defensive Behavior

*Coping behavior is normally expressed via the "style" of the individual, as is other behavior.

When needs are not satisfied by an intrinsically proper (and therefore satisfying) process, the individual may grasp at and become fixated upon arbitrary associations, with non-satisfying objects or modes of behavior, for his need fulfillment. This leads to neurosis, and the satisfaction of these arbitrary "neurotic needs" does not breed health. In fact, it prevents self-realization and creates growing feelings of anxiety and helplessness for the individual as he experiences failure to gratify his basic needs. The unloved may react with anxiety to anything but aloofness from others, the deeply guilty person may demand punishment, and the rash and destructive person may require authoritarian direction to avoid hurting himself. Generally, we see that the neurotic has experienced a high level of need frustration. He develops an irrational defensive orientation with which he reacts to many "psychological dangers" that he may not understand or be able to define. If extreme, such behavior must be dealt with by the professional clinician. However, when evidenced to a milder degree by a subordinate, the superior is challenged to release the subordinate from his neurotic needs by strengthening the satisfaction of his basic needs so that he may grow. A technique for doing this is discussed in conjunction with Generic Hypothesis VII.

What are some other conceptual values that can be derived from this scheme of basic needs? Maslow suggests certain generalized tendencies that he has observed from clinical experience: [7]

PERSONAL ATTRIBUTES	BEHAVIORAL TENDENCY
LOW SECURITY LOW SELF-ESTEEM (THE NEUROTIC)	⟶ WITHDRAWAL, SUBSERVIENCE, MASOCHISM
LOW SECURITY HIGH SELF-ESTEEM (THE POWER HUNGRY LEADER)	⟶ DOMINATING, EXPLOITING, HOSTILE, AGGRESSIVE
HIGH SECURITY LOW SELF-ESTEEM (THE FOLLOWER)	⟶ QUIET, SWEET, SERVING, DEPENDENT
HIGH SECURITY HIGH SELF-ESTEEM (THE GOOD LEADER)	⟶ KINDLY, HELPFUL, SERENE, STRONG

Such classification helps dramatize the need for the supervisor to perceive individual differences and to relate himself to subordinates accordingly. To the extent that we accept the validity of the basic-need approach to analyzing behavior, we may develop a less conventional view of the role of monetary incentives in an organization. Pay becomes a real issue only when it is insufficient to provide basic

[7] *Op. cit.,* pp. 52, 53.

need gratification or when the amount is perceived by the employee as a symbol of rejection or disapproval. Conversely, higher pay, especially for upper-level managers, has meaning more as a status symbol or "way of keeping score" than as purchasing power. An employee will tend to derive security from the presence of "predictable social roles" in the organization. Seniority can serve both as a status symbol and as a source of security. A manager who demands that employees show their loyalty by not striking when their fellow-workers go out and the strike issue is debatable fails to perceive the unreality of his demand. Workers look to their fellow-workers for acceptance; rejection by the group with which we wish to identify ourselves is one of the most potent threats we face. It is unlikely that the manager would seriously consider offering acceptance in his social circle and promotion to a higher position as an alternative for the displaced worker. Yet, this is not meant to imply that workers and work groups cannot be held to high standards of performance. This will be discussed later in the chapter.

Maslow points to an interesting distinction between coping behavior and expressive behavior. He writes:

> Ideal coping behavior is characteristically learned, while ideal expressive behavior is characteristically unlearned. As an example we may take a man in conversation. Conversation has purpose, e.g., he is a salesman trying to get an order, and the conversation is consciously and avowedly brought into being for this reason. But his style of speaking may be unconsciously hostile or snobbish or supercilious and may cause him to lose the order. Thus the expressive aspects of his behavior may have environmental effects, but it is to be noted that the speaker did not want these effects, that he did not try to be supercilious or hostile, and he was not even aware that he gave this impression. The environmental effects of expression, when there are any at all, are unmotivated and epiphenomenal.[8]

Maslow makes the additional observation: "It is certain if one wishes to know about the character structure, the best behavior to study is expressive rather than coping behavior. This is confirmed by the now extensive experience with projective (expressive) tests."[9]

Some have attempted to establish a *fixed* hierarchy of motives as to relative priority or strength. But this appears to be a fruitless and unrealistic ground for generalization. As Dewey and Humber point out, "the motivation of a person at any given time is in large part a

---

[8] Maslow, *op. cit.*, pp. 184, 186.
[9] *Ibid.*

function of the degree of satisfaction of all of the person's motives, both innate and acquired. . . . When asked which motive is strongest, the answer must always be in terms of the value system of particular persons and particular cultures. Universally, there is no strongest motive."[10]

Neurotic Drive vs. Healthy Drive

The point should be made that many executives with outstanding drive, who "know what they want" and go after it with amazing persistence, are actually fired by neurotic tensions and are fixated upon neurotic goals that, though often socially useful, are unrelated to their basic needs. As Richard Smith puts it in talking about such an executive:

Some of his psychological weaknesses, oddly, may be the same characteristics that were responsible for his rise in business. Among engineers and accountants, the so-called "obsessive compulsive" types have often prospered from making a fetish of neatness, order, and "accuracy"; in the same way some patent attorneys have turned a constitutional suspicion of everything and everybody into an asset in drawing up airtight patents. . . . Why doesn't success protect the successful? Sometimes they discover they have spent a lifetime struggling up the wrong mountain. Sometimes, as Dr. Lawrence S. Kubie, the distinguished New York psychiatrist, sums it up, they discover that success does not make friends, that each success increases the strain of a possible failure, and that their preoccupation with activity was simply the burying of unresolved problems—an insatiable *anxiety* not an insatiable appetite for self-expression or achievement . . . as Dr. Fritz Redlich of Yale observes, though success can be the result of a strong neurotic drive, the neurosis will eventually make trouble for the individual.[11]

The success of the low-security, high self-esteem executive is a function of the type of job assignment as well as the organizational climate in which he works. He will certainly thrive better in a lone-wolf or tight-ship, authoritarian operation than he will in one that stresses the development of a permissive atmosphere and long-range human relations values. But, in any event, it is a challenge to his superior to assist him in perceiving and meeting his *real needs* for his own personal good as well as the long-term benefit of the organization. Fortunately, healthy drives toward self-realization provide

---

[10] Richard Dewey and W. J. Humber, *The Development of Human Behavior* (New York: Macmillan Co., 1951), p. 193.

[11] Richard Smith, "The Executive Crack-Up," in William M. Fox (ed.), *op. cit.*, pp. 108, 110; or *Fortune*, May, 1955.

substitute "mainsprings" for the performance of creative and productive work. Though in some situations the neurotically driven executive may look impressive in the short run, he is not as *efficient* nor does he "wear as well in his relationships" for the long pull as the emotionally healthy individual.

GENERIC HYPOTHESIS II
(SOCIAL SYSTEMS AND FORMAL ORGANIZATION)

The basic needs of employees tend to be met through the operation of social systems operating within the framework of formal organization. The social system through its benefits and social interactions provides a sense of belonging and a reserve of emotional support from which its members may draw. Good formal organization provides for productive, coordinated effort through consistent adherence to a clearly defined system of authority relationships, rules, and task assignments.

Formal organization provides the skeleton that informal organization fleshes out. Both are essential and are not necessarily antithetical; they can and should be harmonized so that they complement each other. Informal organization performs many functions. It resists harsh management and changes that threaten employee security; it provides informal leadership to discredit the incompetent formal leader or to fill in the "vacuum" created by him; it supplements formal lines of communication and communicates overtime (the grapevine "smokes") when formal communication fails on matters of concern; it exerts pressure on organizational members for conformity with modes of behavior that may or may not be in the interest of formal organizational goals; it provides support and acceptance for those who respect its values and harsh rejection for those who do not. Informal organization is often unduly influenced by misinformation and caprice. It is the supervisor's job to respect it, study it, influence it constructively, and utilize it.

We often forget that the typical employee spends more waking time in his job environment than in any other. Numerous studies have produced definite correlations between job satisfaction, absenteeism, and turnover and the quality of work group and supervisory relationships. To most rank-and-file employees, the foreman and work group *are* the company in a very literal sense. If the work group and foreman create a work environment that the individual perceives as being positive and need satisfying, he will be *attracted* to this environment and will have positive feelings about the company. He will *not necessarily* be productive with regard to formal organizational goals—as opposed to group goals—unless his group has adopted those goals! It is the job of the supervisor, supported by higher management, to provide the group with the rationale for identifying with formal goals by planning the implementation of formal goals in such a way that individual employee goals are met in the process.

Legitimate formal organizational goals, coupled with sound formal organization, provide the most suitable framework within which purposeful, productive economic group activity can take place. Individual need fulfillment and self-realization cannot take place in a chaotic, uncertain work environment any more than in a chaotic, uncertain society. One of the striking findings reported by cultural anthropologists is that *all* cultures or societies, however primitive, have found it necessary to resort to formal hierarchical systems with definite "chains of command" and sets of rules or laws. The "normal" individuals of all societies perceive, at least intuitively, that informal organization must be supplemented by adequate formal organization if individual and group needs are to be met effectively.

The Need for Varied Stimuli

A suitable job assignment adequately supervised has therapeutic value for the normal individual. It provides him with varied stimuli, an avenue for self-expression, and a means for achieving self-esteem and security. A widely held stereotype holds that the average employee is predisposed to shun work, "goof off," and avoid responsibility. Perhaps this flows from the tendency to attribute to the majority of workers, the observed behavior of a minority—a minority that must be dealt with realistically (as will be discussed) but, nevertheless, a minority. The typical worker approaches his new job with a genuine desire to do what is expected of him and "make good," as a means for satisfying his basic needs. Generally, he does not bring to the job a need for *inactivity* or a need to subvert organization goals. Deterioration of performance and attitudes is usually traceable to negative supervision and work experience.

Psychologist Woodburn Heron dramatized the human need for varied stimuli and activity, rather than inactivity, with a provocative experiment. He paid students $20 a day to lie on a soft bed in a soundproofed, air-conditioned cubicle—with short breaks for food —and *do nothing!* Some stuck it out for six days, while others quit after 24 hours.

When interruptions cease, some of the victims try desperately to think about their studies, or to occupy themselves with intellectual problems. For the most part they fail. Little by little their brains go dead or slip out of control. They cannot concentrate; their thoughts wander aimlessly. Their arithmetic drops to primary-school level.

Strange hallucinations, like waking dreams, creep into their minds. The students see patterns of dots or lines. Then, as the empty hours drag on, livelier visions appear. They may see rows of little yellow men with black caps and open mouths, or a procession of squirrels with sacks on their backs marching across the snow.

As soon as they leave the cell, the hallucinations stop; the squirrels and little yellow men march away forever. But not for hours do the victims get back to normal. They have headaches, cannot study, lose their skill at handwriting. Sometimes such effects continue for 24 hours.[12]

Such reactions have been experienced by prisoners in solitary confinement; undoubtedly this helps to explain why it is regarded as such an extreme form of punishment. It may help to explain the communist "brainwashing" technique. In any event, these results dramatize the individual's needs for stimulating and meaningful experience.

Factors in Effective Communication

One of the functions of informal organization is to supplement formal systems of communication. It is useful to examine some of the factors that contribute to communication failure, for effective communication is an essential requirement for effective supervision. Yet, judging from survey results, it appears that few supervisors are as successful with communication as they think they are. It has been found that, almost to a man, supervisors seriously overstate the adequacy of their communication with subordinates when their private opinions are compared with those of their men.

There are a number of factors that probably bear upon this. Communication can occur any time, not just when we decide that it should, and tone and gesture as well as the character of the sender are often more accurate communicators than words themselves. Typically, we tend to be "students of the boss" more than we are students of our subordinates, for he is a powerful source of need gratification or frustration for us. Changes in the way he says "Good morning," or his failure to say it, and numerous other covert and overt expressions are "read" by us with concern or relief. If he fails to explain a new policy or to take us into his confidence, we

---

[12] Reported in the science section of *Time* Magazine, October 4, 1954.

definitely perceive it as a message! The way in which we interpret it will, to a large extent, be determined by the projection of our own hopes and fears. Yet, if we think about the lot of *our* subordinates, we are likely to think that they are most fortunate to be spared the never-ending task *we have* of reading the boss! We tend to tell our boss "what he wants to hear," but are naïve enough to believe that this does not apply to *our* subordinates in their dealings with us.

Often we give too little consideration to the problems of *acceptance, timing,* and *mode of expression*. Until an individual has achieved some degree of respect and *acceptance* from a group, he cannot expect its members to give much *favorable* consideration to his ideas. When people distrust each other, sheer volume of communication is to little avail. Yet, husband and wife or old friends of long standing can effectively communicate with surprisingly few words! The unaccepted newcomer in a group may even be actively resented and penalized to the degree that his ideas are superior to those of the old hands. After all, experience with the group and its affairs is *supposed* to count for something.

Timing is also important. When people are emotionally upset and fraught with anxiety, it is very difficult for them to be objective and reasonable. Only after they have been given the opportunity to ventilate their feelings and "get things off their chest" will they be truly receptive to rational discussion. Many discussion leaders and committee chairmen fail to perceive this and unrealistically press for calmness and objectivity before encouraging the necessary catharsis to take place. Also, if genuine acceptance is desired for a proposal, the group should have an opportunity to sift and question the "facts" and to "catch up" with the understanding of the proposer. Research has shown that "unanimous decisions" may be *imposed* on a group with surprisingly little effort.[13] When that happens, there is little relationship between voting for, and intelligent acceptance of, a proposal.

The *mode of expression* we use in communicating is equally important. People pay the most attention to messages they understand and perceive as being *relevant* to their needs and fears. It would obviously be a mistake to lecture to a group in German when the group members do not speak German. To a lesser extent we often commit the same error by using inappropriate terminology and illus-

---

[13] For example, see W. M. Fox, "An Experimental Study of Group Reaction to Two Types of Conference Leadership," *Human Relations*, Vol. X, No. 3, 1957.

trations. To the highest degree possible we should try to relate the material we wish to present to the common needs and anxieties of the group. If a given proposal has the net effect of threatening a work group, then serious attention should be given either to revising it or to revising the plans for implementing it.

A perplexing communication problem for the supervisor is the one arising from "misreading" the true feelings or objectives of employees. This stems from the tendency to "take things at face value," inadequate investigation, and insufficient self-knowledge on the part of the supervisor with which to "discount" the effects of his own biases and emotional needs upon his perception. There are many cultural and personal values that constrain us from revealing our basic, unvarnished feelings. If we feel that our foreman is too arbitrary and harsh, we may strike for higher pay or for some rule or benefit he is known to oppose, but we will rarely strike *because our foreman is a bully* through fear of being laughed out of the community! There is considerable evidence to suggest that the majority of strikes are caused by *other* than denial of the demands publicly announced. It is unusual when the true character of an individual grievance is revealed with its first presentation. Thorough and impartial investigation and the clinical approach (discussed in connection with Generic Hypothesis VII) significantly aid the supervisor in analyzing human problems.

There are other important techniques that help managers solve their communication problems. Periodically, each subordinate should be asked to prepare in writing, without assistance, a statement of the formal goals or mission of his group, his own authority and duties, and the authority and duties of his superior. Collectively, these statements will define the nature and scope of communication failure. Through individual and group discussion, the supervisor can lay the groundwork for real unity of purpose and action. Clarification of these matters should also lead to better "self-coordination" and initiative on the part of subordinates, for they will have less fear that what they may do will be judged inappropriate.

Employee Evaluation and Growth

Closely allied to this is the supervisor's need of an effective means for *evaluating* his subordinates. When a formal merit rating scale is used, there is the danger that the supervisor may be unaware of employee activity that should be rewarded. Or individual subordinates may feel that the rating scale does not adequately reflect performance factors associated with their particular jobs. The supervisor can overcome the first problem by withholding his own rating at the time of the merit rating interview until the subordinate has had an opportunity to rate himself. If new information is brought to light, the supervisor can revise *his* rating before offering it to the subordinate. If the subordinate reveals a greatly overrated and unrealistic perception of his performance, then the need for counseling rather than explanation and discussion is indicated. With regard to the second problem—the appropriateness of the merit rating factors for the individual—an entirely different approach may be desirable. The supervisor can guide each subordinate in the preparation of a self-development program and subsequently evaluate the subordinate on the basis of his *own* criteria. Also, he can collaborate with the subordinate in formulating standards for evaluating present performance, the establishment of objectives that are fair and attainable and consistent with the present scope of the subordinate's authority and responsibility. Periodically, the superior can consult with the subordinate to analyze why goals were met or not met and to consider appropriate modification of goals or behavior for the future.[14]

To assure adequate "feedback" of bad news along with the good, the supervisor must create the right "climate" for his subordinates and see to it that they have regular opportunities for contact with him. The supervisor must accept and communicate the premise that growth can take place only as a result of *attempt* and *inevitable* error, that all of us must cope with unanticipated problems and human reactions. Few of us like to "sit on" problems and experience the anxiety that comes from having them hanging over our heads and knowing that sooner or later they will catch up with us. We will be inclined to discuss our difficulties with a superior who, we think, will give us a frequent and objective hearing for both good and bad news, and who, we think, will evaluate us in terms of our *net contribution* to the organization. Perhaps the biggest barrier to this type of superior-subordinate discussion is created by the superior's incli-

---

[14] For further discussion of this approach, with specific suggestions for implementing it, see C. W. Randle and W. H. Monroe, "Better Ways To Measure Executive Performance," *Management Method*, January, 1961. See also "Setting Standards for 'Nebulous' and Top-Level Jobs" in Virgil Rowland, *Managerial Performance Standards* (New York: American Management Association, 1960). Certain problems of control in using this approach are discussed in chap. 14, pp. 380 and 382.

nation to "go off half-cocked," to judge and act prematurely on the basis of inadequate information. The majority of employees have good reasons for their behavior, although first appearances may suggest otherwise. The superior who forces himself always to place a full hearing before final judgment and action in no way abdicates his authority to act. On the contrary, he will enjoy a larger measure of authority as his subordinates grant him greater *acceptance* because of his attempt to be fair and to respect their individuality.

FIG. 8-1

Sociogram for Group of Eight Office Workers

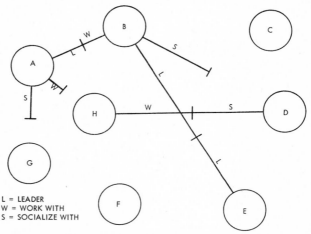

L = LEADER
W = WORK WITH
S = SOCIALIZE WITH

Note: In this partially completed chart, it can be seen that worker A voted for B as leader, B voted for A to work with, D voted for H to socialize with, and so on.

Sociometry

The use of *sociometry* provides the supervisor with a means for better understanding the informal organization of his group and the needs of its members. After carefully discussing the uses to which such data will be put, he can ask each subordinate to indicate three choices: whom (from his work group) he would most like to work for, whom he would most like to work with, and whom he would most like to socialize with. The supervisor can plot the responses in the form of a sociogram (see Fig. 8-1) and can use the information thus gained in making recommendations for promotions, in planning work assignments, and in identifying those who are rejected by the group and who may be in need of counseling. Such ratings were found to correlate well with performance in officer candidate schools during World War II and later.[15]

Generic Hypotheses III and IV are so closely interrelated that they will be discussed together.

GENERIC HYPOTHESIS III (POSITIVE LEADERSHIP)

The pattern of leadership in supervisory positions that will assure the greatest long-run effectiveness is based on cooperation, participation, consultation, consistent adherence to high standards of achievement, and satisfaction for the egos of the rank and file— though this will require the strong leader to restrain his natural drive toward self-assertion and will require all leaders to deal in a firm, authoritarian manner with the maladjusted minority who will attempt to disrupt the group.

GENERIC HYPOTHESIS IV
(POSITIVE VS. NEGATIVE MOTIVATION)

In leadership, positive motivation is superior to negative motivation when the necessary *time, rapport, skill,* and *group environment* are present to make it possible. Otherwise, negative motivation is superior to no motivation or a laissez faire approach. Also, negative motivation must always be applied in the interest of the group to that minority which has proved itself non-receptive to positive motivation. However, negative motivation is most effective when it encourages types of behavior that are rewarded by relief of stress and satisfaction of personal needs.

There is little question that positive motivation is superior to negative motivation when it is *appropriate and can be successfully applied*. These last qualifications are stressed because there are well-meaning extremists who suggest that positive motivation is the only kind that should be employed in virtually all situations. No one will deny that the employee who conforms to a policy because he believes in it, or the student who learns a particular thing because

---

[15] See R. L. French, "Sociometric Status and Individual Adjustment among Naval Recruits," in Dorwin Cartwright and Alvin Zander (eds.), *Group Dynamics: Research and Theory* (1st ed.; New York: Row Peterson & Co., 1953). See also the following articles from *Personnel Psychology:* Raymond H. Van Zelst, "Sociometrically Selected Work Teams Increase Production," Autumn, 1952, pp. 175–85; E. P. Hollander, "Buddy Rating: Military Research and Industrial Implication," Autumn, 1954, pp. 385–393; Joseph Weitz, "Selecting Supervisors with Peer Ratings," Spring, 1958, pp. 25–35; and Wilse B. Webb, "The Problem of Obtaining Negative Nominations in Peer Ratings," Spring, 1955, pp. 61–64.

he is interested in it and can relate it to his needs, is better motivated than those who respond because they have to.

But the conflicting demands of life and our own human limitations make the use of negative motivation essential for coordinated action and individual growth. The medical student may not *enjoy* memorizing bones, neural structure, or medical terminology, but he *must* if he is to be a successful physician. A child is incapable of relating the value of much of his early training to the demands of adult life, yet such training is essential to his future health. Some have defined maturity as that state at which we learn to like to do the things that we know we must do. Certainly, much of our self-esteem and acceptance from others flows from our capacity for self-discipline, our ability to master our passing emotions and impulses and behave in a manner consistent with out *basic* values and needs.

Our rebellion is not to negative motivation per se, but rather to *unnecessary* or *inappropriate* negative motivation. Good discipline is not punitive; its purpose is to influence our behavior along lines that will be beneficial to us as well as to society in the future. Nor should negative motivation be used in situations in which positive motivation is appropriate and can be successfully applied. Our feelings about our parents, school, military service, and our boss are based upon our *net perception* of the behavior we associate with them. It is unlikely that I would have *any* respect for my father had he *never* subjected me to legitimate punishment. My feelings of warmth and affection for him are due to the fact that his relationship with me *as I perceived it* was definitely positive in its *net* impact. A supervisor must be versatile, he must know *when* and *how* to use both positive and negative motivation. He tends to be a positive leader to the extent that he limits his use of negative motivation to situations in which positive motivation is inappropriate or unsuccessful.

When Negative Motivation Is Necessary

Generic Hypothesis IV suggests these kinds of situations. For example, when there is *insufficient time*. No one expects an infantry platoon leader caught with his unit in an ambush to confer with his subordinates as to the best course of action; it is his job to give the right orders and to give them quickly and concisely. Paradoxically, any attempt on his part to be consultative on such an occasion might diminish the respect of his men and jeopardize his effectiveness with them in the future. In fact, unilateral leadership is the only appropriate mode for the occasion and therefore, *is* positive leadership.

Positive motivation is based on a perception of subordinate needs and utilization of means, which are appropriate for him, to satisfy these needs. It is difficult for a supervisor to perceive the needs of a subordinate if he cannot establish rapport—a relationship of mutual trust—or *does not have the skill or insight required.* There are some individuals who "rub us the wrong way" for no apparent reason, and we find it almost impossible to establish rapport with them. And it is not surprising that we often lack the skill to perceive the needs of individuals who are themselves incapable of perceiving them! Even when rapport and perception have been achieved, the supervisor must attempt satisfaction of the subordinate's needs within the framework of organizational constraints. At times, this will not permit the supervisor sufficient flexibility to deal in a positive manner with a particular case.

The long run must be distinguished from the short run. It is very possible for intelligent, authoritarian leadership to outperform positive, democratic leadership over a relatively short span of time or with certain types of temporary work groups. A new, whip-cracking, driving supervisor can exact an amazing amount of work from workers who value their jobs and do not readily see alternative avenues of employment open to them. They will not be happy about it, but their increased output may be sustained for a year or longer. However, the seeds of dissension will have been sown. As frustrations accumulate, subordinates will organize informally to resist and subvert the superior. And, as satisfaction with the work environment decreases, employees will search harder for alternative job opportunities and become less responsive to the threats of their superior. In a very real sense, such a supervisor is spending the "human relations capital" of the organization, and it may take years to re-establish a useful supervisor-subordinate relationship after his departure. It is short-sighted indeed that many top managers *encourage* this ruinous "short cut" to production by paying lip service to the human relations job of their supervisors while basing promotions and bonuses on short-term ability to get out the work.[16]

It takes time for a supervisor to gain the kind of acceptance and build the kind of relationships with his subordinates that will ultimately lead to higher productivity and long-term individual growth. If a *temporary* work group or committee is composed of mature

---

[16] Some important research relating to this has been reported by Rensis Likert in his "Measuring Organization Performance," *Harvard Business Review,* March-April, 1958. For a more complete discussion of this material in addition to other important research findings, see his *New Patterns of Management* (New York: McGraw-Hill Book Co., 1961).

people who share and practice a positive philosophy of leadership, then it will probably function best under such leadership. In other temporary work group situations, however, positive leadership may well be less productive than intelligent authoritarianism. For example, consider a group of casual common laborers hired for a period of three months to do road work. Because of their lack of education and skill, they require close supervision. They perceive this particular job as a stopgap, offering little opportunity for growth, enhanced self-esteem, advancement, or lasting security. It may be that motivation of such a group in terms of threatened deprivation of pay or employment—negative motivation—would be superior to an attempt to develop positive values that are largely precluded by the character of the situation.

Finally, *a positive approach is inappropriate for certain types of employees.* There is the dependable and valuable individual with "high security" and "low self-esteem" who does not want a chance to shape policy or to show what he can do, who *needs* a dependent relationship with his superior. He will feel threatened by attempts to force him out of his shell. He does not want to be on his own. In time, a supervisor may successfully wean such a person away from his dependency, but he should be most careful to avoid withdrawing his support prematurely.[17]

And then there is a troublesome minority group of employees with whom supervisors must eternally cope—the chronic "goof-offs" and troublemakers. These are severely maladjusted individuals who are so insecure and hostile that they will not respond to positive supervision. On the contrary, they are compelled by their neurotic needs to subvert and challenge the authority of the formal leader. They perceive positive leadership behavior as appeasement—the leader is afraid of them—or as an attempt to put something over on them.[18] Though these individuals may be helped by professional counseling, the supervisor has neither the time nor the skill for ad-

---

[17] Likert says: "The available theory and research findings suggest that the best results are obtained when the amount of participation used is somewhat greater than expected by the subordinates, but still within their capacity to respond to it effectively." "Effective Supervision: An Adaptive and Relative Process," *Personnel Psychology,* Autumn, p. 329.

[18] Some researchers, such as W. F. Whyte, stress the role of home background and social environment in accounting for certain nonconformist worker behavior. In discussing "restricters" and "rate busters" he has studied, Whyte points out that the restricters were sons of unskilled industrial workers who had been reared in large

ministering it. It is the supervisor's job to protect his own integrity and the interests of his group. If the troublemaker does not respond to negative sanctions, then he should be fired. Remember, however, that healthy individuals may at times behave like trouble-makers because of legitimate grievances or personal problems. The supervisor who conscientiously attempts a positive approach with all subordinates who behave like troublemakers should have little dif-ficulty in making an accurate diagnosis.

Role of Informality

A popular saying is that "familarity breeds contempt." Machia-velli held this view and many present-day managers seem to accept it. Actually, its incorrectness is worth discussing, for much that we have said about positive leadership is based on assumptions that are in direct conflict with it. What is meant by the term "familarity" in this expression? Presumably, it implies the lack of formality or adherence to formal protocol in subordinate-superior relationships. The position taken in this book is that informality, when coupled with other necessary attributes, is an asset for the supervisor, not a liability. Some of the desirable functional characteristics for effec-tive leadership were presented in the preceding chapter in the dis-cussion of selection criteria. Here, we will discuss those which specifically relate to this matter of familiarity.

Informality should not be confused with the problem of partiality. Effective supervisors do not play favorites, nor do they give their subordinates reason for suspecting that they do. For this reason, a good supervisor does not spend any more time socializing with some of his subordinates than with others, nor does he perform special favors for some as compared with others. Yet, he attempts to be friendly and informal with all of them, to create an atmosphere of acceptance and facilitate communication and consultation. The effective supervisor operates within the framework of policies and orders handed down to him. He does not "pass the buck" by criti-cizing higher management for unpopular undertakings. If he dis-

cities. He states that "... they had been active in boys' gangs. Such activity tends to build loyalty to one's own group and opposition to authority—whether from parents or management." Rate busters on the other hand were largely from farms or small towns, "... where they lived under close supervision or parental authority and had little time or opportunity to develop gang activities and the accompanying loyalty to the gang." See W. F. Whyte *et al.*, *Money and Motivation* (New York: Harper & Bros., 1955).

agrees with higher policy, he tries to influence a change through proper appeal to his superiors. If this fails, and he feels that he can not live with the assignments given to him, he should seek employment elsewhere.

Lastly, the effective supervisor holds his men to high standards of performance which have been set, as far as is possible, through consultation with them. He does not let his feeling for his men interfere with effective discipline or adherence to the job at hand. He invariably demands as much from himself as from his men, and usually more. He stresses high standards because of the realization that employees may be happy and evidence good group morale without contributing to organization objectives. The challenge to the supervisor is to help the subordinate meet his personal needs in the process of carrying out formal organizational objectives and, *conversely, to deny him this need satisfaction if he does not contribute to these objectives.*

The practice of informality *within the framework outlined above* will create respect rather than contempt on the part of subordinates in a stable work group (perhaps not in some temporary work groups). Think of the men you have worked for, for whom you had the most respect; chances are that they were essentially informal in their relation with you! Perhaps the idea that familiarity or informality breeds contempt came from the fact that a weak and incompetent leader often uses friendliness as a means of trying to "buy" acceptance from his subordinates and inducing them to overlook his deficiencies. Such a person is so fearful of rejection that he will disregard his obligations to the organization—and even denounce his superiors—if he feels that this will help him gain the the acceptance of his men. Such a person cannot detach himself from the immediate situation and remain consistently task oriented. It is not surprising that his subordinates often feel contempt for his incompetence and attempts to curry their favor.

The effective supervisor is a healthy individual. He has not suffered need deprivation to the extent that he is incapable of doing what must be done, though this often involves unpleasantness and the meting-out of discipline. He has a sincere interest in his subordinates and their needs but never forgets that their needs must be met within the framework of organizational constraints. He refrains from becoming too greatly involved, in a personal sense, with any of his men through the realization that such involvement can seriously interfere with his ability objectively to meet his obligations to the group and the company.

Generic Hypotheses V, VI, and VII have to do largely with the *clinical job* of the supervisor. Since they are so interrelated, they will be discussed together.[19]

GENERIC HYPOTHESIS V (PERCEPTUAL DISTORTION)

Objective perception of problems and interpersonal relations is distorted by wishes and fears—catharsis will tend to relieve the distortion.

GENERIC HYPOTHESIS VI (PATHOLOGICAL REACTION)

Pathological reaction occurs when an organism is confronted by a situation that it perceives as being impossible to solve or cope with and that it feels it *must* deal with.

GENERIC HYPOTHESIS VII (COUNSELING)

There is a basic clinical approach, available to and practical for the supervisor, that is effective in dealing with perceptual distortion and troubled employees. It is based on the non-directive interview concept in which the interviewer

1. establishes face-to-face rapport with the employee;
2. *listens* as he encourages the employee to talk out his problems without challenge or approval;
3. refrains from prescribing for the employee, but assists him in developing his own solution;
4. follows up by encouraging and assisting the employee in carrying out his *own* plan.

In developing this technique the interviewer can be trained to gain insight into his own behavior so that he may remain emotionally neutral with the employee, and he can learn to identify those cases which should be referred to a professional therapist.

Directive vs. Non-directive Counseling

There are two general schools of counseling theory and practice: the *directive* and the *non-directive*. Comparison of these should provide for a better understanding of the rationale and technique

---

[19] For an excellent discussion of the clinical role of the supervisor see John Pfiffner, *The Supervision of Personnel* (2d ed.; Englewood Cliffs, New Jersey: Prentice-Hall, Inc., 1958), chap. 18.

of non-directive interviewing as a productive counseling tool.[20] The directive approach requires that a professionally trained counselor interview the counselee for the purpose of obtaining adequate information about the counselee's problem; that he thoroughly analyze this information and then *clarify* the nature of the problem for the counselee or prescribe a course of action for him. An underlying assumption of the directive approach is that the counselee is incapable, both currently and potentially, of understanding and solving his own problem—that is why he seeks help from the counselor. Other assumptions are that the counselor can give real understanding of the problem to the counselee through explanation and appeals to his reason and that the counselee will *act upon* the counselor's recommendations if they are understandable and appropriate to the problem!

The theory of non-directive counseling is based on significantly different assumptions. It assumes that the *best solution* to the counselee's problem resides *potentially* within the counselee but that it will remain *unavailable* to him as long as he is too emotionally involved in the problem to see it objectively. As Generic Hypothesis V points out, we are denied objective perception of our problems and interpersonal relations by our wishes and fears. Catharsis—permitting the counselee freely to examine and express his feelings—will remove the "emotional prism" that has distorted the counselee's perception and permit him to view his problem objectively. Once the counselee sees the problem realistically, he is in a position to develop a solution that will adequately take into account his intimate knowledge of the factors and people associated with the situation. It is further assumed that the counselee will not really understand a solution, or be as motivated to put it into practice, if he has not arrived at it through his own thinking. We might say that catharsis releases the counselee from the influence of his neurotic needs sufficiently to let him objectively perceive and cope with his basic needs.

The technique of non-directive counseling seems deceptively simple. Some have labeled it the "two grunts and a groan method"!

---

[20] Reference was made to the value of non-directive interviewing for selection purposes in chap. 5 (see p. 147). When used for selection, the basic technique remains the same. However, the interviewer uses it to gain information about the candidate, which he feels is relevant to the job to be filled, rather than to guide the interviewee to the discovery of his own solution as in counseling. For an excellent reference on non-directive counseling see Carl R. Rogers, *Client-centered Therapy* (Boston: Houghton Mifflin Co., 1951).

It appears to be simply a matter of listening attentively to the coun-selee and encouraging him to talk. Actually, the expert non-directive counselor requires professional training as much as, if not more than, the expert directive counselor. For, though he re-frains from prescribing for the counselee, he does use his insight to guide the counselee along productive avenues of exploration. And the personal demands on the counselor are undoubtedly greater in non-directive counseling; he must conceal his emotions from the counselee, suppress his ego by consistently giving the counselee the center of the stage, and exercise the patience required to wait for the counselee to "catch up" with his thinking and insights into the prob-lem. A counselor must have a large measure of self-knowledge and maturity to meet these requirements effectively. Only to the extent that he is acquainted with his own biases and emotional "sore spots," and is not driven by a need to dominate and impress, can he hope to be an attentive listener and remain emotionally uninvolved with the counselee.

The value of catharsis with regard to group discussion was pointed out earlier in this chapter. When a group member is emo-tionally upset and filled with anxiety, it is very difficult for him to be objective and reasonable. Only after he has been given the opportunity to ventilate his feelings and "get things off his chest" will he be truly receptive to rational discussion.

Emotional involvement, by denying the individual objective per-ception of the problem and its possible solutions, can lead to a level of frustration and anxiety that causes him to view the situation as hopeless and overwhelming. If this condition persists over a period of time, it can produce neurotic and other pathological behavior. Non-directive counseling can be very useful in such cases by making it possible for the individual to cope objectively with his problems and needs, to "see through" his defenses!

Fortunately, the non-directive approach, unlike the directive, is safe in unskilled hands. To the extent that the counselor *refrains* from giving prescriptions and explanations, he will not run the risk of harming the counselee. The professional non-directive counselor will use the method much more productively than the non-professional; nevertheless, the mature supervisor, with practice, will find it to be a most successful tool of supervision. Of course, when the troubled counselee fails to respond to the supervisor's technique or exhibits severe symptoms of abnormal behavior, the supervisor should recognize the need for professional help.

GENERIC HYPOTHESIS VIII ("LAW OF THE SITUATION")

This hypothesis relates to what has been termed the "law of the situation in relation to the solution of business problems": **If time permits, and all relevant facts are collected, studied, and discussed by those immediately concerned, under leadership that encourages impartiality, a solution (the "law of the situation") will emerge that will be acceptable to all. There will be no need to *impose* a solution upon the group through the exercise of formal authority.**

It is important that the conditions prescribed by this hypothesis be met before the "law of the situation" can emerge. There must be positive leadership with genuine participation, that is, a realization on the part of group members that they may significantly influence the final decision. Not only must all relevant facts be assembled; they must also be *effectively communicated* to group members. As was pointed earlier, *timing* and *mode of expression* are most important in communication. We cannot expect anxious, defensive group members to consider the facts objectively until they have had an opportunity to vent their feelings, and we must keep before us the need to "speak their language." If these factors are present—participation, positive leadership, facts, secure people, and adequate time—discussion will produce a sound solution or decision that will be acceptable to all.

This may sound idealistic and rather impractical. Have any groups *actually* functioned on this basis? The Quakers provide a striking example as described by S. Chase:

> Suppose we look in at a typical monthly business meeting. . . . After everyone has had his say, the Clerk drafts a minute—the famous "sense of the meeting" minute in which group opinion is summarized. He reads it to the members for their assent or modification. *There is no formal voting.* Nobody, I am told, has voted in any Quaker meeting, in any country, in three hundred years—except where the law requires it on specific documents. The challenge of the Clerk to the members on the minute, and their response, can perhaps be interpreted as a kind of voting. But when a policy or an action is decided upon, there is no division between majority and minority; the decision is invariably unanimous.
>
> At least nine major principles and procedures appear in Quaker business meetings, though not necessarily all in any one gathering:
>
> 1. *Unanimous decisions.* There is no voting, no minority to nourish grievances and so prevent a real settlement.
> 2. *Silent periods,* always at the opening and closing of meetings, and whenever two opposing parties begin to clash.

3. *A moratorium* (or cooling-off technique) for questions where agreement cannot be reached unanimously, where opposing parties start to form. If they are important questions, they will come up again at future meetings until disagreement ceases and unanimity is found.
4. *Participation* by all members who have ideas on the subject. Experience has demonstrated, says the Book of Discipline, "that the final decision of the group is usually superior to that of the individual." Members pool their knowledge and experience.
5. *Learning to listen.* Again to quote the Book of Discipline: "It behooves them in their meetings to hear with attentive and tolerant minds the messages and views of all members present." Quakers do not go to meetings with minds made up; they go to learn, expecting the right solution to crystallize from the experience of all.
6. *Absence of leaders.* The Clerk does some steering, but he must not interpose his ego or take a dominant role.
7. *Nobody outranks anybody.* Rich and poor, men and women, old and young, have equal status and are expected to participate equally. Everybody has had past experiences, and so everybody has something to give.
8. *Consider the facts.* As emotions are at a minimum, facts and their cool consideration can be at a maximum.
9. *Keep meetings small.* The best size for solving problems is a face-to-face group of not more than twenty persons. Yearly meetings of several hundred, however, are able to use the method.[21]

Chase also refers to other groups that have relied on unanimity:

Councils of the Solomon Islanders do not vote but come to unanimous agreement. William Penn wrote that Indian councils in America forego formal rules of order and "do not speak two at a time, or interfere in the least, one with another," George P. Murdock, who developed the famous Cross-Cultural Index at Yale, says that unanimous agreement is the rule in the councils of many primitive societies.[22]

There is no intention of implying here that unanimous agreement should be the goal of all group deliberation within a business organization. There are significant differences that distinguish the environment of a Quaker business meeting from that of a business organization. The Quakers comprise small, highly selected groups, they draw upon a long tradition of self-discipline and participation; and usually they are not constrained by the serious time limits within which the business executive must operate. Nevertheless, the value of this approach for effective group action should not be

---

[21]Stuart Chase, *Roads to Agreement* (New York: Harper & Bros., 1951), pp. 45–55.
[22] *Ibid.*

underestimated; it is appropriate in many more business situations than it is attempted!

Evidence of the value of this participative approach to problem-solving in business is provided by a number of sources. The so-called Scanlon-type plan has provided for a new order of understanding in labor-management relations when labor and management representatives are mature enough to implement it.[23] Morris Viteles has reported some valuable research findings.[24] Leighton's now classic study of the administration of Japanese relocation centers during World War II is most relevant.[25] And Stuart Chase points out that the board of directors of Standard Oil of New Jersey has followed the rule of unanimity.[26]

GENERIC HYPOTHESIS IX (RESISTANCE TO CHANGE)

Resistance to change is motivated largely by a real or imagined threat to personal well-being. When a change can be perceived as affording greater satisfaction of personal needs than can be achieved without it, it will no longer be resisted. Because of this, the *feelings* associated with a given change must receive just as much attention as do the *logics* associated with the change.

Some people erroneously generalize that change *in itself* is resisted by humans, but it does not take much reflection to disprove this idea. Pay increases and improvements that render working conditions more pleasant are rarely resisted, and there are many other examples that could be cited. When we resist change, we really resist the inconveniences and threatened need deprivation that we, correctly or incorrectly, associate with the change. Many technical assistance experts are amazed when they discover that it is not always easy to "sell" improved practices and equipment in backward areas. A primitive farmer, for example, may fear that a steel plow will poison his soil or that he may lose status with his group because his use of it will imply a disrespect for the traditions and values of the past.

---

[23] See Frederick Lesieur, *The Scanlon Plan* (Cambridge: the M.I.T. Press, 1958). See also Henry Nunn, *The Whole Man Goes to Work* (New York: Harper & Bros., 1953).

[24] See Part Three of Viteles, *Motivation and Morale in Industry* (New York: W. W. Norton & Co., 1953). See also Cartwright and Zander (eds.), *op. cit.*, first and revised (1960) editions, for other interesting experimental data.

[25] Alexander Leighton, *The Governing of Men* (Princeton, New Jersey: Princeton University Press, 1945).

[26] Chase, *op. cit.*, p. 54.

To introduce a change effectively, management must devote as much attention to *emotional reactions* associated with the change as to adequate explanation of the *rational character* of the change. In work situations *the meaning of a change* is as important as, if not more important than, the change itself.[27] Before we can hope for employees to view a change objectively, we must reassure them that they will not be penalized as a result of the change. Even if the change necessitates laying off workers who cannot be absorbed on equivalent or better terms elsewhere in the organization, management has the responsibility of assisting them to find equivalent employment elsewhere. Some firms have made it a practice to carry such displaced employees on the pay roll until they do find other employment, treating this expense as a cost of innovation. It is unlikely that such an outlay will ever equal the first year's saving made possible by the innovation. To the extent that such an expenditure will forestall *future* resistance to change on the part of remaining employees, it is a sound investment indeed!

Of course, the rapid pace of innovation made possible by and *demanded* by automation has made it virtually impossible for some firms to cope adequately with the displaced employee problem. But even in these, management can ameliorate the situation through better planning for change and closer cooperation with public agencies. Most employees are aware of the need for economic change and progress, but they can hardly be blamed for resisting such progress when they perceive that it is taking place at undue personal expense.

Employee participation in the making of changes is most productive.[28] It helps to get employee fears and misgivings in the open, where they can be dealt with. It provides employees with a means for *influencing* changes along lines that are most consistent with *their needs* as well as those of the organization. At the same time,

---

[27] This was one of the findings of the now famous Hawthorne experiments. See F. J. Roethlisberger and W. J. Dickson, *Management and the Worker* (Cambridge, Massachusetts: Harvard University Press, 1939). On page 579, they point out that " . . . changes in technical organization, of course, have consequences in terms of the social structure of a concern. They frequently result in the social dislocation of individuals and groups and disrupt the interpersonal relations which tend to give these individuals and groups their feelings of security and integrity." See also "The Fruitful Errors of Elton Mayo" in W. M. Fox (ed.), *Readings in Personnel Management from "Fortune,"* or *Fortune*, November, 1946.

[28] If, as has been suggested, the employee views the participation as being "legitimate."

it permits employees to develop a genuine understanding of the *need* for a change as well as of the *character* of the change. Several experimental studies have shown that this approach helps management avoid the drop in output and the increases in employee turnover and grievances that *usually* accompany changes in work assignments. These undesirable consequences have occurred even in those cases in which management has carefully planned changes and made every effort to explain them—inviting full employee discussion.[29]

Not only should employees be given the opportunity to participate in the fashioning of a change; but whenever feasible, they should be led to a *group decision* as to its adoption. Group decision establishes the change as a *group goal* and directs group pressure toward individual compliance with it. Even individual decisions for individual action that are *evoked in a group setting* are more likely to be implemented than if they are evoked in private. It has been found, for example, that mentally ill individuals may respond better to group therapy than to individual therapy.[30]

GENERIC HYPOTHESIS X
(MORALE AND COMPANY GOALS)

Good morale in a group is evidenced by the willingness of group members to subordinate their immediate convenience to identification with, and effective implementation of, group goals; good morale contributes to the efficient implementation of formal company goals to the extent that group goals contribute to these formal goals.

Some researchers report that there is no significant relationship between morale and productivity. This is not surprising if one thinks of production *only* in terms of output for the firm. Since morale is a *group* phenomenon, we should think of production in terms of *group goals* if we wish to interrelate the two. For example, it is likely that a work group with high morale will strike quite productively; that is, the group members will carry out their picketing and other assignments with real unity of purpose and diligence. For group goals are not synonymous with company goals. In fact,

---

[29] See Lester Coch and John French, Jr., "Overcoming Resistance to Change," Cartwright and Zander (eds.), *op. cit.* See also French, Ross, Kirby, Nelson, and Smyth, "Employee Participation in a Program of Industrial Change," *Personnel*, November–December, 1958.

[30] For some provocative research findings see Kurt Lewin, "Studies in Group Decision," in Cartwright and Zander (eds.), *op. cit.* (1st ed., 1953).

there is widespread featherbedding and withholding of effort in industry because workers do not see the achievement of company goals as a means to the fulfillment of their own individual needs. When this occurs, management has failed in one of two ways: either it has failed to make it possible for workers to meet their own needs in the process of carrying out company goals, or it has failed to *demand* the achievement of company goals as a *requirement* for individual need fulfillment. The challenge to management is to see to it that company goals are encompassed by group goals. When this occurs, good morale will contribute significantly to improved production for the firm.

We say that good morale is evidenced by the willingness of group members to subordinate their immediate convenience to identification with and effective implementation of group goals. When will group members do this? When they see it as the "price" they must pay for having their individual needs met by the group. The supervisor has an important part in creating the kind of interpersonal relationships and group climate that will facilitate individual need-fulfillment and, consequently, the development of good group morale. In addition to being good at planning and organizing the work of the group, he must be good at human relations.[31]

SOME CONCLUDING REMARKS ABOUT SUPERVISION

Impact of Organizational Climate

Most of this discussion has been directed at the complexity and challenge of the individual supervisor's job. Unfortunately, effective supervision is not assured by the recruitment of healthy and able supervisors. For the individual supervisor and his group do not function in a vacuum. There are strong environmental factors in the organization that have a profound influence on the supervisor.

Among these are the leadership "climate" at the top of the organization, the kind of supervision that the supervisor receives from his boss, and the system of rewards and penalties in the organization (what type of supervisory behavior does it encourage?). These factors have much to do with defining the set of behaviors or "role"

---

[31] Because the "task" and "social" roles of the leader are each demanding in their own right and it is unusual for an individual to be equally strong in both, it has been suggested that *two* leaders be appointed to a group. The "social" leader would be subordinate to the "task" leader and would complement his efforts. It is argued that this will merely provide more formal control over what now takes place informally, i.e., the missing mode of leadership is supplied by the group informally.

that is expected of the supervisor and that significantly sets the stage
for his success or failure.

One of the most dramatic illustrations of how we may be influenced by forces of which we are largely unaware is provided by
experimentation with representatives of groups that are in competition. Each group is given the same problem to work on and is
told that it will win or lose in terms of whether or not its solution
or proposals are accepted as the best by the other competing group
representatives after due deliberation. When the group representatives meet around a conference table, their teams are permitted to
sit behind them and send notes to them on questions they want
clarified. The results are striking and invariable: despite the fact
that a team of impartial judges usually will agree unanimously as
to the "best" solution, the representatives have never achieved such
agreement! Professor Herbert Shepard reports on the results of this
type of experimentation at Esso:

> ... when people are in a competitive situation, they are unable to see
> the points they have in common but they clearly see their differences. ...
> ... We have done this with fifty or sixty groups but we have never
> been able to get a decision. ... Nobody has ever deserted his own group.
> In fact, it is questionable if his life would be worth living for the rest of
> the program if he did. ...
> The interesting thing is that when there are spokesmen representing
> groups in competition, what a spokesman does has very little to do with
> his own character or personality. His behavior is almost completely
> determined by his role as group representative. ...
> ... However, as far as the other participants are concerned, they see
> the spokesman's behavior as a reflection of his personality, rather than
> his role.[32]

This type of finding dramatizes the need for higher management
to appraise realistically the "counterdemands" that groups can exert
upon divisional managers, department heads, and, especially, foremen. Higher managers should encourage and support lower managers in their efforts to develop group values that are consistent with
organizational aims, yet they must realize that some concession
has to be made to the parochial demands of group loyalty. A production vice-president cannot be expected to function with an objective "general management viewpoint" in executive committee
meetings if he is not adequately protected from possible charges of
"betrayal" by the members of his group.

---

[32] Herbert A. Shepard, "An Action Research Approach to Organization Development," *Management Record*, June, 1960.

Supervisory Influence

Another important consideration is the amount of *influence* that the supervisor has with his superiors. From the employee's viewpoint, positive leadership on the part of his supervisor is useful to him only to the extent that it helps to *satisfy* his needs. If the supervisor's recommendations regarding improvement of working conditions, pay increases, promotions, and other matters of importance are largely ignored by higher management, employees will tend to associate him with *frustration* of their needs. To the extent that they attribute his lack of influence to personal incompetence at "handling things," they will lose respect for him as a leader.[33]

The preceding pages have presented a strong case for positive, enlightened supervision. Why isn't this approach more prevalent in industry? Certainly it is not because it is new.[34] As with many international problems in the world today, it is not through want of sound concepts for effective living that we are confounded; it is our *inability to put what we know into practice.* Autocratic supervision, for example, is much *easier* to practice than the type of supervision that has been discussed. It makes far fewer demands for maturity, self-constraint, and self-knowledge. Actually, the way in which we exercise authority in supervising others is a reflection of our basic values and personality structure, to a large extent.

QUESTIONS

1. Do you think that human "ends" are more universal than the means for achieving them? Why or why not? What do people have in common? In what ways do they differ significantly? What bearing do these questions have on the study of effective leadership? Explain.

2. When the personal goals of organizational members are not the same as organization goals, how can the members be induced, most effectively, to carry out the work of the organization?

3. What are the basic needs that all people share? What happens if the satisfaction of these is habitually frustrated or blocked? Is one of these basic needs universally the strongest? Discuss.

---

[33] For an interesting study of the effects of supervisory influence, based on an analysis of several hundred supervisors and several thousand non-supervisory employees, see D. Pelz, "Influence: A Key to Effective Leadership in the First Line Supervisor," *Personnel,* Vol. XXIX, No. 3, pp. 3–11.

[34] See the references to Adam Smith in chap. 1; read Henry Dennison, *Organization Engineering* (New York: McGraw-Hill Book Co., 1931); and "rediscover" the important findings of the Hawthorne experiments (Roethlisberger and Dickson, *op. cit.*). Chaps. 9, 13, and 26 describe how the interview program led to the development of non-directive counseling and chap. 25 provides a summary of over-all results.

4. In what ways can neurosis be an asset in business? A liability? Explain.

5. What role does "formal organization" play in a business organization? What role does 'informal organization" play? Is there any relationship between the two? Explain.

6. Do you believe that the average person would elect to do nothing if his income were adequate and his neighbors uncritical? Explain the reasons underlying your position.

7. "A man's influence upon the thinking and actions of a group is determined for the most part by the quality or soundness of his ideas." What is your reaction to this statement? Discuss.

8. "It has been suggested that the majority of workers who strike for higher pay are really not striking for higher pay." Does this statement make sense? Explain.

9. What alternative to the use of a formal merit rating scale is discussed in this chapter? What are the advantages and disadvantages of this alternative?

10. Under what conditions is a negative approach to motivation likely to be more effective than a positive approach? Why?

11. What is meant by the popular expression, "familiarity breeds contempt?" Is this true in your opinion? Why or why not?

12. "Happy, contented employees are invariably good producers." What is your reaction to this statement? Explain.

13. "There are some people you just can't trust; if you give them an inch they'll take a mile and rub your good intentions in your face." Is this true? Why or why not?

14. Explain the *theory* and *technique* of directive counseling. Explain the *theory* and *technique* of non-directive counseling. What are the significant differences between the two as to theory and practice?

15. "A forty-year-old man, Mr. Smith, sees his middle-aged neighbor, Mr. Jones, make a fool of himself over a woman twenty years his junior, endangering his family unity and his own self-respect. All but Mr. Jones can plainly see that the woman is after Mr. Jones's wealth and position. Mr. Smith tries to advise Mr. Jones as to his folly, but to no avail. Five years later Mr. Smith does the same thing!" Is it reasonable to assume that Mr. Smith is a hypocrite or dishonest? Or is Mr. Smith not very smart? Is there any alternative explanation? Explain.

16. From the standpoint of decision making, what is unique about the Quakers? Would their methods apply equally well to groups within a business organization? Why or why not?

17. If you were assigned the task of introducing steel plows to natives who have never used anything but wooden plows in some far-off land, what steps would you follow? Outline in some detail these steps.

18. Under what conditions will high morale be related to the effective implementation of company goals? Explain.
19. What is meant by the expression "organizational climate?" Is there any relationship between it and supervisory behavior? Explain.
20. When told that a particular army division had the reputation of being a "black sheep," "hard luck" outfit and when shown evidence in the training and combat records that supported this evaluation, a famous general reputedly said, "We'll fix that!" picked up the phone, and replaced the divisional commander on the spot with one of his best officers. What assumptions did he base this action on? Do you think that he was right or wrong? Why?
21. What conflicting organizational demands may confront the production vice-president when he is serving as a member of the executive committee engaged in over-all planning activity? Explain.
22. What is "supervisory influence?" What relation has it to effective supervision? What lesson is implied for the "low-influence" supervisor? Explain.

Section II

ORGANIZATION FOR MANAGING

There are unique organizational requirements associated with each of the organic functions of management. Chapter 9 considers organization for planning in terms of integrated data processing requirements, the modern role of accounting, various planning agencies, and special provision for operations research and long-range planning activity. Organization for performance of the organizing and control functions is discussed in chapters 10 and 11, and chapter 12 presents a description and evaluation of provisions for decentralization at General Motors.

Chapter 9

ORGANIZATION FOR PLANNING

In chapter 2 the importance of planning, the *organic subfunctions of planning,* certain planning techniques, and the unique role that the computer plays in modern planning were discussed. There are still some important questions to consider with regard to planning. When is the acquisition of a computer feasible for a particular firm? How should we organize for maximum utilization of the computer, and how can we use it to strengthen the flow of data and over-all communication within the organization? Is there such a thing as "computer unemployment," and are there unique problems associated with the recruitment, training, and maintenance of computer personnel? What special planning groups can be created to facilitate the performance of planning functions, and what interrelationships should exist among those agencies to assure effective coordination of planning effort? These and other related questions will be discussed in this chapter.

COMPUTER ACQUISITION

The use of computers has made the development of a much higher degree of formalization in planning both feasible and economically desirable. The recent introduction of "solid state"—all transitorized—computers provides even greater appeal to the customer, for these virtually eliminate tube failures and dispense with the need for costly heat-dissipating and weight-bearing installation facilities and high electric power consumption. A computer purchase may prove feasible when forty or fifty full-time workers are engaged in computing, sorting, transcribing, or storing data. Investigation shows that computer application will replace approximately half of this force. Kozmetsky and Kircher point out that:

> Special-purpose information, such as recording an inventory situation, can be obtained by using special systems if the present expenditure or the added value of the information is of the order of about $15,000 to $20,000 a year. Systems have already been accepted that call for a pay-off period of up to 5 years, because of other advantages in speed and accuracy. A number of companies are already buying computer time on a service basis. Rates of $100 to $300 per hour are being quoted....
>
> Detailed installation studies often require 12 to 18 months for one application. The first application generally takes the longest.... Because of this (and other) preparation, the cost of installing the computer is generally equal to the cost of the computer....
>
> The General Electric Company placed their study under the direction of a systems and procedures group ... study showed that a break-even point could be reached when a computer was used as little as 2 hours a day on four clerical operations....[1]

Though they concede that clerical applications have provided some dramatic savings, Kozmetsky and Kircher believe that the *greatest promise* of the computer lies in its potential as a tool for achieving better production planning, market analysis, and over-all top management planning. They stress the value of companies *starting with* a top management operations research approach, even though it may not afford as large immediate savings as a purely clerical approach. This view is shared by many top executives who have had experience with computers. Some of the advantages of this approach will be considered in the discussion of the operations research group as a special planning agency.

INTEGRATED DATA PROCESSING AT SYLVANIA

The introduction of an integrated data processing system—a means for supplying data to users quickly, with desired format and minimal duplication of effort—provides an organization with an important communications tool. Often it leads to significant *unexpected* savings, too! For many firms have neglected thoroughgoing study of their informational needs. They find, in making the required analysis for integrated data handling, many gaps in their

---

[1] George Kozmetsky and Paul Kircher, *Electronic Computers and Management Control* (New York: McGraw-Hill Book Co., 1956), pp. 11, 12, 56, 60, 98. This book is especially useful for firms investigating the purchase of a computer or the installation of an integrated data handling system. Chap. 4, "Studies and Applications of Electric Systems," presents many interesting case studies.

communication system, much duplication of effort, and other inefficiencies. In making such an analysis:

The first step is to define as precisely as possible the various aspects of the availability of information and of the need for information. Next, the volume of data and rate of flow must be measured. Then the communication and processing links can be built.

This means the study will determine the points of use of information, the types of information required at each point, the time when the information is needed, and the forms in which it is desired. These items are then examined to determine overlaps. In this way unnecessary duplication is eliminated and provision of data for several similar needs can be unified.[2]

Some decentralized companies, impressed by the advantages of integrated data processing, shy away from it through fear that it will require, or lead to, centralization of authority. Actually, integrated data processing can *strengthen* rather than weaken the organizational basis for decentralization. At least, this seems to be the case at Sylvania Electric Products, Inc., which established a Central Data Processing Center in 1956.[3] At that time Sylvania was a decentralized company operating nine product divisions (now ten) and one engineering division; with 47 plants (now 45), 18 laboratories (now 22), 27 sales offices (now 32), and 18 warehouses (now 29), in 65 communities (now 70), in 25 states (now more than 30).

In 1951 a movement was started to centralize record keeping in order to reduce over-all clerical expense and take advantage of new developments in mechanization. Until then, records had been maintained at each plant or division headquarters. However, this centralization trend, which led to the establishment of a data processing center, was designed to *strengthen* rather than weaken the company's decentralized mode of operation. Mr. Guest stressed this point when he said:

We believe, and practice this belief, that every decision affecting the operations of the company must be made at the lowest level at which a

---

[2] *Ibid.*, p. 187.

[3] The discussion that follows is based on three published talks on "Administrative Automation at Sylvania" given by Sylvania officials at the Annual Office Management Conference of the American Management Association in New York, October 16, 1956 (the officers were: Leon C. Guest, Jr., controller; E. G. Dunn, manager of the Data Processing Center; and J. D. Gallagher, manager of planning and development at the Center), and an analysis by Robert Gregory, "Sylvania's Data Processing Center," in Malcolm, Rowe, and McConnell, (eds.), *Management Control Systems* (New York: John Wiley & Sons, 1960), pp. 157–68. The talks by Guest, Dunn, and Gallagher are presented in *Administrative Automation through IDP and EDP*, American Management Association, 1515 Broadway, New York, Management Series No. 144, 1956.

good decision (one based on all the facts) can be made. . . . Sylvania's firm belief is that data processing will make decentralization even more effective. The decentralized organization will be able to act more rapidly and with more flexibility. The Data Processing Center, therefore, will become strictly a service department whose responsibility it is to gather information from the operating divisions and to transmit that information at the earliest possible moment to the individual, in the form most helpful to him, who must make the operating decision based on the information so provided.

Of special importance to Sylvania's management was the idea of getting adequate information in *useful* form to decision points at the "earliest possible moment." Mr. Dunn pointed this out by saying: "An awareness by our Board of Directors and Top Management that it was mandatory in future company operations to give all levels of management a look through the forward planning windshield rather than the historical rear view mirror, resulted in the establishment of a Data Processing Center." Mr. Dunn explained that the entire program was built around three basic considerations:

1. A new facility designed to provide for centralization of record keeping for the company *as a whole,* with computer applications to be developed over a five year period to the maximum degree.

2. All company locations tied into the Center by use of a leased private wire system which can handle *both* administrative and data processing traffic on a high volume basis.[4]

3. All applications to be planned and developed as an *integrated system* from its origination at a source anywhere in the Company, to output finalization and feed back of information developed by the computer.[5]

Center Organization

At the time of its establishment the following functions were performed under the supervision of the Center manager:

Methods surveys (planning)	Univac programming
System analyses	Communications:
Forms and machine design	Planning
Univac methods	Operations

[4] The special equipment required for such a communications network was designed by Western Union. The focal point of operations is at the Data Processing Center located in Camillus, New York, near Syracuse. (The paper by Mr. Gallagher provides a very good description of the technical problems involved in setting up the system. See also Robert Gregory, *op. cit.*)

[5] Mr. Gregory points out: "In a well-balanced, integrated program, it is virtually impossible to delineate the boundary between a data-processing system and a communications system. The communications system, in order to function at peak efficiency, tends to lose its identity as a separate unit and becomes, instead, an integral part of the input and output of the data-processing unit itself." *Op. cit.*, p. 158.

Mr. Dunn described the initial service functions of the Center:

Sylvania's decentralized management will be serviced by the Data Processing Center in two ways:

1. Providing facts for decision-making in the proper format and at the right time.

2. Elimination of responsibility by decentralized management for routine clerical operations and reports, thus enabling it to be free to attend to primary responsibilities for planning and effectuating *optimum* return on investment for the operation or operations for which they are accountable.

After almost five years of operation, it is most interesting to examine changes that have been made at the Center and the extent

FIG. 9-1

Sylvania Data Processing Center: 1956 Organization Chart

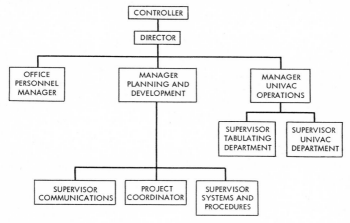

to which initial expectations have been realized. The following discussion is based on data supplied by Mr. J. J. Guidrey, manager of the Center, in November, 1960.[6] The organization of the Center has changed somewhat, though, as Mr. Guidrey points out: "The *over-all* functions and responsibilities of this group remain the same as they were in our beginning days."

It will be noted through reference to Figures 9-1 and 9-2 that there have been several title changes and that there are now five rather than three supervisors reporting directly to the Center manager. One of the five, the supervisor of communications, formerly

---

[6] Sylvania is now a wholly owned subsidiary of the General Telephone and Electronics Corporation. Mr. L. C. Guest, Jr., former controller of Sylvania, is now vice-president and controller of General Telephone.

reported to the supervisor of data processing applications (former title; manager of planning and development). And the fifth represents a new person, coordinator of data processing planning, who provides for liaison and coordination between the planning group at the Center and plant and divisional systems and procedures personnel. Two other new positions are supervisor of the data control department, and chief programmer.

Five Years After

Mr. Guidrey reports:

Up to the present time, the efforts of the Data Processing Center have been primarily directed toward coordination and centralization of finan-

FIG 9-2

Sylvania Electric Products, Inc.
Data   Processing   Center: 1960   Organization   Chart

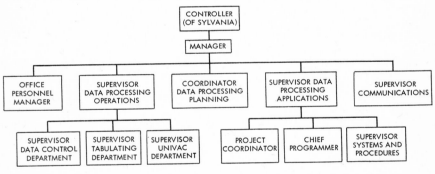

cial and accounting functions applicable to a centralized accounting office. We have expanded in Camillus from one Univac to where we now have two.[7] In these interim years, several complete Tabulating Departments have been moved into Camillus from divisional and plant locations. . . . Included in the list of applications prepared on the computers which we do on a corporate wide basis are:

1. Payrolls and allied reportings,
2. Accounts Payable including vendor check writing and voucher distribution,
3. Accounts Receivable including customers statements, Aging Reports and Statistical Analysis,
4. Personnel Inventory, and
5. General Ledger and Expense Analysis.

---

[7] Mr. Gregory points out: "The goal to have the Data Processing Center break even on a current basis within its first two years of operation was reached." *Op. cit.,* p. 167.

Applications not processed on a corporate basis but only for specific plants or divisions include:

1. Sales accounting, statistics and analysis for two divisions,
2. Material Control for one plant, and
3. Incentive payroll computations for four divisions.

Computer utilization for all of these applications represents well over 600 hours per month.

Mr. Guidrey states:

We feel certain that centralized data processing has definitely made decentralization more effective throughout the company as Mr. Guest had predicted. . . . There has been absolutely no tendency at Sylvania towards centralization of decision making. Decisions are still made at the lowest possible level. The function of the Data Processing Center is to develop information that can be used by management at local operations to guide them in their decision making. . . . We have arrived at the point where our decentralized units would object strenuously to having their routine payrolls, voucher check writing, etc., returned to them.

Elimination of Positions

Up to the present, there have *not* been any middle management positions eliminated in the company, with the exception of tabulating department supervisors and other subsupervisors of divisional and plant accounting functions no longer needed outside the Data Center. As Mr. Guest predicted in 1956, the ratio of clerical workers to all workers has reversed its upward trend; Mr. Guidrey says: "It would appear that additional large volumes of work transferred to the computer will require a disproportionately small number of additional personnel." However, "In no case have clerical layoffs exceeded the assimilation opportunities."

As will be seen, this experience does not bear out the dramatic predictions of such investigators as Leavitt, Whisler, Slater, and Hoos as to the significant organizational changes that would occur when the "computer takes over the office." However, this is not very surprising when we consider some of the unique attributes of the Sylvania situation. Here the Central Data Processing Center serves and, in part, supplements the personnel of *decentralized units*. Also, this *new* facility was established during a period of rapid growth and expansion of the company. In addition, the use of the Center for *non-routine* processing of data has been limited. As Mr. Guidrey points out: "Up to the present time, most of our efforts at Camillus have been directed toward the centralization of accounting functions and any efforts directed toward operations research and fore-casting and decision making have been of a superficial nature."

Program Implementation

From the outset, those responsible for the design and implemen-tation of the program have worked closely with operating personnel. Mr. Gallagher stresses the importance of this:

A basic problem that has hindered the advance of data processing from its inception has centered around the difficulty of establishing proper lines of communications between the data-processing organization and operations personnel, and between the various departmental groups within the data-processing organization itself.

If a data-processing operation is to achieve any measure of success, it must integrate its activities with the operational activities of the com-pany. It cannot consider itself as a separate and distinct entity, apart from the company, functioning as a pure service agency or as a captive consulting facility.[8]

Mr. Gregory points out, specifically, how effective liaison has been maintained with decentralized personnel:

Annual and quarterly meetings are held at Camillus for division con-trollers to cover intensively the entire program including present and future planning. Many meetings at division headquarters are attended by the Data Processing Director to present the program and to answer questions about present and future plans.

All changes in procedures—either simple improvements over present methods or parts of the over-all systems conversion requirements for computer application—are reviewed in detail with local management in advance of the change. We want them to understand what is proposed, why it is proposed, how it will be accomplished, what the effect on local personnel will be, and what benefits will be derived by location, by division, and for the company as a whole. . . . A system is not considered to be operating effectively for turnover to location personnel until it is completely de-bugged throughout all phases from original source to final output.[9]

Plans for Future

Though no management analysis group has been established as yet, such a move remains part of the long-range plan for the devel-opment of the Data Processing Center and the full utilization of its resources. Management may decide to initiate such activity at the divisional level, where decentralized, local, analysis groups, equip-

---

[8] J. D. Gallagher, "Organization of the Data Processing Function," in Malcolm, Rowe, and McConnell, *op. cit.*, p. 121.

[9] Gregory, *op. cit.*, p. 163.

ped with smaller computers, could experiment with various applications and procedures. Later, all or part of the programs could be transferred to the faster and more sophisticated central computer for processing. And perhaps analysis personnel will be maintained at the Center to serve in an advisory or secondary staff capacity to divisional analysis staff members. Mr. Guidrey says:

At present, we are engaged in an evaluation study to determine a replacement for the two Univacs which we presently have installed at Camillus. Our requirements indicate a need for a faster computer with a much larger capacity than we now have available. Our aim is to bring in, at the earliest possible date, a second generation computer which will embody all of the latest computer developments to be used with the most modern techniques available.

THE ACCOUNTING DEPARTMENT: A "DATA PROCESSING CENTER"

An accounting department is a "data processing center" that acts in a service or staff capacity to data users in the organization. Obviously, its effectiveness will depend on how well it can supply users with the data they need, when they need them, and in the most appropriate form. Such service on the part of an accounting department will not "just happen"; it will result only from careful analysis of data needs at all levels in the organization, adequate planning, organizing, and control to meet these needs, and close continuing liaison between accounting and using personnel.[10]

Controllership Foundation Study

Simon and a group of fellow-researchers studied the needs and problems of seven large companies to determine how accounting activities should be organized to provide the greatest service to operating executives and others.[11] Simon provides a good statement of the approach that was followed:

(1) The core of the study was an analysis of the way in which decisions actually were made and the locations of important decision func-

---

[10] Gallagher observes: "Most Companies, from a corporate viewpoint, have found that the potential of the data-processing program can be best exploited where the financial department is held responsible for the developmnt of an integrated systems program because of the over-all interests of the financial department in all phases of the business." "Organization of the Data-Processing Function." *Op. cit.*, p. 123.

[11] Herbert A. Simon, Harold Guetzkow, George Kozmetsky, and Gordon Tyndall, *Centralization vs. Decentralization in Organizing the Controller's Department* (New York: Controllership Foundation, Inc., 1954). A good discussion of the findings is presented by Pfiffner and Sherwood in *Administrative Organization* (Prentice-Hall, Inc., 1960), pp. 390–97.

tions in the organization. . . . By observation of the actual decision-making process, specific types of data needs were identified at particular organizational levels . . . each involving quite distinct problems of communication for the accounting department. . . .

(2) The recommended organizational pattern for the accounting department was built around its task of informing and influencing these operating decisions.

(3) The recommendations for organizational change were to be implemented by bringing about changes in the communication patterns— in the patterns of who-talks-to-whom-how-often-about-what—rather than by formal changes in organization charts.[12]

Three kinds of information were identified by the investigators:

Score card information—to answer the question, "How well am I doing?"

Attention directing—to answer the question of "What problems and situations need looking into?" What is "score card" information for one may be "attention directing" information for another, e.g., his boss.

Problem solving—to supply data necessary for making decisions and solving specific problems.

They concluded that "score card" and "attention directing" informational needs can best be met through a decentralized approach whereby factory accountants and cost analysts are close to operating units. It is essential that operating supervisors have confidence in the standards that are used for "score card" and "attention directing" purposes and that they understand the implications and limitations of the data they receive. Also, operating supervisors must believe that those who supply information are acquainted with their unique data needs and will be responsive to changes in need when they arise. To satisfy these requirements those who supply data must maintain effective liaison with their "data customers."

However, a more centralized approach for the development of "problem solving" data seems desirable. Problem solving needs for accounting data are most frequently encountered in staff units that are responsible for making special studies. To develop data for such units, often it is necessary to start with all the available raw data— for the factory or company as a whole—and to assemble specific figures in response to specific purposes formulated by the using agency. A centralized "special studies" group in the headquarters or factory controller's office could be established for this type of data collection.

---

[12] Herbert A. Simon, *Administrative Behavior* (New York: Macmillan Co., 1957), p. xx.

The research group perceived three major dimensions of the accounting function:

Record-keeping—bookkeeping, report preparation; poses no unique problems as to mode or speed of communication.

Current analysis—provision of appropriate "score card" and "attention directing" information. A decentralized approach with good informal or staff relationships is desirable.

Special studies—provision of data for making decisions and solving specified problems. As was pointed out above, a centralized "special studies" group in the factory or headquarters controller's office probably would provide the best approach.

On the basis of its analysis, the group proposes the following kind of functionalization in the controller's organization of a manufacturing concern:[13]

Financial accounting— all depts.	Cost accounting and current analysis —mfg. dept.	Sales accounting	Special studies at company level—all depts.	Internal audit

Accounting in a Decentralized Firm

With the findings of this study in mind, a productive approach to the performance of accounting functions in a decentralized manufacturing organization would be:

FIG. 9-3

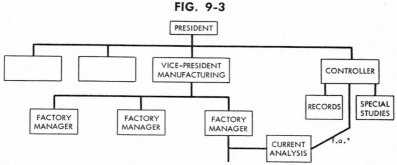

*f.a. signifies functional authority—in this instance, on the part of the controller to specify the nature and frequency of reports from the person in charge of current analysis at the factory level.

[13] Simon, *et al., op. cit.,* p. 71.

With this arrangement, record keeping is centralized. Data—perhaps assembled via an integrated data handling system—drawn from all segments of the company are readily available to the special studies group for special analyses or to company-wide personnel for other purposes. Current analysis activity is placed under the direction of the decentralized factory managers so that the "score card" and "attention directing" needs of factory supervisory personnel may be adequately perceived and served. On the other hand, the headquarters controller should not be left "high and dry." He must have some assurance that accounting personnel assigned to the factories to perform current analysis activities are following prescribed procedures. He must have reliable sources of "attention directing" and "score card" data from below so that he may properly manage his organization and make valuable contributions to over-all company planning as a member of top management. It seems reasonable to assume that these needs will be met if two provisions are satisfied:

1. All personnel who are to be assigned to factory current analysis work must be trained in the headquarters controller's organization or must serve there for a certain minimum period for orientation purposes.

2. The controller has functional authority to prescribe the nature and frequency of reports he requires from such personnel. (As indicated in Fig. 9-3.)

This organizational arrangement encourages current analysis personnel genuinely to serve the needs of factory personnel. Simultaneously, it provides important "feedback" data for the controller without violating the *Principle of Unity of Command.*

One of the men associated with Simon in this study, Kozmetsky, provides some additional comments of interest:

If score-card and attention-getting data are reported as gathered directly to managers, and if problem-solving data are developed from raw data by special staff groups, it is evident that for the first user there would tend to be reporting of data only as required. The "time-schedule" problem of data processing would be minimized.

However, if the data must be used for several purposes, as is usually the case (for payroll, etc.) the duplicate processing required often becomes expensive. There are a number of ways that this "message" problem can be relieved.

The simplest is to report the data in physical terms where possible. Dollarizing the data is time-consuming, expensive, and frequently unnecessary. Some items, such as manpower status, may be handled best by clerks reporting directly to superintendents, as straightforward counts.

If accumulations through time are needed, then the use of counters and of electronic systems may be indicated. . . .

Use of the computer, with its ability to process data rapidly, should not be permitted to encourage managers to ask for data they do not need. In many cases, if a model can be constructed of a particular operation, the manager can operate in terms of key inputs, outputs, and variables in his model.[14]

ORGANIZATIONAL EFFECTS OF THE COMPUTER

Organization for Operations Research

As was pointed out in chapter 2, managers can make use of new planning techniques without the benefit of extensive training in mathematics and statistics. However, a conceptual understanding of operations research techniques and the mathematical approach to business problem solving will obviously facilitate matters. In his attempt to identify variables, assign weights and probability estimates, and speculate as to relationships between factors, the manager will draw upon his extensive experience and knowledge of the business—not on mathematics. However, a conceptual understanding of the *role* of the operations research specialist on the part of the manager will provide for more fruitful collaboration with him and will give the manager a better basis for appraising his effectiveness.

The exact composition of an operations research group will vary, of course, in terms of the type of company and its problems. Presumably, the "hard core" of such a group would include a mathematician-statistician (or both), an economist, a computer analyst and programmer, in addition to appropriate members of management. With the exception of management members and possibly a currently employed economist, it is likely that the other members of the team would have to be recruited from outside the company, and they are hard to find. However, many colleges are now devoting attention to the development of such personnel, and this may help to relieve the shortage.

Computer Personnel: Selection, Training, Assimilation

Robert Slater of John Hancock made the following observations with regard to the problems of selecting, training, and assimilating computer personnel:

Contrary to the commonly held theory, it is not necessary to use only people with long experience in a particular company or industry. . . . In cern with system to be more important than an understanding of the operation we have found an aptitude for computer methods and a con-

---

[14] George Kozmetsky and Paul Kircher, *Electronic Computers and Managerial Control* (New York: McGraw-Hill Book Co., 1956), pp. 177–78.

company's routines as such. This fact will raise two significant issues for management:

1. Since it is so expensive for a business to train computer personnel—and I am talking here about programmers not maintenance people—how can industry make sure of a pool of men and women worthy of the training effort?
2. Since computer people are specialists who can fit easily into any kind of business—they are, in a sense, interchangeable parts, with little to differentiate the systems work in one firm from that in another in their eyes—how can a manager integrate them into his company and hold on to them?[15]

With regard to the first question, he believes that the best prospect will be to look to our educational institutions to assume most of the responsibility. It should be mentioned here that there is an important qualitative factor involved. While present staff can be trained to program in a relatively short period of time, such training will hardly prepare them to "optimize" computer time, that is, to make the most efficient use of the computer, and computer time is an expensive commodity. However, the increasing sophistication of computer design suggests that it will not be long before computers, to a large extent, will be capable of programming themselves and that humans will be able to instruct the machine, for the most part, in "normal" language terms.

With regard to the second question, Slater writes:

I cannot help but believe that many computer specialists are not going to develop any great loyalty to a given company, since their standards of value are different from the usual employee's. Thus, the manager will have to understand and consider their particular interest and preferences, if he is to hold on to them. He is going to have to turn his attention to scientific seminars and other activities of the sort which will interest the computer specialist.[16]

Of course, these observations apply to *present* company research and specialist personnel and, as the professionalization of management develops further, will apply increasingly to *all* management personnel!

Middle-Management Positions

The advent of the computer has had a significant impact on traditional modes for training planning personnel. Use of the computer in conjunction with new planning techniques will relieve managers

---

[15] Robert E. Slater, "Thinking Ahead: How Near Is the Automatic Office?" *Harvard Business Review*, Vol. 36, No. 2 (March-April, 1958), pp. 167-76.
[16] *Ibid.*

of much detail work and minor decision making, but *it will force upward, the decisions that are made* for they will be more important decisions and ones that will draw more heavily upon the experience and seasoning of the executive. Thus, the computer will displace many middle-management jobs and, as Slater points out:

> One source of potential future managers will dry up because there will be no jobs for the apprentices to do while they learn the business.... We have endeavored to recruit a group of computer specialists who do have the inclination to understand and to be interested in *what* is done as well as *how* it is done. On the job they have been encouraged to broaden their knowledge of non-computer aspects of the business through both formal and informal educational programs.

Ida Hoos has reported, on the basis of a study, that many personnel problems are created when the computer takes over the office.[17] She would second the observation by Mr. Slater of John Hancock that the remaining middle-management positions will no longer serve as a training ground and ladder to success for junior executives. She indicates that much of middle management's function in revamped organizations is devoted to monitoring for errors before data reach the computer and handling exceptions not provided for by the program. This kind of work, she believes, offers few opportunities for the exercise of initiative or judgment. Consequently, approaches to executive development may have to be rethought, for the "apprenticeship" jobs of middle management that require data processing and decision making largely by judgment and policy interpretation may be displaced by the computer. This may require that greater emphasis be placed on the "generalist" approach to top-management training and less on the "coaching" method.

This idea that the computer and the new planning techniques will displace many middle-management people is shared by Leavitt and Whisler.[18] They believe that a formal organization chart of the future will look something like a "football balanced upon the point of a church bell," the football symbolizing top management. And at this top level they predict that "individual autonomy, group decision-making, and so on, should arise more intensely than ever. We expect distinctly different methods of remuneration, control, and communication." To the extent that this process takes place and personnel in general, and middle management personnel in par-

---

[17] Ida R. Hoos, "When the Computer Takes Over the Office," *Harvard Business Review,* Vol. 38, No. 4 (July-August, 1960).

[18] Harold J. Leavitt and Thomas L. Whisler, "Management in the 1980's," *Harvard Business Review,* Vol. 36 (November-December, 1958), pp. 41–48.

ticular, are displaced, we may expect to see a shortening or flat-
tening of the church-bell part of the organization; that is, a reduction
in the number of echelons or levels. With this trend we may see a
shift in emphasis away from our present preoccupation with human
relations, communications, and other dimensions of control to
greater concentration on such areas as operations research and decision theory.

Miss Hoos thinks that it is unlikely that organizations making
the transition will be able to absorb or place elsewhere displaced
personnel without extensive outside help. She reports that, for every
five office jobs eliminated, only one is created by automation. And
many incumbents who remain in downgraded jobs believe that they
are "living on borrowed time" and that much of the meaningfulness
and challenge has been taken from their work.[19]

SPECIAL PLANNING AGENCIES

Whether in the form of an executive committee, a board of directors, a long-range planning committee, an operations research group,
or a staff planning agency, the importance of the group approach
to planning will undoubtedly grow in the years to come. The new
planning techniques require that professionally trained personnel,
representing different areas of knowledge and experience, collaborate to "pool" their contributions in modern planning. Much more
will be at stake as decisions become broader in their implications
and there is less time for corrective action because of speedier implementation. Also, it seems reasonable to assume that competitor
"planning teams," professionally trained and equipped, will make
fewer mistakes and will provide less room in industry for those who
still "fly by the seat of their pants." At this point it seems desirable
to examine the character and organizational role of each of several
new and traditional planning agencies.

Board of Directors

As was pointed out in chapter 4, as a company grows larger and
becomes incorporated, it is conceptually useful to distinguish three
levels of top-management activity:

Level I—for Trustee functions (usually performed by the Board of
Directors).

---

[19] For a report of a study of the effects of a changeover to electronic data processing equipment in a light and power company see Floyd Mann and Lawrence Williams, "Observations on the Dynamics of a Change to Electronic Data-Processing
Equipment," *Administrative Science Quarterly*, Vol. 5, No. 2 (September, 1960), pp.
217–56.

Level II—General Management functions (for our purposes in this discussion, to be performed by either an executive committee or a management group).

Level III—Major Divisional or Departmental Management functions performed by division or department heads.[20]

Trustee functions are *judicial* in character and *intermittent* in performance; they have to do with *appraisal* and *approval*. Owners of the business (stockholders) look to the board of directors to safeguard their interests. In addition the board should:

Appraise over-all results and approve major plans.

Control major organizational matters with regard to plant and equipment, large financial outlays, the selection of the chief executive and approval of key personnel appointments.

Decide dividend policy.

Coach and advise management.

To the extent that the new planning techniques will affect the competitive posture and long-range prospects for a firm, it will become more important that boards select and support the kind of chief executives and top-management groups that will fully exploit these opportunities. To do this, boards of the future will have to be well versed (conceptually) in the new planning techniques. Otherwise they will be seriously handicapped in performing their important *review* function. Also, conceptual understanding of the new planning techniques on the part of board members will make possible a new kind of contribution on their part. At present, it is difficult for experienced directors to *impart* their wisdom and judgment to active executives; they can only coach and advise. But with the growing sophistication in model building and the computer's almost limitless memory, we may soon see the first really effective exploitation of collective board experience in the form of model input data.

General Management Group

General management functions are *executive* in character and continuous in performance; they have to do with the over-all management of the company. They include the *initiation* and *formulation* of changes in objectives, over-all operating policies, and plans. General management functions include:

Maintenance and development of sound organization and other tools for the implementation of plans.

---

[20] This classification of top management levels and functions is based on an analysis of the practices of 31 companies by Holden, Fish, and Smith, *Top Management Organization and Control* (New York: McGraw-Hill Book Co., 1951), p. 15.

Coordination and appraisal of divisional or departmental work.
Counseling division or department managers.

When a company is very small, general management functions, along with many other functions, must be performed by the owner-manager. But as soon as the organization develops to the point at which competent managers head up major line and staff departments, the president can form them into a staff *council* or *executive committee* to perform general management functions. Admittedly, it is difficult for such a general management group to assume an *over-all, impartial* view of company problems, since group members are under pressure from their own people to "look after their interests."

As the organization grows bigger and "both jobs" become more complex, the use of an executive committee exclusively to perform general management functions becomes increasingly inadequate. At this stage, if it is feasible, serious consideration should be given to the assignment of general management functions to one or more executives on a full-time basis to supplement the work of the executive committee. Such men will not suffer from "split loyalties," and they can lay the groundwork for the introduction of operations research and other new planning techniques. One such person might well serve in a liaison capacity between an "outside" consulting group and the developing "inside" management planning group.

The use of a general management group, composed entirely of full-time "general" executives, is feasible only in *decentralized* companies large enough to justify the additional cost or overhead. The company should be decentralized, for it is essential to free the general management group from the parochial demands and time pressures confronting the major group, product, or territorial heads who report to it. General management group members must be free to devote their major energies to general management functions. In a large, decentralized company, major group, product, or territorial heads comprise, in many respects, a group of federated, independent company "presidents." The relationship they have with the general management group is similar to the relationship between an average company president and his board of directors. If the company has well-defined objectives, good performance standards, and seasoned divisional personnel, divisional heads need report to the general management group only once or twice a year. The president of the firm (who is ex officio chairman of the general management group) personally handles any emergencies that arise when there is too little time for the group to act.[21]

In smaller companies, in which major divisional or departmental heads report to the president, it would be unwise to have divisional heads report to a general management group, even if the company could afford the additional cost. The activities of functional division heads are more interdependent and subject to day-by-day coordination than are those of major group, product, or territorial heads in large companies. Also, it is more difficult to appraise the performance of one division head relative to others because of the greater interdependence of their activities. There is need for more positive and decisive *individual*, presidential leadership.

However, the new planning techniques require greater emphasis on *group* planning at the top of the organization. Presidents of smaller firms will have to make increasingly greater demands on their executive committee "general management groups" if they wish to remain competitive. For, as predictive and decision models are perfected further, we can expect that the area for important individual planning will significantly decrease. Individuals will make their planning contributions by assisting the general management planning group in the job of determining input factors. The smaller company president, then, will relinquish his role as *chief planner*, providing the firm with long-term guidance based on personal experience, judgment, and intuition. To an even greater extent than before, he will devote his energies to *group leadership* and the *implementation* of planning group programs.

Economic Planning Agency

In deciding upon new objectives or the modification of old ones, the general management group in whatever form it exists, will be greatly influenced by current *planning premises*. As was discussed in chapter 2, the determination of planning premises is the result of forecasting. The importance of this activity cannot be overemphasized. As will be recalled, the first *organic planning subfunction* requires the "determination of key environmental factors and the interrelationships among these factors." The development of predictive models for accurate forecasting is involved and demanding work. It can be turned over to a specialized staff group: an *economic planning agency*. Such an agency, composed of appropriate

---

[21] See footnote on p. 117 for reference to the Du Pont General Management Group.

specialized personnel, does not pre-empt the planning function. It develops essential planning premise data so that the general management group may intelligently define objectives and plan the supporting programs required to carry them out. The head of an economic planning agency would report to the company president who is ex officio chairman of the general management group.

The organizational structure for such a staff planning agency, at an advanced state of development, is shown below: [22]

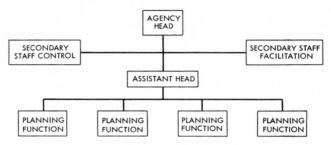

It will be noted that provision is made for "secondary" staff control and "secondary" staff facilitation. Such staff assistance for staff people is required only when continued growth of a staff agency, or the complex nature of its work, requires it. Secondary staff control is provided to coordinate the activities of the staff agency. Secondary staff facilitation is provided to make specialized services or skills available to the planning group, for example, a blueprint or reproduction service or the services of a theoretical mathematician to assist a group of design engineers. Secondary staff control personnel might be used for external liaison in addition to internal control work. It is possible that a secondary staff research group might be established to develop new techniques and refinements for model building or to assist in developing "plans for planning." The assistant head, by taking over his chief's more routine managerial functions, could free him for more creative work or for conferences and consultations with other members of the organization.

Organization Planning Agency

An organization planning agency would be organized along the same lines as the economic planning agency discussed above. It is concerned primarily with the application of the principles and concepts discussed in chapters 3 and 4, "Organization Planning."

[22] Taken from Ralph C. Davis, *The Fundamentals of Top Management* (New York: Harper & Bros., 1951), p. 400.

Holden, Fish, and Smith provide a good résumé of the activities of such an agency:

The primary responsibility of an organization department is, logically, to determine needs, formulate plans, and secure necessary acceptance, cooperation, and support to the end: first, that the company may have the best possible plan of organization to meet its requirements; second, that the appropriate functions, objectives, relationships, and limits of authority may be properly clarified and defined for each level of management, each department, each committee, and each key job; and, third, that the size of the company's organization (manpower) may be kept at a minimum necessary to handle the essential work.[23]

As they point out, this normally involves such specific activities as:

1. Developing an ideal plan of organization to work toward at all times. (Of course, at any given time concessions will have to be made in view of available personnel and the socio-psychological and technological conditions which prevail.)

2. Developing and maintaining an organization manual which defines and clarifies the approved plan of organization by means of charts, job specifications, and similar devices; acknowledging the existence and functions of the uncharted informal organization.

3. Initiating or reviewing proposed changes in the plan of organization, making sure that they are desirable and as far as practicable consistent with the ultimate plan, and recommending appropriate action for the implementation of changes.

4. Making periodic reviews of organization practice to see that it conforms to the plan, or that the plan is amended as needed to meet changed conditions.

5. Making organization surveys to determine essential work, manpower, and organizational requirements.

6. Conduct of job analysis work to obtain data for the preparation of job descriptions and specifications used in conjunction with much of the foregoing work.

7. Design of various systems of control.

This listing is not meant to be exhaustive. But it does point up the character of activities that would be appropriate for such an agency and illustrates the extent to which it would assume functions normally associated with a personnel department. For example, such personnel programs as selection, merit rating, job evaluation, safety, and training draw heavily on job analysis data. Obviously, a personnel manager cannot be concerned with the effective placement, development, motivation, and leadership of employees without being intimately concerned with organization planning. The logics

---

[23] Holden, Fish, and Smith, *op. cit.*, pp. 49–50.

of the situation strongly suggest that the organization planning agency be a part of the personnel organization. It is likely that where this is not the case it is a reflection on the lack of competence or vision of the personnel manager. Certainly, if organization planning is to be performed by a separate agency, the closest kind of liaison with the personnel department will be required to avoid unnecessary conflict and duplication of effort.

Even if organization planning activity is incorporated in the work of the personnel department, as it should be, this separate discussion of such activity seems more than justified. For the importance of organization planning to the well-being of an organization is hard to overemphasize. The late Dr. H. A. Hopf aptly describes one of the advantages of organization planning: "That a business cannot permanently occupy levels of effectiveness higher than those clearly determined by the capacity of its executives is self-evident, but it is not generally understood that the influence of superior organization upon the accomplishments of mediocre executives can raise the enterprise to heights not otherwise attainable."[24]

Operations Research Group

The composition of an operations research group will vary in terms of the type of company and the particular problems at hand. However, the "hard core" of such a group would include a mathematician-statistician (or both), an economist, a computer analyst and programmer and appropriate members of management. The primary function of the group is to assist other organizational units in finding more effective solutions to their problems and in developing more effective means for planning.

It is important that the operations research group be properly placed in the organization to assure its effective operation and yet avoid conflict with existing units and undue duplication of effort. It should be placed near the top of the organization so that it will have access to company-wide data and the necessary support of top management. The head of the operations research group should report to the president, since the latter is ex officio chairman of the general management group or the executive committee. And those who have had experience with organization for operations research

---

[24] Quoted by Ernest Dale, *Planning and Developing the Company Organization Structure,* Research Report No. 20 (New York: American Management Association, 1959), p. 21.

strongly favor the assignment of key jobs in that group to permanent company employees. They believe that consultants should be given key roles in such work *only* during an initial introductory phase or when a company, because of its size, cannot afford an operations research group and must contract for specific undertakings.

At least one member of the general management group should serve as a permanent member of the operations research group. This will help to assure proper liaison and understanding between the group and other organizational elements, such as an industrial engineering or plant layout group, the economic planning group, the special studies group of the controller's organization, the personnel director's group, and so on. It would be impractical for representatives from all such groups, which at one time or another will wish to employ operations research techniques, to be ex officio members of the operations research group. The general management liaison man would keep these groups informed as to the activities of the operations research group and the development of new planning techniques that might be of interest to them. When appropriate, he would arrange for the operations research group to assist a particular group with its own planning and research activity. In other words, the operations research group is not established to *displace* certain groups in the organization; it is established to help them do a better job while assisting the general management group with special studies and top-level planning. By encouraging existing agencies to seek the aid of the operations research group and, at the same time, forbidding that group to "take over" any other group's activities, the danger of conflict can be minimized.

This approach to operations research is in line with that of H. J. Roy, who advocates that "task forces," involving representatives of all departments affected, be set up to go "all the way" with projects that concern them.[25] There are several advantages made possible by the use of departmental representatives. For one thing, the operations research group will find it easier to gain the cooperation of people throughout the organization when it wins the support of departmental representatives who develop a clear understanding of its mission. Also, the group will be able to do a more realistic job of problem definition and data collection through its association with

---

[25] See J. H. Roy, "Operations Research in Action," *Harvard Business Review*, September–October, 1958, p. 120.

departmental representatives. And departmental personnel, in addition to making valuable contributions to operations research activity and the implementation of proposals, have an excellent opportunity to learn about new developments through this kind of collaboration.

Employee-Management Committee

Some companies have experienced phenomenal success with planning committees comprising representatives of labor and top management. These may be referred to as production committees, screening committees, or by other names. The important point is that the truly successful committees have operated in a favorable organizational climate. Employees—committee members and non-committee members—have been provided with a realistic basis for profiting from their efforts.[26] And they *have not been limited as to the kind of problems they can discuss.*

Davenport vividly describes the unique character of a screening committee meeting at the Lapointe Machine Tool Company (the company adopted the Scanlon Plan in 1947):

Like a crack out of a gun the meeting opens with an announcement of the figures for the past month. There follows a roundup by management of the current situation of the company. Then the suggestions are read out, one by one, and debated. A lot of criticism is generated, and is of necessity accepted, since it is all directed to the same end—a better profit. Sometimes the workers throw the book at management, sometimes management points out where the shop has fallen down. Engineers argue against machine-tool operators, foremen attack the engineers for unrealistic blueprints, someone demands better maintenance, management points out that more maintenance means bigger labor costs. In the process of this debate, almost every aspect of the business comes up for discussion. . . .

The meetings are not recorded verbatim. But minutes are distributed to everyone in the plant, and the important points in the debate are carried by the committeemen back into the shop, where they become the subject of further discussion—at the lunch hour, in the evening, or even at the union meeting. The result is that everyone at Lapointe knows the business and takes pride in his particular contribution.[27]

---

[26] For a detailed discussion of how this can be done see Frederick Lesieur (ed.), *The Scanlon Plan* (Cambridge: The M.I.T. Press, 1958). Under the Scanlon Plan, labor and management first agree on a "normal" labor cost for production. Then they devise a means for giving labor the benefit of anything it can save under the "normal" cost.

[27] Russell Davenport, "Enterprise for Everyman," in W. M. Fox (ed.), *Readings in Personnel Management from "Fortune"* (Henry Holt & Co., 1957), p. 12, or *Fortune,* January, 1950.

The question immediately arises: Is such worker involvement realized only in companies that are on the brink of disaster with workers who are fighting to keep their jobs? Or are these committees created and maintained as compensation for grossly incompetent management? Assuming that this approach were tried in an efficient plant with workers who respect the abilities of management and are not afraid of losing their jobs, would a significant contribution still be made? The story of the Adamson Company, a small unionized concern reputedly the most efficient in the storage-tank industry at the end of World War II, provides a partial answer. Shultz reports:

> Mr. Adamson, the company president, had ideas which paralleled Scanlon's. Together with the employees of the firm, they worked out a method for sharing the gains from productivity increases. . . . They set up "production committees" of management and worker representatives and Adamson himself presided over a "screening committee" which discussed and decided on major policy questions. This was a company, then, which had made a profit even in 1932, which paid high wage rates, and which was acknowledged "the best" from the standpoint of efficiency. During the first year of participation under the Scanlon Plan, the workers' average bonus (productivity increase) was 41 per cent. According to Adamson, he made two and a half times the profit he would have made had he remained at the previous level of productivity.[28]

There is little question that employee-management committees, *when properly utilized,* can make a significant contribution in the way of improved planning and motivation. Unfortunately, the requirements for proper utilization are not easy to satisfy. A high degree of competence, emotional maturity, and mutual respect on the part of labor and management representatives is essential. Management cannot try to hide its mistakes, nor can labor overlook *adequate study* of the firm and its problems. An employee-management committee works best when it is part of a plan, like the Scanlon Plan, which realistically rewards participants for their efforts and contributes toward the creation and maintenance of a favorable over-all organizational "climate."[29]

---

[28] George Shultz, "Worker Participation on Production Problems," in Lesieur (ed.), *op. cit.,* pp. 54, 55. For more information on the Adamson case see Joseph N. Scanlon, "Adamson and His Profit-sharing Plan," *AMA Production Series,* No. 172, pp. 10–12, and John Chamberlain, "Every Man a Capitalist," *Life,* December 23, 1946.

[29] For an interesting discussion as to possible limitations and problems see George Strauss and Leonard Sayles, "The Scanlon Plan: Some Organizational Problems," *Human Organization,* Fall, 1957; also reprinted in H. W. Karn and B. von Haller Gilmer (eds.), *Readings in Industrial and Business Psychology* (2d ed.; New York: McGraw-Hill Book Co., 1962).

ORGANIZATION FOR LONG-RANGE PLANNING

Five-Year Plans

In large, decentralized companies, major group, product, or territorial heads function in many respects as a group of federated, independent company "presidents." The relationship they have with a general management group is similar to the relationship between a company president and his board of directors. In this situation, it may be desirable for the general management group to ask each "president" or major head to submit to it a revised five-year plan for his organization each year. This will supply the general management group with invaluable data for its planning activities and its evaluation of divisional leadership. In addition, it will encourage a mode of analysis and questioning on the part of divisional executives that will serve them well in their day-to-day activities and will contribute to their personal growth and initiative. Wrapp reports that one company developed the following "standard" outline for each division's presentation:

The industry	Return on investment
Our position	Location of new facilities
Competitor's activities	Manpower requirements
Sales forecasts	Management controls
Present products	Pricing policies
New products	Appraisal of strengths and weaknesses
Capital investment requirements	Special problem areas [30]
Working capital	

Centralized Control and Service

Under a centralized control and service arrangement, long-range planning in each of the autonomous divisions is undertaken in much the same way as if they were operating as "independent" companies, the only limitation being that divisional planning must operate within the framework of over-all company objectives, policies, capital resources, and planning premises determined by the general management group with the aid of "feedback" data from all divisions. The general management group reviews the five-year plans from various divisions and then synthesizes the approved ones into a coherent, over-all company plan. Through the presentation and defense of their plans, divisional heads compete for company

---

[30] H. Edward Wrapp, "Organization for Long-Range Planning," *Harvard Business Review*, Vol 35, No. 1, (January-February, 1957), p. 44. This article is based on a survey of the planning practices of a number of large and medium-sized companies.

capital allocations and have an opportunity to influence the general management group toward modifying its planning premises or reformulating over-all objectives and policies.

To avoid unnecessary overhead and duplication of that work which can be done more effectively by a headquarters group, certain centralized services are made available to the divisions. For example, basic over-all planning premises and forecast data are developed by a central economic planning agency and disseminated to divisional planners. And specialized headquarters planning personnel are made available, on request, to serve as consultants to divisional planners.

The Medium-Size Firm

What about organization for long-range planning in the smaller firm that has major *functional* division heads reporting to the president? In such a firm, long-range planning should be done by general management personnel—whether as a general management group or as an executive committee—assisted by various staff agencies. Under this arrangement, the general management group delegates or "farms out" some of the planning activity to such agencies as the personnel department, the controller's special studies group, the operations research group, and so on. The general management group coordinates the efforts of these various groups via the dissemination of periodic progress reports or through frequent briefing sessions with group representatives. It is desirable that at least one member of the general management group be made clearly responsible for the proper implementation of this liaison function. Of course, the general management group has the final responsibility for formulating the long-range plans that will be submitted to the president and board of directors for approval.

Getting Started

As Wrapp discovered in his survey of planning practices, it may be useful for a planning group to "get its feet wet" with *limited projects* initially—if they involve long-term commitments and are not primarily oriented toward day-to-day or short-run operations. He lists some of the limited projects that one firm's planning group has undertaken over a period of several years without drawing up a master five-year plan:

Optimum size of main manufacturing facility (a major expansion is now underway as a result of the planning committee report).

Building versus renting home office space (a large office building has now been started).

Employee housing adjacent to main plant (this was undertaken as a company project and subsequently developed into a major rehabilitation project by the community).

Scholarships (a policy on contributing to educational institutions was formulated).

Employee stock purchases (a plan for acquisition of company stock by employees at all levels evolved).

Reappraisal of an existing product (production and sale of this product were discontinued as a result of the planning committee's recommendation).[31]

Wrapp points out that "the chairman's insistence that the committee produce definite recommendations and put them in writing has resulted in a series of carefully documented statements, and as these seemingly unrelated recommendations are accumulated, a very useful background of sales, production, and financial data is being built for a possible over-all company plan."

A long-range planning group will find it productive to apply the *Principle of Limiting Factors.* As will be recalled, this principle states: **In approaching a problem situation with a well-defined goal, it is productive to identify and analyze the sequence of *limiting factors* involved. These are factors that if properly satisfied in appropriate order will permit the accomplishment of the goal.**
The following are among the kinds of limiting factors that should be of special interest to a long-range planning group: anticipated competitor activity; the availability of managerial talent for replacments and expansion; the availability of capital, plant, and equipment; unfavorable economic conditions and other factors that may limit the company's future growth.

The challenges and demands of long-range planning activity will add significantly to the work load of executives involved in it. It may be at this point—the introduction of long-range planning activity—that the larger firm will create a general management group for handling general management functions. The smaller firm may find it useful to add one or two *general management members* to the existing executive committee expressly for the purpose of assisting with long-range planning activity.

SOME GENERAL OBSERVATIONS ABOUT COMMITTEES

We have emphasized the *planning roles* of various types of *committees.* Some management writers challenge this emphasis. They

---

[31] *Ibid.,* p. 45.

believe that committees cannot successfully plan against time limits and that they suffer from other *fixed disadvantages*. Such analyses seem to assume that all committees are essentially alike, for they outline what purport to be *inherent* characteristics of committees, *generally*. Actually, as was discussed in chapter 4, the *caliber* or *quality* of a committee is the decisive factor.

Many of us have contact with *mediocre* committees, which either lack decisive purpose or are sabotaged by unprepared members who use committee time for the pursuit of purely personal goals. Contrast this with the functioning of a permanent committee of seasoned executives who clearly understand the purpose of their planning activity and who do their "homework" on agenda topics *before* each meeting (with the help of background data and special analyses prepared by staff personnel)! We must be cautious in generalizing about the attributes of *all* committees.

Nevertheless, as has been pointed out, a committee does *not* function effectively as a "plural executive" for day-to-day supervision and leadership. *The Principle of Unity of Command* applies to such situations of "continuous" supervision. It does not apply to those situations in which there is "intermittent" supervision, for example, a president reporting to a board of directors, or major group, product, or territorial division heads periodically reporting to a general management group in a large, decentralized company. In such instances of "intermittent" supervision, when the use of a "plural executive" is feasible, it is still essential that all contact between the group and its subordinates regarding personal performance, reprimands, salary, and the issuance of direct orders be handled by the group chairman.

The kinds of planning groups discussed in this chapter *are not* responsible for "continuous" supervision of subordinates. When composed of well-motivated men of high caliber, they provide planning contributions to the organization that no single individual could supply. For two heads *are* better than one, *if* the two heads have common purpose, mature judgment, a thorough comprehension of all data relevant to the problem or topic at hand, and *adequate time for fruitful discussion*. If we eliminate *non-fruitful* committee discussion, this time requirement is surprisingly modest!

QUESTIONS

1. What are the advantages and disadvantages of "renting" computer time? When is it feasible to own a computer? From an organizational standpoint, what should be the place and role of various groups or individuals who use the computer?

2. What is meant by the expression "integrated data processing"? What steps would you follow in designing an integrated data processing system?

3. Will the use of integrated data processing force recentralization of authority in a decentralized company? Discuss.

4. Do you think that the kind of integrated data processing that is used at Sylvania would be useful for other companies with different primary objectives? Why or why not?

5. Is an accounting department a data processing center? Explain. How should accounting activities be organized to best accommodate data customers? What were the three major dimensions of the accounting function that were defined by the Controllership Foundation Research Group?

6. Discuss the different kinds of people you would expect to find in an operations research group? What key factors will determine the composition of such a group at any given time?

7. What do you think of Mr. Slater's concern "that my computer specialists are not going to develop any great loyalty to a given company since their standards of value are different from the usual employees." What factors will have a significant bearing on this? Discuss.

8. What impact will the introduction of the computer have on managerial training? What impact will it have on formal organization? What do Leavitt and Whisler mean when they say that a formal organization chart of the future will look something like a football balanced on the top of a church bell? Explain.

9. Do you feel that the group approach to planning will grow in importance in the years to come? Explain.

10. From the standpoint of planning, what value is there in distinguishing three levels of top management?

11. What is the most logical location in the organization for the performance of organization planning functions? Why?

12. What do you see as the pros and cons of the employee-management committee as a planning agency? Explain your thinking.

13. Discuss organization for long-range planning in the smaller firm that has major functional division heads reporting to the president.

14. State and explain the *Principle of Limiting Factors*.

15. Can we generalize as to the advantages and disadvantages of using committees for planning? Why or why not?

Chapter 10

ORGANIZATION FOR ORGANIZING

Chapter 5 discussed the organic subfunctions of organizing: *the procurement of factors as planned, the establishment of interrelationships among factors as planned, and the development of factors as planned.* By "factors" we mean capital, physical requirements (plant, equipment, and materiel), and personnel. In this chapter certain organizational arrangements that facilitate the performance of these organic subfunctions of organizing will be considered. The discussion will be selective, for many of the organic subfunctions of organizing are performed in *all* organizational units and are not relegated to specific subsidiary organizations. Such functions as the assignment of duties, delegation of authority and responsibility, and the activation of a communications system, procedures, rules, policies, and other bases for accountability and control must be performed in all organizational units.

ORGANIZATION FOR THE PROCUREMENT AND MAINTENANCE OF CAPITAL AND THE DEVELOPMENT OF CAPITAL SOURCES

The size of an organization has much to do with the extent to which financial staff functions are differentiated from line positions. In a small, sole proprietorship, the owner-manager is likely to perform all the financial functions with, perhaps, some clerical assistance and the part-time services of a consulting certified public accountant. As the organization grows in size, we see the evolution of such positions as office manager, treasurer, controller (or comptroller as it is sometimes called), and chief financial officer. We are concerned here specifically with organization for procuring and maintaining capital and developing capital sources. However, there are other important financial functions, such as financial plannning, accounting and data processing, disbursement of funds, credit and collections, budget preparation, and financial control. Since many of these financial functions are interdependent, it will be useful to consider a logical allocation of all of them so that the functions of procuring and maintaining capital and developing capital sources may be placed in proper perspective.

The Controller

The following are among the functions generally assigned to a controller when there is also the position of treasurer in the organization: accounting records, reports, and systems; cost accounting; depreciation policies and methods; developing and maintaining systems of budgetary control; internal auditing; relations with outside public accountants; formulating disbursement procedures for accounts payable and payrolls; preparing and issuing financial statements; complying with government regulations and requests; maintaining inventory control records; administering salary and wage payroll procedures; statistical operations; and tax return preparation and filing.[1]

If either the controller or the treasurer is regarded as the chief financial officer of the company (this is more likely to be the treasurer, as we shall see, in view of the nature of his functions) then one should report to the other and the superior should report to the president. If both are competent and there is insufficient justification for the retention of a chief financial officer to whom both would report, then the controller and treasurer should report directly to the president. There is a departure from this pattern at General Motors (see Fig. 10–1), but for very good reasons! It is such a large, complex company that a division of "chief executive labor" is necessary.

The chairman of the board is the *chief executive officer* of the Corporation and has reporting to him the president; executive vice-president, financial staff; vice-president, legal staff; chairman, General Motors Acceptance Corporation; and president, Yellow Manu-

---

[1] National Industrial Conference Board. "The Duties of Financial Executives," *Studies in Business Policy,* No. 56, p. 25. Of course, financial functions may be *line* or *staff* depending upon whether or not they are *organic business functions* of the company. In our discussion here we assume them to be *staff* as would be the case in a manufacturing concern.

facturing Acceptance Corporation. The chairman of the board is also chairman of the finance committee. The president is the *chief operating officer* of the corporation and has reporting to him three executive vice-presidents, two of which head up the main line organizations of the company. The president is chairman of the executive committee of the board and serves on the finance committee. In turn, the chairman of the board serves as a member of the president's executive committee.[2] As can be seen, this *is* a unique situation. The chairman does *not* function as ordinary chairmen do, and the president, despite his role as chief lieutenant to the chair-

FIG. 10-1

Top Financial Staff Organization at General Motors

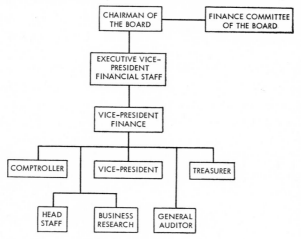

man, retains far more authority and responsibility than most company presidents because of the scope of General Motors operations (see Fig. 10-1).

The Treasurer

The following are among the functions generally assigned to a treasurer when there is also the position of controller: banking relations; the receipt, custody, and disbursement of funds; planning future cash and financial requirements and planning for both short-term and long-term financing to meet them; the formulation of

---

[2] For a fuller discussion of the composition and roles of these and other committees at General Motors see chap. 12, "Organization for Control: Decentralization at General Motors."

financial policies for the company; the maintenance or conservation of capital; the purchase and sale of securities; and, perhaps, the formulation of credit and collection policies (though the granting of credit is clearly a marketing function and should be under the jurisdiction of the chief marketing officer).

The Office Manager

The office manager is a staff specialist who provides technical and facilitative services to such office executives as the treasurer, controller, chief engineer, purchasing agent, chief accounting officer, etc. He is usually responsible for mailing and messenger services, central filing and stenographic services, and the formulation of procedures for coordinating the flow of clerical work throughout the company. Often, the office manager reports to the chief financial officer, for the financial division generates a large volume of clerical work and becomes the point of "most use" of his services.

Some Concluding Observations

As outlined above, it is clear that the treasurer—or the treasurer and the chief financial officer jointly, if there is one in addition to the treasurer and controller—has primary responsibility for the origination of plans for the procurement and maintenance of required capital and for the development of capital sources. Also, he has primary responsibility for the execution of such plans when they have been approved by appropriate line authority. Davis observes:

> The treasurer does not determine the purposes for which available funds shall be expended. This decision is made by the president or the board of directors, on the recommendation of the appropriate committees. The treasurer has a right to question the propriety or necessity of proposed expenditures. This right grows out of his obligation to conserve the company's assets.
>
> The treasurer has the right of decision concerning the execution of arrangements for financing the company's operations. It is presumed that his plans have had the prior approval of the chief financial officer, the concurrence of the finance committee, and the final approval of such higher authorities as may be necessary.[3]

By-passing the President. When there is a chief financial officer in addition to the treasurer and controller, we sometimes find him reporting directly to a finance committee of the board of directors

---

[3] R. C. Davis, *Industrial Organization and Management* (3d ed.; New York: Harper & Bros., 1956), p. 842.

rather than to the president.[4] This stems, probably, from the almost invariable company practice that:

1. Changes in financial structure must be authorized by the board and approved by stockholders.
2. The board handles policies with regard to dividends and surpluses.
3. The board must authorize plans for the significant expansion or rehabilitation of facilities.

Nevertheless, this is a dangerous practice that tends to undermine the authority of the president in two ways: it dilutes or removes his control over one of his major staff executives and his organization, and it encourages the financial committee to abandon its legitimate *review* functions to embark upon active management under the guise of exercising financial control. Also, if the chief financial officer "works" for the board rather than for the president, it is less likely that he will perceive his primary role as one of service to other organizational units as well as to the organization as a whole.

Legitimate Finance Committee Functions. The use of a finance committee by the board to facilitate its work can be most productive as long as it does not effectively *relieve* the full board of its responsibility of passing on important financial decisions and does not serve as a plural executive for the supervision of one of the president's key lieutenants. If the board believes that it must "by-pass" the president with regard to financial matters owing to his indifference or incompetence in this area, the solution is to alter his behavior or replace him, *not* to violate basic concepts of good organization in an attempt to compensate for his deficiencies! Ideally, then, plans for the procurement of capital, the development of capital sources, and, *to a lesser degree,* the maintenance of capital are originated and executed by the treasurer—or treasurer and chief financial officer jointly—under the direction of the president with the review and approval of the board. See Figure 10-2.

Exception to Initiation Rule. One possible exception to the rule that a board should only review and not originate plans has to do with the development of capital sources. To the extent that board members have important contacts in the financial world and they coordinate their efforts with the president and chief financial officer, they may productively *initiate* plans and action in the area of *external* financial relations. However, the spirit of such board member

---

[4] This discussion pertains, of course, to companies that do not have the volume and breadth of activity of a company such as General Motors.

participation should be in terms of supplementing the efforts of the company's officers, *not* displacing them![5]

ORGANIZATION FOR THE PROCUREMENT OF MATERIEL, THE DEVELOPMENT OF MATERIEL SOURCES, AND THE MAINTENANCE OF MATERIEL

The importance of the procurement function varies, of course, with the volume of purchased materiel required by the organization and the skill demanded by the type of purchasing done. In the textile industry, for example, the purchase of wool is an exacting

FIG. 10-2

Organization for the Procurement and Maintenance of Capital

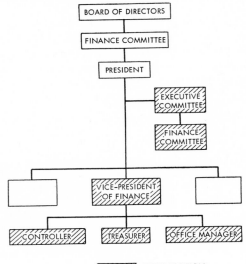

BOARD OF DIRECTORS

FINANCE COMMITTEE

PRESIDENT

EXECUTIVE COMMITTEE

FINANCE COMMITTEE

VICE-PRESIDENT OF FINANCE

CONTROLLER   TREASURER   OFFICE MANAGER

▨▨▨ STAFF POSITION

and important function. The value of wool in a blanket comprises a significant portion of its finished value. Since the price of wool fluctuates widely, buying in quantity at the right time can make the difference between profit and loss for the company. In addition, wool is sold by grades and often by unwashed weight "on the hoof." It takes skill to know whether the wool being bought is at the upper or lower end of a grade and considerable knowledge to know how

[5] For a good discussion of board functioning in this and other respects see Vannevar Bush, "Of What Use Is a Board of Directors," in Edmund Learned, C. Roland Christenson, and Kenneth Andrews, *Problems of General Management* (Homewood, Illinois: Richard D. Irwin, Inc., 1961), pp. 504–13.

many pounds of dust and cockleburs per sheep can be expected from each sheep-raising area in the world under varying conditions! The more important the procurement function is for a given firm, the higher we can expect the head of this activity to be placed in the organization.

Large capital outlays for heavy equipment are planned by top management and, with board approval, are usually made through direct negotiations between top management and the supplier. However, as a firm grows larger, it looks increasingly to specialized staff personnel for the procurement of smaller equipment, raw materials, and supplies. Davis lists the objectives of a major staff supply division:

(a) adequate quantities of the right kinds of materials and supplies, when and where they are needed,
(b) materials whose qualities suit them to their intended purposes,
(c) minimum materials purchase, storage, and transportation costs,
(d) minimum loss from deterioration, obsolescence, or theft of materials,
(e) maximum turnover of inventories in transit and in stores,
(f) a minimum of interference with operations, due to supply failures. . . . [6]

We often overlook the importance of supply activities. As Davis points out:

Many concerns install expensive accounting and cost systems and watch expenditures carefully. Safes or vaults are provided for the cash on hand. An accounting for it must be made to the last penny. On the other hand, stocks of materials, costing large sums, are left with a minimum of protection, and control of these inventories may be very poor. . . . Cash on hand seems more important and real to some people . . . than far greater amounts that are invested in materials.[7]

Organization for Procurement

Davis suggests that the principal phases of supply activity are: (1) procurement, (2) traffic and transportation, (3) storage, (4) materials handling, (5) salvage, (6) inventory control, and (7) materials standardization. Figure 10-3 is based on his organizational approach for these activities.[8] It represents a large firm with a high degree of functional differentiation. In a smaller concern, of course, some of these functions may not be differentiated from

[6] Ralph C. Davis, *Industrial Organization and Management* (3d ed.; New York: Harper & Bros., 1956), p. 571.
[7] *Ibid.*
[8] *Ibid.*, pp. 572, 573.

other line or staff positions, but all of them should be performed adequately by someone. In firms in which procurement is especially important, the position of director of supply often is *separated* from the manufacturing chain of command and *elevated* to the major divisional or vice-presidential level.

FIG. 10-3

Organization for Supply Activities in a Large Firm

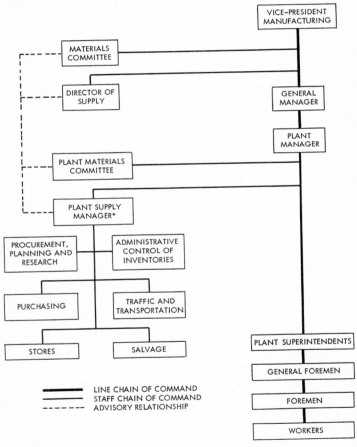

*Often called general or chief purchasing agent.

Davis describes the functions of some of the positions depicted in Figure 10-3:

The plant materials committee ... [is] set up to coordinate the needs and ideas of the organizations that are affected by materials standards. It may coordinate also the thinking of those line and staff groups that are concerned with procurement and supply plans.

The functions of the procurement and research department are those within the scope of its mission, which the director of procurement and supply assigns. These may include such activities as the recommendation of objectives and policies for the supply division. This may require: (1) procurement cost analysis, (2) market research to determine price and supply trends, (3) the study of quality standards in cooperation with the quality manager's organization, (4) the development of inventory plans and standards, (5) the determination of economical ordering quantities, (6) the development of better procedures for procurement and supply, and (7) cooperation with vendors in price reduction.

A distinction should be made, for organizational purposes, between an administrative control and an operative control of inventories. An administrative control has to do chiefly with coordinating the execution of procurement programs, with respect to classes of materials that must be supplied and to the organizations that use them. Staff responsibility for such administrative control should be assigned to the supply division. Operative control of inventories has to do with coordinating the provision of certain materials, as requisitioned, with the needs of the line departments for these materials for specific orders or schedules. This operative control should therefore be assigned to production control. Both administrative and operative inventory control should be coordinated with one another, and with accounting.

The traffic department is under the purchasing agent in many plants, because of the greater volume of incoming materials. . . . Traffic must serve the marketing functions as well as purchasing. . . . The bulk of its work has to do with such activities as classification of materials and product for traffic purposes, the routing of shipments, the provision of cars or trucks by a common carrier, and similar problems.

The functions of the purchasing department are to procure by purchase the proper quantities of what is wanted, for delivery at a certain time and place, at the lowest price consistent with the requisite quality.

The stores department is responsible for the proper storing and piling of materials, the selection of materials handling equipment, the handling and control of stock, the organization and location of storerooms, etc. The general storekeeper . . . , accordingly, is responsible for the operation of our plant warehouses and storerooms. The receiving, internal transportation, and shipping functions may also be placed under his general direction.

The functions of the salvage department are collecting, reclaiming, reworking, and disposing of scrap and waste, and reducing the amount thereof. The work of the department is partly a manufacturing problem and partly a stores problem. . . . The salvage department also handles the sale of scrap, waste, or reclaimed material. It returns to stores any reclaimed material which can be reissued to the shop. . . . Salvage is sometimes regarded as a phase of the stores function.

A director of . . . supply, who reports to the vice-president in charge of manufacturing . . . develops and recommends company procurement and supply policies. The director's office develops interplant procedures for inventory planning and control. This office surveys interplant requirements for like materials. It may integrate company purchasing power by originating corporate contracts for such materials. Such contracts should receive the concurrence of the materials committee, as well as the approval of higher line authority. His office may also initiate the development of standards and specifications for materials that have company-wide use. The director of supply and his staff act as consultants to the supply managers of the various plants, when requested.[9]

Organization for Maintenance

In certain large, continuous manufacturing concerns we see the most dramatic development of automation, the increasing transfer of skills and knowledge from line-production employees to machines. In these companies the importance of maintenance work is unquestioned, for each second of unscheduled down-time of the production system costs an impressive amount. And there is little doubt that maintenance personnel play a crucial role in determining whether or not such organizations will realize the full productive capacity of their automated systems. Managers of automated operations are more likely to be aware of the kind of objectives that should influence organization for maintenance. They are aware of the importance of *preventive* maintenance, the kind that anticipates trouble and avoids breakdowns. They are aware of the need for competent, well-managed maintenance personnel assisted by adequate communications and procedures to assure that needed repairs and adjustments are made as quickly and economically as possible. The need for well-organized maintenance work in other firms is just as real; it is just not so dramatically revealed!

A maintenance department—in firms large enough to have these staff functions differentiated—is concerned with providing good physical working conditions at all times, even though this may require it to operate at less than optimal efficiency part of the time. (For example, the number of maintenance employees will tend to be influenced by peak more than by average maintenance requirements.[10]) The head of the department is often an engineer so that he will have the technical ability to evaluate his subordinates and assist them in planning their work and will be qualified to provide sound advice to higher management as to maintenance needs. In

---

[9] *Ibid.*, pp. 574, 575, 609, 611, 630, 655.

[10] This is an expression of the concept of *Limitation of Staff Economy:* "It is usually necessary that staff functions be performed with less than maximum economy in order that the line functions that they serve may be performed with maximum economy and effectiveness." This concept is discussed in chap. 11; see p. 288.

addition, he must be a competent manager who can pick good men, effectively train and motivate them, and skillfully coordinate their activities. These attributes are especially important to the maintenance supervisor, for his men work largely on their own initiative and there is limited opportunity for him to control their activities via personal supervision.

Among the functions closely allied to and normally assigned to a maintenance department are the following:

1. Prompt performance of emergency repairs.
2. Planned, systematic inspection of plant and equipment to detect present deficiencies as well as to *anticipate* future ones. The making of repairs and adjustments where needed.

FIG. 10-4

Maintenance Organization for a Large Company

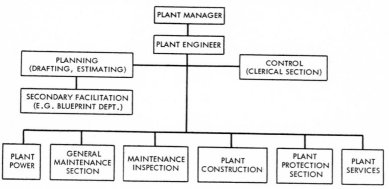

3. Adequate fire protection and other plant protection services.
4. Maintenance of heating, lighting, air-conditioning, power, compressed air (and other service systems assigned to it) in good operating condition at all times.
5. Suggestions for design changes in plant and equipment to accommodate current and future needs of the organization.
6. Maintenance and dissemination of data required for proper accounting, adequate preventive maintenance, and evaluation of departmental activity, and effective orientation of company employees as to the care and operation of equipment.

Of course, the extent to which all these functions are differentiated and assigned to a maintenance department depends on the size of the organization and its unique maintenance problems. Figure 10-4 depicts a suitable maintenance organization for a large company.

ORGANIZATION FOR THE PROCUREMENT, DEVELOPMENT, AND MAINTENANCE OF PERSONNEL

The personnel department is typically the staff agency that assists line management with the functions of procuring, developing, and maintaining personnel.[11] Figure 10-5 depicts a suitable personnel organization for a large firm.

A vice-president of industrial relations has an important role to play in the organization. He should represent a balance of personal attributes and professional skills that will permit him to formulate an effective over-all program, successfully coordinate its many parts,

FIG. 10-5

Personnel Organization for a Large Company

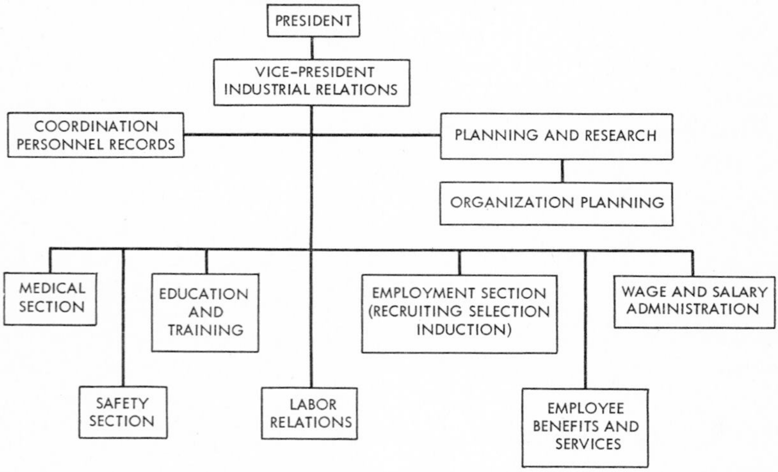

and gain the confidence and cooperation of managers and employees throughout the company. As a member of the president's executive committee, representing a staff agency that should serve all organizational elements without fear or favor, he is expected to make useful contributions to over-all policy decisions. Not only must he keep abreast of the latest research findings in the personnel field (hopefully, his organization will contribute significantly to this research); he must seek out divisional heads and managers, establish rapport with them, study their needs, and generate a desire

---

[11] For a discussion of the stages in the development of a personnel department, from its initial evolution to its ultimate separation and elevation to major divisional rank, see pp. 108–9.

on their part for his department's services. If he has technical competence in addition to administrative skills, he and his personnel organization can make significant contributions to the firm through their work of finding, developing, and conserving human resources. For example, in the area of selection, alone, the kind of contribution made possible by the proper validation of selection instruments was discussed in chapter 5.

Organization for Procurement

The employment section of the personnel department might be organized around the functions of recruiting, receiving, screening (application-blank analysis, interviews, medical examination, tests), and inducting employees. The most important consideration from an organizational standpoint is the danger that staff personnel performing these employment functions may *usurp line authority* and fail to retain a proper *spirit of service* to other line and staff personnel. It is not legitimate for staff personnel to *displace* others with regard to certain functions; it is their job to *strengthen the capability of others* to do their work and to *serve them* in ways that *meet with their approval!*

Parity of Authority and Responsibility. Members of the personnel department, for example, should not be given authority to hire people, for this would violate the *Principle of Parity of Authority and Responsibility:* **The responsibility of any manager or employee should correspond with his authority.** When *authority* for choosing a man is exercised by the personnel department, the supervisor for whom he will work is *not* relieved of *responsibility* for the quality of his performance. To the extent that selection *does* affect quality of performance, the supervisor is denied authority commensurate with his responsibility for performance. This would be similar to telling the coach of a college football team that he will be responsible for the performance of the team next year but will have no say-so in selecting men for the team and assigning them to various positions—that this will be done by a faculty committee of experts in selection. This is hardly an equitable arrangement! Also, if the team does poorly, there will be a tendency for the coach to blame the faculty committee and for the committee to blame the coach. As a result, no real basis will exist for establishing *accountability*— the extent to which responsibility has been accepted and discharged —however, we might suspect that the coach will be encouraged to look for another job next year!

Though the undesirability of this arrangement is obvious in the football example given above, unfortunately it is not so obvious in industry. Time and again we find company personnel persons with the authority to hire. The justification for this, it is argued, rests in the fact that personnel persons are supposed to be experts on selection matters, and those who know the most about something should have the final say-so about it. This is a most unfortunate and widespread fallacy. The owners of the enterprise and their *line* subordinates should and must have the final say-so, if their interests are to be safeguarded and staff personnel are to function harmoniously with them. For, if the business goes to ruin, they, not their staff advisers, will be the prime losers.

Competent owners and their line subordinates know the value of expert advice and service rendered by capable staff personnel. It seems reasonable to say that competitive success today depends in large measure on the effective utilization of staff expertise. Presumably, if a company president and his subordinates fail to draw adequately upon the resources of staff personnel, they and the enterprise will suffer. The solution is to dispose of the president, *not* to delegate more authority to staff personnel! Perhaps discussion of the desirable patient-physician relationship will help to illustrate this concept. The patient pays for the expert advice of the physician. He may accept or reject this advice. If the physician prescribes an operation, the patient may choose to ignore the matter—which is very foolish. Or he may wish to consult with other competent physicians to see whether there is an honest difference of opinion—which often is very wise. Or, if the evidence is rather conclusive and time and expense will not permit further exploration, he may instruct the doctor to proceed. The key point is that the patient normally has the final say-so. After all, as with the company owner, he stands to lose more if things fail to work out than anyone else associated with the venture.

Approved Selection Criteria. This may all sound well in theory, but, as a practical matter, how can we utilize the services of our personnel experts for *selection purposes* without violating these basic concepts? The first requirement is that selection criteria to be used by the personnel department in screening applicants for a given job *be approved*—preferably in writing—by the immediate supervisor associated with the job. This helps assure that the personnel department will use the same criteria that the using supervisor *now* would use in filling his vacancies. With this arrangement the personnel department performs a service for the supervisor *according to his specifications and subject to his control* (that is, the selection criteria cannot be changed or abandoned without his approval). In this way, the immediate supervisor still exercises authority over the selection process as it affects his department, and staff personnel are encouraged to *serve him* rather than unilaterally prescribe for him.

True, it is unlikely that the supervisor, if left to his own devices, would or could have come up with the same selection criteria that the personnel experts derive from detailed job analyses and interviews. But this is the kind of contribution competent supervisors expect from able staff people and for which they are paid. However, it would *not* be a useful contribution if it were imposed. Normally, a competent staff specialist can gain acceptance for well-formulated selection criteria without too much difficulty. If the personnel manager has been successful generally in gaining the confidence and acceptance of company executives, he need not be greatly concerned when an obstreperous foreman attempts to block the work of his men. If necessary, as a last resort, he can advise the foreman's superior of the situation, and usually this will suffice. Of course this "solution" can be abused and must be used with discretion. Staff not only should restrain the desire to impose their ideas upon others but must be careful to avoid creating an *impression* that they wish to do so.

Selection Procedure. Upon receipt of a labor requisition—a form sent by a supervisor to the personnel office describing the type of vacancy to be filled and any special attributes to be met by an applicant—the employment section can take steps to recruit candidates for the job and screen them with approved selection criteria. When one or more applicants are found who appear suitable, they should be referred to the supervisor for whom they will work *for the final selection decision.* The employment section should *not* be given this authority except when it is specifically delegated to it by a particular supervisor in a given instance as a matter of convenience to the supervisor. If a supervisor who has been satisfied with the quality of clerks referred to him by the employment section currently needs one and it is inconvenient for him to interview an applicant, he may have one of his subordinates conduct the interview. Or he may delegate his authority to the employment manager to make the decision *in this particular instance.* The important point is that the *control* of such decision making should *reside* with the supervisor concerned. This will help assure that employment section personnel will use only approved criteria, that they will collaborate with supervisors with regard to changes in criteria, and that they will continue to perceive their role as one of service to, not prescription for, the supervisor.

Some may argue that the average supervisor is not qualified or inclined to conduct an appropriate selection interview, that this requirement is a waste of time. This line of reasoning overlooks the importance of giving the supervisor authority commensurate with his responsibility. And, of course, we can train supervisors to do a better job of interviewing. Actually, however, it is not important whether the supervisor does a good job of applying the approved selection criteria during *his* interview. Presumably, the employment section has done this and *anyone* referred by them to the supervisor will satisfy the criteria. The supervisor and his subordinates, however, are probably the best judges of whether or not a given person will "fit in" with their group. Certainly, if they believe that one of several applicants is significantly stronger in this regard, there is nothing to be lost by applying this additional criterion, and possibly very much to be gained. In addition, having the supervisor make the final selection decision permits a "commitment" to be obtained from him as to the new employee. If *he* has made the final selection decision, it is likely that he will make more of an effort to train and assist the new employee and see to it that things work out. There will be less of a tendency, when the inevitable first mistake is made by the newcomer, for the supervisor to blame the employment section for sending him a lemon.

Promotion from Within. Many jobs can be filled by those who have demonstrated merit while working their way up through the ranks. True, in certain types of activities, such as college teaching, creative design and writing, etc., there is a real danger of "inbreeding," that is, perpetuating and intensifying deficiencies and biases within the organization. However, this danger, though important, should not be controlling. For, in those companies in which it applies, it is likely to apply only to certain departments or areas of activity. There are many advantages to be gained from primary reliance on "internal sources" of labor. To a much greater extent than when we process applicants, we are dealing with *known quantities,* and the impact on organizational morale can be quite favorable. Even when managers subscribe to this policy, they often find it difficult in large organizations to develop *organizational means* for implementing it effectively. One approach would be to punch a card for every employee and, each time there is an opening, run all the cards through to identify those who are qualified, and then pick out those for whom the change would be a promotion and get in contact with them to see whether they wish to apply. A much simpler approach, and one that is quite effective, is the use of *posting*. Merely place detailed job descriptions and specifications for all openings on strategically located bulletin boards and advise those who are qualified and interested to apply to the personnel office by a certain date. It is understood that the personnel office will have to go outside the firm if an acceptable applicant does not present himself before the deadline.

The Personnel Committee. The use of personnel committees at various levels—departmental, divisional, and general management—can do much to assure that nominees for employment or advancement are fully qualified and that deserving candidates from other areas of the organization are not overlooked or discriminated against. Such committees need not consider all appointments but merely those in certain title or salary ranges. They furnish the executive concerned with a list of all candidates who they believe are qualified and from whom he can make his final selection. Though the authority of the committee is limited to passing upon *qualifications* for promotions (or certain classes of raises), it serves a very useful function. By providing an equitable basis for eliminating unqualified candidates from consideration, it permits higher management to delegate more authority for making appointments to lower managers with adequate but unobtrusive control. Plant, divisional, and company personnel directors would be logical chairmen for these committees at each level. If there is an organizational specialist, he should be included along with the executive concerned with the particular appointment under consideration. The staff of the chairing personnel director could serve as a secretariat to the committee to facilitate the collection and presentation of relevant data.

Since pay increases and other forms of promotion are often based on merit ratings, it is useful to have these personnel committees serve, also, as coordinating agencies for the actual work of merit rating. This will help to solve two difficult problems associated with merit rating: (1) the individual supervisor's fear that *other* supervisors will be too lenient in *their* ratings and thus put him at a disadvantage with his employees and (2) the problem of assuring that objective ratings will be made when we are dealing with very small rating groups. When a personnel committee brings together several supervisors, who have some acquaintance with one anothers' employees and work, for the purpose of rating their combined "pool" of subordinates—say 30 or 40—these problems are greatly diminished. Each supervisor observes at first hand *and can help to control* how the other supervisors use the rating scale. The personnel director can expect a more normal distribution of ratings for the larger pooled group of employees or look for a good explanation as to why the group is a "select," above-average one or below-average one.

Organization for Training

In the area of junior executive development, there is perhaps more agreement as to training objectives than there is with regard to means for *implementing* them (though, it should be pointed out, there is still ample disagreement as to objectives, too!) Some large firms, for example, General Electric, have set up training institutions with full-time faculties to give college-graduate trainees one to two years of additional classroom instruction before they are absorbed into the operating organization. Others, such as Ford, believe that openly identifying graduates or others for special treatment and consideration does a disservice to the trainee, in the final analysis, and creates serious tensions in the organization. So Ford does not enter the graduate in a centralized program, but hires him for a specific vacancy and relies primarily upon on-the-job training *supplemented* by off-hours courses, etc., for his development. The editors of *Fortune* point out: "Dangerous or not, it is certainly evident that a centralized training program has a great effect on the trainee's outlook toward work and himself. To put it simply, in corporations with centralized programs, trainees like to talk about managing. In places like Ford, they talk about making automobiles." [12]

These comments were made in 1953; subsequent research findings tend to suggest that the "Ford approach," coupled with well-planned, supplemental training activity, is the more productive. For, in the final analysis, over-all training must remain essentially a *line responsibility* which takes place continuously in a proper *line organization environment*. As was pointed out in the discussion of training in chapter 6, "with the wrong organizational climate, it is quite possible for the supervisor to be less effective after human relations training than before it; the training merely confirms his misgivings about the inadequacies of his boss's approach and under-

---

[12] "Crown Princes of Business," in W. M. Fox (ed.), *Readings in Personnel Management from "Fortune"* (New York: Henry Holt & Co., 1957), p. 51, or *Fortune*, October, 1953.

mines his confidence in company management." [13] If a company has a poor organizational climate, obviously the solution to the problem is to alter the climate, not to attempt to isolate trainees from it!

The most important role for staff training specialists is to dramatize the need for training, define specific training needs, and *strengthen* the *trainer capabilities* of supervisors and executives throughout the organization. Their presentation of specialized subject matter and organization of special courses should always be a an *appendage* to the primary, continuous training effort mounted largely by the firm's line and staff executives. This is *not* to imply, however, that intensive short courses for salesmen, engineers, managers, and other employees are unimportant. These can be most useful for initial orientation, for training in techniques, and for keeping personnel abreast of current technical and business developments. The position taken here is simply that these *alone* will not constitute an adequate training effort.

In the Ford approach, emphasis is placed on the development of competence with a specific assignment, as well as coaching and special training to deal with individual deficiencies turned up by periodic assessments of performance. This approach provides the trainee with a continuing challenge to apply concepts and techniques he has learned and those he is being exposed to in supplemental training activity. Psychologically, he is better motivated and less frustrated, for he has something he can get "his teeth into" with the benefit of useful feedback if he is being properly coached.[14] Most trainees like the idea that their efforts are being carefully and continuously considered by their superiors, preferably by several persons, not just their immediate boss—if this is done in an organizational atmosphere in which self-development is accepted and encouraged on the part of *all personnel*. After all, genuine and lasting development can be the result only of a continuous training process that goes on throughout a man's career. There can be no substitute for the active interest, support, and participation of all managers in a training program, especially those at the top of the organization. The legitimate role of the training director is to assist management in planning, organizing, coordinating, and evaluating training activities and by handling staffing and other arrangements

---

[13] See p. 169.

[14] See p. 166 in Chap. 6 for a discussion of four ways in which the superior can productively coach his understudies.

for specialized presentations, workshops, or short courses. He can help define training needs through consulation with those who do organization planning and job analysis as well as through conferences with those who are currently being trained or have completed certain phases of training.

Guidance from trainees who are currently "in process" can be especially helpful. International Harvester has had considerable success with the use of committees composed of trainees from various levels of the organization, as well as various functional areas, which help define appropriate training objectives and evaluate what is being done. Chapter 8 discussed the value of having subordinates fashion their own "self-development" programs as a basis for personal growth and effective merit rating.[15] Also discussed has been the value of the "assistant to" position as well as the value of delegation of authority for training purposes. In addition, mention could be made of planned rotation through various positions, which helps give trainees a "feel" for different job environments and makes it easier for them to gain acceptance in the organization. Though these organizational considerations can significantly facilitate or hinder productive training effort, they can never serve as a substitute for the prime requirement: top-management leadership, based on sound philosophy and theory, which continuously *expects* and *nurtures* improved leadership throughout the managerial ranks of the organization.

Organization for Maintenance of Personnel

Most human beings are not amenable to "cabbage-like" existence. They thrive on moderate amounts of varied stimuli and challenge. We might argue that there is no such thing as "treading water" in life, that we and our relationships are in a state of either growth or decline, and that the individual who settles for dormancy is, in effect, embarking upon a period of personal decline. Thus it appears to be with marriage, a career, or with life in general! Consequently, what has been said about organization for training applies equally to organization for the *maintenance* of personnel. To the extent that top management creates a climate that encourages and nurtures growth, it is making provision for the conservation and development of human resources. I suspect that if management

---

[15] See pp. 204–5.

merely wishes to "maintain" personnel, it will embark on a period of organizational decline.

To create this climate, management must do much more than merely talk about the values that have been discussed. It must reward supervisors for personal growth and effective coaching of subordinates—even though this may not raise production as much in the short run as whip-cracking might. It must *really delegate authority* to those who are ready for it within the framework of adequate control, and it must design and respond to an adequate system of communications. Perhaps one of the most important requirements for the maintenance of this climate is the willingness of management constantly to re-examine its "ends"—primary, collateral, and secondary objectives—and its means for achieving them. Good human relations must never come to mean the elimination of conflict rather than the introduction of change with a minimum of conflict!

Organization planning, also, plays an important role in the maintenance of personnel. It should be a continuing activity that anticipates personnel and training needs sufficiently in advance to permit them to be met without undue reliance on external sources of labor and "crash" recruitment and training programs. As suggested before, organization planning "belongs" in the personnel department. Too often, it is not placed there, owing to lack of competence in this area on the part of the personnel staff. Perhaps, in the future, management will learn to make more demands on its personnel specialists in this area as well as in the area of adequate statistical analysis of personnel activities.

QUESTIONS

1. How does the job of controller differ from that of treasurer? Is it more plausible that a controller rather than a treasurer be made chief financial officer? Why or why not?

2. Is there any justification for the arrangement at General Motors where the chief financial officer reports to the chairman of the board? If so, what is it? Would this arrangement be desirable for most companies? Why or why not?

3. Discuss the relative importance of each of the objectives of a major staff supply division listed on page 265.

4. Is the importance of proper maintenance activity likely to be appreciated more in an automated factory? Why?

5. What is the concept of *Limitation of Staff Economy?*

6. Is there any particular reason why organization planning should be assigned to the personnel department? (See Fig. 10-5.) Explain.

7. "It has often been felt that the opinion of the most knowledgeable person in a given situation should prevail. For example, if an operation must be performed, the most skilled and experienced surgeon present should have the final say-so as to procedure. In like fashion, the personnel specialist is supposedly the organization's expert on selection. Consequently, he should make final hiring decisions. If he is not competent to do this, he should be replaced." Do you agree with the foregoing statement in whole or in part? Why or why not?

8. How should selection criteria for specific jobs be developed? Explain. Outline a sound selection procedure.

9. How can the use of a personnel committee contribute to the work of merit rating?

10. Which approach—the General Electric approach or the Ford approach—do you think is the more productive for training college graduates? Why?

11. How might management reward supervisors for personal growth and effective coaching of subordinates so that only the deserving are recognized and current productive efficiency is not sabotaged? Discuss.

Chapter 11

ORGANIZATION FOR CONTROL

In chapter 7 ("Planning for Control") the *organic subfunctions of control* were discussed; the *organizational setting* in which control should take place will now be discussed. As has been stressed before, organization structure and the functions of control are but *means* to the end of carrying out the organization's *primary service objectives*. Organization for control must be compatible with organization for other purposes. The process of control (performance of the *organic subfunctions)* must be tailored to the characteristics of organization structure and to the specific needs of the people operating within that structure at any given time.

ORGANIZATION PLANNING
AND KEY FACTORS AND OPERATIONS

Organizations grow and contract in size, people gain in experience and competence, and organizational objectives change. Organization for control must be responsive to these changes or the process of control may cease to be appropriate to current needs. The agency for organization planning[1] must stay in close touch with those groups responsible for cost accounting, operations research, production control, forecasting, data processing, auditing, etc., to assure that its recommendations relating to organization for control will reflect the current needs of the organization in an integrated way. Also, it is the responsibility of organization planners to identify, in collaboration with the representatives of such groups, the

---

[1] See p. 248 of chap. 9 for discussion of a staff organization planning agency. In smaller organizations, of course, these activities would be performed by the president or his appointees.

key factors and operations around which control systems must be established. *Key* factors and operations are those which are especially relevant to the attainment of objectives; those which, if properly controlled, are likely to assure adequate control of many related subsidiary factors and operations. Control must be *selective* to conserve organizational resources and morale. The identification of *key* factors and operations provides a sound basis for selectivity so that "where the risk lies there also lies the control." [2]

FEEDBACK DATA

In addition, organization planners must design control systems that provide for quick and adequate communication of "feedback data" as to input error, deviations from planned performance, and the *status* of *key* factors and operations. For corrective action cannot take place until the comparison function of control has been performed. The comparison function determines where we are relative to where we should be. It cannot be performed without swift communication of relevant operating data in "scorecard" and "attention directing" forms that are suited to the user. The role of the computer and accounting personnel in meeting these needs was discussed in chapter 9. Accounting personnel must be sensitized to their data processing function and their obligation as staff "servants" to perceive and satisfy the needs of data users.[3] Generally, data should flow first or concurrently to the lowest management levels concerned to facilitate the operation of the *Exception Principle*.[4] When programmed with *key factors* of control, the computer can facilitate the operation of the *Exception Principle*, also, by acting as a "sensing unit" to detect and report significant deviations from "normal" that occur at these *key* points.

Input Error

Though the computer is an invaluable tool for data processing, its use seriously compounds the problem of *input error*. Kozmetsky and Kircher report that in several installations "an error on about one punched card in a thousand is customary, requiring extensive

---

[2] The role of PERT in facilitating the identification of *key* factors and operations (in the form of critical paths and events with slack) for project control was discussed in chap. 7 (p. 188).

[3] Direct feedback via instrumentation, mechanical linkage, or the operator's senses will not be discussed, since this is usually quite simple and manageable from an organizational standpoint.

[4] Discussed in chap. 7 on p. 172.

trouble shooting later." [5] They report the efforts of one company to cope with this problem:

Controls were developed at the point where documents originated. The purpose was to ensure that all documents were received in the data-processing center, and also that all information received was processed by the computer. Documents were batched, given a control number, and time and identification logged.

After the materials went through key punch (which was necessary for input), the cards were balanced against a control card on an accounting machine. The control clerk then checked the total with the payroll section to make sure all the data forwarded were received.

Cards were then converted to tape. A tape-control total was prepared and checked against the card total. The first computer run was to sort the data; during this run totals were prepared to balance the data on the tape against the control total.

The extent to which such controls are required cannot be established without study of a particular operation. Because of the nature of an electronic system, introduction of faulty data is often quite costly, so that fairly elaborate control of input is often justified.[6]

Collusion

Since the computer makes possible a drastic reduction in the number of humanly handled steps in data processing, opportunity for separation of duties, to discourage fraud and collusion, is reduced. Kozmetsky and Kircher point out that:

... close control of input tapes, programs, and output records will have to be maintained, with as much separation of duties as possible. If there is any slip-up, a single expert might be able to rerun a tremendous volume of transactions, by old standards, in only a few hours.

A major safeguard against this in most present installations is the fact that the expert would not benefit from such falsification, since he does not have access to disposable assets or to means for mis-directing checks.[7]

1. *A record must be made of all accountable transactions and events.*
   In some cases the record must be precise (particularly for transactions involving outsiders), and in other cases estimates will do. The degree of necessary precision should be determined.
2. *There should be a way for authorization to be recorded.*
   If the proposed electronic system bypasses the manager, or eliminates the paper document, some other means of control—perhaps statistical analysis with rapid feedback—will be established.

---

[5] George Kozmetsky and Paul Kircher, *Electronic Computers and Management Control* (New York: McGraw-Hill Book Co., 1956), p. 110.

[6] *Ibid.*, p. 57.

[7] *Ibid.*, pp. 112, 113.

3. *There should be a means for subsequent checking.*

It appears likely that in many cases this check will not be an actual retracing of data flows, as in some present auditing procedures, so much as a testing of equipment and systems design so as to indicate a high probability that it is performing satisfactorily.[8]

Charts

The flow of feedback data can be facilitated through the use of a carefully planned system of charts. After key factors in a given

FIG. 11-1
Input/Output Control Chart

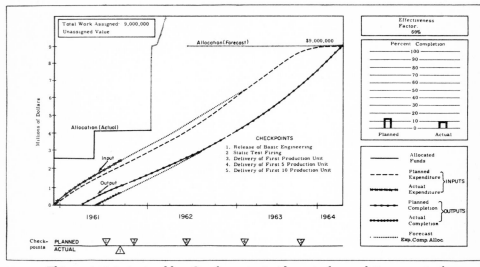

This project is in trouble. On the output side, actual completions are trailing planned completions. On the input side, too much is being spent. Also, it missed its first checkpoint. The Effectiveness Factor, upper right, is based on Actual Output divided by Planned Output, and the Planned Input divided by the Actual Input. The results of each are added together and then divided by 2 giving the E.F. To convert to percentage, multiply by 100.

Source: E. C. Soistman, "Input/Output ... Management's Control at Martin," *Aerospace Management,* April, 1962. In five years of work at Martin's Orlando Division on such projects as Pershing, Lacrosse, Bullpup, and other missiles, 770 million dollars of business has deviated from target cost by only 1 per cent.

manager's operation are identified, charts can be prepared to present current, historical, and projected data relating to these factors in a form that is most convenient for him. For project control, participating executives can collaborate in the design and maintenance—with clerical staff assistance—of a project chart room. When this

---

[8] *Ibid.,* pp. 187, 188.

is done with genuine acceptance by participants, healthy group pressure for prompt corrective action can be generated, since *all* project or unit managers see the charted deviations from "normal" or "expected," not merely the manager immediately responsible. Charts, as with the other media of feedback discussed above, set the stage for the kind of "analysis of results" meetings that produce effective action and individual executive growth. Figure 11-1 presents a chart used by the Orlando Division of the Martin Company for project control. Such charts are kept on display there in a chart room.[9]

STAFF ORGANIZATION FOR CONTROL

The six *Organic Subfunctions of Control*—programming, scheduling, dispatching, supervision, comparison, and corrective action —are discussed in chapter 7. The functions of programming, sched-

FIG. 11-2
Basic Organization for Staff Control

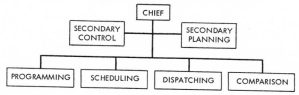

uling, dispatching, and comparison, to a large extent, may appropriately be assigned to staff personnel when the demand for specialization, or organizational size, justifies it. The organization chart for a control staff in an advanced stage of development (or functional differentiation) is presented in Figure 11-2.

The "secondary" staff functions—staff to serve staff—of secondary control and secondary planning need not be differentiated except

---

[9] For some provocative ideas as to the format and content of charts see John Curley, "A Tool for Management Control," *Harvard Business Review*, March, 1951; *How the Du Pont Organization Appraises Its Performance*, "Financial Management Series," No. 94 (New York: American Management Association, 1950); Allen Rucker, "Clocks for Management Control," *Harvard Business Review*, September, 1955; Leland Spencer, "The Profitgraph—Technique and Applications," *National Association of Cost Accountants Bulletin*, Vol. 38, No. 4 (1956); Marjorie Osborn, "Graphic Presentation of Results under a Variable Budget Control System," *National Association of Cost Accountants Bulletin*, Vol. 38, No. 4 (1956); Bernard Whitney and Marion Israel, "A Working Model of the Financial Dynamics of a Business," *Operations Research*, Vol. 6, No. 4 (1958). All but the first two articles appear in B. C. Lemke and James Edwards (eds.), *Administrative Control and Executive Action* (Columbus, Ohio: Charles Merrill Books, 1961).

in very large organizations. R. C. Davis points out: "Any large staff divisions will develop problems of internal coordination and external liaison. . . . It may become necessary to place staff responsibility for them on someone. A function of secondary staff control develops when this happens." [10] Secondary planning is concerned, to a large extent, with the development and refinement of control procedures for the control organization. In smaller firms all or several of the functions depicted in Figure 11-2 are performed by the same person.

For the most part, the boss of a line or staff unit should personally perform the organic control functions of Supervision and Corrective Action and pass personal judgment on the evaluation of his subordinates. Also, in most instances, he should handle dispatching when it involves verbal order-giving. For these functions involve face-to-face leadership and the effective use of authority. Obviously, the manner in which they are executed has much to do with the quality of group performance. The principles of *Unity of Command* and *Parity of Authority and Responsibility* would be violated if these functions were turned over to staff personnel. However, a manager can have staff personnel assist him in the performance of these functions by using them (1) to confirm verbal orders and instructions, (2) to follow the course of corrective action and report back as to its progress, and (3) to assist with the replanning phases of corrective action (this is discussed in chap. 13).

Also, there are times when it is not feasible to supply supervisors with highly specialized skills that are needed only occasionally in their work. Consider, for example, the case of a foreman who supervises the loading or charging of a blast furnace in a steel mill. He has the technical knowledge and skill required to direct normal loading operations. If something unusual comes up, he can seek specialized staff counsel through prescribed channels and then direct his men accordingly. However, suppose that there is an occasional loading formula that requires highly technical knowledge and *instantaneous* control of input factors. In this situation it is desirable to give a specialist (say, a chemist from the research department) *functional authority* to direct the loading crew when the special formula is being used (see Fig 11-3).[11] If the need for this arrangement is clearly understood by the regular foreman of the work group, there is little danger that he will give conflicting orders when

[10] R. C. Davis, *The Funamentals of Top Management* (New York: Harper & Bros., 1951), p. 409.
[11] Functional authority is defined and discussed on p. 92.

the functional supervisor—the chemist—is carrying out his assignment. Since the chemist understands the limited scope of his authority over the work group (applicable only to loading operations requiring the special formula) he will not attempt to establish himself as a "dual," regular boss of the men. In turn, the men have no doubt as to who their boss really is and are not confronted in any significant way with the problem of trying to please two masters.

This arrangement *does* constitute a violation of the "old" unity of command concept requiring that each employee have only one boss all the time. However, if the conditions set forth above are satisfied, it is a "nominal" or meaningless violation. For the advantages of specialization are brought to bear in the most effective

FIG. 11-3
The Use of Functional Authority

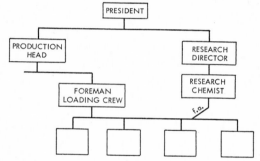

Note: f.a. denotes functional authority.

way, without the disadvantages of duality of command that gave rise to the old concept. For this reason, the *Principle of Unity of Command* is restated in this book: **An employee should receive orders from one "regular" superior only, unless they result from specific functional authority delegations which are clearly understood by the "regular" superior, the employee, and the functional superior.**

Cross-Contacts

A distinction should be made between the use of functional authority and the use of standing orders, procedures, and policies. Generally, functional authority should be used *only* for situations for which some other arrangement is not feasible. Suppose that our loading foreman is faced with a machine breakdown and wishes to summon the repairman without delay. He may be authorized to do so *as a procedural matter* without recourse to functional authority. Perhaps a staff specialist wishes to confer with a foreman or other specialists in another division of the company about a problem of mutual concern without "going through channels" (that is, having the problem relayed up through his boss, over to the other man's boss, and then to the man, and having the answer or solution returned to him via the same route). To facilitate matters and conserve everyone's time, the specialist should be permitted to make direct contact with the other man. But *as a procedural matter,* he should be required to inform his superior as to the nature and outcome of the meeting, and solicit his approval for any proposals or commitments *tentatively* arrived at. Again, the use of functional authority is not required.

Limitation of Staff Economy

Primary service objectives have to do with the creation and distribution of salable utilities. The values that the organization must create to induce the proper implementation of *primary service objectives* are expressed as *collateral objectives. Secondary objectives* have to do with the implementation of primary and collateral objectives with maximum economy and effectiveness. *Staff agencies* are concerned, primarily, with *collateral* and *secondary objectives.* In approaching their *secondary objectives*, staff agencies cannot always assure their own efficiency in the process of supporting the efficiency of line agencies. At times, a staff agency must "overorganize" relative to the *average* volume of work it will be expected to handle. This relationship is expressed in the concept of the *Limitation of Staff Economy:* **It is usually necessary that staff functions be performed with less than maximum economy in order that the line functions that they serve may be performed with maximum economy and effectiveness.** Davis writes:

The maintenance organization is an example of the operation of this principle. In most concerns, there are times when maintenance operatives have hardly enough work to keep themselves busy; but other times they may have to work overtime. Production equipment seldom considers their convenience in breaking down. . . . The size of the maintenance department more nearly approximates the man power necessary to handle the peak load of maintenance work that may reasonably be anticipated, rather than the average load over a period of time. It is unwise, furthermore, to lay off workers during dull times because of the specialized training and experience needed for this work.[12]

---

[12] R. C. Davis, *Industrial Organization and Management* (3d ed.; New York: Harper & Brothers, 1957), p. 366.

DECENTRALIZATION

As organizations grow in size, the complexities and problems facing centralized management grow at a faster rate. Centralized managers become engulfed by the sheer volume of problems referred to them for solution and are plagued by delays and inaccuracies caused by growing "distance"—as to both communication and understanding—between the head office and the "firing line." When a firm is operating in a relatively stable environment with little competition (for example, a railroad during the years before the advent of good roads, buses, trucks, and planes), centralized management can reduce its load to manageable proportions through the extensive use of rules, procedures, and standard practices. This is feasible because centralized management will be confronted, for the most part, by predictable situations. Employees who are not seeking a dependent relationship with their employer probably will not like it, but such an organization can be quite efficient! However, it has two drawbacks: It does not develop leadership, and it is not viable and adaptive to change.[13] For most firms operating in America today, these are, indeed, serious limitations. Change is the order of the day, competition is prevalent, and seasoned managerial talent is hard to come by in our growing economy.

Decentralization, if implemented properly under favorable conditions, permits a firm to expand and enjoy the economies of large-scale operations without losing its flexibility and the opportunities for individual motivation and growth it afforded when it was smaller. Effective decentralization presents many advantages, but they are not easy to come by. In a new organization decentralization will not be feasible until company objectives and policies are well defined and comprehended and managerial capacity for competent leadership, at all levels, is established. For the highly centralized firm a shift toward decentralization presents transitional "pains." It will require that many dependent executives and employees be "weaned" to independence or dropped. It will require a significant revision in the philosophy and behavior of members of top management or their replacement with executives who subscribe to the values of decentralization and are emotionally equipped to delegate authority. The following criteria are essential for successful decentralization.

---

[13] For research findings in support of this see J. C. Worthy, "Organization Structure and Employee Morale," *American Sociological Review*, April, 1950.

1. *Well-seasoned, well-trained executives at all levels who are thoroughly oriented to company objectives and policies.* Decentralization must take place within the framework of over-all company objectives and policies. Every part of the organization should contribute to a harmonious whole.

2. *Decentralization with selective, central control.* Centralized control of such factors as over-all objectives, policies, and procedures, capital expenditures, performance criteria for decentralized units, certain accounting practices, pure research, and certain aspects of collective bargaining. The *specific areas* for a particular company should, of course, be determined by an analysis of the firm's needs. Centralized control, like functional authority, should be applied only to those areas for which it is absolutely essential, for organizational decentralization cannot occur without delegation of authority or managerial decentralization.

3. *Control of subordinate managers by results and consultation rather than by close supervision.* Well-defined performance standards for periodically evaluating decentralized units should be formulated and explained. Within the framework of over-all objectives and policies, each subordinate manager should be permitted to "run his own show." He should be held accountable for results more than for conformity to specific means for achieving them. He should be given freedom and encouragement to "try his wings" and grow. This requires that managers at all levels have the capacity to provide consultative leadership for their subordinates.

4. *Participation by lower-level managers in over-all policy making.* Better policy, as well as better understanding and acceptance of policy, will result if means are provided whereby lower managers can understand and *influence* policy matters that affect them.

5. *Advice rather than prescriptions from general management to divisional management.* Divisional managers should be encouraged to adhere to the concept of completed staff work in making proposals to general management. That is, they should be encouraged to submit *complete* proposals with supporting documentation rather than consult with general management on a more frequent "piecemeal" basis. This will stimulate the kind of initiative on the part of subordinate managers that will contribute to improved analytical skill and personal growth.

6. *Functional authority on the part of central staff units to specify the frequency and content of reports from decentralized staff units.* These reports supply data that will indicate to central staff officers areas for productive research and problem solving. Also, such reports make it possible for the central staff unit head to contribute more productively to over-all company policy making.

7. *Use of the following "force techniques" to assure delegation of authority "down the line":*

a. Broader spans of control where appropriate.

b. Establishment of managerial training positions in decentralized units with the understanding that the company as a whole will bear the burden of any unusual training costs. In this way certain training opportunities are created without making decentralized managers feel that they are being financially penalized as a result.

c. Establish the policy that no manager will be considered promotable, normally, until he has trained a replacement for his present job.

These criteria are useful for decentralizing those operations in the organization which *should be* decentralized. Decentralization is not an "either-or" proposition; only certain operations or parts of an organization may be suited to it. Consider the matter of production control. Where it is necessary to integrate engineering changes in annual models and to keep work in process and inven-

FIG. 11-4
Centralized Production Control

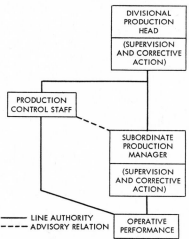

Note: Here, the subordinate production manager is not responsible for the control functions of programming, scheduling, and dispatching. He may or may not be given the comparison function. Of course, he must perform all the control functions for those activities of his department which do not come under the jurisdiction of the centralized production control unit.

tories at a minimum by working close to the demand schedule, it may be desirable to centralize production control under the divisional production head (see Fig. 11-4). If production control were completely decentralized, managers at *each level* under the divisional head would have all six organic functions of control performed under their jurisdiction (see Fig. 11-5). When conditions are sufficiently *stable,* the advantages of centralized production control may well outweigh the disadvantages.

Chapter 9 discussed the design of Sylvania's *centralized* data processing system, which was established to serve the needs of decentralized managers. It was pointed out how it provides for the fruits of optimal computer and communications efficiency along with those of managerial decentralization, simultaneously. Also, the appropriateness of various functions with regard to centralization were discussed. It may be helpful for the reader to review this material to facilitate the development of his "overview" of decentralization.

FIG. 11-5

Decentralized Production Control

decentralized managers. LINE AUTHORITY
ADVISORY RELATION

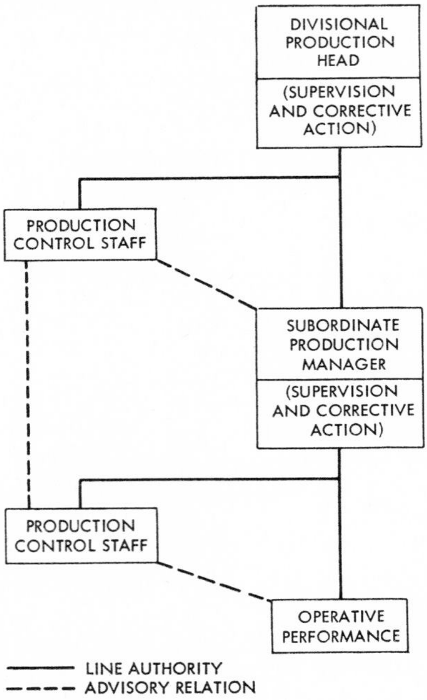

Organization for Decentralized Staff Activity

A decentralized production control staff unit is depicted in Figure 11-5, and reference has been made to decentralization of accounting functions. What about desirable organization for other staff units? For the sake of illustration, let us look at the area of personnel administration. Assume a manufacturing concern with decentralized factories geographically dispersed. Each factory manager reports to the vice-president of production, who in turn reports to the president. There are personnel managers for each factory as well as a vice-president of industrial relations (personnel) who reports to the president. This situation is presented in Figure 11-6.

As shown in Figure 11-6, the plant personnel managers do not "belong" to the organization. This was done purposely, because some important questions must be answered before a useful arrangement can be formulated. Whom should the plant personnel manager *directly* work for? On the one hand, his chief function in the factory is to *serve* the factory manager by assisting him with the performance of factory personnel functions. One could argue that the factory manager should be his boss, since he is the best judge of how well he has been served. Also, if the factory manager is to be judged by results—how well his factory performs—should not he be given authority to supervise the people who determine results?

FIG. 11-6

A Decentralized Manufacturing Firm
(Partial Diagram)

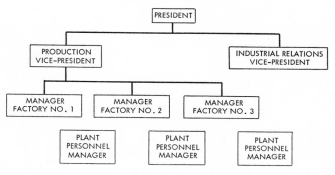

On the other hand, why should not the vice-president of industrial relations be the plant personnel manager's boss? After all, he is the most experienced personnel expert in the company. He could rquire the factory personnel managers to follow good practices and assure some uniformity of personnel practice throughout the company. Also, he would not be left "high and dry" in the home office with no real understanding of what is happening in the field. Through regular contact with the factory personnel managers, he would be in a better position to contribute to top-level policy making.

Fortunately, there is a solution that satisfies all the requirements outlined above. Figure 11-7 illustrates the solution in chart form. The factory manager is the plant personnel manager's boss. This will encourage the plant personnel manager to serve the needs of the factory manager rather than the possibly conflicting needs of the industrial relations vice-president. And it will help give the factory manager authority commensurate with his responsibility for the operation of the factory. However, we will require that factory managers satisfy certain minimum qualifications—formulated by the vice-president's office and approved by the line—in hiring plant per-

FIG. 11-7

Decentralized Personnel Administration in a Decentralized Multiplant Manufacturing Firm

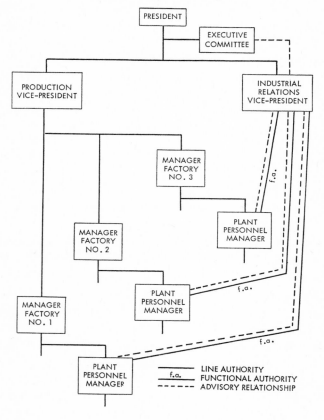

sonnel managers and that *all* factory personnel managers complete a training course under the direction of the vice-president of industrial relations at the home office. During such training the men will receive grounding in over-all company personnel objectives and policies and what are regarded as good personnel practices. To the extent that the trainees *accept* what they learn, they will try to apply it in the factories even though the vice-president is not there ordering them to do so. Of course, all personnel men in the company must comply with those company-wide personnel policies and procedures which have been authorized by the president.

In addition, the vice-president has an advisory relationship with the factory personnel managers. He can keep them informed on new techniques and the home office's latest research and survey findings. At the same time, he puts his research resources at their disposal and is available to them as a consultant. To permit the vice-president to keep abreast of developments in the field, we give him *functional authority* to specify the frequency and content of reports from the factory personnel managers. This supplies him with more *flexibility* than would be provided by a *standing order* specifying the frequency and content of reports. And such use of functional authority presents little danger of encroaching upon the factory manager's authority or of creating confusion.

It was mentioned earlier that the factory managers might hire new factory personnel managers. Actually, the vice-president could be authorized to hire, train, and have on hand as special assistants, several men, at any given time, who would be qualified to be factory personnel managers. Factory managers could then select from this "pool." Whichever approach is used, the key idea here is to have the candidate receive home office training before assuming the duties of a factory personnel manager.

It may be noted in Figure 11-7 that there is an advisory relationship between the industrial relations vice-president and the executive committee. This signifies that the vice-president contributes to over-all policy making. Though they are not shown on the chart, the vice-president has informal advisory relationships with other organizational personnel. If he has reason to believe, for example, that one of the factory managers is irrationally blocking the establishment of a sound personnel program in a factory, he will probably put the matter before the vice-president of production and try to induce *him* to take corrective action. Of course, the kind of success he will experience in these "informal" contacts will depend on the effectiveness of his interpersonal relationships as well as his prestige and demonstrated competence.

There is an important "exceptional case" to the foregoing proposals for decentralized staff activity. This occurs when the idea of formal personnel activity is new to an otherwise mature organization, and considerable resistance to its introduction at lower levels is anticipated. If we send qualified personnel managers out to work for factory managers under such conditions, they may be denied any reasonable opportunity to "show what they can do". In some actual situations, they have either been fired on the spot or put to work as office boys! If the president is willing to throw his full support behind the new personnel chief and his program (if he is not, forget the program), a good argument can be made for having the factory personnel men report directly to the chief (vice-president of industrial relations) during the initial phase of introducing the personnel program (as outlined in Fig. 11-8).

Under this arrangement, there will be less opportunity for the factory manager to ignore or "sidetrack" the factory personnel man-

FIG. 11-8

Centralized Personnel Administration as an Introductory Stage of Development

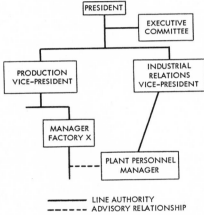

ager. To the extent that the industrial relations vice-president and his men have a sound program to "sell" and use the right approach, they can hope to win over significant portions of the organization to their cause. If this does not occur within a reasonable period of time, the personnel program can be regarded as a failure. Good staff work and counsel are not imposed; they gain acceptance by their merit. The centralized approach described above should be regarded as a *transitional device,* which will be displaced by the decentralized approach as soon as conditions permit.

Decentralization of Purchasing

The analysis for decentralization of personnel administration applies generally to other company-wide staff services, though concessions must be made to the unique demands of the activity and organization. In the case of purchasing, for example, it is feasible to use selective decentralization. The central purchasing office procures those materials which are used by all decentralized units and which, when ordered in large quantities, can be obtained at appreciable savings. All other purchasing is handled by plant purchasing men who report to the factory manager or production head. As with decentralized personnel managers, plant purchasing men are trained by the central staff and are subject to company-wide purchasing policies and procedures that are formulated by the home-office purchasing staff and approved by the president for dissemination.

Problems of Decentralization

If large amounts of authority are delegated, then equally large amounts of responsibility must be delegated also. But, without some means for *establishing accountability,* responsibility cannot be exacted from subordinates in any meaningful way. Professor Davis provides some worthwhile observations with regard to accountability:

Accountability is a requirement or condition under which each member of the organization renders a report on his discharge of responsibilities and is judged fairly on the basis of his record of accomplishment. . . .

Accountability may be established by means of organizational and operational directives. They usually specify the performance standards by which the degree of accomplishment of assigned objectives, both organization and operational, may be judged. . . . The maintenance of accountability is one of the purposes of the control function. . . .

Accountability is an individual rather than a group problem. Divided responsibility and authority necessarily results in divided accountability. The latter leads to friction between superior executives, "buck-passing" by subordinates, and other difficulties. . . . This is one reason why committees are usually kept strictly in a staff capacity in business organization. Individuals are likely to give themselves the benefit of the doubt concerning what constitutes satisfactory performance of their functions when they cannot be held strictly accountable for results.[14]

The need for well-defined performance standards was stressed in our discussion of criteria for effective decentralization. Budgets and profit center control (discussed later in this chapter) are important tools for establishing accountability. In the area of *policy compliance* we need to develop better standards of performance

---

[14] Davis, *The Fundamentals of Top Management,* pp. 320–22.

and means for establishing accountability. A periodic review of all positions in the organization with regard to provisions for establishing accountability should prove most useful.

Decentralization must take place in accord with the *Principle of Unity of Objective:* **The organization as a whole as well as each of its parts provides merely a tool for the achievement of organizational objectives; therefore,** *all* **organization activity should contribute to the attainment of these objectives.** Decentralization can produce undue duplication of effort or conflict of purpose on the part of decentralized units. Price wars, for example, between decentralized units may benefit certain managers in their "showing," but rarely benefit the company. Unjustifiable duplication of research, purchasing, or other effort by decentralized staff units must be avoided. The word "unjustifiable" is used here, for this is a matter of judgment. Some duplication of effort is the necessary price we must pay for the many benefits provided by decentralization.

Of all the criteria for effective decentralization that have been discussed, probably the most important is the quality of over-all leadership. This will determine whether or not a "climate" for executive growth will prevail. Only emotionally healthy men with adequate training and mature judgment can provide it. Unfortunately, such men are hard to come by.

PROFIT CENTERS

The creation of divisional "profit centers" can do much to strengthen and exploit the advantages of decentralized operation. "A profit center is defined as a semiautonomous group of facilities and functions chosen so that profit performance can be the main guide to evaluation of divisional performance and the main guide by which the division manager makes his critical decisions." [15] An example of such a division would be one that orders its own materials, schedules operations, negotiates the sale of its products, utilizes its own staff support, and is free to trade both inside and outside the company for its needs—all, of course, within the framework of over-all company objectives and policies.

A large, multiple product firm functions best as a "small edition" of our competitive, free enterprise economy. In doing so, it profits

---

[15] Joel Dean, "Profit Performance Measurement of Division Managers," *The Controller,* September, 1957 (now *Financial Executive,* published by Financial Executive Institute).

from the same values that have made our nation so productive and protects itself from many of the rigidities and inefficiencies of "bigness." Healthy competition among decentralized "profit centers" motivates and develops managers. It facilitates the development and use of realistic performance standards and sparks a continuing search for improved efficiency. The "profit center" approach facilitates the use of the *Exception Principle* and in other ways contributes to over-all company control without stifling initiative and morale at the divisional level. But, as with decentralization generally, these advantages are not easy to come by. Much planning and refinement based on experience are necessary before this approach can be truly productive in a given firm.

Organizational Requirements

Many potential "profit centers" already exist in the form of functional, product, or territorial divisions. Dean suggests four economic tests to be applied in marking off "profit centers."

1. *Operational Independence.* Unless a division has a large measure of independence it will have inadequate scope to reach decisions on a profit-oriented basis and hence delegation will be defeated. The division manager needs discretion over buying, production, scheduling, inventories, product-mix and pricing. This discretion should be exercised under broad rules of the game established centrally.

2. *Access to Sources and Markets.* Independent access to sources and markets is essential if make-or-buy decisions are to be made correctly. It is also essential for make-or-sell decisions, i.e., choice between selling a product at an early stage of the process or later (e.g., cured vs. uncured hams)....

3. *Separable Costs and Revenues.* Profit centers should be marked off so as to minimize the necessity for cost and revenue allocations, since these are necessarily arbitrary and contentious.

Contribution profits of the division can be defined so as to exclude central and other costs outside the profit center manager's control. But when these controllable profits are too small a part of the total a profit center does no good.

4. *Managerial Intent.* No division's contribution can be measured solely by its profits but this must be a good measure of performance if the division is to be a profit center.

Top management must be resolved to abide by the behavior and performance and the impersonal guidance of the price system which this measure of divisional performance implies.[16]

---

[16] *Ibid.*

Intracompany or Transfer Pricing

Intracompany or transfer pricing has to do with the movement of products, materials, or services into or out of the semiautonomous division. These must be priced in a realistic fashion to provide a basis for sound profit control. Sound transfer prices provide the divisional manager with the economic basis and the incentives for correct decisions. As Dean points out: "They also provide top management with profit and loss information indispensable for evaluation of the results of complex combinations of managerial skills and diverse facilities." [17] It is important that transfer prices *not* be determined by "cost-plus," marginal cost, or other arbitrary methods. These protect the supplying manager from the pressures of competition, and deny the buying manager control over an important aspect of his operations. The greatest degree of realism will be afforded by the use of *competitive, negotiated* transfer prices. These can be instituted by following three simple principles: [18]

a. Buyers and sellers completely free to deal outside or inside the company.
b. Prices determined by negotiation between buyers and sellers with a minimum of arbitration.
c. Negotiators have access to data on alternative sources and markets and have facilities for using the markets.

It is imperative that as much care be used in introducing the concept of competitive transfer pricing as with any change. The transition must be made slowly, for many divisional managers, unaccustomed to this approach, may feel threatened by what they perceive as its implications. Initially, it may be desirable to apply competitive transfer pricing only to certain products or services for which negotiation is not difficult. Temporary price limits may be set along with temporary limits as to the volume of outside trading that will be permissible. But these are temporary expedients. The profit center approach will succeed to the extent that competent, imaginative division managers see it as a positive challenge with significant opportunities for personal growth and reward.

Evaluation Criteria

As Dean points out, *contribution profits as a return on investment* provides the most important guide to top management for evaluat-

---

[17] Joel Dean, "Decentralization and Intracompany Pricing," *Harvard Business Review*, November, 1955.

[18] Dean, "Profit Performance Measurement of Division Managers," *op. cit.*

ing profit center performance. However, as was discussed in chapter 7, there are other important criteria that must be considered in evaluating over-all performance: such factors as market share, research, organizational strength, and executive development. No one knows the relative importance of such factors. As Dean observes:

> The key question is whether the right amount of near profits were sacrificed in attaining these various determinants of distant profits. The answer requires high-level judgment and technical familiarity with the kinds of investment in market franchise, in ideas, in facilities, and in people that are entailed. . . .
> Indeed a good case can be made for not attempting to formalize the standards of profit performance. Instead, leave this to the informal judgment of top management, which must in any event tailor the standard to the individual division and take many dimensions of long-term profit performance into account. . . .
> Par for the profit center course should also take account of economic climate and competitive conditions in the industry. Sometimes this can be done roughly by comparison with the earnings of independent firms of approximately the same product line.[19]

Of course, it must be understood that profit center managers may not increase their profits by practices that drive down total company profits or are inconsistent with company ethical standards. And, in the short run, top management must resist the temptation of placing *too much* emphasis on the *tangible* profit factor. The manager's intent, competence, and environment must be carefully weighed. The autocratic "driver" often can make a good short-term showing at the expense of long-term organizational health. Conversely, certain desirable executive attributes may not "pay off" for an extended period of time, and then in such a way as to elude direct measurement. This is merely a reiteration of the point that executive evaluation cannot be done by rote formula. We must temper our appraisal by "results" with a genuine respect for the following sentiment: "Most men feel that good intentions, perseverance, skills and abilities, initiative, integrity, morality, loyalty to the organization, and consideration for others, when expressed in performance, are also large factors on which rewards, recognition, and 'standing' should be based."[20] High standards of expectation coupled with genuine understanding are likely to induce higher levels of performance in the long run than will a "tight-ship" approach.

---

[19] *Ibid.*
[20] Robert Durand, *Business: Its Organization, Management and Responsibilities* (Englewood Cliffs, New Jersey: Prentice-Hall, Inc., 1958), p. 401.

RESPONSIBILITY CENTERS

Many organizational units that cannot qualify as profit centers can be established as "responsibility centers." These are units headed by individuals who are responsible for earning revenue or for incurring certain elements of cost. Anthony observes that "the several operating and staff departments may each be responsibility centers, and at still lower levels, responsibility centers may consist of sections, subsections, or even, in some cases, individuals who have no one else reporting to them."[21] The rationale for responsibility centers is the same as that for profit centers: to establish an organizational basis for control by results.

Responsibility Center Departmentation

The key attributes of a responsibility center are:

1. The output of the unit must be clearly definable and measurable.
2. The manager of the unit must have sufficient freedom and delegated authority to *influence significantly* many of the factors that affect unit output.
3. Organization of unit activity must be consistent with the *Principle of Unity of Direction:* **There should be *one head* and *one plan* for each group of activities having the same objective.** This is necessary so that *single accountability* for unit performance may be established.

Many service or staff departments do not fully satisfy these requirements owing to the *intangible* (non-measurable) character of much of their output. For example, how can we place a monetary value on the long-range benefits resulting from the conduct of a morale survey by the personnel department? For such activities, "project control" in the form of *stated objectives, time schedules, progress reports, standard costs*, and *budgets* is more appropriate. But responsibility centers *within a staff agency* may be established for those activities which *do* lead to measurable outputs. For example, we *can* measure the savings that result from an improvement in the validity of our selection procedure.

A number of years ago, to gain the advantages of specialization, many department stores separated the functions of departmental buying and selling. When sales in a department were disappointing, the buyer would blame the department manager for poor merchandising skills, and the department manager would retaliate by claim-

---

[21] Robert Anthony, *Management Accounting* (Homewood, Illinois: Richard D. Irwin, Inc., 1956), p. 271.

ing that a merchandising genius would not be able to do much with the items bought at the prices paid. Clearly, here was a case in which single accountability could not be established and in which both buyer and seller were denied the satisfaction of seeing the undisputed fruits of their *individual* efforts. The solution of this problem is to give the department manager freedom to accept or reject merchandise from the buyer and buy on his own account—within certain limits. This arrangement meets our requirements for responsibility center departmentation and contributes to improved morale.

It is also consistent with the concept of "job enlargement" or assignment of whole tasks. We all share a need to feel that what we are doing is meaningful. Numerous studies show that division of labor has often been pushed beyond a point of diminishing returns. For example, a production line approach was established in the central reservation office of a major airline whereby each clerk performed only one or two functions in the processing of each request for space. Output was appreciably below expectations. When employees, at their suggestion, were permitted to process requests from receipt to final disposition, output increased significantly.

Accounting for Responsibility Centers[22]

An accounting system must serve a number of purposes, and, ideally, the processing of data should be tailored to the specific requirements of each purpose. For example, costs charged to a department for *product costing* are unlikely to be the same as those regarded as being controllable. For responsibility center control, we should report only those cost and revenue items for which the department head, or responsibility center head, is held reponsible.

Of course, the responsibility center head rarely has *complete* control over all the factors that determine a particular cost; however, if his actions *significantly influence* the cost, this is sufficient for charging the cost to his responsibility center. The use of *standard costs* helps differentiate between those elements of a cost which may be regarded as controllable and those which are non-controllable for a particular responsibility center. As Anthony points out:

A standard labor cost, for example, presumably states what the cost should be, considering the influence of wage rates, product design, and other factors over which the foreman has no control. Ideally, the differ-

---

[22] For this discussion the author has drawn upon the analysis given by Anthony, *op. cit.*, chap. 14.

ence between standard cost and actual cost represents the effect of actions by the foreman, and it is this difference, or variance, for which the foreman is held responsible.[23]

If, for some reason, non-controllable costs are charged to responsibility centers, they should be clearly distinguished from controllable costs. Preferably, costs should first be reported on a responsibility basis, and then "reshuffled" for product costing, inventory pricing, and other purposes. As has been stressed earlier, the form of data reporting should be consistent with the unique needs and preferences of the data user. A possible format for reports to the foreman of a production responsibility center is given in Figure 11-9.

FIG. 11-9
Drill Press Department*

CONTROLLABLE EXPENSES	AMOUNT				(OVER) OR UNDER BUDGET			
	This Month	This Mo. Last Yr.	Year to Date	Yr. to Date Last Year	This Month	This Mo. Last Yr.	Year to Date	Yr. to Date Last Year
SUPERVISION	$							
SETUP								
REPAIR AND REWORK								
OVERTIME PREMIUM								
SUPPLIES								
SMALL TOOLS								
OTHER								
TOTAL								

PRODUCTIVE LABOR	STANDARD				VARIANCE			
	This Month	This Mo. Last Yr.	Year to Date	Yr. to Date Last Year	This Month	This Mo. Last Yr.	Year to Date	Yr. to Date Last Year
AMOUNT								
HOURS								
PER HOUR								

* Based on a chart developed by Arthur Anderson Associates, presented in the EPA-Bulletin No. 4, 1960.

Note: These controllable expenses do not represent the full burden of the department. They are the expenses for which management holds the foreman responsible. Productive labor is indicated because the foreman is responsible for its efficiency, even though he is not responsible for establishing its budget.

Impact of Cost Charges

The way in which controllable costs are assigned to a responsibility center has a significant impact on the behavior of the person in charge. It will do much to define for him the rules for "winning" or "losing" rewards from his superiors. Management must carefully consider the probable behavioral impact of various approaches to charging costs before selecting one. To illustrate, let us consider the problem of controlling maintenance costs in a factory that has a

---

[23] *Ibid.*, p. 270.

separate maintenance department. The function of keeping build-ings and equipment in good repair is partly the responsibility of operating foremen, who can influence the amount of wear and tear on the facilities, and the maintenance department foreman, who influences the quality and cost of the maintenance work that is done.

Anthony points out that "there are at least a dozen ways in which the costs of the maintenance department can be charged to the several operating departments, and each gives a different 'message' to the foremen as to how they should view their responsibility for maintenance."[24] He presents four possibilities and the implications likely to be conveyed by each:

Method No. 1: Do not charge any maintenance costs to the operating departments.

> *Message:* The operating foreman has no responsibility for mainte-nance costs. He requests the maintenance department to do the work that he thinks should be done, and the maintenance depart-ment has the responsibilty for doing it. The maintenance depart-ment is implicitly responsible for the condition of the equipment. (Note that this system does not motivate the foreman to curb un-necessary requests for maintenance work.)

Method No. 2: Prorate total maintenance costs to the operating de-partments on the basis of the number of direct labor hours incurred in each.

> *Message:* Maintenance costs in total are expected to vary proportion-ately with plant activity. However, the foreman of each depart-ment has no direct responsibility for maintenance work, and the maintenance department, as in the first method, has full responsi-bility. The operating foreman is told what is his "fair share" of total maintenance costs incurred.

Method No. 3: Charge departments for each job they have done at a prescribed amount for each type of job.

> *Message:* The foreman is responsible for situations that create the need for maintenance work, such as machine breakdowns. The maintenance department is responsible for the cost of doing a given maintenance job. The foreman therefore need not be con-cerned with the efficiency with which maintenance men work, once he has requested that the job be done, since he will be charged a prescribed amount no matter how much is actually spent in doing the job.

Method No. 4: Charge each department for maintenance work at a prescribed hourly rate for each hour that a maintenance man works in the department.

---

[24] *Ibid.*, p. 272.

Message: The foreman is responsible both for situations that create
the need for maintenance work and for the time taken by the
maintenance people to do the work. Presumably, he has some
control over the work of the maintenance men. He may, in some
situations, even be authorized to hire outside maintenance people
if he believes that they will do the work less expensively than the
rates charged by the maintenance department.

Management must select that method which, when coupled with
other stimuli, will encourage the kind of total behavior it wants. It
must avoid creating the impression that performance evaluation is
done by rigid formula. To the extent that management collaborates
with responsibility center heads in defining objectives, and demonstrates its intention of equitably evaluating the *total man* in his *total
work environment,* there should be little danger that a sound mode
of cost allocation will prompt behavior inimical to company interests. Also, thoroughgoing "post mortems," on a consultation basis,
as to why objectives were not realized will help improve future performance and dispel any feeling on the part of a responsibility center manager that he is merely a "victim of circumstances." It should
be apparent that in the discussion of "organization for control," as
with organization generally, concern is with the *art* more than with
the *science* of management!

ORGANIZATION FOR BUDGETING

Budget making is an important tool of control as well as of planning. In addition to encouraging adequate analysis and preplanning
of all operations, it contributes to the motivation of managers by
requiring them to *commit* themselves as to future performance.
Also, it facilitates the performance of the *comparison* function by
providing standards against which actual outcomes may be measured. Budget making facilitates the coordination of such related
functions as sales, production, purchasing, and inventory storage. It
facilitates the delegation of authority without loss of control and
provides a means for uncovering weaknesses and deficiencies in the
organization. And the analysis required for formulating flexible
budgets (budgets for different volumes of operation to facilitate
easy adjustment to non-forecasted sales levels) gives the budget
maker insight into the *dynamics of his organization,* that is, an ap-
preciation of how various factors in his organization (for example,
space, labor, and material requirements) are affected by changes

in output levels. It is apparent, then, that budgetary control is an *important complement* to profit-and-loss or "results" control.

Criteria for Effective Budgetary Control

Though a number of these factors have been discussed before, it is useful to reiterate them because of their impact on organizatonal requirements for effective budgetary control. The following prerequisites are essential to successful budgeting:

1. *Top Management Support.* Budget making is a demanding and sometimes frustrating process. It cannot be done properly unless organizational resources and considerable quantities of managerial time are committed to it *on a continuing basis.* This is not likely to ccur without genuine, sustained support on the part of top management.

2. *Well-defined Standards.* Budget makers must be supplied with clearly defined objectives and policies based on the development of sound planning premises and realistic forecasts. Though flexible budgeting provides some margin for error, confidence in the use of budgets is likely to vary directly with the adequacy of planning data. Budget makers should have the opportunity to influence top management in its definition of objectives and policies on the basis of their expectations.

3. *Budget Making by Budget Implementer.* If a person is to be responsible for compliance with a budget, he should assume a major role in developing it. Standards that are self-imposed are by far the most effective. Of course, the budget maker must be realistic and provide for an adequate level of aspiration within the framework of organizational constraints. Though his budget must be reviewed and approved by his superior, he should be the primary initiator and defender of it. He should have access to his superior and various staff persons for assistance and guidance in his budget making.

4. *Effective Flow of Feedback Data.* Provision must be made for promptly communicating revisions in standards in the light of actual experience and changing conditions. Also, budget makers must be supplied, promptly, with feedback data on actual vs. budgeted performance for their areas of responsibility in the form most suited to their individual needs.

5. *Periodic Post Mortems.* If the budget maker is to profit from experience and accept the equity of the budgetary approach, he must be given the opportunity regularly to analyze his performance with the *constructive* assistance of superiors and staff personnel. He must feel that the emphasis in such meetings is on corrective action rather than on pinpointing blame.

The Budget Administrator

"Responsibility budgets," developed by individual budget makers, must be recombined into various "program budgets" and an "over-all budget" for the company. A particular "program budget," for example, " . . . might be arranged by product lines and show the anticipated revenue and costs associated with each product. This type of budget is useful in examining the over-all balance among the various programs of the business."[25] For effective control of budget making, top management needs some basis for determining whether or not a particular budget is realistic and is based on the anticipated use of good procedures and practices. This work is time consuming and demanding. It is useful for management to draw on the services of a staff person or agency for assistance with budget administration.

The budget administrator acts in an advisory role to budget makers and to top management. He should *not* be given authority to originate "responsibility budgets" or to *approve* any budgets. His chief functions are to do useful "spade work" and to *guide* those who approve them. He can assist managers in determining the realism of budgets by maintaining data as to *past* performance by the same unit and past performance by similar units. He can advise managers as to more efficient procedures and practices that have been used in the past or are currently used elsewhere in the organization. He can assist budget makers in analyzing their operations for the purpose of flexible budgeting on the basis of his experience with others in the organization.

Since standard costs should vary with volume of output, also, he can assist managers with the determination of these for various levels of operation. He can compile "learning curve" data that show decreases in man-hours per unit required with increases in the quantity produced, so that standard costs and budgets may be adjusted accordingly. These activities, along with the function of recombining budget data for various purposes, make the budget administrator's job an important one indeed.

Capital Outlay Budgeting

It is essential that some centralized control be exercised over capital outlays in excess of a certain amount. For outlays over the prescribed amount—the specific "cutoff" point being determined by what is feasible for the given organization—the general management group should formulate the budget. It does so on the basis of its long-range planning in conjunction with its analysis of various proposals presented by subordinate managers. However, decentralized

---

[25] *Ibid.*, p. 326.

managers should have the right to initiate plans for capital outlays *below this amount* with assurance of approval, unless some obvious defects are turned up by higher management review. For lower managers will have little chance to grow if they are denied the authority to try things their way. Without genuine delegation of authority, there can be no genuine decentralization of managerial effort.

For all capital outlay budgeting, whether above or below the "cutoff" point, a thoroughgoing analysis of expected return and other values to be realized should be prepared. Periodically, a searching analysis should be made of the actual outcomes as compared with the anticipated outcomes. These post mortems are necessary for maintaining realism in the planning of capital expenditures and for permitting managers to profit from their experience. Normally, data required for such analyses will be "lost," or become hopelessly confounded by other factors, unless specific plans are made for their collection. Dean reports:

One company recently instituted a profit audit of all major projects that had been put into service in the preceding year. On a third of these projects it was found that the earnings had been over-estimated by an average of 25%, including one new product investment aggregating several hundred thousands of dollars which was rendered obsolete by a competitive development two weeks after it went into production. On another one-third of the audited projects, the available data were found to be inadequate to the task of checking on the original estimates.[26]

Limitations

Budgetary control, as with the other tools of control that have been considered, cannot be used mechanistically if we are to realize its potential benefits. After all, it *is* nothing more or less than a *tool*, which can be used or misused. Managers are "learning organisms." If they discover that fortuitous savings this year will bring a pat on the back *and* irrational cutting of their budgets next year, they will probably devise ways in which to spend the difference and forego the back-patting. If managers perceive that undue emphasis is placed on staying within the budget, come what may, they may press for unwarranted staff assistance—to reduce *their* costs—and let *quality* of effort go by the board.

These possibilities for budgetary abuse stress the need for budget review sessions that are constructive rather than punitive. Those who

[26] Joel Dean, "Measuring the Productivity of Capital," *Harvard Business Review*, Vol. XXXII, No. 1, (January, 1954), pp. 120–30.

do the reviewing must never lose sight of those factors in managerial performance which simply cannot be defined in budgetary terms. *Arbitrary* budget cutting is a superficial device for improving total performance. It tends to induce "improvements" in certain areas at the expense of other areas. Unfortunately, this reality is too often *not* apparent in the *short run.* Some managers actually are rewarded for a net deterioration in total performance! The budget review session provides an opportunity for superiors, through consultative management, to improve the competence and motivation of their subordinates.

EMERGENCIES

Urgent situations can arise when decentralized authority must be *temporarily recentralized.* The risks involved may be so high that it is necessary for the most experienced, ranking, line executive to assume personal command of the situation. In effect, the chain of command is temporarily *shortened,* and intervening managers step aside to serve as *staff aides* for the duration of the emergency. Of course, as soon as the emergency passes, decentralized authority should be re-established with displaced managers resuming their normal managerial functions. R. C. Davis describes such an emergency situation:

> The writer was once on the floor of a large locomotive repair shop when an error in judgment by a craneman placed the lives of some twenty-five mechanics in jeopardy. The shop superintendent immediately took command of the situation and directed personally the action required to avert the danger. The foremen who were normally in charge of operations in the particular area acted temporarily as his aides.[27]

Some critics of the armed services argue that they could be managed much more efficiently in peacetime if they were more decentralized. To the extent that the primary mission of our armed services is to function effectively *during time of war*, this criticism is misplaced. To a large degree, war is an unending sequence of emergencies. Today, more than ever before, our armed services must be prepared to go into action on a moment's notice. They must train and organize their personnel to function as they must in war. It would be chaotic, indeed, if they were to develop two significantly different modes of organization—one for peace and one for war—and try to change expeditiously from one to the other on a moment's notice! Here, the point is reiterated that decentralization must be

---

[27] Davis, *The Fundamentals of Top Management,* p. 311.

applied to an organization, and within an organization, on the basis of a careful analysis of the unique conditions that exist.

MULTI-INTEREST SITUATIONS

Certain activities, such as product design or materials standardization, are of vital concern to personnel from *different divisions*. A basic problem is to provide for *adequate control* of such activities without *imposing* decisions upon those who will be significantly affected by them and will be partly responsible for results flowing from them. Consider the matter of product design. To the extent that changes will require major risks or large capital outlays, the final decision should reside with the general management group under the direction of the president. But the preliminary "spade work" leading to major proposals and the approval of minor changes should be delegated to a coordinating agency at the divisional level.

Such an agency, in this instance, would be a product design committee under the chairmanship of the head of the manufacturing or sales division. Or, if the company has the services of a general management man, the chairmanship might be given to him. Competent line and staff members from the sales and manufacturing divisions and other relevant organization units would comprise the committee. It would have the authority to call upon appropriate staff assistance when needed. Concurrence of the committee would be required for the approval of minor changes or the submitting of proposed major changes to the general management group. Any group affected, however, would have the right to appeal the committee's decision to the general management group. On an informal basis, *cross-contacts* among personnel concerned with product design would help to supplement and facilitate the work of the committee.

THE CENTRALIZED CONTROL UNIT AT KOPPERS

Much has been written about the central control unit of the Koppers Company.[28] It was established by General Somervell, who took over as president of the company in 1946. He described the role of the control section as follows:

... the work of the Control Section is divided into four main subdivisions: Planning and Policies, Organization, Reports and Statistics, and

---

[28] For examples see Harold Koontz and Cyril O'Donnell, *Principles of Management* (New York: McGraw-Hill Book Co., 1959), pp. 677–81, and R. C. Davis, *Fundamentals of Top Management*, pp. 417–25.

Procedures. It assists in guiding and coordinating performance throughout the company, in appraising results, and in correcting unsatisfactory conditions. It reviews with staff departments and operating divisions the objectives and program of the company. It is continuously engaged in guiding and coordinating performance through bettering our organization, through the formulation of policies, through the development of inter-unit procedures, through progress reports, and through audits. It assists in correcting unsatisfactory conditions through careful analysis of problems and discussion of their various aspects with the units involved, and works with them in the development of solutions.[29]

In practice, the functions of the unit exceeded those we usually associate with a staff agency.[30] Control staff personnel were concerned with *corrective action,* a control function normally assigned to line managers. They did not have formal authority to issue orders to lower managers, but their "suggested" modifications usually had the force of law owing to the known support they received from the president. They had authority to make on-the-spot investigations *on their own initiative.* In addition, they could make thoroughgoing audits and organization studies of entire units or divisions. And monthly appraisals by the control staff of actual vs. planned divisional performance left little breathing room for divisional managers to run their own shows in terms of *end objectives.* Jerome writes:

> The ultimate ends for which divisional managers felt responsible were such things as market share or a predetermined rate of return. The Control Section's continued demand for explanations of variations from outdated programs only succeeded in keeping everyone on edge. Top management's apparent concern about these monthly variations led divisional managers to question whether their performance was being wisely measured.[31]

Today, the situation has changed. The control section functions more as a staff agency should. Its head reports to the vice-president of finance rather than to the president. Divisional managers are held accountable more for over-all performance and less for detailed compliance with monthly goals. Management is placing greater emphasis on profit centers that go right down to the plant level with return-on-investment as the chief performance measurement.

---

[29] General Brehon B. Somervell, *Organization Controls in Industry,* "General Management Series," No. 142 (American Management Association), pp. 6–7.

[30] Much of this discussion is based on the definitive analysis of the control section provided by W. T. Jerome III, *Executive Control—The Catalyst* (New York: John Wiley & Sons, 1961), chap. 15.

[31] Jerome, *op. cit.,* p. 254.

Thoroughgoing reviews of performance are now made *annually*.[32] Also, a top-level policy committee meets with division managers each quarter to discuss, informally, their progress toward planned objectives, with the head of the control section sitting in. However, whether or not the division manager chooses to revise his program, in light of the discussion, is now left up to him.

General Somervell saw the control section as a necessary device for pulling together a loosely knit federation of almost "independent" companies, which he found when he assumed command. Evidently, previous top management had not clearly defined over-all objectives and policies, nor had it made adequate provision for the control of decentralized units through periodic review of results relative to well-defined standards. He found that many decentralized managers, as a result of this operating environment, were not doing an adequate job of long-term and short-term planning and control. He found, in addition, that many of the decentralized units were poorly organized for current operations as well as for the kind of growth that was promised by the postwar boom. General Somervell had every reason to seek changes that would spur decentralized managers to more productive effort and would integrate the work of decentralized units with over-all objectives.

We cannot question the need for change, or the legitimacy of the goals that were established. However, we can question the *method* that was used to effect change! General Somervell believed that he had to recentralize a large measure of decentralized authority and turn it over to a central control staff, composed of highly competent people, to control operations effectively. Undoubtedly, he thought of this as a *transitional arrangement*, which could and should be modified after lower-level managers had become thoroughly indoctrinated in new modes of behavior and demonstrated their competence with them. As we have seen, the arrangement *was* modified,[33] and there is evidence that the original control staff succeeded, to a large extent, in altering the behavior of subordinate managers along desired lines.

However, this was not accomplished without considerable grumbling; it required a long period of time, and there may be some question as to the "carry-over" effects—with decentralized authority

---

[32] *Ibid.* Jerome obtained this information from a company officer.

[33] Though this was done after Somervell's death. It is interesting to speculate as to whether or not he would have supported the changes at the time they were made.

restored—as well as to the future impact of residual resentments that were generated during the transitional period. It is interesting to speculate as to whether or not as much *or more* could have been accomplished, with fewer undesirable side effects, through the use of a competent general management group operating with the kinds of tools for effective decentralization that have been discussed. Such an approach would have avoided the dangers of assigning inappropriate functions to a staff agency, and it would have provided for change within the framework of an existing decentralized mode of operation. Quite possibly it would have encouraged decentralized managers to learn their lessons more readily and in a way that would have contributed more to their own personal growth and enthusiasm.

QUESTIONS

1. "Organizations grow and contract in size, people gain in experience and competence, and organizational objectives change." Do you think that organization for control must be responsive to these changes? Why? In what ways?

2. What are *key* factors and operations? Are they relevant to the design of a control system? How?

3. In what way is the *Exception Principle* related to control? Explain.

4. In what ways does the use of a computer encourage fraud and collusion? What steps can be made to reduce the risk?

5. Discuss some of the advantages resulting from the use of charts. Are there any dangers or possible disadvantages? Discuss.

6. Which organic subfunctions of control should not be assigned to staff personnel? Why? What are "secondary staff" functions?

7. Explain what functional authority is and outline the requirements for its proper use. Describe a situation in which the use of functional authority could be desirable and explain why.

8. What are cross-contacts, and under what conditions should they be made?

9. "Every staff agency should operate at optimal efficiency at all times." Is this a correct statement? Why or why not?

10. Under what conditions can a highly centralized organization be very effective?

11. List and discuss those criteria which must be satisfied before successful decentralization can occur.

12. Discuss the relationships that should exist among a vice-president of industrial relations, a decentralized plant personnel manager, and a decentralized plant manager: (1) when formal personnel activity is well established in the company, (2) when formal personnel activity

is new to an otherwise mature organization. Draw formal organizational charts for these two situations and explain them.

13. What is the distinction between *responsibility* and *accountability?* Explain.

14. Can or should duplication of effort be avoided entirely in decentralization? Discuss.

15. What are the conditions that must be satisfied for the establishment of a *profit center?* Discuss. What are "transfer prices," and how should they be determined?

16. What is a *responsibility center* as contrasted with a *profit center?* What kind of control can be applied to those organizational units which produce "intangibles"? Explain how it operates.

17. What are standard costs? In what ways are they useful?

18. Review the methods outlined by Anthony on pages 305 and 306 for allocating maintenance costs. What kind of behavior do you think should be elicited from foremen? Will this depend on the type of organization or its goals? In what way? Explain.

19. Outline the criteria for effective budgetary control without reference to the text. What should be the role of a budget administrator?

20. What were the advantages and disadvantages of General Somervell's approach to introducing change in the Koppers Company? Do you think that his goals could have been achieved more effectively some other way? Explain.

Chapter 12

ORGANIZATION FOR CONTROL: DECENTRALIZATION AT GENERAL MOTORS

General Motors is the world's *largest* manufacturing corporation with more than $8 billion in assets, 52 per cent of the United States car market, 11 per cent of the car market outside the United States, and 1962 first-quarter profits of $374 million.[1] In addition, it has unquestionably been, and still is, one of the world's most consistently successful organizations! Since many of the observations in chapter 11 about decentralization have been put into practice at General Motors, it will be useful to examine in some detail just how this has been done.[2]

EARLY PROBLEMS

... Prior to 1921 there existed no real concept of sound management in General Motors. Operations were neither integrated nor coordinated. There was no consistent policy with respect to product programs. Frequently, poor judgment was exercised in making capital expenditures and establishing production schedules. The Corporation did not have a properly developed research and engineering staff nor any sound concept of budgetary control. The central administration did not exercise adequate control over the operations of the individual divisions. ...

Even before the crisis of 1920 materialized, Mr. Sloan [who was elected president in 1923] was very conscious of the need in General Motors for

---

[1] Figures are from *Time*, May 18, 1962, p. 85.

[2] The following presentation is based on charts and materials supplied by the General Motors Corporation, personal interviews with General Motors executives, and other sources as indicated. The author is especially grateful for the assistance rendered by Mr. Maurice Wyss.

a new and clearly defined concept of management philosophy. He had observed that much time was being consumed in solving detailed administrative problems and in meeting the critical situations which were constantly arising.

He recognized that too great a concentration of problems upon a small number of executives limited initiative, caused delay, increased expense, reduced efficiency and retarded development.

He realized that centralization, properly established, makes possible directional control, coordination, specialization, and resulting economies. He also realized that decentralization, properly established, develops initiative and responsibility; it makes possible a proper distribution of decisions at all levels of management, including the foreman—with resulting flexibility and cooperative effort, so necessary to a large-scale enterprise. His objective was to obtain the proper balance between these two apparently conflicting principles of centralization and decentralization in order to obtain the best elements of each in the combination. He concluded that, to achieve this balance so necessary for flexibility of operation, General Motors management should be established on a foundation of centralized policy and decentralized administration "to divide it into as many parts as consistently as can be done, place in charge of each part the most capable executive that can be found, develop a system of coordination so that each part may strengthen and support each other part; thus not only welding all parts together in the common interests of a joint enterprise, but importantly developing ability and initiative through the instrumentalities of responsibility and ambition—developing men and giving them an opportunity to exercise their talents, both in their own interests as well as in that of the business." [3]

Mr. Sloan possessed a quality of insight into the organizational problems of General Motors that was truly remarkable for his time. But effective administration requires more than broad conceptualization; it rests, also, on the ability clearly to define *specific* objectives and supporting policies and the leadership skill necessary to generate meaningful support for them. Fortunately for General Motors, Mr. Sloan had these qualities. In addition, he was fortunate in having the services of Donaldson Brown, also a man of considerable foresight.

THE "BROWN" SYSTEM

Brown devised a sound system for financial planning and control—similar to the one he had devised for Du Pont before joining General Motors—which contributed greatly to Sloan's goal of selective centralized control with decentralized initiative. A partial de-

---

[3] From presentation by Harlow H. Curtice, president of General Motors, before the Subcommittee on Antitrust and Monopoly of the U.S. Senate Committee on the Judiciary, December 2, 1955.

scription of this system is provided by excerpts from an article he
wrote in 1924:

> . . . Space does not permit the presentation of a complete outline of the
> forecast scheme. A brief description is necessary, however, since it is
> through this that the Finance and Excutive Committees are kept informed
> and thus enabled to exercise such control as may be needed from time
> to time.
>
> In December of every year, each division is required to present an
> outline of its view of probable operations for the succeeding year, em-
> bodying estimates of sales, earnings, and capital requirements. These
> outlines are in three forms, i.e.: "pessimistic," representing a minimum
> expectation; "conservative," representing what is considered a likely
> condition, and "optimistic," representing what the name implies, with
> production and sales capacity as a limitation. . . .
>
> Definite forecasts are submitted monthly, on the twenty-fifth of each
> month, by each division, covering the current month and the succeeding
> months. These forecasts cover sales and production each month, and
> indicate the amount of investment at the end of each month in plant,
> and working capital items, and also outstanding inventory commitments.
> If these forecasts are accepted they constitute authority for each division,
> respectively, to proceed upon the manufacturing schedule and to make
> forward commitments for materials up to the requirements of the fore-
> cast, in the judgment of the division manager. Special authority is re-
> quired from the central office to cover any commitment beyond the
> requirements of these authenticated forecasts. . . .
>
> . . . Experience has led to the establishment of standards of working
> capital requirements in relation to volume of business and the forecasted
> investment in receivables and inventory is carefully checked against
> such standards, allowance being made for seasonal fluctuations. The
> tendencies of manufacturing costs and of selling and administrative
> expenses are observed, and profits are analyzed, with reference to the
> pricing policy laid down as governing the operations of a given division.[4]

The question should be raised: Why quote at such length from an
article written in 1924? Other than historical interest, what relevance does it have to General Motors today? The answer is found
in the remarkable fact that, after some thirty-seven years, the system is still being implemented in essentially its original form.[5] And

---

[4] Donaldson Brown, "Pricing Policy in Relation to Financial Control," *Management and Administration*, Vol. 7, No. 2 (February, March, and April, 1924), p. 4.

[5] Ralph C. Mark, comptroller of General Motors, provides some additional detail about the annual forecasts. In a talk, later printed in *The Federal Accountant* (Vol. 2, No. 4), he made the following comments:

"... In the fall of each year every division estimates for the coming year its sales in units and dollars, costs in detail, profits, capital requirements and return on invest-ment. The raw material for these estimates includes the cost of rearranging a depart-ment; it includes estimates of sales potential and distribution costs; time studies partly because of it, General Motors' profits have pretty much moved at a planned pace over this entire period. Brown's reports forced managers throughout the company to develop an analytical approach to planning and to strive constantly to improve the accuracy of their forecasting. He and Sloan saw that, without realistic, workable standards against which to gauge managerial performance, there would be no real basis for establishing accountability: the extent to which individuals discharge their responsibilities. It seems reasonable to assume that the establishment and maintenance of this system all this time partly explains the high caliber of executive personnel and performance that General Motors has enjoyed through the years.

Brown also realized the value of studying the *dynamics* of his organization in terms of the impact of changes in volume of operation on various standards and profit expectations. He saw the value of this for sound pricing decisions and financial planning as well as for assuring *equitable* evaluation of managerial performance. Figure 12-1 presents some of the results of his analysis. Pages 321-24 provide a sampling of charts in current use at various levels in General Motors.[6]

PARTICIPATION WITH DELEGATION: FACT OR FICTION?

In view of the foregoing, one might well challenge the degree to which subordinate executives at General Motors *in fact* do have real authority and freedom to "run their own show." The extensive system of reports and reviews could easily be expanded to a point that would leave little room for individual initiative and decision making. To a large extent, the answer rests with the degree of subordinate management participation in over-all planning, the degree of de-

---

prepared by the Work Standard Department; burden rates derived from information furnished by the manufacturing people, and so on through the whole organization.

"This budget is a complete income statement for each division, and is consolidated for the entire corporation... Cost is in complete detail for each product line and so developed that we can easily convert for any change in the economic cost level. Similar detail is developed for the investment items—working capital, (cash, receivables, inventories), plant and equipment, prepaid expenses—all related to the expected level of operations.

"In these annual budgets, fixed and non-variable expenses are treated separately from variable so that the figures can be readily adjusted for changes in volume at any time during the year." (See definitions for fixed and variable costs in chap. 13, p. 352).

[6] Of course, charts must be used with discretion. For a good discussion of what can happen when proper judgment is not used see Frank Jasinsky, "Use and Misuse of Efficiency Controls," *Harvard Business Review*, July–August, 1956, pp. 105–112, or Fremont Shull and A. L. Delbecq (eds.), *Selected Readings in Management* (Homewood, Illinois: Richard D. Irwin, Inc., 1962), pp. 190–98.

FIG. 12-1

Profits, Capital Employed, and Return on Capital*
(At Four Different Volumes of Business)

ITEM	AMOUNT						(Standard Volume)	
	55,000		50,000		40,000		30,000	
	$ 1,250		$ 1,250		$ 1,250		$ 1,250	
Annual Sales, Units		. . . .		. . . .		. . . .		. . . .
Net Selling Price Per Unit								
PROFIT AND LOSS STATEMENT:		Ratio to Sales		Ratio to Sales		Ratio to Sales		Ratio to Sales
Annual Sales, Amount	$68,750,000	1.000	$62,500,000	1.000	$50,000,000	1.000	$37,500,000	1.000
Factory Cost of Sales	55,000,000	0.800	50,000,000	0.800	40,000,000	0.800	30,000,000	0.800
Gross Factory Profit	13,750,000	0.200	12,500,000	0.200	10,000,000	0.200	7,500,000	0.200
Commercial Expense	3,950,000	0.0575	3,800,000	0.0608	3,500,000	0.0700	3,200,000	0.0853
Net Profit Before Application of Overabsorbed or Unabsorbed Net Burden	9,800,000	0.1425	8,700,000	0.1392	6,500,000	0.1300	4,300,000	0.1147
Overabsorbed Burden	1,875,000	0.0273	1,250,000	0.0200	. . . .	. . . .	. . . .	. . . .
Unabsorbed Burden	. . . .	. . . .	. . . .	. . . .	. . . .	. . . .	1,250,000	0.0200
Actual Net Profit	$11,675,000	0.1698	$ 9,950,000	0.1592	$ 6,500,000	0.1300	$ 3,050,000	0.0813
CAPITAL EMPLOYED:		Ratio to Sales		Ratio to Sales		Ratio to Sales		Ratio to Sales
Cash	$ 3,437,500	0.0500	$ 3,125,000	0.0500	$ 2,500,000	0.0500	$ 1,875,000	0.0500
Drafts and Accounts Receivable	6,875,000	0.1000	6,250,000	0.1000	5,000,000	0.1000	3,750,000	0.1000
Raw Material and Work in Process	9,167,000	0.1333	8,333,000	0.1333	6,667,000	0.1333	5,000,000	0.1333
Finished Product	4,583,000	0.0667	4,167,000	0.0667	3,333,000	0.0667	2,500,000	0.0667
Gross Working Capital	$24,062,500	0.3500	$21,875,000	0.3500	$17,500,000	0.3500	$13,125,000	0.3500
Fixed Investment	15,000,000	0.2182	15,000,000	0.2400	15,000,000	0.3000	15,000,000	0.4000
Total Investment	$39,062,500	0.5682	$36,875,000	0.5900	$32,500,000	0.6500	$28,125,000	0.7500
RETURN ON CAPITAL EMPLOYED (annual rate), Per cent	29.89		26.98		20.00		10.84	

Note: Commercial Expense Comprises (a) Fixed Expenses (b) Partially Controllable Expenses and (c) Controllable Expenses.
* Brown, op. cit., p. 15.

centralization of staff activity, the extent to which company-wide activities are centralized, the *selectivity* of central controls, and the qualities of subordinate management. We will now examine certain aspects of the organization structure and functioning of General Motors with these questions in mind.

VARIOUS CHARTS USED AT GENERAL MOTORS

LABOR EFFICIENCY REPORT

DAILY EFFICIENCY REPORT

DEPT. _Press Room_ _____Date _____

GROUP	HOURS		EFFICIENCY		REMARKS
	Standard	Actual	Daily	To Date	
601	145	150	97%	96%	
602	56	75	75%	70%	Faulty Material
					– Follow Up
					With Purchasing
612	80	80	100%	99%	
Total Dept.	530	550	96%	96%	

This report shows the efficiency attained for each working day by direct labor in each group within a department or division. It is made available to foremen early on the day following the day reported.

BURDEN EFFICIENCY REPORT

DAILY PLANT REPORT

DEPT. _Assembly_ _____ DATE _____

( ) Brackets indicate loss	TODAY			MONTH TO DATE SAVING
	ORIGINAL BUDGET	ACTUAL	SAVING	
INDIRECT LABOR	$ 396	$ 416	($20)	$210
SUPPLIES & TOOLS	341	333	8	84
HEAT, LIGHT, POWER	144	154	(10)	105
MAINTENANCE & REARRANGE	228	240	(12)	126
EMPLOYE BENEFITS, TAXES, ETC.	188	198	(10)	(105)
LOSSES, ERRORS, ETC.	39	38	1	(11)
FIXED CHARGES	158	156	2	21
TOTAL – BURDEN – VARIABLE	$1,494	$1,535	($41)	$430

While this illustration is for a department (at which level the report is most used), these reports are made out for entire plants and divisions. The budget figures have been adjusted for volume, therefore the variances do not reflect volume differences. Supplemental analyses are furnished whenever conditions call for them.

PROFIT, LOSS AND INVESTMENT REPORT

DIVISION "A"
PROFIT AND LOSS AND INVESTMENT
MARCH 19—

	7 MONTHS 19—		VARIANCE	COMMENTS
	ORIGINAL BUDGET	CURRENT OUTLOOK		
PROFIT & LOSS	$	$	$	
NET SALES	21,000	19,500	1,500	Steel Strike
FACTORY PROFIT	3,150	2,730	420	
% OF NET SALES	15%	14%		
DISTRIBUTION EXPENSE	1,050	1,100	50	
PROFIT	2,100	1,630	470	
% OF NET SALES	10%	8%	2%	
INVESTMENT				
CASH AND RECEIVABLES				
AMOUNT	5,200	5,200	—	
TURNOVER	6.9	6.4		Stock Piling
INVENTORY				Material Due
AMOUNT	6,000	6,500	500	To Strike
TURNOVER	5.1	4.4		
NET FIXED INVESTMENT				Delayed
AMOUNT	7,800	6,500	1,300	Delivery
TURNOVER	4.6	5.1		Of Presses
TOTAL NET INVESTMENT				
AMOUNT	19,000	18,200	800	
TURNOVER	1.9	1.8		
% RETURN	19%	15%	4%	

This report (for divisional top management and higher executives) shows turnover rates on an annual basis. Inventory includes raw material, work in process and finished product. Net fixed investment consists principally of plant and equipment less accrued depreciation.

LABOR AND BURDEN VARIANCE CHART

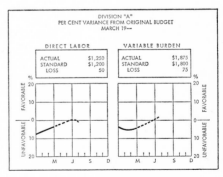

This chart, for a division, presents another way of displaying labor and burden variances. The broken part of the line represents the forecast and is the collective result of what the operating people say they are going to do for each of the next four months.

Note: The charts and comments on this page are either taken from or directly based on Ralph C. Mark, *The Federal Accountant*, Vol. 2, No. 4.

UNIT COST SUMMARY   SALES—PROFIT LINE CHART

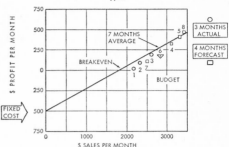

DIVISION "A"
SALES-PROFIT LINE CHART
19--

DIVISION "A" UNIT COST SUMMARY FEBRUARY 19--			
	ORIGINAL BUDGET	ACTUAL JAN.	FEB.
SELLING PRICE	$14.00	$14.00	$14.00
FACTORY COST			
MATERIAL (direct)	4.20	4.19	4.22
LABOR (direct)	2.15	2.20	2.18
BURDEN	4.25	4.35	4.30
OTHER	1.10	1.19	1.15
TOTAL FACTORY COST	11.70	11.93	11.85
FACTORY PROFIT	2.30	2.07	2.15
% PROFIT TO SALE	16.4%	14.8%	15.4%

This report, aimed primarily at senior division personnel and higher executives, compares the budgeted costs of each product with actual costs. Burden includes cost of supervision, maintenance, processing supplies, utilities, taxes, depreciation, and the like. "Other" costs include such items as overtime and night-shift premiums, cost-of-living allowance, engineering, tooling, etc.*

This "break-even" chart is one of the best known charts around General Motors. It shows, graphically, the break-even point—in this example, about $1,800 per month or 60% of budgeted sales. The line is drawn through the budgeted sales-profit point, in this example, $300 profit for $3,000 in sales. Therefore, the line shows the budgeted or standard profit at any volume. This chart is used by top division and higher executives.†

    *Unit cost estimates are prepared for each part, and budget projections are based on the total of these estimates. This cost estimate is a base from which to measure actual performance and, in addition, serves as a check on competitively set prices.

    †For discussion of the break-even chart see chap. 13, p. 352.

    Note: The charts and comments on this page are either taken from or directly based on Ralph C. Mark, *The Federal Accountant*, Vol. 2, No. 4.

Top Committee Organization

It may be recalled that Donaldson Brown made reference to the Finance and Executive Committees. In the first excerpt from his article he pointed out that a brief description of the divisional forecast reporting scheme would be necessary since "it is through this that the Finance and Executive Committees are kept informed and thus enabled to exercise such control as may be needed from time to time." Figure 12-2 shows these committees in relation to the board. The Executive and Finance Committees are the two principal committees of the board, composed entirely of board members, which pass on all major issues in the field of policy and administration. The Finance Committee is chaired by the chairman of the board, who is also the chief executive officer of the corporation. It has delegated authority to act for the board in determining the financial policies and affairs of the corporation. The Executive Com-

VARIOUS CHARTS USED AT GENERAL MOTORS

RETURN ON INVESTMENT REPORT   TOTAL INVENTORY AND TURNOVER

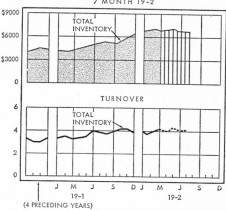

DIVISION "A" RETURN ON INVESTMENT CALCULATION 7 MONTHS 19-- FORECAST		
	ORIGINAL BUDGET	CURRENT OUTLOOK
(P x T = R)		
SALES	21,000	19,500
PROFIT	2,100	1,630
P . . . % TO SALES	10%	8.4%
X		
INVESTMENT	19,000	18,200
T . . . TURNOVER ON SALES	1.9	1.8
=		
R . . RETURN ON INVESTMENT	19%	15%

In evaluating and comparing divisional performance, return on investment has proved to be the best common denominator. It measures not only the profit performance of an operating unit or product but also its utilization of capital—how well a unit controls its inventories, receivable collections, and other use of capital. Return on investment is the most fundamental factor with respect to the financial control of General Motors.

This is a standard inventory chart showing, historically, the inventory dollars on the top and the inventory turnover on the bottom. The broken part of the line represents the forecast position. There are many variations of this chart—raw materials, process, finished product against a normal or budget position, etc.

Note: The charts and comments on this page are either taken from or directly based on Ralph C. Mark, *The Federal Accountant*, Vol. 2, No. 4.

mittee is chaired by the president of General Motors, who is also the chief operating officer of the corporation. It has delegated authority to act for the board in determining operating policies. The Administration Committee is also chaired by the president. It is charged with the responsibility for making recommendations to the president with regard to the manufacturing and selling activities of the company and with regard to any other matters referred to it by the president or the Executive Committee. The Administration Committee and the policy groups provide major "pipelines" through which the ideas and reactions of subordinate line and staff executives may "bubble up" to the top level of the company.

Of the nine policy groups, the following four are concerned with products or operations: Canadian, General Engine, Household Appliances, and Overseas. The other five are concerned with specific functions, as indicated in Figure 12-2. Each is normally chaired by

VARIOUS CHARTS USED AT GENERAL MOTORS

CASH AND CASH INVESTMENT

TOTAL CASH AND CASH INVESTMENT
7 MONTHS 19-2

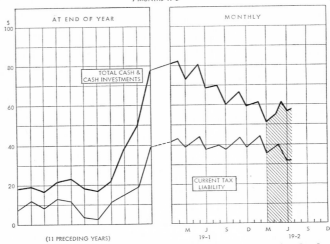

This chart provides data for those at the policy level who are responsible for the company's financial stability. One of its uses is in connection with investment. Rather than permit cash to lie idle, tax certificates, short-term paper, etc., are purchased. In actual practice it is formulated on a daily basis and is invaluable in helping to determine cash and investment policy.

Note: The charts and comments appearing above are taken from or directly based on Ralph C. Mark, *The Federal Accountant,* Vol. 2, No. 4.

FIG. 12-2

Top Management Committee Organization at General Motors

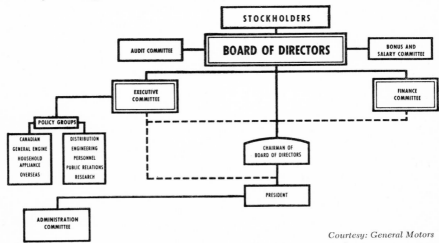

Courtesy: General Motors

the central office staff executive whose function is directly related to the interests of the group. Meetings of these policy groups are regularly scheduled, and their members include top operating executives and divisional as well as staff executives, whose balanced experience is brought to bear on policy recommendations. The two other committees of the board, the Audit Committee and the Bonus and Salary Committee, are composed of board members who are not members of management.

A look at the composition of the following groups will help to explain the effective exchange of ideas that takes place among them:

Board of Directors
(27)

Nine do not serve on committees, and, of these 9, none is a member of management, although 4 are former members of management. The others represent large stockholder interest and include men with broad experience in business and finance.

Finance Committee
(11)

(Line) Chairman: chairman of the board (chief executive officer of the corporation)
A. P. Sloan, Jr., honorary chairman of the board

MANAGEMENT MEMBERS

(Line) President (chief operating officer of the corporation)
(Staff) Executive vice-president, operations staff
(Staff) Executive vice-president, financial staff

NON-MANAGEMENT MEMBERS

Six, including 1 former president and a former chairman of the board (Note: all the foregoing are board members)

Executive Committee
(10)

Chairman: President
(Line) Chairman of the board
(Staff) Executive vice-president, operations staff
(Staff) Executive vice-president, financial staff
(Note: In addition to being members of management, all the foregoing are board members.)
(Line) Vice-president, car and truck group
(Line) Vice-president, Dayton, household appliance and electromotive group
(Line) Vice-president, accessory group
(Line) Vice-president, Overseas and Canadian group
(Line) Executive vice-president, automotive and parts divisions
(Line) Executive vice-president, other operating divisions

Administration Committee

(18)

Chairman: President
The Executive Committee plus the 8 non-board, line members of management listed below:

General managers of 5 car divisions
General manager, GMC truck and coach division
General manager, Fisher Body division
General manager, GM Overseas Operations divisions

FIG. 12-3

Board of Directors

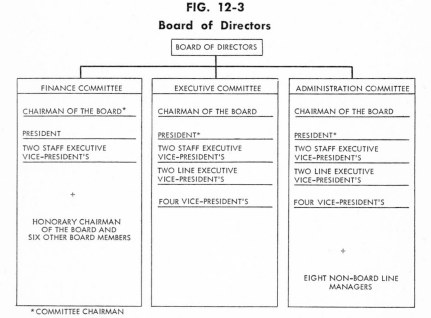

* COMMITTEE CHAIRMAN

Note: The titles above represent the *same* individuals whenever they reappear, e.g., the 4 V.P.'s on the Executive Committee are the *same* 4 V.P.'s on the Administration Committee.

Committee Interaction

Figure 12-3 dramatizes the interlocking character of these groups. One team of four (the chairman, president, and two staff executive vice-presidents) serve on *all* four: The board, the Finance Committee, the Executive Committee, and the Administration Committee. They help to coordinate effectively the thinking of each group with the other. In addition, all group vice-presidents, some staff vice-presidents, and all executive vice-presidents, have offices on the same floor in the Detroit General Motors Building with the office of the president and one of the offices of the chairman of the board. Cross-contacts, impromptu meetings, and other forms of informal interaction are encouraged. Consequently, these men form a general management group "team" which can productively gather and process ideas and feedback from the various sources within the company they represent as well as from the non-board "pipeline" groups in contact with them.

This is not to imply that General Motors is run by a big, happy team. The chairman of the board *is* the chief executive officer of the corporation, and he and his chief lieutenant, the president, *do* provide decisive leadership! But it is leadership that by tradition and inclination brings out and draws upon the best thinking of highly competent subordinates. Undoubtedly some of General Motors' leaders have been more adept with and inclined to this kind of leadership than others, but most of them have been products of "the system." This indoctrination, coupled with their "admission" to leadership by directors who very much know about them and what is going on and know what values they wish to preserve, should provide some very real constraints to excessive deviation from the traditional path! The chairman may very well have his way, but this is likely only to the extent that "his way" proves to be the best one available.

Staff Decentralization

Top management at General Motors clearly distinguishes between line and staff positions. Figures 12-4 and 12-5 illustrate this. Staff vice-presidents have no direct authority over line units or their departments, line or *staff*. Many staff vice-presidents and their central office units perform services and research for their decentralized staff unit counterparts. The relationship that exists generally meets the criteria of organization for decentralized staff activity that were discussed in chapter 11. Most divisions have the following counterpart staff departments: engineering, public relations, financial (comptroller), and personnel.

Divisional Autonomy

Just how much latitude for "running his own show" does a division general manager have? For the purpose of illustration, we will consider a typical car division of the company with top-level organization as depicted in Figure 12-6.

Subject to company-wide policy and reporting constraints and the centralization of certain activities, the general manager acts much

FIG. 12-4
General Motors Line Organization

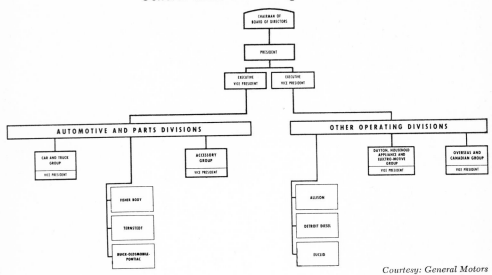

Courtesy: General Motors

FIG. 12-5
General Motors Line and Staff Organization

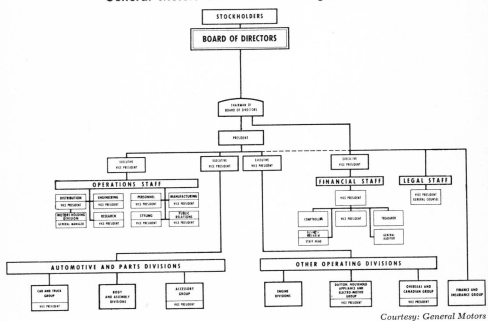

Courtesy: General Motors

like the president of an independent firm. And a large one at that, for each car division is a sizable enterprise in its own right. For example, the Chevrolet Division, alone, recently had a bigger share of the United States market than the entire Ford Motor Company! As can be imagined, the general manager must have considerable leadership and organizing ability to sustain such an operation efficiently.

Each division designs,[7] develops, manufactures, and merchandises its own products. With the exception of centrally purchased steel, tires, and glass, each division purchases its own materials and component parts—in some cases from other divisions, but in many more cases from more than 30,000 outside suppliers! Purchasing deci-

FIG. 12-6

Top-Level Division Organization

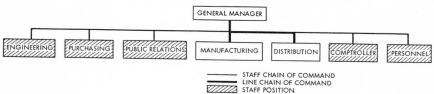

sions, of course, are based on such factors as quality, price, and dependability of supply. Each division develops its own manufacturing processes and methods, hires and trains its own employees, and is responsible for good industrial citizenship wherever it operates.

As was shown in Figure 12-6, divisional staff personnel report to and are directly responsible to the general manager, *not* to their central staff counterparts. The general manager may, and usually does, send his people to training programs provided by central staff groups, but for the most part, this is not mandatory. Actually, the plant managers under the divisional manufacturing head have considerable responsibility, too. Generally, each will have the following men reporting to him: a comptroller, a personnel director, an inspector, a purchasing agent, and a manufacturing superintendent.[8]

---

[7] Styling activity at the divisional level is necessarily restricted. The central styling staff develops all car styles through the use of three basic body shells, and there is a corporate desire to maintain a certain "GM image" in all styles. However, the central staff does work closely with the divisions, and division general managers have a very real opportunity to influence the styling of their lines.

[8] The position of sales manager is omitted because distribution, normally, is handled by the division sales staff.

Centralized Activities

As for centralized activities, we have already mentioned certain aspects of purchasing and styling. In addition, there must be uniformity of accounting procedures and controls in the various operating units so that higher management may evaluate performance effectively and collect those data necessary for over-all planning and control. Financial planning is largely centralized, and divisions are subject to audits by the central comptroller's staff. But these audits are limited to the accounts and records of the division; they are not broad, all-inclusive audits of divisional activity. General audits are conducted, when necessary, by the staff of the division manager's boss, the group vice-president, and *not* by higher-placed agencies.

Legal activity, collective bargaining, fundamental or pure research, and defense research activities are also centralized. The central manufacturing staff coordinates planning for the inflow of basic materials; handles all matters pertaining to the purchase, lease, and disposition of real estate for the divisions, and renders assistance in matters involving construction and alterations. This staff, also, through committee meetings, directs and coordinates the group efforts of divisional technical personnel, where problems of mutual interest are discussed and solutions arrived at. Last, divisional managers are subject to constraints, also, with regard to pricing, capital outlays, salary changes above a certain level, and bonuses.

A SUMMING-UP

Figure 12-7 presents the over-all organization of the company, which we have "taken apart" for our discussion. We have seen how General Motors, through selective decentralization of functions, well-defined standards, and an effective communication system of interlocking committees, has satisfied many of our criteria for successful decentralization. Effective decentralization results from careful analysis and planning. It is the product of the art rather than the science of management. It is certainly not a "way of life" to be indiscriminately applied to all firms under all conditions. Nor is it realistic to define it simply as the absence of centralization. Loosely controlled "federalism" or "anarchy" does not characterize successful decentralization. In this regard, it is useful to recall Mr. Curtice's remarks about General Motors' early period: "Prior to 1921 there existed no real concept of sound management. . . . The central administration did not exercise adequate control over the operations of the individual divisions." [9] Effective decentralization was achieved only by the introduction of *appropriate centralization!*

To asure unity of over-all purpose in the decentralized company, we must require that each decentralized unit operate within the framework of carefully defined over-all objectives, policies, and per-

FIG. 12-7

Organization Chart, General Motors Corporation

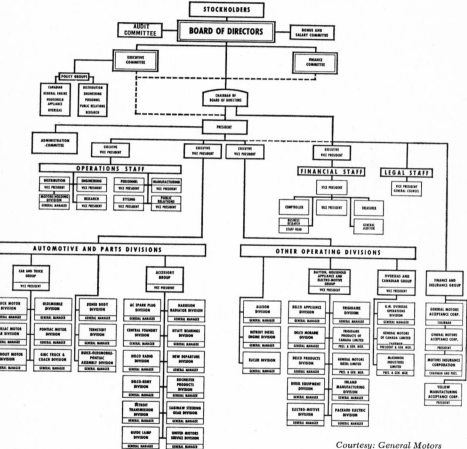

Courtesy: General Motors

formance standards. No decentralized manager can be expected to see the "big picture" as well as centralized managers can. His ideas for capital outlay may be excellent, but other proposed allocations, unknown to him, may be even better. And, surely, no one divisional manager should have the power to make decisions that could jeop-

[9] See p. 316.

ardize the well-being of the whole organization. Still, given the kind of restrictions we have discussed, there is ample room for the decentralized manager to gain a large measure of autonomy and opportunity for growth through demonstrated competence.

General Motors has succeeded in creating an excellent "formal organizational climate" for decentralization. But does the necessary "informal climate" created by high-level executive attitudes still prevail? Is it still permissible for decentralized managers to take issue with centrally determined "facts"? As Dale puts it, "Is the retention of the influence of some of the 'founding fathers' beyond the age sixty-five a partial indication of the difficulty of ideological transference?" He goes on to point out:

> Being "founding fathers" and collaborating over several decades, these men were able to maintain the framework of "decentralized operations and coordinated control" by oral tradition and to interpret, amend, and improve it as times and personalities changed. Those who built up the concept lived within its boundaries without too much difficulty. . . . The feeling of real satisfaction concomitant with success may well stifle further initiative and generate resistance to change and to the new ideas requisite for continuance of the growth of a business and to keep it up-to-date.[10]

These are provocative questions for which only time can provide definite answers. However, there is certainly no evidence *to date* that General Motors has lost any of its drive, flexibility, or capacity for success. Perhaps this is due to powerful forces in the company that tend to counter those which rightly concern Dale. For example, General Motors has the kind of prestige, people, and resources to attract top-flight personnel. And divisional managers who are under pressure to improve their showing are likely to use this recruiting power for all it is worth. Highly competent newcomers can supply a division with new skills and ideas that often lead to dramatic improvements in performance. Such "breakthroughs" literally start a chain reaction throughout the organization, owing to the number of *comparable* divisions and the well-defined performance standards that exist. Undoubtedly, some executives would like to "lock in" on the status quo and coast along on past achievements, but generous executive bonuses and promotional opportunities at General Motors are not based on these criteria. And the performance criteria by which divisions are judged go beyond the factors depicted earlier in the charts. For example, the central engineering staff operates the General Motors Proving Grounds where comparative tests are

---

[10] Ernest Dale, *The Great Organizers* (New York: McGraw-Hill Book Co., 1960), pp. 106, 107.

made of GM products and those of competitors. This is done to inform higher management of general progress and standing, and to assist the divisions in meeting their responsibilities with regard to the quality and performance of GM products. For the most part, a divisional manager at General Motors has "no place to hide"!

But Dale is concerned with a very real danger. Sustained success can stultify initiative and render an organization less viable. Effective decentralization is not something that is "done" at a particular point in time and then put aside; it is a *continuing process,* which requires sustained dedication to its basic requirements on the part of top management. At least until now, top management at General Motors has evidently been well aware of this challenge!

QUESTIONS

1. To what extent do you think that General Motors has put into practice the criteria for effective decentralization that were presented in chapter 11? Be specific; match each criterion with evidence presented in chapter 12.

2. What role do you believe that sound organization has played in the success of General Motors since the early twenties? Discuss.

3. What contribution did Sloan make? What contribution did Brown make?

4. What important purpose does duplicate committee membership serve? Explain.

5. Do you think that a proper balance between constraints and freedom has been struck for divisional general managers? Discuss. Make a list of all activities that are centralized and review the explanations given. Do you think that all these should be centralized to the extent that they are? Explain your thinking.

6. Do you agree that effective decentralization is more the result of the *art* than the *science* of management? Explain.

7. Do all parts of General Motors have the same organic business functions (those functions which represent the creation and distribution of salable utilities)? For example, would the General Motors Acceptance Corporation (which in effect is a finance company) have the same organic business functions as the parent General Motors Corporation, which is engaged primarily in manufacturing operations? Discuss.

8. What do you think of the arrangement at General Motors whereby the chairman of the board is the chief executive officer of the corporation and the president is the chief operating officer of the corporation? Discuss.

9. Do you think that other automobile companies should copy General Motors' formal organization in detail so that they may improve their chances for success? Why or why not? Explain.

Section III

CONTROL
OF
MANAGING

Chapters 13–15 are concerned with control of the performance of the organic functions of management. Chapter 13 considers certain factors that have to do with the control of planning, such as the economic accuracy of planning data, break-even analysis, the allocation fallacy, and provisions for adequate coordination of planning effort. Chapter 14 explores such areas as the use of learning curves, evaluation of personnel and training programs, the organization audit, and other factors related to the control of organizing activity. Chapter 15 examines the problem of controlling the performance of the organic subfunctions of control, or providing for control of control.

Chapter 13

CONTROL OF PLANNING

Control has to do with making events conform to plans and other standards. In this chapter we are specifically concerned with control of planning: making *planning activity* conform to sound planning procedures and other standards for planning. Of course, before we can expect good planning to take place in an organization, we must have adequate *time* and *resources* set aside for it and we must adequately *motivate* our planners to do a good job.

TIME AND MOTIVATION

Listing of the time requirement here may seem odd. Actually, time is a very scarce commodity. Often, too scarce for most executives. Surveys show that the average executive spends from one-fourth to one-half of his time in conferences! Requests for information on the part of the home office and the public seem to grow like Topsy, if not properly controlled. And, of course, there is the administrative routine of day-to-day operations and face-to-face supervision. It is not surprising when a harassed executive permits these demands to encroach upon time he should reserve for careful study, analysis, and planning. Some feel that at least a third of the executime's time should be reserved for these important functions. This is not likely to happen unless steps are take to *make* it happen.

Preparation for adequate control can start with a "time study" of each executive's working day. This should be done at the *executive's invitation* to help free him of unnecessary burden, certainly not to reflect upon his management methods. Often, such a time study will reveal, especially at the foreman level, that the company

337

has been "penny wise and pound foolish" with regard to giving adequate clerical and other assistance to managers in the face of mounting "routine" demands upon their time. That is, the company has lost more than it has saved by denying adequate assistance. It has missed the economies and opportunities that would have flowed from adequate planning and has paid the manager an excessive wage for his hours devoted to routine clerical detail. These studies usually reveal that many things that the manager is doing can appropriately be turned over to subordinates or other agencies. This type of study can and should be applied to the board of directors and various committees as well as to individual managers, to see whether they are performing functions they should not perform and whether they are in legitimate need of staff assistance. Observation and analysis of the minutes from past meetings will facilitate the study of groups.

The problem of motivation is equally important. Where long-range planning has not been practiced in an organization, for example, there are bound to be strong resistances to the thorough analysis of current operations and divisional and departmental *capabilities* it requires. Many executives will regard this as an unwarranted intrusion upon their private domain. In addition, such planning *is* hard work, and those uninitiated in its values are likely to question the value of diverting the effort required from their more pressing daily problems. A prime motivational requirement for adequate planning is genuine support or "push" from the top. Lower-echelon planners must be convinced that their findings and recommendations receive careful consideration and significantly influence top-level planning. Also, top management must set an example of excellence in its planning activity and reward subordinate managers for superior performance in this area *not* just for results per se. Effective control by results refers to results that are well planned, not results that are the product of chance, undue risk, or improbable action. As has been suggested before, regularly scheduled, properly used "post mortems" can do much to stimulate and improve sound planning at all levels in the organization.

REVIEW OF OBJECTIVES

There is a real need for *periodic review* of the firm's primary, collateral, and secondary objectives, for the organization's capabilities as well as market conditions and opportunities are constantly subject to change. In addition, there are forces at work that tend to pervert legitimate organizational objectives. For example, to the extent that competitive pressure diminishes for a given firm, personnel associated with it may modify the firm's primary service objectives to further accommodate their personal goals. One noted tea manufacturer reportedly operated a boat-building branch in his firm because of his interest in yachting. Many presidents have been known to impose uneconomic growth on their companies as a means of enhancing their personal prestige and power. Some absentee stockholders have forced illegitimate goals and practices on firms to make it possible for them to get in and get out fast with a quick profit and leave their successors with little but an organizational shambles. Admittedly, in the absence of competitive pressures, it may be difficult to control these tendencies on the part of powerful board or top-management personnel. However, there is "constraining value" in the periodic review that dramatizes unjustifiable shifts and makes it more difficult for them to occur through default.

Management has the problem of balancing short-term goals against long-term goals. It must determine how much profit to withhold from current distribution to invest in growth and those factors which will enhance future strength. Management must decide to what extent it will invest its time and energies in building the reputation of the firm as opposed to innovation or productive efficiency. It must decide to what extent a given goal is *relevant* to primary service objectives *or merely a reflection of personal goals.* The criterion of return on investment or productivity of capital provides an important yardstick for measuring the relative costs of various alternative uses of the firm's resources. If a given undertaking is admittedly "uneconomic," it is still instructive for management to determine the cost of it in terms of profits forgone through alternative uses of the same capital.[1] Probably what most managements try to do is obtain "adequate" profits coupled with what they perceive as the proper "mix" of other goals and values.

Periodically, a searching analysis should be made of the actual outcomes as compared with the anticipated outcomes. That is, the original evaluations of alternatives in terms of investment value or "investment forgone value" should be closely checked. Through the *anticipation* of such analysis by organizational members, we can hope to control *current* over-all planning activity to some degree.

---

[1] For a detailed discussion of this approach see Joel Dean, "Measuring the Productivity of Capital," *Harvard Business Review,* January, 1954.

Through application of the lessons learned through such analysis, we can hope to improve the quality of over-all planning in the future. Obviously, this type of planning post mortem should be used at all levels of the organization.

A productive review of objectives must be based on accurate, up-to-date forecast data and the planning premises derived from them. These data must be effectively disseminated to lower-echelon planners—in suitable form—*along with clear explanation of higher-level plans,* so that *meaningful* planning may take place *throughout* the organization. This last point may seem too obvious to mention. It seems apparent that divisional planning should take place within the framework of company plans, departmental planning should take place within the framework of divisional plans, and so on. In reality, few executives in business today can define their departmental or divisional goals in terms that would be acceptable to their superior or colleagues! Far too little attention in most organizations has been given to *periodic* review and comprehensive definition of objectives and policies *at all levels.* If you are skeptical of this, try the following experiment. Ask the president of a firm and his vice-presidents each to prepare, independently, a *detailed* statement of the objectives of the firm. Then compare their writeups! Ask several board members to do the same. Compare these with the others! If you have subordinates, ask each of them to prepare—again, independently in writing—a statement of the goals of the department and the goals associated with their position. Check to see whether the goals they have listed for the department have any resemblance to the ones you have jotted down and whether or not the sum of their individual goals equals the departmental mission! This will dramatize our widespread failure to set the stage for productive self-coordination, individual initiative, and individual planning through *adequate review* and *explanation* of objectives—a simple but very effective control of planning activity that few of us elect to use in our everyday affairs. Could it be that we fear the possibility that we may *not* be able to agree on objectives? If so, we should not be as surprised as we usually are when we encounter differences of opinion as to the *means* for carrying out *largely undefined* goals!

"ECONOMIC" ACCURACY OF PLANNING DATA

The importance to planning of fast dissemination of accurate, adequate data to data users in a form most suitable to their needs has been discussed several times.[2] An important control aspect is the avoidance of *excessive* accuracy in planning data in terms of *time* or *expense* requirements. Often, it is difficult for those who process data to be *both* prompt and accurate. There is growing awareness in organizations of the value of distinguishing data processing for planning purposes from data processing for record-keeping purposes. Approximations or estimates that vary from actual data within known limits may be almost as useful for certain planning purposes as the actual data. When this is true, and these estimates or approximations can be computed for planners in a fraction of the time required for actual data, *they become immeasurably more useful to the planner.* Of course, when managers need and receive reports of this type, they should be aware of their limitations, and such data should not be used in the preparation of financial statements or in situations in which actual data are necessary.

The extent to which planning data *under certain conditions* may incorporate appreciable error and still be of considerable value is dramatized by the findings of a research team who studied production scheduling in a paint factory. The team reports:

> The complete cost function for production and employment scheduling was developed by adding the components [discussed earlier].... The mathematical generalization was then applied to the specific situation in the paint factory by inserting numerical values representing estimates of the various costs involved.
>
> Some of the estimates were drawn directly from accounting data or obtained through statistical treatment of accounting data. Other estimates such as those for the intangible costs of delayed shipments, were subjective. Here it is important to note that *the accuracy of the estimates was not a critical consideration.* An analysis of the effect of errors as large as a factor of two—*that is, overestimating specific cost elements by 100% or underestimating them by 50%—indicated that use of the resultant decision rules would incur costs only 11% higher than with correct estimates of costs* [italics supplied].[3]

The team reports another finding that points up the need for a proper *balancing* of objectives: the need to expend planning resources and effort in a manner that will do the most *net* good.

The decision rule with the moving-average forecasts saved $173,000 annually against factory performance. *For this stage in the history of*

---

[2] For example see pp. 247–40 of chap. 9.

[3] Melvin Anshen, Charles Holt, Franco Modigliani, John Muth, and Herbert Simon, "Mathematics for Production Scheduling," *Harvard Business Review*, March, 1958, p. 54.

this plant, greater savings could have been secured by making optimum use of crude forecasts than by improving forecasts .... the decision rule with perfect forecasts had lower costs than the same rule with the moving average forecasts in the 1949–1953 period—by 10%, or an average of $59,000 annually. This difference, which is entirely attributable to better forecasting, is a sizable one but only about a third as large as the other saving [italics supplied].[4]

The point should be made here, also, that the *cost* of producing better forecasts may not be equal to the savings made possible by them! The value of accuracy in forecast or other planning data should be analyzed. We can go back in time and apply our decision rules to data of varying degrees of accuracy and determine what the impact would have been on outcomes. Our goal is to find the "economic" level of accuracy for planning data for each application. This level will vary, of course, with the relative "utility of accuracy" for the kind of planning in question and the cost and time requirements for achieving accuracy in that kind of planning.

STANDARDS FOR CONTROL

For successful control of planning activity, we must have well-defined standards for planning. Unfortunately, too little attention has been devoted by most organizations to this important requirement. The following discussion of standards for planning is certainly not intended to be exhaustive. As more is learned about the *organic subfunctions of planning,* we can expect the formulation of important additional standards.[5]

Plans for Planning

Most of us have been exposed to a listing of the steps of the so-called "scientific method" in the form given below or some variation thereof:

1. Define the problem and its limiting factors.
2. Collect and analyze relevant data.
3. Formulate and test tentative solution hypotheses.
4. Evaluate findings and select a solution.
5. Apply the solution.
6. Make follow-up evaluation and refine the solution.

These steps provide, in effect, a "plan for planning." Now, we have a more sophisticated "plan for planning" in the form of the

---

[4] *Ibid.,* p. 57.

[5] Here standards for planning activity are being discussed, *not* standards to which plans must conform. For those see pp. 177–88.

organic subfunctions of planning, which were discussed in chapter 2. They are:

1. Determination of key environmental factors and the interrelationships among them.
2. Search for and identification of *relevant* alternative objectives and determination of all the *relevant* possible consequences associated with *each* alternative objective.
3. Determination of objectives (the result of subfunctions 1, 2, 5, 6, 7, and 8).
4. Search for and identification of *relevant* alternatives for the achievement of objectives and determination of all the *relevant* possible consequences associated with *each* alternative.
5. Assignment of numerical value to the consequences of each alternative in terms of their positive or negative contribution.
6. Ordering of those consequences which are *dependent* (and those which they are dependent on) in terms of one or more natural sequences and the assignment of *conditional* probabilities to them. Assignment of probabilities to independent consequences.
7. Determination of the *expected value* for each alternative (this will equal the sum of the expected values for the branches of the dependent consequences "tree" added to the expected values for consequences not in the "tree").
8. Determination of the optimal alternative or set of alternatives from those which have been identified in view of the objectives and the risks involved.[6]

Each planning group in an organization should give careful consideration to the formulation of an even more thoroughgoing set of steps and procedures for specific types of planning. Such analysis not only will tend to improve the general effectiveness of planning activity but will also provide an important means for orienting newcomers to the planning group and permitting them to profit from the past experience of the group. In addition, as with the cockpit checklist for airline pilots, plans and other standards for planning will provide a useful control for helping to assure that important considerations have not been overlooked, inadvertently, even by experienced planners.

Completed Staff Work

The concept of completed staff work provides a standard or control for assuring that staff planners will develop reports and data in a form most useful to the managers they serve without unduly involving the manager in their preparation. By "completed work,"

---

[6] For further discussion of these *organic subfunctions of planning* see pp. 31–38.

is meant reports or data from the staff planner *as finished products,* with well-supported recommendations if they were called for. In this form, the manager can either accept the work or hand it back to the staff assistant for correction of deficiencies. Implementation of this concept requires genuine delegation of the details of coordination and methodology to the staff specialists. Otherwise, the manager cannot conserve his time and avoid doing most of the work himself in the final analysis.

This is *not* to imply that the staff planner should not have contact with the manager he is serving. Obviously, some contact is necessary. The important consideration is the *character* of this contact. The question is, is it used to supply needed information and further definition of the goals desired rather than to permit the staff planner to place the initiative for implementing the work back upon the manager he is presumably relieving of this chore? The following guides will help to assure the proper relationship:

1. Clear definition by the manager of the detailed objectives of the undertaking and any general methodological framework within which he expects the staff planner to work.
2. Agreement with the staff planner as to the frequency and nature of progress reports.
3. Delegation of sufficient authority and supply of sufficient resources to the staff planner to permit him to carry out his assignment.
4. As suggested above, consultation with the staff planner that supplies him with needed information, further definition, or reassurance as to the goals desired and, possibly, the benefit of the manager's own experience. The important thing is that the staff planner retain the initiative and responsibility for the project until he has developed it into finished form, ready for approval.

As Allen points out. "If the subordinate writes a memorandum *to* his chief, this is not completed work. However, if he writes a memorandum for his chief to send to someone else, and if he so presents his views that his chief can make them *his* views simply by signing his name, this is the best meaning of completed work."[7]

In addition to relieving managers of much planning work, application of the concept of completed staff work helps to *develop* staff personnel in ways that make them more useful to the organization. Certainly, the training value of the concept will be enhanced if staff personnel can be *sensitized* as to the value of completed work in

---

[7] Louis A. Allen, *Management and Organization* (New York: McGraw-Hill Book Co., 1958), p. 148. Allen applies the concept of completed staff work to other activities and line subordinates as well (see pp. 145–48 of his book).

the eyes of those they serve. An interesting means for doing this is described by M. G. Holmen, of the System Development Corporation:

> In our System Training Program, one of the ways we deal with this is to have the battle staff positions filled temporarily by people from the subordinate jobs. After dealing with a mass of unrelated paper they go back to their jobs and send up organized data instead of bits and pieces; and the numbers of pieces of papers and bits of information that come up are much fewer. They realize the need for correct kind of staff work, after having tried to operate at that level during some exercises.[8]

GENERAL COORDINATION OF PLANNING EFFORT

By "coordination" is meant the effective *synchronization* of related activities so that common purpose may be realized expeditiously. It will be recalled that a procedure is defined as a set of complementary and *sequential* relationships among functions, physical factors, and personnel for the accomplishment of specific subgoals within the framework of formal organization structure. In addition to serving as a useful *standard* for indicating how certain activities should be done, a procedure is an important *tool of coordination,* with its emphasis upon the *sequential* aspects of activity. A procedure is a type of plan, and procedures for planning are, in effect, plans for planning that help to assure the general coordination of planning effort.

This section will be concerned with certain aspects of *organization* and *procedure* for coordination of planning activity that have not been discussed before. It should be recalled, however, that these topics are *not* new! In several chapters, such as "Plans for Planning," "Organization for Planning," and "Organization for Control," such aspects have been discussed as the organic planning functions, the role of participation, the use of interlocking committees, adequate liaison between specialized planning agencies, and so on. Effective coordination of planning activity requires the effective *management* of planning activity—that it be carefully planned, organized, and controlled.

Secondary Staffs

In several organization charts provision for secondary staff planning and control has been seen. Figures 13-1 and 13-2 provide examples. Such staff assistance *for staff people* is required only when

---

[8] D. G. Malcolm, A. J. Rowe, and L. F. McConnell (eds.), *Management Control Systems* (New York: John Wiley & Sons, 1960), p. 119.

continued growth of a staff agency, or the complex nature of its work, requires it. Secondary staff planning personnel, among other things, are concerned with the development and refinement of planning procedures for their agency. Secondary staff control personnel, among other things, are concerned with the effective implementation of these planning procedures. In a staff *planning* agency (Fig. 13-1), secondary staff planning personnel are concerned, also, with analyzing and modifying the agency's organizational structure to facilitate the performance of its planning activities. As can be seen, secondary planning and control staffs provide for effec-

FIG. 13-1
Staff Planning Agency

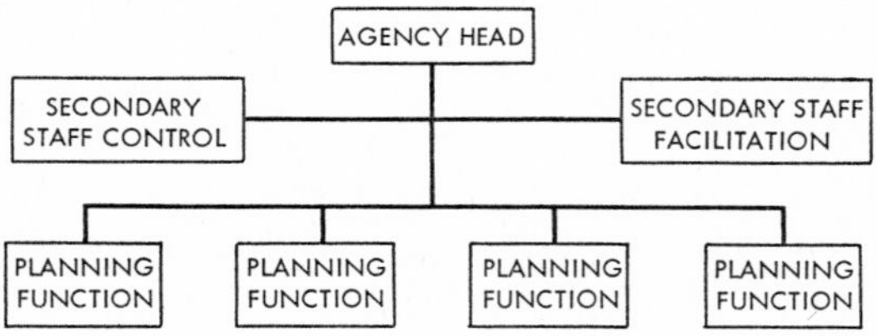

FIG. 13-2
Staff Control Agency

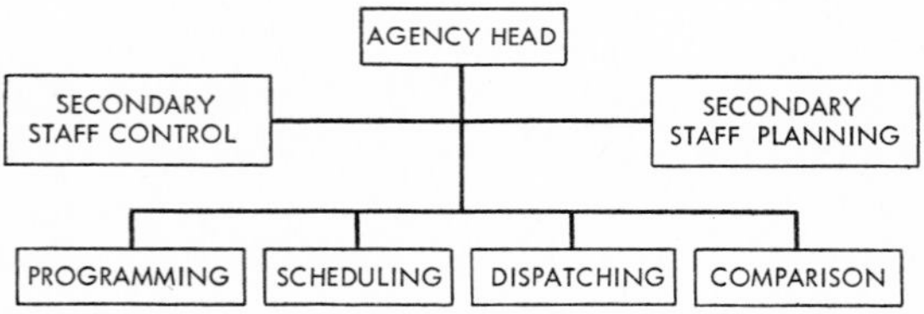

tive coordination of planning activity within staff agencies. They can help to lay the groundwork for effective coordination of over-all company planning through adequate liaison with *other* agencies in the oganization. This will provide valuable feedback data that will permit any agency to be more productive in planning its own activities as well as in working with other agencies toward the achievement of company goals. Another organizational device for helping to achieve this end, the planning coordination committee, will be discussed next.

Planning Coordination Committees

Rarely do we question the need for production scheduling and control. We know that different components for the finished product require different "lead times" for completion before they can play roles at the right *time* and *place* in final assembly operations. The need for accurate synchronization or coordination of effort is quite apparent in the case of a symphony orchestra; it is not difficult to visualize the chaos that would occur without it. Actually, we have the same need with regard to planning activity. The "mission" of each organizational unit flows from the determination of over-all organizational objectives. Varying amounts of time are required by different organizational units to develop detailed plans for their part of the total job. Some organizational units cannot *start* work on their plans until they have received the finished plans of other units. Consequently, we must take into account these "lead times" and phasing problems to avoid chaos in the planning area. We should schedule the work of planning and subplanning with the same care as we schedule production. We should devote the same attention to coordination in this area as we do to the production area. A good means for accomplishing these ends is through the creation of a planning coordination committee. The purpose of the committee is *not* the same as that of a regular staff planning agency. It is to provide for the *coordination* of the planning activities of the various staff and line groups it represents.

The committee chairman might well be an "assistant to" the president, the divisional manager, or the plant manager, depending on the level we are dealing with. It is useful if he is also chairman of the central planning group in his organization, as shown in Figure 13-3, with the title, "Plant Planning Group Chairman." He will have much influence on the quality of the committee's *plans for coordination* and the degree to which they are properly implemented. He may serve as the liaison man between his committee and special planning groups such as the operations research group and the controller's special studies group.[9] Obviously, he should be well versed in the details and scope of the mission or project to which the planning groups represented on his committee are contributing. He should encourage his committee periodically to evaluate its performance. Have most planning schedules been met without sacrifice of quality? Can planning procedures be improved? Are *all* data required by the members supplied to them *in time* and in the *desired form?* How can the coordination of planning activity be improved?

---

[9] See chap. 9 for a discussion of these and other special planning groups.

Programming

From chapter 7, it will be recalled that programming is one of the *organic subfunctions of control.* It is concerned with the *routine* collection, sorting, and assignment of data as planned. It involves the collection of information—often from various sources in the organization—that users will require and the recasting of this information into the form most useful for the user. Here, we are concerned with the collection, processing, and dissemination of *planning data.* As is shown in Figure 13-3, programming accounts for

FIG. 13-3

Flow of Plans Data to and from Plant Control Staff

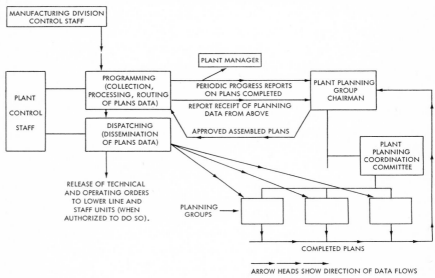

the collection and processing of planning data. As will be discussed next, the *organic control subfunction* of dispatching has to do with the dissemination of the data.

Dispatching

In chapter 7 it was pointed out that dispatching is concerned with the *release of authority:* authority regarding *how* to act as well as *when* to act. It was indicated that the mechanics of delegating authority are supplied by the dispatching function. The release of approved technical orders, standard operating procedures, policies, standard practice directives, specifications, and other such instruments indicates to organization members *how* they are authorized to act when the time comes for them to act. Authority as to *when* to act is released via the dispatching function in the form of operating orders or standing orders. A *planning schedule,* for example, has the force of an operating order when it is approved by proper line authority and released to lower echelons via the dispatching function. In addition, the dispatching function can be used for the release or dissemination of *planning data* to lower echelons.

Office of Record and Issue [10]

It is useful to use staff control agencies at various organizational levels as "offices of record and issue" for planning data. As discussed above, this will be accomplished primarily through the control functions of programming and dispatching. All changes in plans affecting the organization to which the control agency is attached—for example, the plant, if we are dealing with the plant control staff—should clear through the agency's programming section so that it may maintain up-to-date records at all times. This will enable the programming section to provide periodic progress reports on plans completed to the plant manager and the chairman of the plant planning group. Also, the programming section can report the receipt of plans information from a higher control staff's dispatching section to the chairman of the plant planning group, for example, over-all planning premises and forecast data developed by the central economic planning agency.

Staff and line agencies that develop plans are supplied with appropriate planning data by the dispatching section of the plant control staff. Their representatives meet as members of the plant planning coordination committee—probably chaired by the chairman of the plant planning group—to provide for effective coordination of planning effort, as discussed before. The completed plans of these line and staff agencies flow to plant planning, where they are synthesized and released to the plant control staff after approval by appropriate line authority. There they will remain in storage until specific orders for dissemination to lower units are given or they will be disseminated on the basis of standing orders as technical or operating orders. In either case, before the dispatching section actually disseminates the planning data, the programming section

---

[10] The author has borrowed freely from R. C. Davis' analysis for this discussion. See his *The Fundamentals of Top Management* (New York: Harper & Bros., 1951), chaps. 17 and 18.

recasts them in the form prescribed by lower-level users and routes the data according to approved procedure.[11] These data flows and activities are summarized in Figure 13-3.[12]

COMPARISON, CORRECTIVE ACTION, AND PLANNING

Comparison is the *organic subfunction of control* that has to do with evaluation of completed action to see how well it has conformed to plans or other standards. When comparison reveals a discrepancy between actual and planned performance, the stage is set for activation of the last *organic subfunction* of *control:* corrective action. Corrective action is concerned with getting things back on course or, if necessary, changing the course. Sometimes it involves new planning. It is this aspect that the discussion here will be concerned with: the requirement of new planning and *effective control* of this activity.

Much corrective action does not require new planning. For example, the supervisor may correct a faulty work procedure on the part of one of his subordinates, or he may find a machine needing some adjustment and take care of it on the spot. Or he may find it necessary to change his plans but still not engage in new planning activity. For plans may be changed only as a result of new programming or scheduling activity. Or, to the extent that well-defined alternatives are available to him, the supervisor need engage only in decision making—selection from alternatives—and not planning (for planning involves problem solving—search for alternatives— also). Of course, if he is faced with a situation that has been anticipated and for which a clear-cut plan of action is available, there is no problem solving or decision making involved in the modification of plans. Control of these aspects of corrective action will be discussed in chapter 14.

When effective corrective action *for non-recurring problems* requires that the supervisor engage in new planning, no unique control problem is presented. The supervisor is merely starting the cycle of *organic management functions* again: of planning, organizing, and controlling the work of others. Our general discussion about planning for planning (chapter 2) and control of planning

---

[11] If the planning data are to go to a lower-level control staff—as in Fig. 13–3, where the flow is from a division control staff to a plant control staff—it may be preferable to have the *recasting* of data take place in the lower-level control staff's programming section. This is a matter that warrants study in each individual case. The desired approach should be clearly defined in writing in the procedures manual.

[12] The head of the control staff should be held responsible for setting up an adequate procedure for the *recall* of obsolete technical orders and other materials disseminated by his dispatching section.

(this chapter) would apply. When corrective action *for recurring problems* is needed, however, a unique problem of planning control arises. Davis refers to the removal of specific or non-recurring interferences as involving the "operative phases" of corrective action. He regards the elimination of recurring interferences as involving the "administrative phases of corrective action," because it tends to be *organizational* in character and requires creative planning.[13] He lists the following as the operative and administrative phases of corrective action:

1. The operative phases
   a. Prompt investigation of the causes of the deviation.
   b. Decision concerning the required corrective action.
   c. Prompt direction for correcting the situation in accordance with the decision.
   d. Close supervision of corrective action to insure that it is taking place in accordance with instructions and is effective.
2. The administrative phases
   a. Further investigation of recurring difficulties to determine the basic factors, either human or physical, that are responsible.
   b. Disciplinary action, either positive or negative, as the situation requires.
   c. Creative planning to prevent a recurrence of the situation.
   d. Reorganization of the situation and the introduction of the planned measures.[14]

A unique control problem is associated with the administrative phases of corrective action because they normally involve the participation of personnel other than the immediate supervisor in the creative planning required. The first requirement for effective control of this type of planning activity is provision of some means for alerting appropriate planning groups in the organiaztion to the fact that a recurring problem exists. There are two bases for doing this. One is provided by the comparison section of the control staff. It receives data on operations from several sources: inspection reports, regular feedback data, emergency calls, special reports by analysts, and so on. These data are used to evaluate progress and to set the stage for corrective action. They should be analyzed periodically by the control staff for interferences that tend to recur. Such interferences should be reported to those planning groups which take part in the administrative phases of corrective action. This is important, for higher-placed planning groups, through receipt of such reports from *all* lower-level control staffs, not only will perceive recurring prob-

---

[13] Davis, *op. cit.*, chap. 19.
[14] *Ibid.*, p. 731.

lems in a bigger organizational setting but will be in a better position for expediting corrective action through recommendations to higher line authority. This is especially true if the corrective action requires organizational changes involving several subordinate units and could not be authorized by any *one* of their chiefs.

The other basis for alerting planning groups to the existence of recurring problems is to see to it that they are supplied with copies of all inspection reports, special studies reports, and other instruments that *evaluate operations.* As in the control staff, these data should be analyzed periodically by the planning group for interferences or problems that tend to recur. Reports of such recurring problems—along with recommendations for their solution—should be sent to a higher-level planning group. This is desirable so that organizational solutions may be developed by the highest level concerned with a problem. By dealing with a problem in its broadest organizational setting we can avoid *unnecessary* duplication of effort and organizational improvisation.

THE BREAK-EVEN CHART

The use of charts in facilitating control was discussed in chapter 11 (see p. 284). Charts are quite useful in expediting the control of planning activity, since they help us to visualize interrelationships among important factors and to develop a more clear-cut frame of reference for decision making. The break-even chart is an especially useful tool of planning control; it permits us to see at a glance the impact on profits of any anticipated volume of sales and the effect that *changes* in costs or selling price will have on the "break-even point" and profits. The break-even point (see Fig. 13-4) is the volume of sales point at which the *total revenue line*—normally, from sales—*crosses the total expense line.*

Fixed, Variable, and Semifixed Costs

Profit is influenced significantly by sales volume (total revenue) in our break-even chart, because we "spread" our *fixed* and *semifixed* costs over more units of production as we increase sales. If I rent a store for $100 per month, the $100 is a fixed cost—it occurs in the same amount each month whether I make no sales or 1,000 sales during the month. It is called a "fixed" cost in the sense that it does not vary with changes in my level of sales *over a given range* (in this instance the number of sales I can make without having to move into a bigger store and thus pay a higher rent). Examples of fixed costs are fire insurance premiums, land taxes, and other costs that do not vary with changes in the level of production throughout the volume range permitted by the capacity of my facilities.

Variable costs are those which vary directly with changes in the level of production. If a worker is paid 10 cents for each unit he produces, this is an example of a directly variable labor cost. The cost of the raw material required by each unit is also a directly

FIG. 13-4

Break-Even Chart

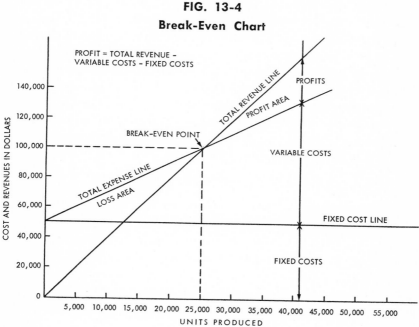

variable cost, *if it remains the same* per unit throughout the range of production volume we are concerned with. Obviously, if we give the worker a *graduated* bonus per unit as his production climbs, or if we enjoy an increasing quantity discount for raw materials as production volume goes up, then these cease to be *directly varying* costs.

In actual practice, we find many costs that do just this. They vary with changes in volume of production, but not directly. These are called *semifixed* costs. For example, consider the cost of the services of an hourly paid janitor or foreman. The cost will remain the same over a given part of our full production range, that is, we pay the janitor or foreman the same whether ten or twenty men are working in the department. However, when *more* men are working, we either have to put these men on overtime or give them assistants.

So there is a cost response to changes in production level, but it tends to be "lumpy" in character.

Of course, in the foregoing discussion of *fixed, semifixed,* and *variable costs,* a "reasonable" *time* frame of reference is assumed. For, as Durand points out:

> If time is short enough, all costs are fixed; it takes time to adjust expenditures, and goods already made cannot be affected. If time is long enough, all costs are variable; a man deciding whether to go into a given business, to expand capacity, to reduce capacity, or to retire from the field, is in position to change some or all of the most "permanent" of cost items.[15]

Developing Chart Data. Reference to Figure 13-4 will reveal that there is no mention of *semifixed* costs. This omission is intentional, for the value of determining the character of *each semifixed* cost probably would not be worth the effort required.

Although individual cost items tend to "jump" in response to volume changes and are affected variously by special factors in the situation, large groups of costs (totals and major subdivisions) often show a much smoother response to volume changes; irregularities balance out. By applying correlation techniques to totals obtained from past experience, a simple "straight-line" relationship between volume and cost totals often can be worked out so that total cost can be stated as approximately equal to a fixed sum (fixed cost) plus so much per unit produced (variable cost).... Any "margin of error" computed for the data on which the relationship formula was based, holds only for the range of volumes included in the study. Both fixed and variable costs will change in time; what was true yesterday may not hold today and may be expected to change tomorrow. Further, the relationships are not what *should be;* they are only what *were.* This limits the value of such estimates as standards.[16]

Break-Even Analysis

The following equation is made obvious by Figure 13-4: Profits = Sales[17] − Fixed costs − Variable costs. Suppose that we wish to determine the acceptability of the "break-even point" for a business, given the following information:

> Anticipated sales $160,000
> Fixed costs 50,000
> Total variable costs = 50% of sales.

---

[15] Robert Y. Durand, *Business: Its Organization, Management and Responsibilities* (Englewood Cliffs, New Jersey: Prentice-Hall, Inc., 1958), p. 361.

[16] *Ibid.,* pp. 361, 362.

[17] If we make the simplifying assumption for our purposes that sales provide the only source of revenue.

Our problem is to determine the level of sales at which the business will just "break even." We can use the equation as follows: We know that at the "break-even point" there will be no profit, so "profits" in the equation will equal zero. The total of fixed costs is given as $50,000 for any level of sales we anticipate, so we merely enter this amount in the equation. We do not know sales (S) for the "break-even point," so we will simply enter this as S. We know that the total of variable costs will equal 50 per cent of sales, so we enter this as .50 S. Now the "break-even point" can be found as follows:

$$0 = S - \$50,000 - .50\ S$$
$$0 = .50\ S - \$50,000$$
$$\$50,000 = .50\ S$$
$$S = \$100,000 \text{ (the "break-even" level of sales)}.$$

With anticipated sales of $160,000, the "cushion" of $60,000 for a reduction in the level of sales before hitting the "break-even point" looks encouraging. Whether or not this is adequate, of course, depends on the *degree* of fluctuations in sales volume the firm can reasonably expect on the basis of past experience and future expectations.

If a firm finds that, for any given future period, its expected minimum level of sales will be well above the anticipated "break-even point," it may profit by measures to *reduce* variable costs that require *increases* in fixed costs! Figure 13-5 illustrates this. Both tables contain the same four levels of sales. In the initial arrangement, fixed costs were given at $50,000 and variable costs determined at 50 per cent of sales. In the lower table, we see that fixed costs have been increased $20,000 to effect a reduction in variable costs to 40 per cent of sales (one way to do this would be through some form of mechanization that would reduce direct labor costs). The impact of this change on profits is apparent. Obviously, the revised arrangement generates more profits *for the same level of sales* than does the initial arrangement.

As a result of this type of analysis, Terry has formulated the "Principle of Variable and Fixed Cost Relationships to Profit Potential": **For a given enterprise, the lowest variable and highest fixed costs consistent with a break-even point which is less than the smallest probable total sales result in the maximum profit potential.**[18]

---

[18] George R. Terry, *Principles of Management* (Homewood, Illinois: Richard D. Irwin, Inc., 1960), p. 610.

However, there are definite "costs" associated with the changes that have been discussed. The "break-even point" was *raised* $16,666.66. This will impose a heavier penalty in the event of an unexpectedly large future drop in sales. And the equipment acquired, or alteration of facilities—whatever the increase in fixed costs represents—may well render management less *flexible* for adapting to future conditions. The course of action that a particular firm

FIG. 13-5

Initial Arrangement

FIXED COSTS	VARIABLE COSTS (50% OF SALES)	TOTAL COSTS	SALES	PROFITS	PROFITS AS % OF SALES
$50,000	$ 50,000	$100,000	$100,000	0	0
50,000	100,000	150,000	200,000	$ 50,000	25%
50,000	150,000	200,000	300,000	100,000	33 1/3%
50,000	200,000	250,000	400,000	150,000	37 1/2%
(Break-even Point = $100,000)					

Reduced Variable Costs and Increased Fixed Costs

FIXED COSTS	VARIABLE COSTS (40% OF SALES)	TOTAL COSTS	SALES	PROFITS	PROFITS AS % OF SALES
$70,000	$ 40,000	$110,000	$100,000	$-10,000	-10%
70,000	80,000	150,000	200,000	50,000	25%
70,000	120,000	190,000	300,000	110,000	36 1/2%
70,000	160,000	230,000	400,000	170,000	42 1/2%
(Break-even Point = $116,666.66)					

should take will depend, of course, on careful consideration of *all* such key factors and their consequences. As was pointed out earlier, break-even analysis, made with the aid of the break-even chart, facilitates control of planning activity by helping us to visualize interrelationships among important factors and by helping us to develop a more precise frame of reference for decision making.[19]

---

[19] This, incidentally, is similar to the kind of contribution that is made by PERT in relation to the control of planning for complex projects. PERT provides a significant frame of reference and helps us to visualize interrelationships among important factors through identification of critical paths and events with slack. It permits us to plan event "trade-offs" that are most relevant to the "on schedule" completion of projects with optimal economy. (PERT is discussed on pp. 50–54 and 188–89.) For further discussion of what can be done with "break-even" analysis see Allen W. Rucker, "'Clocks' for Management Control," *Harvard Business Review,* September–October, 1955.

THE ALLOCATION FALLACY

Our chief cost accountant is alarmed! He has "proof" that the average cost of producing Product C is *higher* than the selling price and recommends that we drop Product C immediately. Also, he has heard that the sales manager is thinking seriously of taking a big foreign order for Product B at a price *below* its average production cost. And, to add insult to injury, when he places this startling news before the president, the president replies that Product C is, in fact, profitable, but not as profitable, perhaps, as a new one (Product X) would be; that, whatever the case, the answer will *not* be found in the cost accountant's data! Obviously, something is amiss here, and, as will be seen, the trouble can be traced to the "cost allocation fallacy."

The chief cost accountant works with a cost accounting system that is designed to allocate a "fair share" of all production costs (*variable, fixed, and semifixed*) to each product. For example, the "cost" of Product C probably includes charges for utilities, rent, and taxes, the amount of these charges being determined by some basis such as the number of square feet of floor space required to produce Product C. Such a system of cost allocation is necessary so that inventory valuation and cost of sales data will reflect *total* production costs associated with the product. But product costs so obtained are *not* valid for the kind of decision making that our chief cost accountant has engaged in. He might have been far less alarmed, perhaps even optimistic, had he thought in terms of *differential costs,* as did the sales manager and the president.

Differential costs are those associated with different alternative courses of action: if we do such and such, what *differences* in cost will be involved? Our cost accountant became alarmed over the "cost"-price relationship for Product C because he failed to consider *differential costs* and assumed that all costs associated with Product C would be *saved* if it were discontinued. The correct approach would have been to determine all the *actual* savings that would result from discontinuing Product C. For example, will we actually save the amount charged to Product C for utilities, rent, and taxes? Will the floor space released actually be used for something else? Will the amount of the president's salary charged to C be saved? Obviously not, at least to the extent that these charges are now made. Whether or not Product C should be continued depends on two considerations: (1) whether the revenue produced by it is greater than the *differential costs* required to produce it and (2) whether or not there is another product, as the president suspects, which should be produced in place of Product C because of an even more favorable *differential cost*–revenue relationship.

The sales manager may do well to take the foreign order for Product B at a price *below* its average production cost (based on a full allocation of accounting charges), provided that the added revenue will top the *differential costs* involved, the sale will not jeopardize the firm's prospects for continuing to sell at a higher price in the domestic market, and there is currently no better offer or more attractive alternative utilization of Product B production facilities in view. Of course, if the anticipated revenue just covers the *differential costs* required, and there are no other alternatives in sight, there may still be incentive for taking the order in terms of various *intangible factors*. The added production might mean the difference between work and layoff for many men, it could have a profound impact on the economy of a small town, good reception of the product in the foreign market could lead to more lucrative orders in the future, and so on.

Our chief cost accountant is almost convinced. And to show that he clearly understands the differential cost approach, he points out that the cost of making the differential cost study for Product C is a perfect example of a *differential cost* that must be covered by revenue from Product C to justify keeping it. Unfortunately for our accountant's morale, even this is not true. The cost of the differential cost study is a *sunk cost,* not a *differential cost.* That is, this expenditure is now an accomplished fact and is *not* contingent upon continuing or not continuing Product C in the future! For this reason it should be *disregarded* in making the decision as to whether or not we will keep Product C. Sound planning requires the *accurate* definition of available alternatives and their consequences. Understanding of the "allocation fallacy" on the part of planners can do much to prevent the unintentional introduction of error in their work.

SOME CONCLUDING REMARKS

Operative or lower-level plans should be derivatives of administrative or higher-level plans. However, administrative plans should be realistic and useful. Those at the upper levels who fashion them should have the benefit of feedback information from lower levels so that their over-all plans truly will accommodate the needs of the lower echelons and will be enriched by ideas flowing from them. Wrapp describes the kind of error that is often made in this regard:

> During the production subcommittee's study of the possibilities of expanding plant facilities, such factors as comparative costs, ease of distribution to markets, and availability of raw materials were considered. The group assumed that the management organization could adjust to whatever proposal it devised, and only after it had settled on a plan was a personnel subcommittee invited to prepare supporting programs for a management staff and a work force.
>
> If, from the start, a personnel subcommittee had been studying the ideal expansion plan, considered from the standpoint of organization and personnel, it might have added an additional dimension to the production group's deliberations and thus have helped it to come up with a more practical proposal. As it was, the personnel subcommittee simply "planned" within the limits set down by the other subcommittee.[20]

Needless to say, when a subsidiary group *knows* that its thinking has had an impact on the planning of a higher group, it is likely to develop more enthusiasm for the goals that are formulated. In addition, the subsidiary group is likely to tackle more enthusiastically the job of devising derivative plans for such goals.

This is not the first time the importance of participation has been stressed in this book. But it is especially important for the effective control of planning. As business problems become increasingly complex and time pressures mount, there is little question that two, or many more, *competent* heads—drawn from various levels of the organization—are better than one for planning activity! Chapter 12 discussed how General Motors provides for participation in planning through a network of interlocking planning committees (see chart on page 324). Also, the use of planning committees for multi-interest situations was discussed (see p. 311). However, we must remember that these are organizational devices that can facilitate productive participation but will not assure it. The caliber of people getting together and the quality of leadership provided them will be the critical factors. We must avoid making the mistake of the production subcommittee described above. We must avoid merely inviting staff or subsidiary organizations in to devise means for *implementing* our goals or subgoals; we must give them a real opportunity to *influence* and *enrich* our thinking and our plans.

---

[20] H. Edward Wrapp, "Organization for Long-Range Planning," *Harvard Business Review*, January, 1957, p. 41.

Because planning, especially for the inexperienced, is a slow, painful process, there is a temptation to turn the job over to specialists or outside consultants and let them do the "dirty" work and produce the recommendations rather than have them assist us. Often we will not have confidence in the experts and their recommendations, and this will destroy the usefulness of their findings for us. Sometimes the experts may be *too brilliant* and go 'way over our heads. I suspect, as someone suggested, that we prefer to live with problems we cannot solve rather than with solutions we cannot understand. Wrapp reports a case that may be of this type:

The chairman of the board of Company D hired an economist to develop a five-year plan. The economist brought three assistants with him. This group conducted extensive interviews and investigations in the company and drew upon sources close to the industry, such as the trade association, investment bankers, and government agencies. Within about eighteen months, the economist made a four-hour presentation outlining a master plan to the board of directors, which is composed mainly of the top officers in the company. The meeting broke up after a brief discussion, and the chairman asked that each member of the board study the 450-page report written by the economist and his staff. At the time this article was written, six months had elapsed since the initial presentation, but discussion of the report had not been resumed.[21]

But, even if the experts come up with highly useful recommendations that we do understand and have confidence in, we will lose out on some important values if we do not effectively utilize our own people in planning. If we merely have them stand on the sidelines and "watch" the experts, this will hardly lead to executive growth—the kind of growth that should eventually generate over-all plans that will be significantly superior to those formulated by "outsiders" taking the initiative. For, as our people dig into the planning job and begin to produce results, they are bound to develop a better "feel" for the organization and its problems than any outsider can ever possess. This is not to suggest that our planners should shun the valuable planning services and assistance that outsiders can provide. It is simply a question of who assists whom. Our people should definitely be in the driver's seat, but they must have *earned* their right to be there through demonstrated competence in planning. We can encourage the development of this competence by setting high standards of expectation, by creating opportunities for real participation, and by tangibly rewarding those who excel.

---

[21] *Ibid.*, p. 43.

QUESTIONS

1. What is an executive "time study"? What value is there in making one?

2. The president of a large company expresses the view: "We pay for results, not excuses!" What would be the probable impact of this attitude on the quality of subordinate planning activity? Explain. Can subordinates be motivated to plan well in a "control by results" environment? How?

3. Discuss the advantages associated with a periodic review of primary, collateral, and secondary objectives.

4. What do we mean when we say that management has the problem of balancing short-term goals against long-term goals? Explain.

5. What is meant by the "economic" accuracy of planning data? How can we determine what the economic accuracy level is? Be specific.

6. What is a "plan for planning"? Why should one be formulated?

7. Explain the concept of *completed staff work*. What are its advantages and limitations?

8. What is the difference between a primary (regular) staff position and a secondary staff position?

9. When we refer to a staff control agency as an "office of record and issue," what do we mean? Are there any advantages to the organization in using a staff control agency this way? What are they?

10. What are the "operative phases" of corrective action? The "administrative phases"? Are there any unique control problems associated with either the "operative" or "administrative" phases? What are they?

11. Draw a break-even chart without reference to the text and explain what each part represents. Demonstrate with your chart that Profit=Total Revenue — Variable costs — Fixed costs.

12. Distinguish each from the others: *Fixed costs, variable costs,* and *semifixed costs.*

13. Why are *semifixed costs* omitted from a break-even chart?

14. State and explain Terry's "Principle of Variable and Fixed Cost Relationships to Profit Potential."

15. What is the "allocation fallacy"? Is it wrong to charge a product with its "fair share" of overhead? Why or why not?

16. What are differential costs? Are they ever the same as *variable costs?* List the differential costs of taking a 500-mile trip in your automobile.

Chapter 14

CONTROL OF ORGANIZING

Chapters 5 and 6 discussed the *organic subfunctions of organizing:* the procurement of factors, the establishment of interrelationships among factors, and the development of factors, as planned. This chapter is concerned with provisions for adequate *control* of these functions, as well as with control of organization planning, for it is through organization planning that the specific goals of organizing activity are established and against which the effectiveness of organizing activity must be evaluated.

ORGANIZATION PLANNING

Organization planning is concerned with the specification of desired authority, responsibility and communicative relationships among functions, physical factors, and personnel for the purpose of achieving company goals. Organization planners must content with such questions as: What functions will have to be performed? When, by whom, where, and how? What equipment and facilities will be required and by whom shall they be utilized? What kind of relationships among organization personnel will be desirable, and what provisions in the way of policies, procedures, communication systems, and so on, will be needed to facilitate effective coordination of effort? What kinds of informal group and individual values will be desirable for the company, and how can they be encouraged?

Effective organizing activity cannot take place until these questions are carefully dealt with. And, as has been stressed throughout this book, these questions cannot be adequately dealt with until the primary service objectives of the firm are spelled out in some detail. For we have discussed many useful guides for the design and functioning of an organization, *given a set of primary service objectives.* A basic requirement for the effective control of organizing activity, then, is to see to it that those who are responsible for organization planning stay in close touch with the changing pattern of organizational goals.

What are some of the means by which we can hope to provide *continuing* knowledge about and understanding of goals to members of the organization? A number have been suggested in preceding chapters. Certainly, the development of an adequate system of communication and participation stands high on the list. Those engaged in organization planning and organizing activity should be asked to explain the *specific* goals they wish to achieve through their work and their understanding of the relationship of these to organizational goals. Each manager in an organization, from the top on down, may find it productive to request, periodically, that his subordinates prepare—in writing and without assistance—a detailed statement of the objectives of their department or unit. When he compares these with his own written version and then strives for some measure of consensus, he will create an important basis for the effective planning and performance of organizing activities.

Assuming that goals are well understood, what are some of the other measures we can take to assure proper control of organization planning and organizing activity? The remainder of the chapter will be devoted to a discussion of certain concepts and techniques that should prove useful.

PROCUREMENT OF FACTORS (AS PLANNED)

Procurement of Required Capital, Plant, Equipment, and Materiel

Control of the procurement of equipment and materiel—seeing to it that an advance provisioning of required items is provided on schedule and as planned—poses certain problems that are not readily apparent. Those responsible for procurement normally do more than merely buy needed items; they are concerned also with the following types of activity:

Research and development with regard to alternatives that are available.

Follow-up to assure proper delivery.

Inspection of incoming items to see whether they measure up to specifications.

Adequate coordination of effort with other organizational units such as traffic and transportation, stores, and accounting.

Collection and analysis of data about various suppliers and general market and product development trends.

The use of policies, rules, and procedures that incorporate appropriate forms and records can do much to facilitate the control of these activities.[1] But perhaps the most challenging problem here from a control standpoint is to reap the benefits of centralized procurement service and still genuinely serve the *unique* needs of internal organization "customers." Sometimes staff procurement specialists become so enamored with the prospect of "good deals" and with their criteria for selecting suppliers that they lose sight of their main objective: to facilitate the achievement of primary service objectives with maximum economy and effectiveness rather than to aim for economy and efficiency as "ends" in themselves!

Suppose, for example, that we want a given piece of equipment. We may not have an *absolute* set of specifications in mind; we do, however, have in mind certain performance capabilities that perhaps only someone else trained in our area of specialization can appreciate. If we had the time and opportunity to talk with various suppliers, we might find equipment that would more adequately satisfy our requirements than we had expected and, possibly, at a lower price, too. If our purchasing procedures are too rigid and we do not have effective communication with those who do the actual work of procurement, we may be forced to settle for less than we had anticipated.

How can this happen? Well, the purchase requisition (or request) used may require complete specifications, but these may be quite inadequate for conveying a full understanding of the *uses* to which we plan to put the equipment. If the purchasing manager is forced to adhere to our specifications unyieldingly, he may be forced to pass up good opportunities. On the other hand, if he is permitted to overlook certain requirements—unless he is a specialist in our area—it is unlikely that he will have a "feel" for their relative importance and may obtain something that we regard as unsuitable. In part, this problem can be handled through the use of specialists for various types of purchases and the development of procedures that provide for interaction between the buyer and the man he is

---

[1] Along with periodic review of such indexes as average cost of processing purchase requisitions, proportion of small orders, proportion of rush orders, late deliveries, and so on.

serving. And in the purchase of many standard items, it really does not arise.

But the most important basis for the effective control of procurement lies in the concept of this as a *service function* when it is performed by staff personnel. And this leads to the need to distinguish between the desirable degree of *centralized procurement activity* as opposed to the desirable degree of *decentralized procurement decision making*. It is unlikely that an "across the board" arrangement can be made. Specific provisions will have to be fashioned in terms of classes of items to be procured or units to be served, or both. The important point is that the evaluation of procurement activities be made on the basis of actual service rendered to each user and that the economies of centralization be constantly balanced against the "costs" of such centralization as are outlined above.

Sensing Units. We are not only concerned with control of procurement activity per se but also with control of that phase of organization planning—the making of equipment replacement and other procurement decisions—that activiate it. In chapter 5, means for evaluating various alternatives were discussed, but one important requirement was not explored: *control to assure that useful alternatives come to our attention.* The use of "sensing units" and periodic review of "internal investment opportunities" (in the form of replacements, modifications, or additions to physical assets) can do much to meet this need.

By "sensing units" we mean persons specifically charged with the duty of watching for such opportunities as they develop. This applies to opportunities both inside and outside the firm, though here should be stressed the importance of monitoring *outside* developments, for it is in this, more than in the monitoring of inside opportunities, that most companies tend to be deficient. It is customary to provide for efficiency engineers, systems analysts, consultants, operations researchers, and other such specialists to explore our "inside" opportunities, but, often, little attention is devoted to providing for the *competent* and *systematic* surveillance of "outside" opportunities.

Managers may say, "Well, we expect our personnel, as a matter of course, to keep us informed as to developments and opportunities in their areas of specialization." Unfortunately, this approach is not likely to produce the motivation or coverage that a carefully planned program of surveillance will. An important requirement is that our "sensing units" pick up useful information in time for us to exploit it fully. Sources for such information include technical journals, special departments and feature stories of other publications, and contacts with research personnel and counterpart personnel from other firms. Careful planning should define the scope and nature of sensing work to be done and prescribe the division and assignment of this work to various members of the organization. As with any assignment, adequate "tools," whether in the form of periodical subscriptions or expense money and released time to make appropriate contacts, should be provided for those responsible. Regular meetings with "sensing units" will provide for an exchange of ideas and also for periodic "post mortems" to assess the quality of results achieved.

This device, the "post mortem," is probably the most useful tool for controlling the procurement of plant and capital. The *anticipation* that a thoroughgoing analysis of "what was done relative to what could have been done" will be made later can do much to stimulate more productive *current* action. Also, such sessions, if properly conducted, can do much to facilitate the development of *improved* procedures and techniques, as well as to guide us in properly rewarding those who make significant contributions. The need for remedial action may be apparent when a "post mortem" reveals that a "sensing unit" missed a vital piece of information or the chief financial officer "missed" an opportunity for negotiating a much better loan for the company than was actually obtained.

Learning Curves. On pages 134 and 135 various considerations were examined that bear upon the decision that manufacturing and other firms must make with regard to "making" or "buying" various component parts or services. Here, our concern is with an aspect of the control of this kind of planning for organizing that is quite important: adjustment for the impact of non-trainee learning curves. These curves are also very important for control of the more generalized organization planning activity of forecasting labor, equipment, and materiel requirements for anticipated future output. And they are essential for the making of realistic pricing decisions. The term "non-trainee" learning curves is used because reference is to learning that is experienced by seasoned employees when they undertake the production of a new product rather than learning that is associated with training. "Trainee" learning curves will be discussed later in the chapter when control of the development of personnel is considered.

The existence of "non-trainee" learning curves was discovered in the aircraft industry during World War II. It was found that the number of direct labor hours required per airplane declined significantly—and at a seemingly regular rate—with the continued production of a particular model. And, surprisingly enough, when another model of essentially the same size and complexity as the preceding one went into production, the direct labor requirement per plane increased to approximately what it had been for initial production on the preceding model! Frank Andress reports that the armed forces became so interested in this phenomenon that they sponsored a study (by the Stanford Research Institute) of direct labor input required for the majority of all aircraft produced during the war. He reports:

As a result there was developed a series of learning curves which represented the *average* experience for various categories of airframes—fighters, bombers, and so forth. Although these curves were all different in terms of their starting points (i.e., the labor input for the first plane of a particular type), the great majority had one characteristic in common: their *rate* of improvement. It was this fact, essentially, that started speculation about a general theory of learning curves.

The rate of improvement which was found to hold true for the operations covered by the survey was such that, once production on a plane got going, the 4th unit required about 80% as much direct labor as the 2nd; the 10th 80% as much as the 5th; the 200th, 80% as much as the 100th; and so forth—in each case a reduction of 20% between doubled quantities. Because this *rate* of improvement seemed to prevail so consistently, it was concluded that the aircraft industry's rate of learning was approximately 80% between doubled quantities. That standard is applied to this day in analyzing a variety of procurement, production, and costing problems within the industry and within particular companies.[2]

Of course, all the reduction in direct labor hours required is not due to "pure" learning on the part of workers, nor will such "dramatic" curves be obtained, necessarily, for other industries. Andress explains:

. . . A distinction must be made between (a) learning in the literal sense, on the part of both workers and management, but primarily the former, and (b) a whole series of other factors, among which management innovations appear most significant. These casual factors operate

---

[2] Frank J. Andress, "The Learning Curve as a Production Tool," *Harvard Business Review*, Vol. XXXII, No. 1; reprinted in B. C. Lemke and James Edwards (eds.), Administrative Control and Executive Action (Columbus, Ohio: Charles E. Merrill Books, Inc., 1961), p. 344.

sometimes in combination and at other times in opposition. To this extent, the learning curve is more of an empirical method for charting all the various forces which work on labor hour input than it is a truly scientific device.

The significant fact is the consistent behavior of the curve, which indicates that of the various factors learning in the literal sense is the predominant influence. . . . Moreover, the more opportunities there are for learning, the steeper the curve, as the experience of the aircraft industry demonstrates: Approximately 75% of the total direct labor input in the industry is assembly; the balance is represented by machine work. In assembly work there is a relatively large scope for learning; in machine work the ability to reduce labor hours is greatly restricted by the fact that the machines cannot "learn" to run any faster. Accordingly, when the proportion of assembly work is less, the reduction of labor input is slower. For example, in the case of operations made up of approximately three-quarters machine time and one-quarter assembly time (the reverse of the usual situation in the aircraft industry), the approximate rate of learning has been found to be 90% rather than 80%.[3]

It is beyond the scope of this discussion to examine various learning curves and their formulas and the kinds of analyses that may be made through their use (for the interested reader, the article by Andress provides a good start). However, it should be stressed that such curves are important, when conditions permit their formulation, for the effective control of procurement planning, financial planning, production planning, price-setting, and similar activities. Obviously, they must be taken into consideration, where applicable, for the development of *realistic* standard costs and other performance standards. And productive comparisons might be made through time between a given company's curve and the appropriate industry curve.[4] Andress suggests that companies in the following industries, to name a few, may well find it profitable to formulate and utilize learning curves: electronics, home appliances, residential home "project" construction, shipbuilding, and machine shops (and in others where direct labor and product innovation are significant).

Flexible Budgets. An important additional tool for the effective control of procurement planning as well as control of procurement activity is the flexible or variable budget—formulated for each responsibility and profit center—that specifies the anticipated behavior of costs at various levels of volume or output. Obviously, development of the kind of learning curves that have just been discussed

---

[3] *Ibid.,* pp. 346 and 347.
[4] The existence of these curves could also help to produce more accurate expected time estimates for the PERT approach to project planning and control (see p. 50).

(and those for control of the development of personnel, which will be discussed later in this chapter) provide an important basis for the formulation of more realistic flexible budgets. In addition, as was discussed in chapter 4, it may not be long before we will be able to use formulas, derived from the kind of research Haire has done, to project "target organizations" for the future and predict, with surprising accuracy, the capital, personnel, and physical requirements needed for their effective implementation.

In the meantime, flexible budgeting will be greatly facilitated by improved knowledge as to how each line and staff organization in the firm grows and contracts. As has been noted, with good practice they grow and contract at *different* as well as *changing* rates with over-all company growth. Analysis of historical growth data for the firm, break-even charts, and learning curves provide a basis for fashioning sounder flexible budgets, standard costs, and other standards necessary for the effective control of planning and organizing activity at varying volumes of business activity. Since often "time is of the essence" in providing for the effective control of planning and organizing activity, it is important that flexible budgets and other "flexible" standards be formulated *prior* to the initiation of procurement planning, wherever possible.

Procurement and Maintenance of Required Personnel

A number of the concepts and techniques that will be reconsidered in this section were discussed in chapter 5. These are so essential for adequate *control* of the procurement and maintenance of personnel that reiteration and further expansion of them seems appropriate.

Validation. In using validation procedure (discussed on pp. 142-145), we often have a problem in obtaining a validity coefficient in which we can have confidence, one that is "usable" for planning and controlling selection activity. This problem arises when we have to validate a selection instrument using scores from only thirty or so applicants, initially. Say we obtain a correlation or validity coefficient of .50 when we correlate these scores with realistic performance data. Does this mean that the validity of the instrument—its ability to *predict* success or failure for groups of applicants in the future—*is* .50? Unfortunately, owing to the likely presence of sampling error, we really don't know!

The problem might be stated this way. The smaller the sample size, the larger the expected sampling error, that is, the less probable it is that our sample of thirty scores is *representative* of the set of scores we would obtain from either a larger sample of applicants or the population itself (all the applicants who may apply in the future for the kinds of positions we are filling). The only value in obtaining the correlation coefficient as a measure of the predictiveness of a selection instrument is in terms of its usefulness in selecting future groups or "samples" of applicants. If we *knew* the correlation coefficient that would have been obtained if a very large number of applicants had been tested simultaneously, there would be no problem, for we would know the validity of the test with only minor estimating error. Unfortunately, we must *estimate* the true validity of the test, given only the "evidence" provided by a small sample of thirty which we know is subject to error. And, unless we get a value (correlation or validity coefficient) in which we can have a reasonable level of confidence, we cannot use Taylor-Russell tables (see pp. 141 and 142) with confidence and enjoy the advantages made possible thereby in controlling the planning and execution of procurement activity. How can we obtain a validity estimate from such a small sample in which we *can* have reasonable confidence?

One workable approach is provided by the concept of confidence or fiducial limits.[5] If these are computed at two standard errors for the correlation coefficient obtained (which must represent a linear relationship) and *the coefficient that represents the lower limit is taken as the current validity of the selection instrument,* chances are, approximately, only 2½ in 100 that with lower limits arrived at in this way, the *true* validity coefficient for the selection instrument will be less than the lower limit! At one standard error, chances are approximately 16 in 100. As we obtain scores from more applicants to add to the thirty we started with, the influence of sampling error will diminish and the correlation coefficient representing the lower fiducial limit at one or two standard errors will tend to increase. Though the *true* validity of the test will not have changed—unless factors contributing to its validity have changed—the "usable" validity coefficient in which we can place some confidence and with which we can utilize the Taylor-Russell tables will have increased.

-----

[5] It is beyond the scope of this book to examine the detailed steps involved in computing fiducial limits for correlation coefficients; the reader should refer to any one of a number of good statistics books. One word of caution is in order, though: when the correlation coefficient obtained is moderate to large and the sample from which it is obtained is small (as in our example of thirty scores), Fisher's Z Transformation will have to be employed before the standard error of the linear correlation coefficient can be computed.

Continuing validation checks will also contribute to the control of procurement activity by providing a basis for testing whether or not achieved validity levels are maintained with the passage of time; for the validity of a selection instrument may be lowered by a number of circumstances. New personnel may not properly administer a previously valid test or interview procedure. Significant changes in the requirements of the jobs for which we are selecting applicants may occur without our knowledge. Security problems may arise, that is, information as to the manner with which tests or other selection instruments are scored may "get out" and permit applicants deliberately to slant their responses. And, of course, if initial validation were done with present employee scores rather than with applicant scores, we must correlate applicant scores with performance criteria (when we can obtain them) to be sure that what is valid for distinguishing successful performance on the part of *employees* is also valid for *predicting* successful performance on the part of applicants. Often, the two do not go hand in hand, at least not to the same degree.

The concept of validation also should be applied, on a continuing basis, to the evaluation of *sources* of applicants. Is there a significant difference between the performance of employees, as a group, who were recruited from High School A as compared with High School B, or as compared with private employment agency referrals or those attracted by newspaper ads? A simple and effective way to answer this question is to segregate employees as to source and compute the average performance of each such group. If differences in average performance are revealed, then they may be subjected to statistical tests to determine the probability that they are due to chance (sampling error) or are "significant," that is, that employees obtained in the future from one or more sources are likely to do better than employees from other sources, other things being equal. If one source seems to be superior to others, it may be more intensively cultivated. And as the sample size of employees from it and other sources grows in size, repeated testing will reveal with improved "odds" whether or not the differences among groups are, in fact, significant.

From a control standpoint, perhaps, the most important observation that can be made here is one that was made earlier in this book. Knowledge of the kind of basic statistical tools and concepts discussed here and in chapter 5 is essential for the proper conduct of a procurement program, *and top management must recognize this.* For, undoubtedly, one of the chief reasons why so many personnel specialists do not understand and use these essential tools is that *no one has ever demanded it of them!*

Merit Rating for Selection. It is useful to distinguish, for our purposes, two distinct uses of merit rating: *measurement of performance and facilitation of personal growth.* For a merit rating system that does one well does not necessarily do the other well! We are concerned here with merit rating for the measurement of performance to produce performance scores (validation criteria) for the validation of selection instruments and for guiding us in awarding promotions and pay increases.

If all employee contributions were directly quantifiable and measurable, there would be no need—for purely evaluation purposes—for merit rating systems comprising employee characteristics and generalized contributions (initiative, dependability, accuracy, personality, etc.). Or, if typically made *over-all* supervisory ratings were known to be reliable and reflect genuine contribution, there would be no need for merit rating systems—for purely evaluation purposes.

The reason for developing merit rating systems that include numerous rating factors is to *avoid* the generally observed unreliability (and consequent invalidity) of *over-all* judgmental ratings by supervisors by having them direct their attention to specific rating areas and thereby reduce bias. Tiffin has found, however, that this device is somewhat illusory in that the various factors typically do not represent independent rating areas. Through intercorrelation analysis of systems with up to twelve rating factors, he has found that there are really only two basic areas in which independent rating occurs: present performance and promotability.[6]

Here we have a real dilemma! We are almost back to over-all judgmental ratings, which we wish to abandon because we suspect that they are unreliable. We are forced to use the merit rating approach because we cannot measure all the specific contributions being made by the employee. *How can we validate the merit rating system?* How can we know that its ratings truly reflect employee worth and can be used for promotional decisions and as validation criteria for the validation of other selection instruments? Is there

---

[6] See Joseph Tiffin and Ernest McCormick, *Industrial Psychology* (4th ed.; Englewood Cliffs, New Jersey: Prentice-Hall, Inc., 1958).

any way out of this dilemma? Is there any way at least to get *reliable* over-all ratings to serve as validation criteria and for other purposes when there is little hope for obtaining more direct measurements of specific contributions?

We do know that a high degree of agreement (reliability and *presumed* validity) is possible when men are asked to identify *outstanding* and *very poor* employees and supervisors, that the biggest area of disagreement (unreliability and invalidity) has to do with evaluating the remaining "middle" group. Unfortunately, the use of only the extreme scores as validation criteria presents certain statistical problems that preclude the computation of a "lower fiducial limit" validity coefficient. The use of "employee comparison rating," however, provides a solution. Tiffin describes it:

With this plan, all employees reporting to a given supervisor are arranged into pairs, each man being paired with every other. The pairs of names are assembled into a small booklet and the supervisor goes through the booklet, looks at each pair of names, and checks the man in each pair who is better in over-all job performance. If more than 25 men are to be rated by one supervisor, this method becomes unwieldy because of the excessive number of pairs he must go over. With N men, the number of pairs is equal to $N(N-1)/2$. Thus with 25 men to be rated, the number of pairs is 300. While even this number might seem excessive, a supervisor can go through 90% of the pairs very rapidly and check one or the other in a second or two. The average supervisor can check 300 pairs of names in not over 15 minutes.

Time and again this method of rating has shown greater agreement between different supervisors rating the same men than any other rating system we have used.[7]

Such over-all ratings often provide the only practically obtainable performance scores to use as validation criteria for validating merit rating systems as well as other selection instruments.[8] Later in the chapter, in the discussion of *merit rating for development,* consideration will be given to the compilation of anecdotal data about employees that could well serve as a basis for obtaining even more reliable and valid "employee comparison ratings."

Probationary Status for Supervisory Personnel. Few, if any, selection procedures have perfect predictability. Often we can do a much better job of predicting failure than of predicting success,

---

[7] Joseph Tiffin, "Six Merit Rating Systems," *Personnel Journal,* January, 1959.

[8] For discussion of how to translate comparison ratings into scores see chap. 7 of J. P. Guilford *Psychometric Methods* (2d ed.; New York: McGraw-Hill Book Co., 1954).

for many of the "intangibles" that are required for success are not as easy to measure as many of the more "tangible" known requirements. To take an extreme case for example, it is much easier to predict who will *not* be an all-American football player than it is to predict who will be! Of course, if we can take a good prospect and objectively observe his playing behavior over a reasonable period of time, we will be in a much better position to evaluate his chances for success. The probationary period in employment is designed for this purpose, to permit us to acquire more meaningful evidence before we offer permanent employment to an applicant.

In practice, the probationary concept is often abused—especially with regard to managerial positions where good placement is so crucial—and understandably so. A new supervisor (recruited from outside the organization) cannot be placed in limbo; he must be invested immediately with some authority and status unless the work of his department is to be seriously curtailed, and each subordinate, through necessity, is forced to established some kind of relationship with him. If he has *any* competence, though not the level hoped for, strong forces will be generated to retain him beyond the probationary period. Management will wish to avoid the inevitable disruption of the subordinate group that another change would create. Certain subordinates and associates will speak up in behalf of his retention if for no other reason than the security of having a "known quantity" in the position. And those who hired him may feel a strong obligation to give him "every reasonable chance" in order to repay him for personal inconvenience in accepting the position and to avoid the serious blow to his feeling and chances for re-employment that probationary discharge will entail. Also, they may find it difficult to evaluate, fairly, the influence on his performance of those who for reasons of their own do not wish the "newcomer" well. In a very real sense, the use of probationary status for managerial personnel is not as feasible as is its use for non-managerial personnel, for the many interdependencies that are tied to a managerial position tend to discourage the kind of detachment and freedom of action that was intended.

The advantages of the probationary concept for managerial personnel have a better chance of realization through use of the "assistant to" position, when an organization is big enough to justify it. The "assistant to" usually serves as a general staff assistant to the president or a major division head. He may be used for liaison purposes, fact-finding, and special study work. Or the "assistant to" position may be used to introduce a new function "under the wing" of the boss. The important point from a procurement standpoint is that this position will provide a much better chance for really enjoying the advantages of probationary status. The organization can look the candidate over and he can "show what he can do" relatively unhampered by the kind of commitments that go with assignment to a specific managerial position. And often it will be discovered that the man is much more suited for some managerial position *other* than the one we are grooming him for! Since the "assistant to" spot is generally looked upon as a steppingstone to something else, "discharge" from it—suggestion that the "assistant to" look elsewhere for employment—does not create the same "face saving" problems as does discharge from a regular supervisory position.[9] Of course, in the case of probationary promotees from within, the problem may be less complicated. In many situations the "acting head" designation permits the prospective promotee to "try out" the job and to "decline it" if he wishes, reverting to his "regular" position.

Disposition of Inadequate Personnel. At any given time in an organization we may have a number of older, inadequate people in important staff and supervisory positions, people who have "let down" or become less adaptive with the passage of time or who became established in the organization when its standards were less demanding. The question here is what should be done with them. There is genuine merit to the concept of rewarding *faithful service* per se and in demonstrating to employees that we have some compassion for the plight of those who, in a sense, have become the "victims of circumstances" as a result of changed demands and technological innovation.

An important consideration from a control standpoint has to do with deciding how far we can go in the direction of accommodation in any given case. Actually, it is a matter of evaluating the "costs" of any course of action, *in terms of the maintenance of general organizational values* as well as in terms of personal or departmental efficiency. Kozmetsky and Kircher report that one firm, after making such an evaluation, "decided to spend $25,000 to retire certain employees so as to improve the administrative process of approving sales commitments. Their study indicated that, by affecting the personnel changes, the company would save approximately $100,000

---

[9] For further discussion of the "assistant to" position see the footnote references on p. 167.

a year from reduced investments in inventory as well as from smoother production volume." [10]

Holden, Fish, and Smith in their survey of the practices of thirty-one companies found the following types of accommodation to be in use:

1. Premature retirement on pension or cash settlement.

2. Assignment to some special work, such as consultant, where advantage can be taken of the man's background and experience without impairing the organization's effectiveness. In such cases an impressive title, avoiding any inference of line responsibility, is frequently bestowed and full compensation is often continued, thereby tending to preserve morale. In one concern, the salary is the eventual pension, and payments to the pension fund are continued on the old basis, so that this rate will continue for life.

3. Elevation of certain major executives with long service to less strenuous "elder statesmen" jobs, making way for more active, younger men in key managerial positions.

4. Assignment of each such case to the vice-president in charge of industrial relations who is personally charged with responsibility for and given wide latitude in working out an equitable solution. He may even take the individuals onto his own payroll if necessary.[11]

The Morale Survey. To maintain personnel properly, we must keep channels of communication open and periodically assess the status of the organization, in addition to providing opportunities for varied stimuli and growth. In practice, attempts are often made to assess morale or attitudes in an organization apart from an assessment of the organization itself. When this is done, much otherwise valuable information and effort is relatively wasted, for attitudes are in part caused by and in turn influence many of the interdependent factors in the organizational environment. Rensis Likert, director of the Institute for Social Research at Michigan, stresses this point, and he has had as extensive experience with the systematic measurement of organizations as anyone in America.[12] Consequently, any discussion of attitude or morale surveying will be deferred until the end of the chapter, when it will be considered as merely one facet of the organization audit.

---

[10] George Kozmetsky and Paul Kircher, *Electronic Computers and Management Control* (New York: McGraw-Hill Book Co., 1956), p. 150.

[11] Paul Holden, Lounsbury Fish, and Hubert Smith, *Top-Management Organization and Control* (New York: McGraw-Hill Book Co., 1951), p. 127.

[12] See Likert, "Measuring Organizational Performance," *Harvard Business Review,* March–April, 1958, and chap. 13 of his *New Patterns of Management* (New York: McGraw-Hill Book Co., 1961).

ESTABLISHMENT OF INTERRELATIONSHIPS AMONG FACTORS (AS PLANNED)

Various instruments have been discussed for effecting the assignment of duties and the delegation of authority and responsibility: job descriptions, organizational manuals, charts, policy manuals, standard operating procedures, technical orders, standing orders, and so on. Concern here is with adequate *control* of this activity.

Office of Record and Issue

Obviously, some realistic provision must be made for keeping up to date the organization, procedure, and policy manuals, job descriptions, technical orders, and other informational materials that are disseminated throughout the organization. When an organization is large enough to support a staff control agency, then it is the logical unit to function as an "office of record and issue" for these materials as well as for planning data, as was outlined in chapter 13. The task of keeping such informational materials up to date will be accomplished primarily through the control functions of programming and dispatching, as illustrated in Figure 13-3 on page 481.

When an organization is not large enough to support this kind of staff assistance, it is essential that *some individual* be given the responsibility for initiating and coordinating this kind of activity. He must be provided with the wherewithal (functional authority, approved procedure, and personal assistance, if necessary) to recall obsolete materials and simultaneously to replace them *promptly* with current materials. The word "promptly" is stressed, for there are few things more demoralizing than for subordinate supervisors to learn about developments from the union or their men, or for them to discover that they have expended considerable energy on *inappropriate* planning activity! The use of loose-leaf binders from which pages can be easily removed provides an effective and inexpensive basis for facilitating revision.

Feedback Information

Also, some provision must be made for alerting us *from below* to the fact that such informational instruments may be obsolete or no longer appropriate. At the beginning of this chapter one way to generate such feedback information was suggested: each manager in an organization, from the top on down, can request periodically that his subordinates prepare—in writing and without assistance—

a detailed statement of their duties, authority, and responsibilities. *In addition,* he might ask them to indicate any problems they have had in attempting to comply with rules, procedures, and policies, any lack of clarity or seeming conflict they have encountered in using them.

Also, provisions should be made for the periodic evaluation of procedures, rules, policies, technical orders, job descriptions, functional authority delegations, and other such informational instruments. The ultimate criterion for evaluating any of these is *contribution to primary service objectives.* In addition, we must consider such criteria as conflict or undue duplication with each other, understandability, and maintenance of an adequate degree of organizational flexibility.

Objectives change, personnel change, and available equipment, materiel, and the physical environment change; should it be surprising then, that the instruments utilized for the purpose of defining desirable relationships among required functions, physical factors, and personnel must undergo periodic content change if they are to remain effective? Of course, as we have suggested many times before, one of the primary bases for assuring current and appropriate job assignments, policies, rules, procedures, etc., is to provide for continuing and effective participation from below in their formulation. The provision of this, however, is more the result of *net organizational climate* than the product of any single activity or program!

Leadership Specialization

To be an effective manager is quite a challenge! In chapter 5 the generalization was made that there are three basic areas of competence that managers must have: technical skill, human skill, and conceptual skill. The "clinical" role, among others, that the supervisor must assume and the attributes of maturity, self-knowledge, and perception that are required for sustained success in supervisory activity were discussed in chapter 8. Elsewhere, the kind of conceptual skill and technical knowledge that managers must have has been examined. Realistically, all this adds up to a pretty big order, and there are few, indeed, who can really fill the bill on most of these counts. Any practicing manager will readily agree that there is a chronic shortage of such talent in the business world. And the outlook is for an even greater shortage relative to demand in the future as the professionalization of management advances with accelerated progress in the various sciences.

It is rare that managers possess *equal* competence in all three areas of managerial skill. Many competent managers can be characterized as being *more* "task oriented" than "people oriented" or more "people oriented" than "task oriented." A possible way in which we can provide for even more effective management in an organization is to utilize the concept of *dual* leadership within the framework of sound organizational practices. We could appoint a "task leader" *and* a "social leader" for each group, with one being subordinate to and compatible with the other. Such an arrangement has shown promise on an experimental basis, but more investigation is needed to determine its feasibility in a "real life" organization.[13]

DEVELOPMENT OF PERSONNEL (AS PLANNED)

In Chapter 6 the idea was stressed that *effective control of the development of organizational personnel must flow from the top of an organization. A trainee must receive the kind of behavior from his boss that he is expected to practice with his subordinates.* It was pointed out that good human relations must start at the top of an organization and permeate downward, *not* at the foreman level and permeate upward! With the wrong climate, it is quite possible for a supervisor to be less effective *after* human relations training than before it, the training having confirmed his misgivings about the inadequacies of his boss's approach and undermined his confidence in company management. At best, any positive effect that training may have on his behavior will tend to "wear off" with the passage of time if it is not supported and encouraged by his work environment. Not only does the behavior of an individual supervisor tend to mirror that of his boss; all supervisors in an organization are significantly influenced by the distinctive "climate" or pattern of leadership that is unique to that organization. If a company provides a poor climate for development, obviously the solution to the problem is to alter the climate, not to attempt to isolate trainees from it!

Genuine and lasting development can be the result only of a continuous training process that goes on throughout a man's career.

---

[13] The value of this approach in conference leadership has been suggested by the findings of Robert Bales and others of the Laboratory of Social Relations at Harvard University. See Bales, "In Conference" *Harvard Business Review,* March–April, 1954.

There can be no substitute for the active interest, support, and participation of *all managers* in a training program. The four-method understudy approach (discussed on p. 166) is an essential tool of this continuous training process, and by necessity it must be utilized by "bosses" rather than by staff specialists. The legitimate role of a training director is to assist management in planning, organizing, coordinating, and evaluating training activities and to handle staffing and other arrangements for specialized presentations, workshops, or short courses. He can help define training needs through consultation with those who do organization planning and job analysis as well as through conferences with those who are currently being trained or have completed certain phases of training.

In the final analysis, if management is to realize its development goals, it must do more than merely talk about the values we have discussed. It must *tangibly reward* supervisors for personal growth and effective coaching of subordinates—*even though this may not raise production as much in the short run as a whip-cracking, "tight ship" approach*. It must *really delegate authority* to those who are ready for it within the framework of the criteria discussed in chapter 11, and it must design and respond to an adequate system of communications. Perhaps one of the most important requirements for the creation and maintenance of a proper "climate for development" is the willingness of management constantly to re-examine its "ends"—primary, collateral, and secondary objectives—and its means for achieving them. *Good human relations must never come to mean the elimination of conflict rather than the introduction of change with a minimum of conflict.*

Actually, the ideas expressed above are merely reiterations of what has been stressed previously in this book. But these general requirements are so essential to the effective control of development activity that, until they are satisfied, many of the specific control measures that will be considered below will be relatively unproductive and premature.

Merit Rating for Development

Earlier, merit rating for measuring performance was discussed. Here our concern is with merit rating for development. A new and promising approach (briefly discussed in chap. 8) involves having supervisors guide their subordinates in the preparation of written self-development programs and subsequently evaluate them in terms of their own criteria. We will consider certain problems of control that must be solved if this approach is to be really productive.

First of all, it is essential that the employee's self-development program deal with specific, concrete goals that are attainable for him and that are not too numerous for him at any given time. It is not enough simply to select certain goals from a man's job description. The statement of goals should come from the subordinate and should be meaningful to him. His self-development proposal should, whenever possible, spell out *how* he plans to attain his goals and on the basis of what timing or schedule. To help supervisors throughout the organization to assist their subordinates in the formulation of realistic development programs and to assure some uniformity of practice for rating purposes, a procedure should be established whereby a copy of each man's self-development program is sent to the personnel office and periodic meetings are arranged by that office for the purpose of discussing techniques for guiding employees in the formulation of their programs and the development of general standards for evaluating them.

Perhaps the personnel office could assist supervisors in designing a form to which all employee development programs could be "transferred" for comparative and rating purposes. We know that the *evaluation* of a group of employees by several supervisors has many advantages over evaluation by a single supervisor, *provided* that they know enough about the men to rate them. If each supervisor were to keep an accurate, running anecdotal record of critical behavioral incidents reflecting success or failure relative to each subordinate's development goals and this were made a part of each man's record, a workable basis for group ratings would be provided. Such an anecdotal record would also serve as a valuable aid to the supervisor in his review sessions with each subordinate. Obviously, it is important to have observational data to supplement the statements of subordinates about the degree to which they have achieved or not achieved their goals.

Perhaps it would be more accurate to refer to the kind of merit rating interview under consideration here as a form of *structured coaching.* For certainly the idea of a scheduled annual or semiannual interview should be abandoned, to permit discussion of performance at a time when it will be most meaningful to the employee —as soon as possible after he has reached or failed to reach a goal. Actually, what is suggested here is an *elaboration* of the four-method understudy approach that provides for adequate control of it in practice. There might be some real merit in divorcing evaluation for pay and promotional purposes from such interviews—to maintain a more "permissive" atmosphere—except when group-formulated employee comparison ratings are made periodically on the basis of employee development program data and anecdotal data supplied by each supervisor. Then the subordinate's rating can be discussed as something *apart* from the week-by-week or month-by-month evaluation of his development efforts.

But suppose that an employee does not wish to formulate development goals? What if his performance is satisfactory and he professes no desire to become promotable or qualified for a significant pay increase? Certainly, we will always need more "Indians" than "chiefs," and there is nothing illegitimate about an employee feeling this way. However, our approach still serves the important function of forcing him to commit himself openly to this position and, possibly to re-examine his position. Many employees would like to have their cake and eat it too. They would welcome the fruits of effort without having to earn them. It is hard for us to be objective about our real contributions when our aspirations tempt us to rationalize away our shortcomings. If a man is periodically forced to face reality and to state his development goals—or absence of them—in writing, he is less likely to make unreasonable demands or to delude himself when promotion time comes round.

Evaluation of Training Programs

Employees must be trained in specific skills, knowledge, and techniques to do their jobs properly whether we make formal provisions for this activity or not. Generally speaking, *formal* training effort based on accurate identification of training needs, careful planning, and the utilization of proper tools is more productive than *informal* provision for training, provided that it is properly controlled. The basis of proper control lies in the measurement of results. To evaluate a particular program, we must have some means for obtaining post-training evidence of the *extent* and *persistence* of change that may be attributed to the program. What are some specific techniques for doing this?

The "pay-off" of many types of training is tangible and readily observable. For example, if we have conducted a class in blueprint reading, we can administer a work-sample test of blueprint reading facility to the trainees and also to a similar group of workers who did not receive the training. Presumably, any difference in score obtained by the trained group is attributable to the training received, and the value of this difference can be balanced against the cost of the special program. This approach is useful wherever we can directly measure output—good or defective units produced, breakage, scrappage or consumption of materials, number of words typed with percentage of errors, time required to perform an operation satisfactorily, and so on—or other desirable values created by training, such as reduction in accidents, absenteeism, and turnover rates for trained as opposed to untrained groups.

We can plot learning curves for both formally trained and untrained "average," "below average," and "above average" operators (see Figures 14-1 and 14-2). The cost of training can be determined and compared with the savings it generates in terms of reduced training time as well as the other criteria mentioned. And, of course, the effectiveness of *new* training techniques or new instructors can be ascertained in the same fashion. Incidentally, such learning curves can serve as valid selection instruments, too. Learners who start and remain on the "below average" learning curve are not likely to become average or above-average operators; they can be released or transferred to other work after the first few weeks of their probationary employment. An approach that would be applicable to other jobs would be to plot "time required to perform a task" on the ordinate of the graph in place of "average hourly production." [14]

In the case of training programs that are designed to impart knowledge alone, we can resort to the classical device of the teacher: the written examination. It may be desirable to administer tests of comprehension to new employees on the content of the employee manual and other informational materials and presentations given to them. After a series of discussion meetings, supervisory personnel might be quizzed on their understanding of such things as, the union contract, rules, policies, and procedures, or whatever was presented to them. Though the use of tests will not indicate the *value* of transmitting information to employees, it will certainly provide essential feedback information to indicate how well we are attaining our communication goals.

---

[14] The learning curves presented in Figures 14-1 and 14-2 are hypothetical. Reference to appropriate journals and books on industrial psychology will yield a wealth of actual learning-curve data for various types of jobs or operations.

Undoubtedly, we have our biggest problems when we try to evaluate human relations, leadership, or general executive development training activity. One company has successfully used a periodic oral examination to review and evaluate the progress of each executive trainee and decide whether or not he is ready for the next phase of his program. Line and staff officers, representing areas in which

FIG. 14-1

Formally Trained Operators

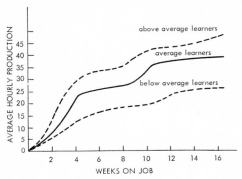

FIG. 14-2

Untrained Operators

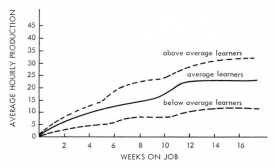

the trainee has presumably gained competence since his last review, probe the trainee's knowledge and skill. When deficiencies crop up, they plan specific remedial action in the form of special assignments and provisions for individual instruction and coaching.

In the area of human relations training, some measure of the impact of training can be obtained by having trainees prepare "before training" and "after training" analyses of the same case material. A complex human relations case is passed out before the training begins; the trainees are asked to analyze the case thoroughly in writing, being careful to explain their thinking: What problems do they perceive, why are they problems, and why or how did they arise? They might also be asked to formulate recommendations for disposing of the problems they have examined. The case is not discussed during the training program, and the trainees are requested not to consider it further. At the end of the course, the case is redistributed with the same instructions. When trainees complete the second write-up, their first write-ups are returned to them and they are asked to compare the two and to prepare a written analysis of the differences, if any, that they perceive. We can also attempt to gain some measure of the impact of human relations training by observing the behavior of trainees on the job and through feedback information—in sociometric or other form—obtained from those who serve with the trainee or are under his supervision.

THE ORGANIZATION AUDIT

In various places throughout this book, specific types of audit (formal examination) activity have been discussed. For example, in chapter 13 an audit was discussed of how executives spend their time to determine whether the encroachment of routine demands has left too little time for planning and other managerial activities that are more in keeping with their abilities. Stress has been put many times on the need for periodic auditing of primary service objectives and determination of whether or not collateral and secondary objectives, as well as rules, policies, procedures, organizational structure, organizational climate, and other "tools" for attaining primary objectives, are still in tune with these objectives and with one another.

Though audits for specific areas and activities of the organization are necessary to make the control of organization planning and organizing activity *feasible*, it is most important for an organization to undertake, periodically, a *comprehensive organization audit*. For an over-all examination of the organization will provide some understanding of the interplay and *net impact* of interdependent organizational factors. Of course, this consideration is more related to certain types of audits than to others. As was suggested earlier in the chapter, it is particularly relevant to the making of morale or attitude surveys. When these are made, apart from an examination of the organization itself, much otherwise valuable information and effort is relatively wasted, since attitudes are in part caused by, and in turn influence, many of the interdependent factors in the organizational environment.

In auditing the behavioral and other facets of an organization, we must be very careful from a *methodological* standpoint. Likert points out: "It is commonly assumed, for example, that if persons are asked why they behave as they do, the reasons given are valid statements of the motivational forces at work. This assumption, unfortunately, is incorrect." [15] He goes on to state:

A related error occurs in the interpretation of data. For example, if employees say that the thing they like best about their job situation is the clean, well-lighted space in which to work, it does not follow that this factor is most important in producing favorable over-all attitudes. It is even possible that those who give this as their first choice have the least favorable over-all attitudes toward the company. Similarly, the items which are reacted to least favorably cannot be interpreted as the variables which are most important in producing unfavorable over-all attitudes.

. . . Whenever an organization suddenly and for the first time is given a large volume of measurements dealing with a wide array of variables, the members of the organization feel so completely overwhelmed that they find it difficult to analyze and use the data. They often reject the entire process as a consequence. As with so many good things, it is unwise to do too much too rapidly. Experience in introducing this kind of measurement into an organization has shown that it is desirable to start with measurements of a limited number of variables first. Additional variables can be added as the persons using the measurements acquire skill in interpreting and applying the measurements and want more data to help them in guiding their operation.

. . . As in accounting, professional assistance is needed in setting up the measurement program and in laying out the analyses to be made. Once the program is launched and experience is obtained in using the results, professional assistance other than occasional consultation may no longer be required. [16]

In the way of a "checklist," the following are among the questions that should be considered in the conduct of a comprehensive organization audit:

1. Are primary, collateral, and secondary objectives clearly defined and understood? Are collateral and secondary objectives properly *related* to primary service objectives and to each other?

2. Are the organic business functions of the enterprise—and consequent line and staff positions—properly identified in view of possibly changed

---

[15] Likert, *New Patterns of Management*, p. 195.
[16] *Ibid.*, pp. 195, 220, 196.

primary service objectives? Should changes in the placement of certain line and staff positions in the organization be made in the light of shifts in emphasis in primary service objectives?

3. Are all rules, policies, procedures, job descriptions, allocations of authority, functional authority, and responsibility *clearly defined, consistent with each other* at all organizational levels, *understood,* and *still appropriate* in view of *current* objectives?

4. Is the rationale of functionalization and departmentation defensible in the light of current objectives and good organizational practice? For example, is there undue duplication of effort? Has specialization been pushed too far in areas where job enlargement would be more appropriate? Are spans of control appropriate in view of specific circumstances in each organizational unit?

5. Have executives sufficient time for planning and other important managerial activities? Have they been supplied with adequate staff assistance? Putting it another way, have those staff positions evolved which should have evolved? Have those staff positions which should have been separated and elevated been separated and elevated?

6. Are the criteria for effective decentralization being satisfied (see pp. 289–311)? For example, are decisions being made at the lowest organizational level that is feasible? Are decentralized staff positions properly related to the decentralized units they serve *and* the central unit? Are there provisions for interlocking committees and other organizational devices for facilitating genuine lower-level participation in policy making and other types of planning? Are profit and responsibility centers properly identified? Do budget-making procedures generate self-imposed standards that are meaningful?

7. Is there adequate organization for quick, efficient data processing to serve the special needs of data customers throughout the organization as well as the over-all needs of central planning groups? Are all reports and informational materials essential, and are they kept reasonably up to date? (An analysis of the daily flow of documents can be very useful in this respect.)

8. Is organization for long-range planning effective? Are adequate provisions made for liaison between planning agencies in the form of liaison personnel, informational instruments, and multi-interest committees? Are these committees as well as other committees still essential? Does an individual or agency function as an "office of record and issue" to perform programming and dispatching functions with regard to the recasting and dissemination of informational instruments? Are organizational provisions made for "sensing" important external developments? Are those data required for meaningful post mortems retained in the proper form? Are data relating to ratios and other control standards retained in the proper form? [17]

---

[17] Certain useful data can be obtained from external sources. For example, the periodical *Personnel* annually publishes data on personnel ratios for different sized firms, and data on financial ratios can be obtained from numerous sources.

9. Are performance standards for all areas of activity well defined and understood? Are control systems well defined, properly selective, and efficient? Is adequate provision made for the *initiation* as well as the *termination* of activities? Can accountability be established for all positions?

10. Are data relevant to the various rates of growth of various organizational units being compiled and retained? If long-term reduction in the total volume of operations has occurred, has the organization been *contracted* properly throughout? Have adequate provisions been made for the continuous performance of organization planning functions and for the effective dissemination of sound organizational concepts to appropriate personnel throughout the organization?

11. Does an organizational climate conducive to personal growth prevail? Are provisions made to integrate managers throughout the organization with staff personnel for the performance of personal development and training functions?

12. Do data obtained for the checklist questions given above in conjunction with those obtained about the attitudes and behavior of organizational members, when properly interpreted, indicate that the formal and informal organizations are compatible and are properly articulated, that organizational personnel perceive that their needs are being met in their respective jobs, and that the total organization is a reasonably viable and effective instrument for the attainment of primary service objectives?

On the basis of findings derived from such a comprehensive organization audit, management will be able to identify organizational limiting factors and then will be in a position to plan for effective remedial action to dispose of them.

QUESTIONS

1. In what ways is it a problem to "reap the benefits of centralized procurement service and still genuinely serve the *unique* needs of internal organizational 'customers'"? Discuss.

2. What are "sensing units"? Is the need for them a reflection of poor morale or initiative on the part of organizational members? Why or why not?

3. What is a non-trainee learning curve? Discuss various uses that may be made of it. For what type of company or industry is a learning curve likely to be obtainable and useful? Why?

4. Explain what a flexible budget is?

5. Is the validity coefficient obtained from correlating selection instrument scores with performance scores the same as the "usable" coefficient for planning and controlling selection activity? Explain. If not the same, how can the "usable" coefficient be computed?

6. Describe, step by step, the procedure you would follow to evaluate various *sources* of employees.

7. Is it useful to distinguish between merit rating for the measurement of performance and merit rating for the facilitation of personal growth? Why? Describe an approach or combination of approaches that you think would satisfy the requirements of *both* measurement and growth facilitation.

8. Should a merit rating system for measurement purposes be valid? Why or why not? If you think that it should, explain how you would validate it. What would be your validation criteria? Defend the use of these criteria.

9. Discuss the possible advantages and disadvantages of using the "assistant to" position for introducing new executive personnel into an organization.

10. Do you believe that demonstrably inadequate personnel should be discharged whatever their status or length of service? Why or why not?

11. What are the various instruments used for effecting the assignment of duties and delegation of authority and responsibility?

12. Why do some people suggest that we appoint *two* leaders for each group? How would they label these two leaders? Would this violate the concept of unity of command? Explain.

13. Describe general requirements for effective supervisory training in an organization. Can these always be satisfied? How?

14. If we use the "self-development program" approach to merit rating for development, how can we provide for some uniformity of practice and interpretation of results on the part of our supervisors? Explain.

15. What is a trainee learning curve? Discuss various uses that may be made of it.

16. Your personnel director protests that he has no means for evaluating the effectiveness of various training programs he has conducted. Describe various approaches to evaluation and the kinds of training activity for which they are most appropriate.

17. What is an organization audit? Would there be any need to conduct one if every manager were doing his job properly? Why or why not?

Chapter 15

CONTROL OF CONTROL

Control has to do with making events conform to plans. It is the *organic management function* of coordinating the work of others so that objectives are achieved. This chapter is concerned with "control of control," seeing to it that those activities which relate to control are planned and performed effectively.

IDENTIFICATION OF KEY FACTORS AND OPERATIONS

It has been pointed out earlier that control cannot be feasible and economical unless it is *selective* in terms of *key* factors and operations. For the effectiveness of control does not increase in proportion to the *number* of control points. In fact, simply increasing the number of points will have the effect, usually, of *decreasing* the effectiveness of control. For control costs money, and excessive or unjustified use of it exerts a decidely negative influence on the general productivity and viability of an organization. In planning for and in implementing systems of control, it is important to see to it that *key* factors and operations are, indeed, "key"—not as of yesterday, but currently—so that there will not be *in fact* two general approaches to control: one that is formally prescribed and one that is actually utilized because it is workable.

How can we determine whether or not we are dealing only in terms of *key* factors and operations? Certainly, much of the information from the organization audit (discussed at the end of the preceding chapter) will prove useful for this purpose when it is properly organized and interpreted. Also, it is useful to analyze, periodically, *what would have happened* if we had utilized fewer or different sets of key factors and operations. Could we have achieved the same degree of control with *fewer* "keys," or could we have improved the level of control through the use of *different* "keys" at no more, and possibly lower, expense? It will help, too, if we avoid creating the impression in an organization that present systems of control are somehow "sacrosanct" and stress the idea that these are tools for the attainment of objectives that can and should be re-examined whenever there is dissatisfaction. Some may protest that this invitation is "too open," that it will encourage many to complain about a prefectly workable and valid system. But this overlooks the important fact that no system is better than the implementation it receives. Dissatisfaction may stem from *incompetence* and *misunderstanding* as well as from system defects. We wish to take effective remedial action *whatever* the difficulty.

PROGRAMMING

Programming is concerned with the *routine* collection, sorting, and assignment of data: the plans data, organization data, and control data required for the controlled execution of plans. It involves the recasting of information (on a preplanned basis) into a form that is most suited to the user, and it may involve decision making on a preplanned basis (but not problem solving).

The organization requirements for the performance of these activities have been considered in the discussion of the role of an "agency of record and issue." [1] From a control standpoint we want to be sure that those who are responsible for programming are kept informed as to the *current* needs of information users. Data from the organization audit as well as periodic analyses as to the appropriateness and current use being made of various reports, forms, etc., will help to reveal whether any unnecessary or inappropriate information processing and dissemination activity is taking place and whether programming activities are being performed with sufficient promptness.

Newcomers to an organization should be impressed with the idea that staff programming personnel are providing a service—at a very real expense—to serve *their* informational needs, that they are *not* under obligation to continue receiving information in a form desired by their predcessors if they have an alternative form that is workable and of greater meaningfulness to them. This is not to

---

[1] See p. 349.

imply that every new data user should be given a "blank check" in this regard, since *undue* proliferation of forms, reports, etc., in an organization is wasteful and breeds confusion. But most organizations seem to err in the direction of *discouraging* productive innovation on the part of information users. New and old managers often find it easier, and more judicious for their own well-being, to accept the informational instruments given them without complaint, even though they know that they will never look at half of them and that they will have to rework others and obtain additional information on their own initiative before they can manage their departments properly!

One company tried to curb the preparation of unnecessary information by periodically *delaying* the issuance of routine reports, etc., and then waiting to see who complained about not receiving them. Unfortunately, such a "cure" may be worse than the disease. The fact that an information user fails to complain does not prove that the information is valueless to him *at other times* or that it would be valueless *if presented in a different form or if he were doing his job properly!* A much better approach is to create a "climate" and procedures that will encourage productive collaboration between data processors and data users.

SCHEDULING

Scheduling has to do with the *translation* of planned time requirements and completion dates into actual calendar dates. This is a simple activity and a relatively easy one to control. Aside from eliminating clerical error, control of it has to do largely with assuring that specific activities and programs are, *in fact*, scheduled, because a surprisingly large number of activities, especially those of research and other staff agencies, will remain unscheduled—formally—if this need is not consciously met.

True, owing to the difficulty of accurately planning for the scheduling of many activities, managers are reluctant to commit themselves to specific dates. And, when we press them to do so, they are likely to complain that we are trying to tie them down and to take to four decimal places that which cannot be taken to one. But this complaint should be directed only at poor planning for scheduling and the improper evaluation of deviations from schedule. Schedule dates themselves are goals or standards against which to measure performance and the adequacy of planning; they are essential to control. Adjustment for the impact of uncontrollable factors and uncertainty should be made in planning for scheduling, *not* scheduling per se.[2]

DISPATCHING

Dispatching is concerned with the *release of authority:* authority regarding *how* to act as well as *when* to act. The mechanics of delegating authority are supplied by the dispatching function. The release of approved technical orders, standard operating procedures, policies, specifications, and other such instruments indicates to personnel *how* they are authorized to act when the time comes for them to act. Authority as to *when* to act is released via the dispatching function in the form of written or verbal operating orders and standing orders. A schedule has the force of an operating order when it is approved by proper line authority.

The use of "offices or agencies of record and issue" for the performance of programming and dispatching activities was discussed earlier. Whether or not staff personnel or managers have performed the dispatching function, with either written or verbal directives, the proper implementation of this important control activity is of concern. Are directives communicated adequately and with proper timing? Do managers and those who serve them in the performance of this function have access to and profit from appropriate feedback information as to the adequacy with which it is being performed? Control of the dispatching function will be facilitated by analysis of specific instances in which improper action can be traced to the faulty receipt of orders.

It may not be hard to remedy procedural or other organizational defects that have interferred with the proper performance of the dispatching function on the part of staff control personnel, but when poor dispatching is traceable to inadequate supervisory behavior, short of firing the offender, we may find it more difficult to take effective corrective action. For to the extent that this behavior is a product of the personal needs of the supervisor, it will not be as amenable to the "logics" of the situation. Nevertheless, we cannot ignore it. On a broader scale, in considering the control of supervision and "control of control" generally, we have to contend with this same problem, which will now be considered in the discussion of control of supervision.

---

[2] For an illustration of how this can be done in project planning see the discussion of PERT, pp. 50–54. Any one of a number of industrial management books will provide information as to useful ways for doing this in schedule planning for production.

SUPERVISION

Supervision has to do with the effective motivation of men—the face-to-face direction of individuals and groups. To supervise successfully, a manager must have a large measure of self-knowledge, an understanding of individual and group behavior, and the character, courage, and skill to profit therefrom. Various factors that contribute to the effective performance and control of supervisory activities have been discussed previously, especially in chapter 8. Effective control of supervision is so important to the well-being of an organization—and to control in general—that it will be worthwhile to reiterate some of these considerations here along with the presentation of some new ones.

Standards

The control of supervision at lower levels must start with control of supervision at the top of the organization. Top management, far more by its actions than by its pronouncements, will set the "climate" for supervision and the role expectations for supervisory behavior. Top management must give careful thought, not only to the kinds of supervisory behavior that it believes are productive, but to those kinds that *it* can live with and practice on a day-in and day-out basis. It should then be willing to formalize in writing its position with regard to *standards of supervision* and to design the organization and its system of penalties and rewards to encourage the type of behavior desired. Too often, and too humanly, top management is not willing to appraise the productiveness of its own supervisory behavior or commit *itself* to standards that it wishes to impose on lower-level managers. Standards for subordinates, if they are to be meaningful and taken seriously, must be *practiced* by top-level personnel; they cannot be successfully "imported" from outside the organization and imposed on others by "non-practicing" supervisors.

The implications of this should be clear. Top management cannot hope to improve the quality of lower-level leadership by sending subordinates off to human relations courses until it is willing to understand, accept, and practice the content of these courses, or step aside to make room for top management that will. Some may object to this by saying that it is comparable to telling a group of autocratic, rigid top managers to go out and shoot themselves if they are not willing to do the "impossible," that is, if they are not willing to alter their basic outlook about people and their every-day mode of supervision. Actually, this misses the point of the fore-going comment. It relates to the kind of situation in which top management wishes to improve the quality of lower-level supervision by expecting subordinates to behave in ways that are *different* from its behavior. Autocratic leadership, under certain conditions, *does* get results and it tends to create the kind of organization that is supportive to its rationale. The autocratic leader is better advised to prescribe standards of supervision for his organization *that he can accept and practice* than to risk the disruptive effects of a "double standard."

It is important that we establish standards of organization that support and facilitate the attainment of our standards of supervisory behavior. Many organizational concepts that can be drawn upon for doing this have been discussed in the chapters on organization planning, organization for planning, organization for organizing, and organization for control. For example, the criteria for effective decentralization (presented on pp. 289-311) are felt to be realistic organization standards that must be met if we wish to encourage the kind of behavior that decentralized managers must practice to be successful. The reality should be kept in mind that *such standards are meaningful only to the extent that rewards and penalties are based on evaluations that are made relative to them.* It does little good to base promotions on one set of standards and to pay extensive lip service to others, however desirable or lofty they may sound. We must guard against the temptation to establish and use only those standards which reflect immediate and direct contribution to short-term goals or we will discourage attention to equally important areas of contribution. We should consider, also, such factors as the quality of planning activity, proper use of authority and influence, ethical conduct, effective discipline, compliance with policies, etc., capacity for growth, the ability to develop individual subordinates and groups, and so on.

Evaluation

Assuming that top management has fashioned *honest* standards for supervisory behavior, which it believes will most productively contribute to the attainment of primary service objectives and which it is willing to be evaluated relative to, from what sources can management obtain the necessary data with which to evaluate performance in relation to these standards?

If we have planned well for data processing, information relating to various quantitative standards, such as budgets, standard costs, return on investment, and other ratios, etc., will be readily obtainable. For our other standards, we can obtain much useful information from self-development program progress data, post mortem data relating to analyses as to why deviations from planned performance have occurred, and the organization audit. Also, properly conducted "exit interviews" often can throw light on the adequacy or inadequacy of supervisory behavior in meeting employee needs. They are especially useful if conducted several weeks or months after the employee has left and secured employment elsewhere. It is more likely that he will then reveal his true feelings and will be more objective about the reasons surrounding his separation from the company.

Undoubtedly, one of the most important considerations in evaluating supervisory behavior—and one that will be considered at greater length in the discussion of control of the comparison function, generally—is to recognize the unreality and unworkability of a mechanistic or "formula" approach to it. There is *not* a one-to-one correspondence between good supervisory behavior and desirable outcomes, although, naturally, we assume that there is some correspondence between them. What may seem "successful" in the short run may well be creating dissension for the long run. Favorable outcomes are often granted or denied the supervisor through the operation of factors largely beyond his control. In evaluating a man's supervisory behavior, we should be concerned with the degree to which he is using what we regard as "good form" in his day-to-day activities; we should be concerned much more with his "batting average" than with specific instances of success or failure.

There are too many ways that supervisors can contrive to deny the value of supervisory control to the organization if they observe that only a few standards actually count; that *results* relative to them count for everything and *effective behavior* relative to them counts for nothing!

Corrective Action

As was suggested earlier, it may be difficult to alter behavior that is the product of the personal needs of the supervisor rather than merely the result of misunderstanding or ignorance of requirements. To do it, we must create a type of climate that will induce the supervisor to re-examine his behavior and then we must encourage him to explore and experiment with alternative modes that will be more productive for him. And we should structure the "compulsions" of his work environment to reinforce and sustain him in his new behavior.

Ideally, it would be desirable for supervisors to gain "insight" or genuine understanding as to the rationale of their non-productive behavior as the best means for "emancipating" them from the need for that behavior. Unfortunately, this is not likely to be achieved by the majority of supervisors in the best of human relations training programs. However, such programs, when supported by the right supervisory climate, *can* induce improved behavior on the part of supervisors. When coupled with appropriate on-the-job coaching, human relations training will tend to sensitize the supervisor to other viewpoints and to the existence of other ways of doing things and will tend to increase his sense of adequacy and afford him an opportunity for the release of tension. With the passage of time and the greater accumulation of experience in such an environment, the supervisor *is* likely to gain some measure of personal insight. When this occurs, he may become a *net contributor* to the organization's permissive atmosphere, as opposed to a net withdrawer from it. Such results, of course, can be realized only after this kind of training has been pursued over an extended period of time.

One of the most effective ways for altering supervisory behavior in the *short run* is to structure the "compulsions" of the work environment so as to produce behavior that is productive for the organization and, in turn, is productive for the supervisor (in that it will tend to generate better interpersonal relationships between him and his men). Is this really true? Is there any evidence that this is more than wishful thinking? Actually, the strength of non-punitive "compulsions" has been demonstrated in several studies. The impact of role expectations on the performance of representatives of groups in competition was discussed briefly on page 222. What group spokesmen did had very little to do with their own character or personality!

Stuart Chase reports the findings of a study of various United States air forces in the European theater during World War II:

A flier had one chance in four, yet morale was good. Why? The psychologists found that good leadership was certainly one reason, but another was even more important: the sense of being *a member of a group in which flying and fighting were the only accepted ways of behaving.*[3]

And Dewey and Humber cite an example illustrating the impact of role expectations on the behavior of a man. They refer to Chester A. Arthur, who became President of the United States upon the death of President Garfield:

> Arthur had been the pet of the New York political machine, and many, if not most, of the men "in the know" expected one of the worst, most corrupt administrations in American history.... However, his administration was a pleasant surprise to the supporters of good government. The roles he played were quite in keeping with the status assigned to the office of the President. He responded to the attitudes which he knew the populace had toward the occupant of the President's chair.[4]

The findings of leadership studies conducted at Ohio State led Carroll Shartle to conclude that "less than half" of leadership performance "could be ascribed to the man and a little over half to the demands of the particular job." [5] In one study, predictions were made as to how naval officers would behave in *new* positions (1) based on their performance in their preceding jobs and (2) based on the performance of their predecessors in the same new positions. A most provocative finding was that *we can predict the behavior of the new incumbent almost as well on the basis of his predecessor's behavior in the job as we can on the basis of the new incumbent's performance in his preceding job!* [6]

Granted, then, that we can mold behavior to some extent through the use of external influences, what are some of the "compulsions" we should work with? The usefulness of supervisory group ratings of subordinate self-development programs has been discussed. Perhaps these same groups of supervisors could meet to analyze also the perceived needs of their subordinates as well as the informal organizational values of their groups. Are such values in conflict with formal goals? Why? What needs is the formal organization failing to meet? When changes must be made, what kind of repercussions can be anticipated, and how can these be eliminated or

---

[3] Stuart Chase, *The Proper Study of Mankind* (New York: Harper & Bros., 1956), p. 55.

[4] Richard Dewey and W. J. Humber, *The Development of Human Behavior* (New York: Macmillan Co., 1951), p. 143.

[5] Carroll L. Shartle, *Executive Performance and Leadership* (Englewood Cliffs, New Jersey: Prentice-Hall, Inc., 1956), p. 94.

[6] Ralph M. Stogdill *et. al., A Predictive Study of Administrative Work Patterns* (Bureau of Business Research, The Ohio State University, Research Monograph No. 85, 1956), p. 68.

moderated? What are the implications of sociometric data collected from the groups? Not only will good staff and line leadership in the conduct of such sessions train supervisors in new techniques; it can—*by inducing "group decisions" to utilize "findings" in daily contacts*—influence them to engage in more perceptive and productive supervisory behavior.

In addition to these suggestions, it may be useful to review, periodically, the amount of "influence" that supervisors actually have with their superiors in terms of the number of requests they have made and the proportion denied. Pelz's findings were referred to on page 223. He pointed out that if a supervisor's recommendations regarding improvement of working conditions, pay increases, promotions, and other matters of importance are largely ignored by higher management, employees will tend to associate him with the *frustration* of their needs. An examination of why a supervisor has not been very successful in this regard will point the way to desirable remedial action. And, as has been suggested earlier, there are other ways in which superiors can strengthen the influence of their subordinate managers by giving due attention to the role of status symbols and their relations with subordinate managers in the presence of *their* subordinates.

Obviously, supervisors must have the *time* to engage in those supervisory activities that may not produce an immediate "payoff," activities that often are displaced by the pressure of other demands. An analysis of how supervisors spend their time may suggest the need for more clerical help and other kinds of assistance. With regard to counseling, the fear is frequently expressed that subordinates will leave little time for anything else if the door is really opened to them. Experience has shown that, after a possible initial surge, the time required for this will be quite reasonable and manageable, provided other factors in the situation are satisfactory.

Even the physical dispersion of individuals and offices can have a significant impact on the structuring of informal organizational relationships. From the discussion of General Motors, it may be recalled that all group vice-presidents, some staff vice-presidents, and all executive vice-presidents have offices on the same floor in the Detroit General Motors Building with the office of the president and one of the offices of the chairman of the board. Cross-contacts, impromptu meetings, and other forms of informal interaction are encouraged thereby. Consequently, there is created a general management "team," which can productively gather and process ideas and feedback information from the various sources they represent within the company as well as from other "pipeline" groups in contact with them.[7] Of course, it is a common practice, when subordinates are physically dispersed throughout the country in decentralized units, for superiors to engage in regular "circuit riding" to assure the kind of face-to-face contact with their men for which there is no effective substitute.

A training technique for sensitizing supervisors to the *need* for effective listening skills—though it will not necessarily make good listeners of them—is to require them in training-session discussions to "play back," accurately and to the preceding speaker's satisfaction, what has been said before them prior to making their own contribution. And if supervisors fail to delegate authority, we have the kind of "force techniques" discussed on pages 290 and 291, which are designed to encourage delegation through the application of rewards and penalties.

Wage and Salary Administration

Finally, not to be overlooked is a most important tool for controlling supervision: wage and salary administration. Pay becomes a real issue to all employees when it is insufficient to provide basic need gratification or when the amount is perceived by employees as a symbol of rejection, disapproval, or inequitable reward. Supervisors are especially concerned with being supplied with the monetary wherewithal to attract, to hold, and properly encourage good subordinates. One of the best ways to *pervert* a merit rating system in an organization and to breed general discontent is to permit starting wages to get out of line with the market and *especially* with regard to the *relative position* they should hold with other rates in the organization. The only way in which a rational wage structure can be maintained through time is by the use of formal job evaluation coupled with sound concepts of wage and salary administration. The point system should be used, for it is the only one that can be validated effectively.[8]

---

[7] For a discussion of the impact of physical dispersion on friendship formation in a housing development see Leon Festinger, "Group Attraction and Membership," in Dorwin Cartwright and Alvin Zander (eds.), *Group Dynamics* (Evanston, Illinois: Row, Peterson Co., 1953), p. 92.

[8] See William Fox, "Purpose and Validity in Job Evaluation," *Personnel Journal,* October, 1962, and any one of a number of books on job evaluation for a discussion of the planning and implementation of a wage and salary program incorporating the point system. For an interesting discussion of top-management compensation see Perrin Stryker, "How Much Is an Executive Worth," *Fortune,* April, 1955, and the other works cited by Stryker in that article (the article is reprinted in William Fox

Philosophy and Practice

Though the factors discussed above for control of supervision are useful if they operate in a proper over-all climate, they will never serve as a substitute for effective top-management philosophy and practice. Shultz and Whisler imply this with an interesting anecdote:

> ... At a recent conference, a young manager described in some detail the refinements of technique by which he claimed to be able to evoke from his subordinates "in free and permissive discussion" precisely the decisions he wanted. He concluded, "The important thing is that they get the *feeling* of having participated, even though the decision had really been made by me."
>
> Let us grant that such techniques may, so long as the deception succeeds, gain their objective. But at what cost? Is everyone in the management group indoctrinated in these skills? Is there a gentlemen's agreement not to use them on each other? The young man just quoted disavowed the use of such tricks on any but the "lower" levels of management, presumably the ever-suffering foreman. This disavowal only makes the entire conception even more unpalatable. *In contrast, the harsh and undisguised authoritarian stands a frank and honest fellow.*[9]

And James C. Worthy, of Sears, Roebuck and Company, provides us with an excellent closing statement:

> There is no easy way to improve employee relations. Basically, the problem is moral and ethical. Attempts to deal with it without facing up to this fact are sterile. The material advances represented by higher wage scales, shorter hours, generous employee benefits, and better working conditions are all important, but none of them goes to the heart of the problem. And the heart of the problem is the hearts and souls of the individual men and women who comprise American industry.[10]

COMPARISON

Comparison involves the evaluation of completed action to see how well it has conformed to plans or other standards. Comparison has been discussed in relation to control of supervision. Some addi-

(ed.), *Readings in Personnel Management from "Fortune"* (New York: Henry Holt & Co., 1957). Also of interest, the study to test the effects of wage incentive conducted with the Hawthorne experiments. See chap. 6 of F. J. Roethlisberger and W. J. Dickson, *Management and the Worker* (Cambridge, Massachusetts: Harvard University Press, 1939). On page 160 is found the observation that ". . . the efficacy of a wage incentive was so dependent on its relation to other factors that it was impossible to consider it as a thing in itself having an independent effect on the individual."

[9] George P. Shultz and Thomas L. Whisler, *Management Organization and the Computer* (Glencoe, Illinois: Free Press, 1960), p. 127.

[10] James C. Worthy, *Big Business and Free Men* (New York: Harper & Bros., 1959), pp. 133, 134.

tional considerations having to do with the *general* control of this function will now be discussed.

Formulating and Interpreting Standards

Comparison cannot occur without standards, since comparison has to do with determining where we are relative to where we should be. Standards—in the form of specifications, plans, policies, procedures, budgets, etc.—define where we should be. Consequently, part of the discussion of control of comparison is appropriately concerned with assuring the proper formulation and interpretation of standards.

One way to encourage the development of appropriate standards and assure some understanding of them is to permit those who use them, and are evaluated relative to them, to *participate* in their formulation and periodic review. This is especially important with regard to those standards which can never, in any sense, be absolute. For example, standard costs are useful standards, but they certainly are not free of error. They should change with variations in volume, and these variations must be carefully studied to be even partially understood. The allocation of many indirect charges is largely a matter of judgment and open to question. And the impact of variations as to the quality or cost of materials as well as variations in other factors must be taken into account if such standards are to be used effectively.

In the same vein, we cannot expect to use an oversimplified concept of efficiency—such as time actually spent to do a task relative to standard time—and at the same time maintain the confidence of employees and an environment for real contribution. For, realistically, efficiency involves other factors, such as quality, tool costs, staff services consumed, space utilized, inventory levels, and so forth. Perceptive supervisors and employees know this, and their participation in the definition of standards will help to avoid serious oversights. In meeting with them we must demonstrate our desire to consider all relevant factors in evaluating performance or they will be encouraged to unbend every effort simply to "improve their scores." This can be done, and often is done, at the expense of primary service objectives!

Measuring "Where We Are"

Before we can perform the comparison function, we must accurately determine "where we are." That is not always easy. In the case of staff agencies, many of the intangible values being created are quite difficult to measure. However, if we do not attempt to measure them, we can be reasonably sure that the agency will divert its energies to better rewarded, though possibly less important, activities. Consider, for example, measurement of the achievement of a public relations department. One company placed considerable emphasis on the number of letters it received in response to publicity releases by its public relations department. Would this encourage the department to do a good public relations job for the company or would it encourage the department to design releases that would stimulate letter writing? The use of periodic reports that indicate progress relative to a *number* of criteria (as was discussed on page 184) would be much more fruitful.

We must be quite careful in ascertaining the "achievement" of various divisions of the same company or the "achievement" of similar companies on the basis of accounting data! Good accounting practice permits considerable variation in the handling of such matters as inventory pricing, depreciation, the allocation of fixed costs, and so on. Overhead and depreciation costs can act as "substitutes" for direct costs. As Durand points out, "If our competitor's direct labor costs are less than ours, we would be interested in his wage rates, his methods of production, what materials, machines, and tools he uses, and his training programs."[11] The extent to which variation owing to accounting practice can occur is dramatized by Marquis Eaton, a former president of the American Institute of Certified Public Accountants:

> I suspect it would come as something of a shock to some people to realize that two otherwise identical corporations might report net income differing by millions of dollars simply because they followed different accounting methods—and that the financial statements of both companies might still carry a certified public accountant's opinion stating that the reports fairly presented the results in accordance with "generally accepted accounting principles." [12]

Speed vs. Accuracy

In determining "where we are," we must also keep in mind the *speed* with which this can be done. For time is of the essence in

---

[11] Robert Y. Durand, *Business: Its Organization, Management and Responsibilities* (Englewood Cliffs, New Jersey: Prentice-Hall, Inc., 1958), p. 398.

[12] From an address presented to the Illinois Society of Certified Public Accountants, June 7, 1957 (printed in *Financial Reporting in a Changing Society* [New York: American Institute of Certified Public Accountants], p. 9).

avoiding unnecessary deviation from standards and in making corrective action appropriate to the situation that exists. Part of the problem has to do with the speed with which data necessary for comparison can be processed and disseminated. Consideration has been given to the importance of the computer, coupled with a well-designed system of integrated data processing, in making it possible to prepare and distribute data quickly and economically to various personnel in the organization in a form most suited to their needs. Another important means for reducing the time factor is often overlooked: analysis of the required accuracy that reports for control purposes must have. Suppose, for example, that we can estimate our level of sales, on the basis of sampling or analysis of incomplete returns, within 5 per cent of the actual figure a week earlier than that figure will be available. Those who use this figure for control purposes may decide that the amount of controllable error present is relatively unimportant and that the time saved is quite significant. Analysis can reveal where the cost of such early estimate reports is more than offset by savings resulting from earlier evaluation, and the balance between time saved and permissible controllable error can also be established.

Several aspects of the problem of controlling performance of the comparison function have been considered. A hard but realistic truth that must be faced is that good evaluation or comparison is often difficult and demanding of the best analytical skills that can be mustered, especially in evaluating human performance. It must be kept in mind at all times that the *legitimate* purpose of such evaluation is to establish accountability for actions so that we may know whom to reward, whom to correct, and whom to discharge— *not* whom to punish in a punitive sense!

CORRECTIVE ACTION

Corrective action is concerned with getting things back on course or, if this is not feasible, changing the course or schedule through new planning. Corrective action often involves new organization planning for the purpose of fashioning organization changes to assure that recurring deviations from standards will be less likely to recur in the future. It has been pointed out that we must have properly prepared and disseminated standards, means for comparing performance relative to them, and bases for establishing accountability before the stage is set for corrective action. Here some additional aspects of the control of corrective action that were not discussed in the section on supervision will be considered.

Need for Analysis

Much corrective action entails simply the application of pre-planned procedures or alternative plans. For example, if the belt on a machine becomes loose, there is a prescribed procedure for adjusting it. Or corrective action may involve no more than routine decision making: the supervisor is aware of several well-defined alternatives for handling a deviation and is also aware of the specific criteria that he should utilize in making a choice. Effective control of these types of corrective action is based largely on the adequate formulation and dissemination of various informational instruments and periodic review as to their current applicability and the extent to which they are properly understood.

In the area of less routine corrective action, the quality of analysis that should precede it is of concern. Are supervisors sensitive to the various factors that may be affected by, and the repercussions that may flow from, various contemplated actions? Whenever applicable, do they think in terms of a "step" approach to corrective action? That is, do they think in terms of the rate of change that the organization can handle? And do they consider the added control and flexibility afforded by being able to modify each subsequent step in terms of feedback information as to the outcomes of the preceding step? In other words, do they think in terms of a sequence or chain of "limiting factors" that stands between them and their corrective action goal whenever they are confronted with the need for more than "one-step" remedial activity? Control of this is partly assured by selection of supervisors with the capacity for such analysis and by training that incorporates periodic post mortems of past corrective action taken. Such post mortems are especially useful for improving the performance of staff personnel who are responsible for recommending organization changes to eliminate recurring deviations (see p. 351).

"Operation Bootstrap"

The dangers of one type of corrective action must be kept in mind at all times. This is corrective action designed to up-grade the over-all performance of an organization "overnight." It is often attempted by a new manager or administration that is convinced that people are "goofing off" or simply are not being pushed hard enough. Such an "operation bootstrap" is usually quite unrealistic and most disruptive to organizational morale and the *net contribution* of personnel. A few individuals may in fact be "goofing off," but utilization of such across-the-board action rather than *selective* corrective action is just as harmful as are blanket cuts in the area of budgetary control. If pressure is brought to bear for improvement in only one area of performance without the appropriation of additional resources, supervisors may accommodate to this by letting up in other areas, and the chief damage done comes from the consequences of improper performance of the comparison function by management. But when a general increase in all dimensions of performance is demanded, even more serious damage is done. Supervisors and other employees think that they are being victimized by the "ratchet principle" or "speed-up." They lose confidence in the integrity of superiors and tend to combine forces to resist the threat, both overtly and covertly.

If, in view of its resources, the over-all performance of an organization is in fact below par, nothing short of wholesale discharge and reorganization can *productively* alter the situation "overnight." The conviction that this can be done is fostered by a willingness to overlook the serious consequences that will be generated, but may not be readily apparent, in the immediate short run. For it is as impossible to turn an existing organization in its tracks as it is a whale! But this characteristic is really more of an asset than a liability. It takes time to build an effective organization, and it must be done in terms of specific goals and "steps." But this process creates desirable forces, which tend to stabilize the organization, render it more manageable, and provide it with staying power in times of stress.

Use of Outsiders

Another consideration for the control of corrective action is quite important. It has to do with the occasional need for utilizing qualified personnel from outside the organization. This need flows in part from two observable tendencies that characterize many long-term organizational members: inability to see the forest for the trees and inability to become prophets among their own people. Frequently, a competent consultant—unfettered by involvement in the traditions and pressures of the organization—can supply productively fresh viewpoints to old problems or recognize the *significance* of factors in a situation that are known but not properly appreciated by insiders. Even if he does no more than confirm the good judgment of an insider, this can supply the additional influence or prestige needed by the insider to gain acceptance of, and action on, his proposal. Jerome summarizes these ideas very well by pointing out that "to be *aware* of a situation is one thing, to recognize the *significance* of that situation is something else; and, finally, to gain *corrective action* is still another matter . . . the psychological impact of the outsider's contribution should never be minimized."[13] Of course, when corrective action is actually taken, it should be taken by, or under the direct personal guidance of, those in command who are responsible for outcomes.

SOME CONCLUDING REMARKS

Organization planners should review regularly the appropriateness of control systems in the organization and the effectiveness with which they are functioning. Control systems are too often evaluated in terms of their efficiency, *given* the rationale for their initial establishment. A "step back," periodically, to examine the *current desirability* of this rationale is often productive. Such questions as the following should be raised: What would happen if this system of control did not exist? If we were starting from scratch in designing control for these activities, how would we do it? Could these control activities be performed by machines that either exist or are potentially designable; if so, could they do them economically? Can we apply the concepts of statistical quality control, based on sampling, to these activities? And so on. As was suggested above, the utilization of competent outsiders in the conduct of such reviews can be most useful.

Overcontrol

Evidence of the value of this kind of analysis is provided by the experience of a large firm that operates several hundred retail stores. For many years, it had been standard procedure for each sales clerk in each store to count the cash in her register every night and then turn it in to the store cashier, who, in turn, had to count it, issue a receipt, and place it in the store's safe. The procedure, in reverse, was repeated each morning. The purposes of this procedure were to discourage dishonesty on the part of the clerks, to turn up shortages before they became acute, and to safeguard cash against rob-

---

[13] William Travers Jerome III, *Executive Control—The Catalyst* (New York: John Wiley & Sons, 1961), p. 190.

bery. Considerable study had been given to devising ways for improving the efficiency with which this procedure was implemented, and some very real improvements had been made. But for many years no one had questioned the *need* for the procedure—at least in this form—as an adequate basis for control!

Finally, someone did. He proposed that they experiment with a new approach to control in several of the stores: have the girls check in only once a week, for counting purposes, and then make unannounced spot checks in those stores where the weekly count revealed significant deviation from normal. He estimated that the loss rate under this new system could be many times the loss rate under the old and still amount to decidedly less money than the added cost of the old system! As a matter of fact, the loss rate did not increase, sales clerks welcomed the new system with enthusiasm, and customers were quite pleased with the added attention and service they received around closing time. Unfortunately, this kind of "overcontrol" is much too common.

Undercontrol

There is one area of "undercontrol," however, that is causing increasing concern today: control of corporate management by widely dispersed and relatively non-influential "little" stockholders, in the absence of strong proprietary interests or competitive pressures. One of the prime functions of a board of directors, representing ownership interests, is to provide for independent review of the performance of the president and his top-management team and to decide how this performance will be rewarded. In the absence of large stockholders, there is an opportunity for operating management to elect itself or its agents to the board for the purpose of rubber-stamping its decisions and perpetuating itself in office. Of course, over a period of time this will tend to put the firm at a competitive disadvantage, but, in the short run, who will protect stockholders from the dissipation of accumulated assets in the form of excessive bonuses and fringe benefits for executives? Determination of top executive salaries is a matter of judgment; in the absence of significant ownership representation on the board, is it ethical for managers to evaluate themselves for the purpose of determining their own rewards?

It might be well, and in the interest of maintaining a healthy climate for the preservation of private enterprise in our country, for our more socially responsible, professional managers to bring pressure to bear on certain of their colleagues to make provisions for adequate independent review of their activities when this does not exist. As a matter of policy, some firms already appoint to their boards a number of prominent, capable, "independent" directors to assure that such review will be maintained. Possibly, independent "industry association directors" could be appointed by trade associations to perform the more limited function of participating in the determination of top-level salaries and benefits. Or, as the professionalization of management progresses, we may see the day when appointees of professional associations will perform this service.

In the meantime, there are a number of measures that might be taken to strengthen the likelihood of independent review. More use can be made of cumulative voting, whereby small stockholders can concentrate all their votes for only one position on the board.[14] Greater pressure might be brought to bear on institutional investors —who represent almost a third of the value of all issues on the New York Stock Exchange—to take a more active interest in the management of companies in which they have stock, for many of these men have the capacity and time for developing the kind of expertise needed to influence constructively the firms they have an interest in. Dale suggests that institutional investors might act in concert

> ... through the formation of a nationwide association of institutional investors for the purpose of selecting and appointing their own representatives to the boards of companies in which their combined holdings are large. . . . (The expense could presumably be met easily because of the substantial allowance for administrative expenses of institutional funds.)[15]

Another possibility suggested by Dale is for the SEC in proxy fights to permit the reimbursement of expenses for the dissemination by minority interests of information to *all* stockholders when the minority group is sufficiently strong and the information it wishes to distribute is sufficiently relevant to the issues at hand.[16] What-

---

[14] Under the "majority rule" system, each stockholder can cast as many votes as he has shares for each director to be elected. Under "cumulative voting," the stockholder can cast all his votes (number of shares held times number of directors to be elected) for only one director, if he wishes. In this way, minority stockholders can hope to get *some* representation on the board.

[15] Ernest Dale, *The Great Organizers* (New York: McGraw-Hill Book Co., 1960), p. 214. Dale presents a provocative discussion of the issue of independent review, from which the author has drawn. See chap. 6 and the Appendices to chap. 6. Also read chap. 20 of Richard Eells and Clarence Walton, *Conceptual Foundations of Business* (Homewood, Illinois: Richard D. Irwin, Inc., 1961).

[16] *Dale, op. cit.*, p. 206.

ever the solution to the problem of independent review is, it is certainly a matter worthy of the attention of our leading business statesmen.

Administrative Viewpoint

In concluding this chapter on control of control, it seems appropriate to say a word about "the administrative viewpoint." Board members, and especially those who perform general management functions, are primarily concerned with what is termed "administrative management": the *over-all* management job of fashioning the organization into a balanced whole, holding it together, and leading it into the future. The effective administrator must develop and maintain an administrative viewpoint. That is, he must keep before him the concept that the organization as a whole, as well as each of its parts, provides merely a tool for the achievement of primary service objectives and he must attempt to achieve a balance among the various activity areas of the business so that these areas are stressed in proportion to their contribution to primary objectives.

This is a challenging assignment. But for that matter, all management is challenging! It is hoped sincerely that this book has whetted your desire to explore further the challenges and opportunities it affords.

QUESTIONS

1. A supervisor was overheard to say, "Tell them what to do and then see that they do it by checking up on them every step of the way." What is your opinion as to this approach to control? Explain the reasons for your position.
2. What kind of analysis would you make to determine the *appropriateness* of a system of control? Explain the reasons for your approach. How would you determine the *effectiveness* with which the system is being utilized? Again, explain the reasons for your approach.
3. What reasons might "newcomers" to an organization have for, in effect, contributing to a reduction in the effectiveness with which programming activities are performed? Explain. How can we avoid this?
4. Is it important that activities be scheduled? Why?
5. A personnel director indicates that the president of his company is very autocratic and refuses to delegate much authority to anyone because he says that they are not ready for it. He has a plan for remedying this situation, which he thinks he can "sell" to the president. He wants to set up a special training program for supervisors—utilizing the services of a human relations expert from a local university—so that they will become better managers and thus more

deserving of the confidence of the president. What do you think of this plan? Discuss.

6. "I've heard a lot about the need for good human relations and I suppose that people do feel better if you pamper them. But it's a cold, hard fact that results are what keep you going relative to your competitors and this is what we pay our managers for every working day in the year. The streets of failure are paved with good intentions!" What do you think of this statement by the president of a company? Discuss.

7. What is "insight"? In what way is it related to the control of supervision?

8. Discuss ways in which we can structure the "compulsions" of the work environment to produce behavior that is productive for both the organization and the supervisor.

9. Though we don't like to say it, our basic purpose in studying the concepts and techniques of supervision is to learn how to *manipulate* people effectively. Do you agree or disagree with this statement? Discuss.

10. Is it easier to define "where we should be" than to measure "where we are"? Give the reasons for your answer.

11. A report that cannot be used for the preparation of financial statements because it contains errors may be quite useful for control. Is this true? Why or why not?

12. What contribution can an outside consultant make that a competent insider cannot make? Explain.

13. Under what conditions is it possible for corporate management to avoid independent review of its activities? Do you think that this is a serious problem? Why or why not?

14. What is "administrative" management? Do you believe that administrative skill is something that exists, and can be developed, apart from technical skill? Explain.

APPENDIXES

Appendix I

BASIC MANAGEMENT PRINCIPLES

A science is developed through the systematic accumulation of knowledge based on and related to the discovery of *general truths*. The science of management is new, but it is progressing. Listed below are the more important general truths, principles, and hypotheses that underlie modern management art and science. (The classification used is quite arbitrary; many of them belong in more than one category.)

PLANNING

Generic Planning Premise. Planning requires a selection from alternatives for the establishment of goals and the means for achieving them. Since the evaluation of alternative goals presupposes a value system, *planning involves ethics*.

Principle of Limiting Factors. In approaching a problem situation with a well-defined goal, it is productive to identify and analyze the sequence of limiting factors involved. These are factors that, if properly satisfied in appropriate order, will permit the accomplishment of the goal.

Principle of Optimality. An optimal policy has the property that, whatever the initial state and initial decision are, the remaining decisions must constitute an optimal policy with regard to the state resulting from the first decision.

ORGANIZING

The Scalar Principle. An unbroken chain of direct authority relationships from superior to subordinate must be developed from the top to the bottom of the organization.

415

Unity of Objective. The organization as a whole, as well as each of its parts, provides merely a tool for the achievement of organizational objectives, therefore *all* organization activity should contribute to the attainment of these objectives.

Unity of Command. An employee should receive orders from one "regular" superior only, unless they result from specific functional authority delegations that are clearly understood by the "regular" superior, the employee, and the functional superior.

Parity of Authority and Responsibility. The responsibility of any manager or employee should correspond with his authority.

Principle of Functional Emergence. The tendency of a given function toward differentiation and independent grouping tends to vary directly with (1) the degree of dissimilarity between the particular function and the functions with which it is grouped, (2) the degree of correlation between its growth and development and the growth of the organization as a whole, and (3) the tendency of the function to become increasingly complex and technical with growth.

The Principle of Staff Authority. A staff executive should not have authority to supervise line personnel (only his own personnel) or issue orders to the line unless he is authorized to do so by a specific allocation of functional authority.

Law of Functional Growth. The complexity of functional relationships tends to increase in geometric progression as the volume of work that the organization must handle increases in arithmetic progression.

Graicunas' Theorem. The complexities of managing tend to increase in geometric progression as the number of subordinates increases in arithmetic progression.

CONTROL

Unity of Direction. There should be *one head* and *one plan* for each group of activities having the same objective.

Principle of Harmony of Objective. Though the personal goals of the people associated with an organization frequently are not the same as primary organization goals, organization goals often can be conceived and implemented in such a way as to satisfy these personal goals within the framework of necessary organizational constraints.

Limitation of Staff Economy. It is usually necessary that staff functions be performed with less than maximum economy in order that the line functions that they serve may be performed with maximum economy and effectiveness.

Exception Principle. To conserve the time and ability of executives, each decision should be made by the lowest manager in the organization who has the necessary competence, authority, and prestige. Also, only significant deviations of actual from planned performance should be brought to the attention of the responsible executive.

Personnel Coordination. Promotions, wage changes, and formal disciplinary action should always be approved by the executive immediately superior to the one directly responsible.

Principle of the Fixation of Responsibility and Authority. The process of delegation relieves the responsible executive of none of his responsibility, authority, or accountability.

Generic Hypothesis I (Universal Needs). Though employees act in terms of their *belief systems* (and effective leadership must operate through these systems), they have the *same basic needs.* (Ends are more universal than the means for achieving them, since means are largely determined by local culture.) These universal need characteristics support a pattern of leadership that can be applied successfully in a wide range of human activity.

Generic Hypothesis II (Social Systems and Formal Organization). The basic needs of employees tend to be met through the operation of social systems operating within the framework of formal organization. The social system through its beliefs and social interactions provides a sense of belonging and a reserve of emotional support from which its members may draw. Good formal organization provides for productive, coordinated effort through consistent adherence to a clearly defined system of authority relationships, rules, and task assignments.

Generic Hypothesis III (Positive Leadership). The pattern of leadership in supervisory positions that will assure the greatest long-run effectiveness is based on cooperation, participation, consultation, consistent adherence to high standards of achievement, and satisfaction for the egos of the rank and file, though this will require the strong leader to restrain his natural drive toward self-assertion and will require all leaders to deal in a firm, authoritarian manner with the maladjusted minority who will attempt to disrupt the group.

Generic Hypothesis IV (Positive vs. Negative Motivation). In leadership, positive motivation is superior to negative motivation when the necessary *time, rapport, skill,* and *group environment* are present to make it possible. Otherwise, negative motivation is superior to no motivation or a laissez faire approach. Also, negative motivation must always be applied, in the interest of the group, to that minority which has proved itself non-receptive to positive motivation. However, negative motivation is most effective when it encourages types of behavior that are rewarded by relief from stress and satisfaction of personal needs.

Generic Hypothesis V (Perceptual Distortion). Objective perception of problems and interpersonal relations is distorted by wishes and fears—catharsis will tend to relieve the distortion.

Generic Hypothesis VI (Pathological Reaction). Pathological reaction occurs when an organism is confronted by a situation that it perceives as being impossible to solve or cope with and that it feels it *must* deal with.

Generic Hypothesis VII (Counseling). There is a basic clinical approach, available to and practical for the supervisor, that is effective in dealing with perceptual distortion and troubled employees. It is based on the non-directive interview concept in which the interviewer:

1. Establishes face-to-face rapport with the employee.
2. Listens as he encourages the employee to talk out his problem without challenge or approval.
3. Refrains from prescribing for the employee but assists him in developing his own solution.
4. Follows up by encouraging and assisting the employee in carrying out his *own* plan.

In developing this technique the interviewer can be trained to gain insight into his own behavior so that he may remain emotionally neutral with the employee, and he can learn to identify those cases which should be referred to a professional therapist.

Generic Hypothesis VIII (Law of the Situation). This hypothesis relates to what has been termed the "law of the situation in relation to the solution of business problems". If time permits and if all relevant facts are collected, studied, and discussed by those immediately concerned under leadership that encourages impartiality, a solution (the "law of the situation") will emerge that will be acceptable to all. There will be no need to *impose* a solution on the group through the exercise of formal authority.

Generic Hypothesis IX (Resistance to Change). Resistance to change is motivated largely by a real or imagined threat to personal well-being. When a change can be perceived as affording greater satisfaction of personal needs than can be achieved without it, it will no longer be resisted. Owing to this, the *feelings* associated with a given change must receive as much attention as the *logics* associated with the change.

Generic Hypothesis X (Morale and Company Goals). Good morale in a group is evidenced by the willingness of group members to subordinate their immediate convenience to identification with, and effective implementation of, group goals; good morale contributes to the efficient implementation of formal company goals to the extent that group goals contribute to these formal goals.

Appendix II

SOME QUESTIONS FOR BUSINESSMEN[1]

The following questions are designated to facilitate the examination by American businessmen of their ethical standards and performance. They are intended to illustrate the kinds of questions that must be identified and considered by each business enterprise if it is to achieve compliance with those high ethical standards that derive from our heritage and traditions. Every reader will think of others. No single list can possibly encompass all of the demands for ethical judgments that must be met by men in business.

1. General Understanding:

Do we have in our organization current, well considered statements of the ethical principles that should guide our officers and employees in specific situations that arise in our business activities, both domestic and foreign? Do we revise these statements periodically to cover new situations and changing laws and social patterns?

Have those statements been the fruit of discussion in which all members of policy-determining management have had an opportunity to participate?

Have we given to our officers and employees at all levels sufficient motivation to search out ethical factors in business problems

---

[1] From the booklet, *A Statement on Business Ethics and a Call for Action*, published by the U.S. Department of Commerce, Washington 25, D.C.

and apply high ethical standards in their solution? What have we done to eliminate opposing pressures?

Have we provided officers and employees with an easily accessible means of obtaining counsel on and resolution of ethical problems that may arise in their activities? Do they use it?

Do we know whether our officers and employees apply in their daily activities the ethical standards we have promulgated? Do we reward those who do so and penalize those who do not?

2. Compliance with law:

Having in mind the complexities and everchanging patterns of modern law and government regulations:

What are we doing to make sure that our officers and employees are informed about and comply with laws and regulations affecting their activities?

Have we made clear that it is our policy to obey even those laws which we may think unwise and seek to have changed?

Do we have adequate internal checks on our compliance with law?

Have we established a simple and readily available procedure for our officers and employees to seek legal guidance in their activities? Do they use it?

3. Conflicts of interest:

Do we have a current, well-considered statement of policy regarding potential conflict of interest problems of our directors, officers and employees? If so, does it cover conflicts which may arise in connection with such activities as: transactions with or involving our company; acquiring interests in or performing services for our customers, distributors, suppliers and competitors; buying and selling our company's securities; or the personal undertaking of what might be called company opportunities?

What mechanism do we have for enabling our directors, officers and employees to make ethical judgments when conflicts of interest do arise?

Do we require regular reports, or do we leave it to our directors, officers and employees to disclose such activities voluntarily?

4. Entertainment, gifts, and expenses:

Have we defined our company policy on accepting and making expenditures for gifts and entertainment? Are the criteria as to occasion and amount clearly stated or are they left merely to the judgment of the officer or employee?

Do we disseminate information about our company policy to the organizations with which we deal?

Do we require adequate reports of both the giving and receiving of gifts and entertainment; are they supported in sufficient detail; are they subject to review by appropriate authority; and could the payment or receipt be justified to our stockholders, the government, and the public?

5. Customers and suppliers:

Have we taken appropriate steps to keep our advertising and sales representations truthful and fair? Are these steps effective?

How often do we review our advertising, literature, labels, and packaging? Do they give our customers a fair understanding of the true quality, quantity, price and function of our products? Does our service as well as our product measure up to our basic obligations and our representations?

Do we fairly make good on flaws and defects? Is this a matter of stated policy? Do we know that our employees, distributors, dealers and agents follow it?

Do we avoid favoritism and discrimination and otherwise treat our customers and suppliers fairly and equitably in all our dealings with them?

6. Social responsibilities:

Every business enterprise has manifold responsibilities to the society of which it is a part. The prime legal and social obligation of the managers of a business is to operate it for the long-term profit of its owners. Concurrent social responsibilities pertain to a company's treatment of its past, present and prospective employees and to its various relationships with customers, suppliers, government, the community and the public at large. These responsibilities may often be, or appear to be, in conflict, and at times a management's recognition of its broad responsibilities may affect the amount of an enterprise's immediate profits and the means of attaining them.

The problems that businessmen must solve in this area are often exceedingly perplexing. One may begin his reflections on this subject by asking—

Have we reviewed our company policies in the light of our responsibilities to society? Are our employees aware of the interaction between our business policies and our social responsibilities?

Do we have a clearly understood concept of our obligation to assess our responsibilities to stockholders, employees, customers, suppliers, our community and the public?

Do we recognize and impress upon all our officers and employees the fact that our free enterprise system and our individual business enterprises can thrive and grow only to the extent that they contribute to the welfare of our country and its people?

INDEXES

NAME INDEX

A

Alderson, W., 22
Allen, L. A., 344
Allport, G., 195
Ammer, D. S., 161n.
Andress, F. J., 367, 368
Andrews, K. R., 164n., 264n.
Anshen, M., 341n.
Anthony, R., 181, 186n., 302, 303, 306, 308
Arbous, A. G., 147n.
Argyris, C., 22
Arthur, C. A., 398

B

Baker, A. W., 104, 105, 106, 120
Bales, R. F., 150, 379n.
Barksdale, H. M., 147
Barnard, C. I., 33, 194
Barnard, I., 162–63
Barnes, R., 22
Barth, C., 15
Bass, B. M., 146n.
Bavelas, A., 22
Bellman, R., 50
Bennett, E., 160n.
Bowman, C. H., 22, 42n., 43, 49
Brandeis, L. D., 17
Brothers, L. A., 39
Brown, D., 317–18, 319–20, 322
Brownlee, O. H., 40
Burth, H. E., 168n., 169.
Bush, V., 264n.

C

Cartwright, D., 29n., 207n., 218n., 400n.
Chamberlain, J., 253n.
Chapman, R., 152n.
Chase, S., 216–18, 397–98
Christenson, C. R., 264n.
Churchman, C. W., 28n.

Clark, J. M., 22
Clothier, R. C., 140
Coch, L., 220n.
Cohen, K., 147n.
Cooke, M., 15, 22
Copernicus, N., 13
Coppinger, J. M., 28n.
Curley, J., 285n.
Curtice, H. N., 316–17, 330–31

D

Dale, E., 30n., 87n., 97, 98, 146–47, 165–67, 250, 332–33, 409
Dantzig, G., 22
Davenport, R., 252
Davis, R. C., 3n., 22, 69–70, 82–83, 91, 104–6, 108n., 122, 135, 158, 174n., 248, 262, 265–68, 286, 288, 297, 310, 311n., 349n., 351
Dean, J., 22, 138n., 298–301, 309, 339n.
Degan, J., 160n.
Delbecq, A. L., 32n., 171n., 187n., 319n.
Dennison, H., 223n.
Despelder, B. E., 104n.
Dewey, R., 198–99, 398
Dickson, W. J., 219, 401n.
Dimock, M. E., 30
Drucker, P., 22
Drury, H. B., 19n.
Duncan, D. C., 147n.
Dunn, E. G., 231n., 232, 233
Durand, R. Y., 130, 131, 132–33, 301, 354, 403

E

Earl of Halsbury, 39
Eaton, M., 403
Edwards, J., 285n., 367n.
Eells, R., 177–78, 409n.
Einstein, A., 21
Emerson, H., 12, 15, 21, 94

427

SUBJECT INDEX

A

Absenteeism and turnover, 200
Acceptance, authority through, 90
Acceptance, personal, in communication, 203
Accountability
  corrective action and, 176
  decentralization and, 297
  defined, 157
  Principle of Parity of Authority and Responsibility and, 271
  responsibility center departmentation and, 302–3
Accountants, factory, 238
Accounting
  data processing role in, 237–41
  in a decentralized firm, 239
  major functions of, 239
  organization for, 237–41
  variations in practice of, 403
Accuracy, economic, 404
Accuracy in planning, excessive, 341
Acid test (ratio), 182
Active staff, 107
Adamson Company, 253
Administrative management, 112
Administrative viewpoint, 410
Algorithm (in GPS), 46
Allocation of costs fallacy, 357–58
American Institute of Certified Public Accountants, 403
Analog computer, 40
Analog models, 43
Analysis of costs, 357
Anxiety
  communication and, 204
  and counseling, 215
  and merit rating, 205
  neurosis and, 197
Approximations in planning, 341
Art of management, 1, 6, 56, 84, 306
Assignment of duties, 154
"Assistant to" position
  in coordination of planning, 347
  nature and value of, 167

"Assistant to" position—*Cont.*
  for probationary status, 374–75
Attention directing information, 238
Audit
  organization, 385-88
  profit, 309
Authority
  centralization of, 166
    in emergencies, 310
  decentralization of; *see* Decentralization
  delegation of, 157, 165
    via dispatching function, 175, 348–50
    force techniques for, 290
  formal
    defined, 88
    role of, 87
    ultimate source of, 88
  functional, 92, 94–96, 239, 287, 290, 295
  to hire, 271
  informal or acceptance, 90, 206
  parity of with responsibility, 158
  of staff personnel, 272
Autocratic leadership
  when applicable, 207–11, 395
  easier than democratic, 223
  relative to democratic, 207–23, 301
Automation
  feed back and, 174
  impact on employment, 219
  maintenance and, 268
  organizational effects in the office, 241–44

B

Behavior, factors which influence, 196
Belief systems, 192
Belonging, 200
Board of directors
  administrative viewpoint of, 410
  by-passing the president, 262

431

*This book has been set on the Linotype
in 11 point Caledonia, leaded 2 points, and
10 point Caledonia, leaded 1 point. Section
and chapter numbers are in 30 and 24 point
Karnak obelisk; section and chapter titles
are in 30 and 24 point Tempo Bold Con-
densed. The size of the type page is 27 by
46½ picas.*